Everyday French Cooking

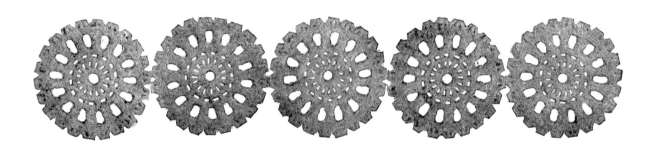

HENRI-PAUL PELLAPRAT

Everyday French Cooking

Henri-Paul Pellaprat,
formerly Senior Professor in the Schools
of Cooking and Confectionery of the "Cordon Bleu", Paris

Collins *LONDON AND GLASGOW*

TEXT PRINTED IN GREAT BRITAIN BY WM. COLLINS SONS
& CO. LTD. GLASGOW
ILLUSTRATIONS PRINTED IN SWITZERLAND
BY IMPRIMERIE CENTRALE,
LAUSANNE

SBN 00 435145 2

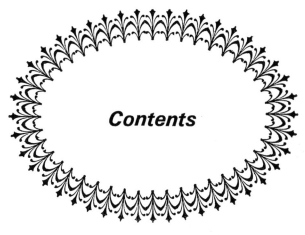

Contents

We are indebted to:

THE HOTEL CARLTON SENATO, MILAN
THE HOTEL-GRITTI-PALACE, VENICE. THE CONFISERIE KRANZLER, FRANKFURT
Messrs. LACROIX, Pâté and Delicatessen manufacturers, Frankfurt
MANUEL & CIE, Delicatessen merchant and Pastry shop, Lausanne
THE RESTAURANT MÖWENPICK, ZURICH
THE PARKHOTEL, FRANKFURT
who contributed the various dishes illustrated in this book

BÉARD INC., MONTREUX . CHRISTOFLE, PARIS, LONDON AND NEW YORK
MAPPIN AND WEBB, PARIS AND LONDON
STEIGER, LAUSANNE AND BERN
whose silverware was kindly placed at our disposal

STEIGER, LAUSANNE AND BERN
RICHARD GINORI, VENICE, PARIS AND NEW YORK
ATELIER D'ART "AU PRINTEMPS" IN PARIS
for the loan of crockery, chinaware and glass

MR. JEAN FROEHLICH, MR. ERIC MULLER-GRUNITZ, MR. MARIO ANSALDI
photographers

Acknowledgements:
MADELEINE DECURE, ANNE-MARIE FROEHLICH, ANNIE JACKSON, MARGARET LITTLE,
DOMINIQUE MONOD, ALICE ROHRER, CHRISTINE WATT, FRANCOIS D'ATHIS, WALTER BICKEL,
OCTAVE BRUST, CLAUDE DESARZENS, WILFRED FANCE, MARC FATIO, DAGOBERT FEHLMANN,
PIERRE GLEIZE, CHARLES GOETZ, CESAR GOSI, PAUL HEINZ, ANNE JACKSON, XAVIER MAIER,
PIERRE MENGELATTE, LÉON MICHAUD, FLAVIEN MONOD, LUIGI MORANDI, GILBERT ROHRER,
HERBERT SEIDEL, CHARLES VAUCHER, STEFANO ZACCONE

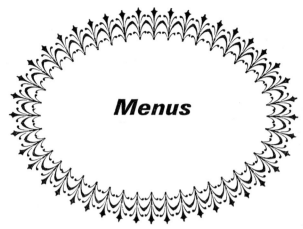

Menus

In the past, formal meals consisted of ten to twelve courses, but nowadays even a menu of six to seven courses has become exceptional. This change has taken place as a result of altered eating habits, social and economic necessity and the fact that people do not have the time nowadays to make or even eat elaborate meals.

A family meal usually consists of three courses and for special occasions and entertaining four or five courses. Planning menus for any occasion depends on several factors and the following list of points should prove helpful.

1. Do not serve the same kind of meat or poultry twice at any one meal.

2. Consider the colour and flavour of each dish and make sure that these harmonise.

3. Vary the garnishes you use.

4. Vary methods of cooking—for instance—never serve poached chicken after poached fish. Take into consideration the texture of the foods to be served, for example do not serve a cream soup and then a creamy dessert.

5. Consider the number of people to be served, the help available and the individual tastes of guests if you happen to know them.

6. Try to serve food, especially fruit and vegetables, when it is in season.

7. If three or four courses are to be served it is easier for the cook/hostess to serve at least two cold dishes which can be prepared in advance.

8. Do not repeat outstanding flavours or particular ingredients.

9. Remember to serve hot foods very hot and cold ones really cold.

One cannot discuss the subject of meal planning without mentioning the subject of nutrition. Most people know that milk, meat, eggs, cheese and fish supply us with protein which is important for the growth and repair of body tissues. You should serve at least one protein food at every meal. Carbohydrates in the form of sugar and the different types of starches provide energy and bulk to the diet. A balanced diet should include plenty of fresh vegetables and fruit to ensure all the vitamins and minerals are supplied.

The subject of nutrition is fascinating and people are becoming more aware of the importance of applying sound nutritional principles to everyday eating habits. However it can be generally said that there is little danger of people who eat three conventional meals a day suffering from malnutrition.

Below is a guide to help you to plan main meals for guests or special occasions.

Lunch

1. Either cold *hors d'œuvre*, or an egg or fish dish.
2. A hot roast dish (joint of meat, poultry or game) or garnished grill. In summer, cold meat or poultry with salads.
3. Either a sweet, ice cream, stewed fruit or pastries.
4. Cheese.

Dinner

1. Either clear or thick soup, or single *hors d'œuvre* (such as melon or smoked salmon).
2. Either fish, a hot *entrée* or a vegetable dish.
3. A roast with vegetables. If the *entrée* is substantial, serve a simple cold dish with salad.
4. Either a hot or cold sweet, ice cream or a selection of fresh fruit.

Family Menus

Cream of Celery Soup	*Cheese Soufflé*
Stewed Veal with Vegetables	*Cold Beef Niçoise*
Latticed Apple Tart	*Strawberries and Cream*
Poached Eggs with Ham or Bacon	*Leeks with Vinaigrette Sauce*
Oriental Chicken Pilaf	*Veal Medallions Veronese*
Buttered Leaf Spinach	*Green Salad*
Fruit	*Apricot Croûtes*
Niçoise platter	*Stuffed Tomatoes Piémontaise*
Grilled Lamb Cutlets	*Hake à l'Anglaise*
Buttered French Beans	*Steamed Potatoes à l'Anglaise*
Potato Straws	*Green Peas Ménagère*
Strawberry Mousse	*Stewed Fruit*

Party Menus

Lunch	Dinner
Shrimp Cocktail	*Italian Pasta Soup*
Roast Fillet of Beef	*Fillet of Sole with Mushrooms*
Ratatouille Niçoise	*Duck with Orange*
Château Potatoes	*Potato Purée Mousseline*
Pears with Chocolate Sauce	*Pineapple Ninon*

Culinary Craft

There are few foods which are eaten in the raw state and do not require some method of cooking. It is important to understand the basic methods of heat transfer or cooking in order to carry them out successfully. Many of us are familiar with these basic methods, but do not always understand the underlying principles.

BOILING

Strictly speaking, in boiling, food is supplied with heat by water only. There are very few occasions when food is actually "boiled", although we tend to refer to "boiled beef" or "boiled fish". Most of the time we are referring to the simmering process. The practical difference between these two terms can be measured by the amount of surface movement of the water. The difference in actual water temperature is almost negligible—rapid boiling takes place at a temperature of 212°F or 100°C, while simmering requires a temperature of 190°F or 97°C. In simmering, the surface of the liquid is merely agitated and bubbles break gently on the surface, in one place only. Whereas in boiling, the surface is turbulent and bubbles break continuously all over the surface.

When food is cooked by boiling or simmering, soluble substances such as proteins, mineral salts and meat juices dissolve out into the water. In order to prevent this loss, meat is usually immersed in boiling water for the first few minutes to seal the surface pores. The temperature is then lowered, and the meat simmered for the cooking period. Simmering is essential to eliminate loss of nutrients, loss of character and colour, and also loss of texture and flavour of food.

Vegetables are usually put in boiling water at first, to conserve the flavouring and colouring substances. Here again, cooking is continued at simmering point.

STEAMING

In this method of cooking, heat is transmitted by steam, not water. It is used for non-fatty foods such as fish, some kinds of meat, vegetables, potatoes, cereal products, etc. Steaming involves a different process from boiling; the effect of hot steam on food substances is different from that of boiling water; for example, fat is the only food substance that is dissolved out.

Vitamins are affected in exactly the same way as by boiling; those sensitive to heat or soluble in water are destroyed or become less active according to the degree of heat and length of time for which they are subjected to it. Mineral salts are practically unchanged.

Steaming is an ideal method of cooking, for the texture of food is generally lighter and more digestible than foods cooked by any other method.

Steaming is recommended for non-fatty fish, poultry and light puddings. The essential points to note about steaming are to maintain the rate of water evaporation by keeping the water boiling steadily. When necessary, add fresh boiling water, and ensure that the steamer has a tightly fitting lid to prevent the escape of steam.

"ÉTUVÉE" COOKING

This method is often confused with steaming. The difference is that "étuvée" cooking involves the use of both steam and a little liquid (water, stock, wine, etc.), and sometimes fat, as heat conductors. In addition, cooking takes place in a tightly closed pot. The moisture from the steam and the actual cooking liquid both act on the food. The advantage of this method in comparison with steaming is that the food retains its flavour very well and slightly tougher fibres can be thoroughly cooked. The addition of fat to the liquid as a heat conductor is of basic importance in this method.

"Etuvée" cooking is essentially a long slow cooking process, and may be used for the cheaper and tougher cuts of meat. It is important that the food is covered with a tight-fitting lid so that the self-basting action of the condensing steam may be maintained. With few exceptions, a great variety of foods may be cooked in the same fat without their taste being passed from one to another. New substances are formed during cooking which result in the formation of a tasty, savoury crust.

The so-called "glazing" of vegetables is based on the principle of "étuvée" cooking. The vegetables or other foods are cooked in fat and liquid until the latter has almost completely evaporated. When the pan is shaken, the food is covered with a shiny coat of fat and reduced liquid. If the glazing process is continued beyond this point, braising begins, putting an end to "étuvée" cooking. The amount of food to be cooked is very important. If it is small, a *sauté* pan or saucepan with a lid is usually sufficient.

OVEN-ROASTING

In this case fat and hot air serve as heat conductors. It is important to subject meat, especially, to fierce heat at first to sear the surface and seal in the juices. The food must be basted frequently with the fat to prevent the outside crust becoming too dry. If the food is subjected to fierce heat for too long, particularly from underneath, it soon burns. The heat must therefore be lowered after a crust has formed, and the meat must be cooked at between 300° and 350°F. The joint will shrink a good deal if it is cooked at a higher temperature than this. In a closed oven the accumulated steam acts as damp heat. If a joint with a crisp surface is required, there must be adequate heat above it and proper provision for the escape of steam. It helps too, if the joint is placed on a rack to allow hot air to circulate freely. Fat joints, such as spare rib or loin of pork, ham, etc., which should have a crisp surface, are scored before cooking. The changes that take place when food is roasted are the same as in "étuvée" cooking.

SPIT-ROASTING

In spit-roasting, dry heat is used, so that the food has to be basted frequently with fat to prevent the crust becoming too dry. The meat is first exposed to fierce heat, which is reduced when the outside crust is golden-brown. Different types of spits have different methods of regulating the heat. Before spit-roasting, the joint or bird is seasoned lightly and brushed with fat or butter. The changes produced by spit-roasting are the same as in oven-roasting.

Some modern spits have a glass door in front to close them up. Steam accumulates inside and produces damp heat; in the absence of dry air, proper spit-roasting is impossible.

GRILLING

In grilling, too, the heat conductor is hot air. Generally, grilling is confined to small pieces of meat, such as chops, tournedos, steaks, etc.; small fish, trout, whiting, fish fillets,

4

etc.; and small birds which are cut into two or more pieces depending on their size. Grilled foods should be juicy and tender and have a slightly puffy appearance when cooked.

Before grilling, the food is brushed with oil or clarified butter. The grill must be pre-heated to ensure quick coagulation of the surface proteins. Fish, especially flat fish, should be dredged with flour before being brushed over with oil. This helps to form a protective crust and reduces the risk of breaking the flesh. Fish and chicken are often coated with bread-crumbs before being brushed with oil or clarified butter. Whenever food to be grilled has been floured or coated with breadcrumbs, the use of a double grilling rack, pre-heated and oiled, is recommended. The food can then be turned more easily, being held firmly inside the double rack.

Pieces of meat are turned frequently to keep the juices flowing and to prevent drying up. If fairly thick cuts of red meat are being grilled, the heat should be turned down once a crust has formed on both sides, to prevent the latter drying out or charring. The food should be basted with oil occasionally while it is grilling. White meat (veal, lamb, chicken) is nearly always cooked and crisped at one and the same time. The heat therefore must not be too fierce. This also applies to fish fillets and small whole fish.

Most grills have an arrangement for the fat to drain off along a groove into a container. Either charcoal, electric or gas grills may be used. There are various methods of altering the height of the grill.

SHALLOW FRYING OR SAUTÉING

This method is used for small pieces of fish, meat, game or chicken. "*Sauter*" means to toss food in hot fat in a tall or shallow pan without a lid. As the heat only reaches the under-side of the food, the latter has to be turned and stirred now and again. The hot fat quickly coagulates the surface proteins and lightly browns the outside of the food, which brings out the flavour. Some of the juices are invariably drawn out of the food and are deposited on the bottom of the pan, where they are lightly caramelised.

When both sides are golden-brown, the heat must be lowered to prevent charring. Meat to be cooked in this way should always be put in very hot fat. If it is not hot enough, the proteins escape, the meat becomes sodden and insipid, losing its goodness and flavour. Care must also be taken to make sure that the juices adhering to the bottom of the pan are only caramelised and do not become too dark. When the cooked food and the fat have been removed, the pan should be rinsed out with liquid (wine or stock), and scraped with a wooden spoon to loosen the deposit. The liquid is then reduced and used to make the sauce. If the deposit is too dark it is unusable, as it would make the sauce bitter. A shallow saucepan or a frying-pan may be used for small quantities of food to be cooked by the "*sauté*" method.

BRAISING

Braising is one of the most commonly used methods of cooking. The most important point in braising is the correct formation of a crust round the food. To achieve this, the food is put in very hot fat and lightly browned all round, including the ends.

Sufficient liquid (water, stock, wine, sauce, etc.) is added to come about a quarter of the way up the food. The pan or casserole is then covered and the food is left to simmer.

Three heat conductors are involved in braising—liquid, fat and steam. The heat only penetrates the food very gradually and the latter should be turned several times. The best procedure is to wait until the liquid has been so much reduced that only fat is left, then to turn the food several times in the fat and pour some more liquid over it. The braising pan should not be left uncovered for too long, and the liquid should not cook too quickly.

For successful braising an ovenproof dish or pan with a tightly fitting lid is required and the food should be cooked in a moderate oven, where it is surrounded by heat on all sides.

FRYING

Whatever fat is used for frying, it must be hot enough for the food to absorb very little of it. The fats in the food itself may, however, combine with the frying fat.

If the instructions for frying are followed carefully, a perfect crust is formed right round the food. The heat must be regulated according to the type of food to be fried. Some general rules to follow are that only small quantities of food are fried at one time and the fat must be kept hot. Frying is only used for small fish or pieces of meat, potatoes, vegetables, etc. Soft foods coated with breadcrumbs—*croquettes* in particular—should be fried in very hot fat so that a protective crust forms immediately to prevent the inside disintegrating. Other foods, however, should be cooked and browned at one and the same time. Some foods such as potato straws, matchsticks or crisps are fried once only, while *soufflé* potatoes and chips are blanched first of all and then fried in two stages. It is essential always to keep separate frying fat for fish; also that the fat must be kept clear by straining after use. Well-fried food should be golden or light-brown in colour, free from grease and crisp on the outside.

POACHING

Poaching is cooking food in a liquid at a temperature just below boiling point. The liquid must never boil.

This method is used for large fish, large birds, hams, etc., and also for small fish and fillets, small cuts of meat and birds. Large fish like salmon, carp or turbot are put in a fish-kettle and covered with cold water or cold *court-bouillon*. It is brought rapidly to the boil and the fish is then poached until it is cooked through. A flat buttered pan is used for small fish and fish fillets, chicken breasts, etc. After seasoning, the food is put in the oven with a little liquid (wine, stock, etc.), covered with buttered or oiled paper or foil.

Care must always be taken to use only the minimum amount of liquid required for poaching. Small cuts are put on to cook in a little liquid only and large ones are barely covered.

GRATINATING OR AU GRATIN COOKING

"Gratinating" means producing a brown crust on a dish. There are three ways of gratinating—completely, quickly and lightly.

To gratinate completely, the raw food, which is often cut up small, is put in a buttered, ovenproof dish on a bed of sauce. It is then covered with a *gratin* sauce, sprinkled with soft white breadcrumbs and melted butter or oil, and baked in the oven. The most important part of the dish is the sauce. There must be enough of it for the food to cook in it. The sauce binds and covers the food during cooking, but it should not become soup-like. Cooking and browning take place at the same time; this means that the oven must be used for this method of gratinating.

The quick gratinating procedure is the same, except that the food has to be well cooked beforehand. Either a hot oven or a salamander may be used.

The commonest of the three methods is gratinating lightly, which is mostly used for pasta dishes. The pasta should be bound with a sauce or sprinkled with soft white breadcrumbs or grated cheese, or a mixture of the two and butter. The heat should not be too fierce, so that the cheese can melt slowly and combine with the butter. These dishes are put in a moderate oven to form an even, golden-brown crust.

OVEN TEMPERATURE CHART

In the vast majority of recipes in this book we have given both a description of the heat of the oven and also the exact temperature in Fahrenheit degrees and the gas mark. However, you will probably find the oven temperature chart overleaf useful, as individual ovens do vary. It is important to remember, of course, to pre-heat ovens for at least 15 minutes before use.

DESCRIPTION OF OVEN TEMPERATURE	ELECTRIC TEMPERATURE IN °F	GAS TEMPERATURE IN MARKS
Very cool oven	225–250°F	$\frac{1}{4}-\frac{1}{2}$
Cool oven	275°F	1
Cool oven	300°F	2
Warm oven	325°F	3
Moderate oven	350°F	4
Fairly hot oven	375°F	5
Hot oven	400°F	6
Hot oven	425°F	7
Very hot oven	450°F	8
Very hot oven	475°F +	9

Useful Hints

Beating Egg Whites

The bowl used for beating egg whites must be free from all traces of grease. When whites are beaten they should be 2–3 days old and as cold as possible.

Clarifying Bouillon

Beat up a little cold *bouillon* (stock) with some egg white and pour the *bouillon* over it after warming the latter slightly. Bring to the boil, stirring continuously, cover and leave to stand. When the egg white has all risen to the top and the *bouillon* has become clear, strain through a tammy cloth or piece of unstarched damask.

Cooking Meat

If you want to sear cut-up meat or poultry for stews, or *sauté* chicken, brown the meat or chicken in separate batches. If it is heaped up in the pan, its juices will escape and it will not brown. The main thing is to seal in the juices quickly, in very hot fat.

Cooking Chicken

To test whether chicken is cooked, turn it over and let a little juice run on to a white plate. If the juice is clear, the chicken is done. If it has traces of blood in it, allow the chicken to continue cooking.

Deep Frying Fat

If your deep frying fat has an unpleasant smell, heat it, drop one or two quartered onions or some potato peel into it and fry them well. Strain the fat through a fine sieve.

Chestnuts

To skin raw chestnuts, make a slit in them on both sides, place them on a baking sheet sprinkled with water and put them in a hot oven, 425°F or Gas Mark 7. The chestnuts split open after a short time, and the outer and inner skins may then be easily removed.

Curdled Mayonnaise

Add the mayonnaise drop by drop to a spoonful of boiling water, stirring all the time with a whisk.

Burnt Food

To rescue food which has burnt slightly, transfer it to a clean saucepan, but do not stir it or scrape off the food remaining at the bottom or sticking to the sides of the burnt pan.

Onions
When peeling and chopping onions, pour a little vinegar over them to prevent your eyes watering.

Curdled Butter Sauces
Sauces such as *Hollandaise, Béarnaise*, etc. tend to curdle if stored in too warm a place. If a sauce has curdled, pour a little cold water into a saucepan, tilt the pan and begin beating the sauce into the water, a little at a time.

Soufflés
To make a *soufflé* rise properly, whip the egg whites to a very stiff snow and fold them into the panada quickly and lightly. The whites should be added when the panada is lukewarm. Butter the mould.

A *soufflé* rises and sinks again if the oven is too hot, if it is not cooked right through, or if the whites have not been folded in thoroughly.

Tomatoes
To skin tomatoes, put them in boiling water for one minute.

Wine
Never add wine of any kind to a sauce without first cooking the wine and reducing it by half.

Wine used to flavour jelly should be added when the jelly is cold but before it has set.

Basic Preparations

FORCEMEATS

FARCE DE PORC PÂTÉS OU GALANTINES ★ PORK FORCE-MEAT FOR PÂTÉS OR GALANTINES

This is made of lean and fat pork for *pâtés*, and of pork, veal and fat bacon for poultry and game galantines.

1. **For Pâtés:** Mince 1¼ pounds lean pork and 1¼ pounds fat unsalted bacon; pass through the mincer 2 or 3 times, using a fine blade. This will yield about 1½ pounds of forcemeat.
2. **For Poultry Galantine:** Make in the same way as for *pâtés*, using 12 ounces lean pork, 12 ounces lean veal and 1½ pounds fat bacon. Finely minced meat from the chicken legs may also be added. Forcemeat for galantine must be even finer than that for *pâtés*.
3. **For Game Galantine:** Add a little of the meat, or blood, or just the crushed liver of the game. Season with ⅓ ounce *pâté* seasoning per pound of forcemeat.

Farce à Gratin ★ Gratin Forcemeat (Liver Pâté)

6 oz fat green bacon; 9 oz liver (chicken, game or calf's liver); 1 tablespoon altogether of shallots, parsley, thyme, and bay leaf.

Chop the bacon very finely, melt it on the stove and when it is almost entirely melted add the thinly sliced liver, browning quickly to prevent loss of blood. Add the herbs and shallots as soon as the liver is stiff. Toss for another 2 minutes, pound in a pestle and mortar or the liquidiser with the fat, and pass through a sieve. Keep in a cool place, well-covered with oiled paper. This forcemeat is delicious and ready to serve because it is already cooked. It is better made with chicken or game liver than with calf's liver.

Used for stuffing game or as a spread on *canapés*, and served as *hors d'œuvre*.

MARINADES

Marinade Crue ★ Uncooked Marinade

Place the meat to be marinated in a dish. Cover with plenty of sliced carrots, onions and shallots, a pinch of crushed peppercorns, some juniper berries, 1 or 2 cloves, and some parsley, thyme and bay leaf. Salt lightly and add 1 bottle of white wine and

$\frac{1}{4}$ pint vinegar and sprinkle the top of the meat with oil to prevent the part which is not covered by the marinade from turning black. Put in a cool place and turn several times. Let small pieces (cutlets, *noisettes*, etc.) stand for 24 hours, larger pieces (leg of venison or boar) for 2 or 3 days, according to size.

Cuite * *Cooked*

The same ingredients as above, but boil the vegetables in the white wine and vinegar for 15 minutes, using a little more of each liquid to allow for evaporation. If one is in a hurry for the marinated meat the marinade may be poured over the meat while still boiling hot, provided the latter is fresh. In this way a leg of venison will be perfectly marinated in 24 hours and a small piece in 4 or 5 hours.

Spices and Herbs in the Kitchen

Allspice (*berries*)
Forcemeat, savoury pie fillings, pork products.

Aniseed (*seeds of the anise plant*)
Cakes and pastries, manufacture of liqueurs.

Balm (*leaves*)
Sauces, spring vegetable soup, salads.

Basil (*leaves, branches*)
Sauces, soups, omelettes, fish dishes, meat, pork products, game *pâté*, herb vinegar. Italian cooking.

Bay (*leaves*)
Fish stock, marinades, sauces.

Borage (*flowers, leaves*)
Vegetable soups, *galette* (flat cake) bases, salads.

Burnet (*leaves*)
Herb soups, young leaves for salad.

Cardamon (*seeds*)
Curry, exotic dishes, breads, cakes.

Celery (*leaves*)
Soups, herb-flavoured dishes, garnish for cold dishes.

Chervil (*leaves*)
Fish stock, sauce *Vinaigrette*, soups, salads, garnish for cold dishes.

Chives (*leaves*)
Sauces, soups, raw vegetables, fish and meat dishes.

Cinnamon (*bark*)
Sweet dishes, cakes and pastries, flavouring for punches and liqueurs, spiced wine.

Cloves (*flower buds*)
Fish stock, marinades, sauces, cakes (spice loaf, or French gingerbread).

Coriander (*seeds*)
Fish marinades, sauces, exotic dishes, pork products, cakes and pastries, liqueurs.

Cumin (*seeds*)
Ground: sauces, fish, roast mutton, mushrooms, turnips, sauerkraut, salads, cakes. *Whole:* manufacture of certain kinds of cheese, liqueurs.

Curry (*powder, a mixture of spices*)
Curry sauces, veal, mutton, lamb, poultry, *pilafs*, exotic rice dishes.

Dill (*branches*)
Marinades, fresh herb soup, sauce for crayfish, salads, pickled gherkins, garnish for cold dishes.

Fennel (*seeds*)
Cucumber salad, marinade for gherkins, manufacture of liqueurs.

Garlic (*bulb*)
Marinades, sauces, soups, roasts, mutton stew, salads.

Ginger (*pieces of root*)
Exotic dishes, confectionery, cakes and biscuits.

Horseradish (*root*)
Marinades, hot and cold sauces, pickles.

Hyssop (*leaves*)
Sauces, roasts, raw vegetables, salads.

Juniper (*berries*)
Game, sauerkraut, flavouring for spirits (gin).

Lovage (*leaves*)
Soups, pork products.

Mace (*husks*)
In small quantities in mixed spice.

Marjoram (*leaves*)
Sauces, soups, potato dishes, Italian cooking, pork products.

Mint (*leaves*)
Soups, sauces (Mint sauce), roast mutton and game, vegetables, preparation of liqueurs.

Mugwort (*flowers*)
Sauces for roast dishes, especially roast goose, duck and pork.

Mustard (*seeds*)
Meat dishes, pickles.

Nasturtium (*seeds*)
Flavouring for pickled gherkins and wine vinegar.

Nutmeg (*kernels*)
Sauces, soups, vegetables, mashed potatoes.

Onion (*bulb*)
Extensively used in cooking.

Paprika (*fruit*)
Sauces, flavoured butter, meat and fish dishes, sprinkling on certain sauces and dishes.

Parsley (*branches, leaves*)
Bouquet garni, soups, *maître d'hôtel* butter, as a garnish either chopped or whole, for sprinkling on vegetables, fish meat and savoury dishes.

Pepper (*seeds*)
Condiment universally used in cooking.

Pimento (*seeds*)
Marinades, pork products, preserved meat.

Poppy (*seeds*)
Cakes, breads and rolls.

Rosemary (*leaves*)
Sauces, fish soups, roasts (mutton and pork), poultry, game, pork products, potatoes, herb vinegar.

Rue (*leaves*)
Marinades, omelettes, salads.

Saffron (*flower stigmas*)
Bouillabaisse (fish stew), *risotto*, *pilafs*, exotic dishes, cakes.

Sage (*leaves*)
Fish (*tench*), veal, Italian specialities, forcemeat for fatty meat (e.g. pork), mixed herbs.

Saltpetre
Brine for preserving meat.

Savory (*branches*)
Sauces, herb soups, meat, French beans.

Shallot (*bulb*)
Very extensively used condiment.

Southernwood (*leaves*)
Fish, meat, salads, pickled gherkins.

Sweet Cicely (*leaves*)
Same as chervil.

Tarragon (*leaves*)
Marinades, sauces, soups, omelettes, roast meat and poultry, salads, tarragon vinegar and mustard, garnish for hot and cold dishes, pickled gherkins.

Thyme (*leaves, herb*)
Marinades, *bouquet garni*, sauces, soups, meat, roasts, vegetables, potatoes.

Vanilla (*seed pods*)
Sweet dishes, cakes, pastries and biscuits.

Wild Marjoram (*leaves*)
Sauces, roasts, Italian cooking.

SPICE MIXTURES AND SEASONINGS

For Roasts

$\frac{1}{4}$ *oz cloves;* $\frac{1}{2}$ *oz thyme;* $\frac{1}{4}$ *oz bay leaf;* $\frac{1}{2}$ *oz parsley;* $\frac{1}{4}$ *oz pepper;* $\frac{1}{2}$ *oz marjoram;* $\frac{1}{4}$ *oz basil;* $\frac{1}{2}$ *oz rosemary.*

Pâté and pie seasoning

$\frac{1}{4}$ *oz rosemary;* $\frac{1}{4}$ *oz cinnamon;* $\frac{1}{2}$ *oz bay leaf;* $\frac{1}{2}$ *oz ginger;* $\frac{1}{4}$ *oz savory;* $\frac{1}{4}$ *oz sage;* $\frac{1}{2}$ *oz mace;* $\frac{1}{2}$ *oz basil;* 1 *oz nutmeg;* $1\frac{1}{4}$ *oz coriander;* $1\frac{1}{4}$ *oz thyme;* 1 *oz cloves;* $1\frac{1}{4}$ *oz marjoram;* $1\frac{1}{4}$ *oz pepper.*

Do not crush dried spices too finely and use only in small quantities.

Spices to be used with roasts may be ground more coarsely and mixed directly with the salt. These two spice mixtures may be made up in large quantities and stored in airtight jars or tins, ready for use.

Glossary of Cooking Terms

Like all trades and professions, cookery has its own technical terms. They include everyday words which everyone understands, but which have quite a different meaning when used in cookery. An outline of this specialised terminology is given in the little dictionary below.

Aspic Savoury jelly, or cold food set in jelly.

Bain-marie A device for keeping foods hot or cooking them very gently. A large pan is half-filled or filled with hot water and placed over gentle heat. One or more saucepans or basins can be stood inside it so that their contents can be cooked very gently, or kept hot.

Bake blind To bake pastry cases for flans, tarts or tartlets, before filling, by covering them with a piece of greased greaseproof paper and half-filling with rice, dried beans or fruit stones.

Barding To cover meat or poultry with slices of fat bacon before roasting, to prevent the flesh from drying up.

Bind To add egg, flour, cornflour, etc. to a liquid to thicken it, or to add a liquid, egg or melted fat to a mixture to hold it together.

Blanch To cook partially, e.g. vegetables or meat; to cook green vegetables in boiling water in such a way as to preserve their natural colour; to put in cold water and bring to the boil, in order to whiten or remove a strong flavour or excess saltiness from food.

Bouchées Small cases of puff pastry.

Bouillon A rich, strong clear stock of game, poultry, meat or vegetables.

Bouquet garni A bunch of herbs—usually parsley, thyme, bay leaf and celery tied together, cooked in the pot with the other ingredients and removed before serving. Other herbs, such as tarragon or basil, are occasionally called for in a recipe.

Braising Method of cooking in a covered pan or casserole with a little liquid.

Brochette Meat, onions, mushrooms, etc. cooked on a skewer.

15

Brunoise	A mixture of vegetables cut into very small dice, then cooked in fat.
Canapé	Small fancy-cut slices of bread which can be buttered, fried or roasted, and used as a base for a savoury or *hors d'œuvre*.
Caramelise	To melt sugar and cook until it reaches a straw colour, or to coat with caramel.
Clarify	To clear or purify. Butter is clarified by melting and straining it; *bouillon* or consommé, by beating it over heat with some egg white.
Consommé	A clear soup made with meat or chicken stock.
Court-bouillon	Stock used for cooking fish.
Couverture	A special type of chocolate used for sweet dishes, cakes, pastries and confectionery. It contains a minimum of 35 per cent cocoa butter and a maximum of 50 per cent sugar.
Croustade	A case of pastry or fried bread.
Croûtons	Toasted or fried bread cut into various shapes for *canapés*, or diced as a garnish for soup.
Daube	Meat stew cooked in red wine.
Duxelles	Chopped mushrooms cooked in butter with chopped shallot and used as a forcemeat.
Entrecôte	Steak cut from the ribs of beef.
Etuvée	Method of cooking in a covered pan with a given amount of fat, but little or no liquid.
Flame (flambé)	To coat food with a spirit and set it alight.
Forcing bag	Cone-shaped cloth bag to which nozzles of various shapes and sizes may be fitted for piping.
Fumet	A concentrated stock of meat, fish, game or vegetables such as mushrooms, greatly reduced and used to give extra flavour to some sauces.
Glaze	Any substance used to give a glossy finish to certain meat dishes, vegetables, sweets and savouries, e.g. brushing with beaten egg.
Julienne	Vegetables or other foods cut into thin, match-like strips.
Larding	The insertion of small strips of pork fat larding bacon (lardoons) into the flesh of meat, poultry or game before cooking, to prevent its drying out while roasting. A special larding needle is used for the purpose.
Liaison	Binding or thickening agent, used in soups and sauces.
Macerate	To soak a fruit in wine or liqueur to impart flavour.

16

Marinade	A liquid containing seasoning, herbs and spices in which various foods, especially game, are steeped to give them flavour and make the flesh more tender.
Mask	To coat with a sauce.
Mirepoix	A basic preparation used as a foundation for certain sauces, braised dishes, etc. It consists of diced carrots, onions, celery and ham or bacon gently cooked in butter.
Mousseline	A small, individual *mousse* usually made in an egg-shaped mould.
Pare	To prepare or trim.
Poach	To simmer a food very gently in liquid at 194–203°F.
Praline nougat	Ground almond rock, used for flavouring and decoration.
Pré-salé	A description of origin, which means "salty meadows by the seashore", referring to the pastures of the Breton coast. The grass is supposed to give a specially good flavour to the lamb and mutton.
Quenelles	Meat or fish forcemeat made into small oval shapes and poached.
Reduce	To boil a liquid, such as a sauce or stock rapidly, uncovered to make it more concentrated by evaporation.
Refresh	To pour cold water over vegetables, fruit or meat after they have been blanched.
Roux	A paste made by cooking fat and flour together; it forms the foundation of most sauces. See also page 19.
Salpicon	A mixture containing various ingredients, such as flavouring vegetables, ham, fish or meat, cut into dice, finely minced or shredded, and bound with sauce. Used to fill *vol-au-vent* cases, *canapés* etc.
Sauté	To shallow fry lightly in hot fat, shaking the pan frequently.
Scald	To pour boiling water over food.
Score	To make shallow cuts in the surface of meat or fish.
Sear	To brown meat quickly in a little hot fat to seal in the juices.
Spatula	A wooden tool with a flat blade for beating and mixing.
Suprême	The best or most delicate part, e.g. breast of chicken.
Sweat	A term used to describe meat or vegetables being given a preliminary cooking in fat until beads of juice start to pearl on the surface.
Tammy cloth	A fine woollen cloth used for straining sauces, soups, etc.

Truss   To tie a bird's legs and wings in position with string by means of a trussing needle, which is passed right through the bird.

Work   To mix a paste with the hands or a tool so that all the ingredients are combined.

Zest   The thin coloured outer skin of citrus fruits (lemons, oranges or grapefruit).

Sauces

Sauces play a very important part in cookery; they add flavour, colour and texture to other dishes. Stock and *roux* form the basis of most sauces.

ROUX * *ROUX*

Roux is the most common thickening for sauces, stews and soups. It may be cooked until it is white, blond or brown, and is usually made of nearly equal quantities of flour and fat.

The method is to melt the fat slowly in a saucepan and when it has just melted draw the pan off the heat and add the sifted flour. Stir until the mixture is smooth and then cook, stirring constantly, to the required colour.

It is important that:

1. The mixture of flour and butter or fat is never cooked too quickly, even if one is making a brown sauce. The flour must be cooked gently, otherwise the fat will burn and blacken it, giving it a bitter taste.

2. The *roux* should never be dry, i.e. contain too much flour for the amount of fat. A *roux* must always be slightly liquid, otherwise you will have difficulty in making a smooth sauce.

3. The hot *roux* should never be moistened with boiling liquid, for if the pan is hot the mixture will start to boil before the *roux* has been diluted. The sauce will be too light and the *roux* will granulate into small lumps which will not dissolve.

4. A whisk should always be used.

LES SAUCES DE BASE BRUNES * *BASIC BROWN SAUCES*

Sauce *Demi-glace* forms the foundation of all brown sauces. It is often served combined with Madeira, port, tarragon, mushrooms, etc.

Thickening brown sauces with cornflour or potato flour.
Mix the cornflour, plain flour or potato flour with a little cold water or Madeira, depending on the sauce, and add some of the boiling liquid, stirring all the time. Then add the boiling liquid to this thin paste, stirring all the time.

Sauce Demi-glace * Basic brown sauce

1½ oz lard or dripping; 1 oz flour; ½ pint pot-au-feu or bouillon; 1 tablespoon concentrated tomato paste or 2 skinned, crushed fresh tomatoes without their seeds; seasoning.

Make a *roux* with the flour and lard. Cook it over gentle heat until it browns *stirring all the time* to prevent the flour burning, as this would give the sauce a bitter taste. Whisk in the *bouillon* gradually; add tomatoes or paste and continue whisking until the sauce comes to the boil. Simmer without stirring for 1 hour, skimming frequently to remove surface fat. Correct consistency by adding more *bouillon* if necessary. Strain. Add 1 ounce fresh butter in small pieces, making sure that each piece is melted before adding the next. This sauce should thicken, but not become too thick.

LES SAUCES BRUNES COMPOSÉES * DERIVATIVE BROWN SAUCES

Sauce Bercy * Bercy sauce

¼ pint sauce Demi-glace; 6 tablespoons white wine; 1 chopped shallot; juice of half a lemon; 2 teaspoons chopped parsley; ¾ oz butter.

Boil the white wine rapidly with the chopped shallot to reduce it. Before it is completely reduced, remove the pan from the heat and stir in the *sauce Demi-glace* and the butter. Add the lemon juice and chopped parsley.

▣ Bordelaise * Bordelaise or Marrow

½ pint sauce Demi-glace; 2 oz beef marrow; 1 small teaspoon chopped shallots; ¼ pint red wine; 6 crushed peppercorns; 1 sprig thyme; 1 oz butter.

Toss the chopped shallots for a minute in butter. Moisten with red wine; add crushed peppercorns and a sprig of thyme, and reduce to ⅓ quantity. Add *Demi-glace*, simmer the finely diced marrow and keep on one side of the heat for another 10 minutes without boiling. Stir in the melted marrow, which will be floating on top. Serve with grilled meats.

▣ Chasseur * Chasseur

½ pint sauce Demi-glace; 4 tablespoons white wine; 4 oz mushrooms; 1 small teaspoon tomato paste; chopped chervil and tarragon; 2 tablespoons olive oil; 1 shallot.

Lightly brown the minced mushrooms in hot oil, add a finely chopped shallot and the white wine. Reduce to half and add the *sauce Demi-glace* and tomato paste. Add a pinch of chopped chervil and tarragon. This sauce is served with chicken, grilled meats and game.

▣ Chevreuil * Venison

The same sauce as *sauce Poivrade* for game, but reduce with red wine instead of vinegar. Season with cayenne and a little sugar.

▣ Colbert * Colbert

For ¼ pint: 4 oz butter; 3 tablespoons meat glaze; chopped parsley and tarragon; juice of 1 lemon.

Melt the butter and meat glaze, mix together and leave until cold. Add the herbs and lemon juice, salt and pepper. Serve as an accompaniment to grilled meat and fish.

Sauce Diable * *Devil*

For ¾ pint: 2 shallots; 1 oz butter; ¼ pint dry white wine; ½ pint sauce Demi-glace; Worcester sauce.

Fry the chopped shallots to a pale golden colour in butter, add the white wine and slowly reduce by half. Add the *sauce Demi-glace*, which should be fairly thick. Simmer for a few minutes, then add a pinch of chopped chervil and flavour with cayenne pepper and a dash of Worcester sauce. Serve with grilled chicken and pigeon.

▣ à l'Estragon * *Tarragon*

Infuse a pinch of chopped tarragon in *sauce Demi-glace* for 5 to 6 minutes and serve without straining. This sauce is suitable for eggs, escalopes and chicken. Sprinkle the meat with fresh chopped tarragon when serving.

▣ Gratin * *Gratin*

½ pint sauce Demi-glace made with fish stock; 2 oz finely chopped mushrooms; 2 chopped shallots; ¼ pint white wine; ¾ oz butter; 1 small teaspoon tomato paste; chopped parsley; seasoning.

Simmer raw mushrooms in butter, add the chopped shallots and the white wine; reduce to half and add *sauce Demi-glace* with a little tomato paste and chopped parsley; season.

▣ Italienne * *Italian*

2 oz chopped raw mushrooms; 2 oz diced cooked ham; 1 chopped shallot; ¼ pint white wine; ½ pint sauce Demi-glace; 1 tablespoon Tomato sauce; chopped parsley; 1 tablespoon olive oil.

Brown the mushrooms slightly in oil. Add the lean, finely-diced ham and a chopped shallot and cook for 2 minutes. Moisten with the white wine. Reduce by half, add the *sauce Demi-glace*, Tomato sauce and a little chopped parsley. Season and simmer for 5 to 6 minutes.

▣ Lyonnaise * *Lyonnaise*

½ pint sauce Demi-glace; ¼ pint white wine; 1 finely chopped onion; butter.

Toss the finely chopped onion in butter without allowing it to brown, moisten with the white wine, reduce to half and add the *Demi-glace*. Simmer for 10 minutes, and sieve or tammy. This sauce is served with meat or vegetables, mainly liver and artichokes. It may be strained or served with the onion in it, according to taste.

▣ Madère * *Madeira*

¼ pint Madeira; ¼ pint sauce Demi-glace; 1 tablespoon meat glaze; seasoning; 1 oz butter.

Cook Madeira and meat glaze till reduced by half. Stir in *Demi-glace*, and boil up. Whisk in butter, in small pieces. Season to taste.

▣ Périgueux * *Truffle*

4 tablespoons Madeira; ½ pint sauce Demi-glace; 1 oz chopped truffles; ½ oz butter.

Reduce the Madeira by half. Add the *sauce Demi-glace* and cook for 10 minutes. Skim well, remove from the heat, add the softened butter and the finely chopped truffles.

Sauce Piquante * *Piquant*

½ pint sauce Demi-glace; 4 tablespoons vinegar; 2 tablespoons white wine; 1 tablespoon chopped shallots; 1 oz thinly sliced gherkins; chopped parsley; 1 oz butter.

Toss the chopped shallots in butter, moisten with the vinegar and wine and reduce by three-quarters. Add the *Demi-glace* and simmer for 15 minutes, then sieve or tammy. When about to serve the sauce add a few sliced gherkins and a little chopped parsley.

▣ Poivrade * *Pepper sauce for Game*

For approx. ¾ pint: 8 oz game trimmings; 4 tablespoons olive oil; 1 carrot; 1 onion; 2½ tablespoons vinegar; 1 pint sauce Demi-glace; 4 tablespoons marinade; 6 pepper-corns; thyme; bay leaf; parsley. Cooking time: 1½ hours.

Fry the game trimmings in a little oil. Add the carrot, onion and herbs. Brown slowly, add vinegar and reduce completely. Add the *sauce Demi-glace* and the marinade. Add crushed peppercorns and cook gently for 1 hour. Skim off the fat, strain, and season well.

▣ Robert * *Robert*

½ pint sauce Demi-glace; ¼ pint white wine; 1 chopped onion; 2 tablespoons tomato purée; 1 small teaspoon strong mustard; ¾ oz butter.

Reduce the white wine by half with the chopped onion, without colouring. Add the tomato *purée* and *sauce Demi-glace* and cook for 15 minutes. Skim the sauce and add the mustard and butter to finish. Remove from the heat and serve.

LES SAUCES BLANCHES * *WHITE SAUCES*

White sauces may be made with *bouillon*, stock of the meat to be served, water or milk, or with fish stock.

The best known white sauce is the *sauce Velouté*, which is the foundation of most white sauces just as *Demi-glace* or brown sauce is the foundation of most of the darker-coloured sauces.

LE FUMET DE POISSON * *FISH STOCK*

A *fumet* is used to add flavour to a fish sauce. Make the stock as and when needed, with the trimmings and bones of the fish used. Place the trimmings in a saucepan with 1 or 2 onions, a sliced shallot, some mushroom trimmings or stalks, a little parsley and a few peppercorns. Moisten with ¼ pint good quality white wine and an equal quantity of water. Salt lightly, bring to the boil, reduce the heat and simmer for 25 minutes. Strain through a fine sieve. (See section on fish for the way in which to use the stock).

THICKENING AGENTS FOR WHITE SAUCES

The principles of thickening a white sauce with egg yolks are very little understood. It is important to remember that where egg yolks are used to thicken any liquid in which there is no flour, and the liquid is boiled, the mixture will curdle. If however there is even a small amount of flour in the liquid and the *liaison* is properly made and whisked, the sauce will not curdle even if it is brought to boiling point.

Mix the egg yolks thoroughly in a small bowl with 2 or 3 tablespoons of the cold liquid which is to be thickened. Then add 3 or 4 tablespoons of the boiling liquid one at a time, stirring rapidly all the time and using a small whisk. The *liaison* may then be added to the remaining hot liquid, beating well all the time whilst the mixture is brought to boiling point.

LES SAUCES DE BASE BLANCHES * *BASIC WHITE SAUCES*

Béchamel * *Béchamel*

1 oz butter; 1 oz flour; ½ pint milk, flavoured with onion, carrot and bouquet garni.

Make a *roux* with the flour and the butter. Cook for a few minutes without letting it colour and add the milk very gradually. Whisk until it boils and add salt and pepper. Simmer for 15 minutes. The sauce should be rather thick. *Béchamel* is not usually prepared in advance.

▣ Blanche Ménagère ou Bâtarde * *Plain white or Bâtarde*

This replaces *sauce Hollandaise* in everyday cookery. *Hollandaise* is rather expensive for daily use. It is served with fish, eggs, artichokes, asparagus, cauliflower, etc., and only takes 5 minutes to make.

1 oz butter; 1 oz flour; ½ pint hot (but not boiling) water; 1 egg yolk.

Melt butter in a saucepan. Remove from heat and stir in flour and without cooking moisten with the water. Add salt, ground white pepper and egg yolk. Whisk briskly over heat until it comes to the boil. Remove sauce from heat and add the desired amount of butter. There is no absolute rule for this—one may add from 2 to 5 ounces depending on the richness required. Complete with a dash of lemon juice or vinegar and do not allow to boil again.

▣ Veloutée * *Velouté*

1 oz butter; 1 oz flour; ½ pint bouillon.

Make a *roux* and cook over low heat for 2 minutes without letting it brown. As soon as the *roux* begins to froth, gradually add the *bouillon*. Whisk until it comes to the boil and then simmer for 25 minutes. The sauce should be a little thicker than *sauce Demi-glace*. Skim, removing all the fat, and strain through a fine sieve. Add either egg yolks, cream or other ingredients (see the recipes that follow).

LES SAUCES BLANCHES COMPOSÉES * *DERIVATIVE WHITE SAUCES*

Aurore * *Aurore or Rosy*

½ pint sauce Béchamel or Velouté; 1 tablespoon Tomato sauce or purée; 1 oz butter.

This is *Béchamel* or *Velouté* mixed with Tomato sauce to give it a rosy colour. Butter is added when the sauce has been removed from the heat. Served with eggs, poultry, etc.

Sauce au Beurre Blanc * *White Butter*

4 *tablespoons vinegar or white wine vinegar; 1 large shallot; 4 oz butter;*
seasoning.

This sauce is served mainly with pike, but also with other fish. Reduce vinegar or white wine vinegar with coarsely chopped shallot. When only a trace of vinegar remains in the pan remove the shallot with a fork. Take the butter, wash it in cold water, stir it until soft, adding pepper and salt, and put it in the slightly cooled saucepan. Beat well with a whisk without letting the butter melt. This sauce is sometimes made with a reduction of muscadet, a dry white wine from the Nantes region.

▣ Blanche à l'Estragon * *White Tarragon*

Make a *sauce Velouté* with chicken stock, thicken with an egg yolk and add a large pinch of freshly chopped tarragon. If the sauce is to be served with a boiled chicken, put a bunch of tarragon in with it while it is cooking.

▣ aux Câpres * *Caper*

Add a few chopped capers to a plain white sauce; it is unnecessary to add lemon juice or vinegar. The egg yolk may also be omitted.

▣ Chivry * *Chivry*

½ *pint chicken Velouté; 6 tablespoons white wine; a bunch of chervil;*
parsley; tarragon and chives; 1 oz Ravigote butter.

Infuse herbs in wine for a few hours. Strain and add to *Velouté*. Finish with *Ravigote* butter.

▣ Crème * *Cream*

½ *pint sauce Béchamel; ¼ pint thick cream.*

Stir the cream into the *sauce Béchamel* and serve.

▣ Crevette ou Joinville * *Prawn, Shrimp or Joinville*

2 *oz prawns or shrimps; ½ pint fish Velouté; 3 tablespoons cream; 2 oz*
butter; 1 small pinch Cayenne pepper; 1 small truffle.

Shell the prawns or shrimps, add shells to the hot *sauce Béchamel*, boil for 2 or 3 minutes and strain through a fine conical sieve. Season with salt and cayenne pepper and add the fresh cream and beat in the butter. Add chopped shrimps and finely shredded truffle. Optional: add a few drops of carmine to colour the sauce pink.

▣ Curry * *Curry*

For 2 pints; 1 large onion, finely chopped; 1 medium-sized apple, grated;
2 *oz butter; 2 oz flour; 2 level teaspoons curry powder; 1 piece dried orange peel, finely chopped;*
1 *small clove garlic, grated; 1½ pints brown stock; 3 tablespoons tomato purée; 1 tablespoon*
dessicated coconut soaked in 6 tablespoons milk for 15 minutes.

Fry the chopped onion lightly in butter. Sprinkle with the flour and curry powder without browning. Add the apple, brown stock and tomato *purée*. Stir until boiling. Add a moderate amount of salt, the garlic and the orange peel. Cook over low heat for 40 minutes. Add the strained coconut milk and boil up a little. Do not strain this sauce, which is used for cooking Anglo-Indian style dishes—beef, mutton, lamb, chicken and firm-fleshed fish. These are always served with Creole rice.

Sauch aux Groseille à Maquereau * Gooseberry

½ lb green gooseberries; 4 tablespoons water; 4 tablespoons white wine; ¼ pint sauce au Beurre Blanc.

Cook to soften the gooseberries in water. Drain off liquid and finish cooking in wine. Sieve or liquidise and add *purée* to the *sauce au Beurre Blanc*.

▣ Mornay * Mornay or Cheese

½ pint sauce Béchamel; 1 egg yolk; 1½ oz grated cheese.

Make the *sauce Béchamel*. Remove from the heat and stir in the egg yolk and cheese, mixing well. When cheese is added to a sauce or other mixture it must not be over-mixed, otherwise the mixture turns into an elastic paste. Fold gently with a spoon, never with a whisk. Do not let the mixture boil again and use at once.

▣ Moutarde * Mustard

Add 2 level tablespoons "made" mustard to ½ pint Plain white sauce at completion of cooking and without allowing to boil again. The yolk of egg may be omitted.

▣ aux Oeufs Durs * Hardboiled Egg

Mix 2 chopped hardboiled eggs with ½ pint *sauce Béchamel*. Season with salt, pepper and chopped parsley. Served mainly with boiled cod.

▣ Poulette * Rich Mushroom

½ pint sauce Velouté; ¼ pint fresh cream; 1 egg yolk; juice of half a lemon; 2 oz finely sliced mushrooms; 2 level teaspoons chopped parsley.

Boil the *sauce Velouté* with the mushrooms for 10 minutes. If preferred strain through muslin, and then bind with the cream, previously mixed with the egg yolk. Finish off by adding the lemon juice and chopped parsley.

▣ Smitane * Sour Cream

2 tablespoons finely chopped shallot; ½ oz butter; ¼ pint white wine; ½ pint sour cream; lemon juice.

Cook shallot in butter until golden brown. Add wine and reduce to a quarter. Stir in cream and boil for 2 or 3 minutes. Strain, and sharpen with lemon juice.

▣ Soubise * Onion

½ pint sauce Béchamel; 3 oz finely sliced onions; 1 oz butter or 4 tablespoons fresh cream.

Blanch the sliced onions in butter in a saucepan. Add the very thick *Béchamel*. Season, simmer and strain. Heat again and add butter or cream. Serve with braised mutton, sweetbreads or eggs.

Sauce Suprême ⋆ *Rich Chicken*

1 *pint sauce Velouté;* ¼ *pint cream; juice of* 1 *lemon; a pinch of pepper;* ½ *oz butter.*

Make a *sauce Velouté* with chicken stock and add the cream. Reduce rapidly, mixing all the time with a spatula to prevent the sauce from sticking to the pan; continue until the sauce is very creamy and coats the spatula. Remove from the heat, add the butter, lemon juice and pepper.

▣ au Vin Blanc ⋆ *White Wine*

½ *pint fish stock;* 1½ *oz butter;* 1 *oz flour;* ¼ *pint cream;* 2 *egg yolks; juice of half a lemon.*

Make a white *roux* with the butter and flour. Add the fish stock, cook for 5 minutes, remove from the heat and bind the sauce with the cream, previously mixed with the egg yolks. Lastly add the lemon juice.

LES SAUCES FINES ⋆ *FINE BUTTER SAUCES*

Béarnaise ⋆ *Béarnaise*

3 *tablespoons white wine;* 6 *oz butter;* 3 *tablespoons vinegar;* 2 *egg yolks;* 1 *chopped shallot;* 1 *tablespoon each chopped chervil and tarragon;* 3 *crushed peppercorns.*

Reduce the white wine and vinegar in a small saucepan with the shallot, a pinch of chopped chervil and tarragon and the crushed peppercorns. When the liquid is reduced by two-thirds, strain it through a very fine sieve into another small pan containing 2 egg yolks, 1 ounce of softened butter and a pinch of salt. Place this pan in a *bain-marie*, making sure that the water in the latter is not too hot (remove from the heat as soon as the water is more than hand-hot). When the egg yolks have thickened to a cream, remove the pan from the *bain-marie* and gradually add the softened butter cut into small pieces, stirring all the time with a small whisk. When the butter has begun to blend with the sauce, put the pan back into the *bain-marie* to keep the contents hot. Do not overheat, otherwise the sauce will curdle. Add the remaining chervil and tarragon at the last minute.

▣ Choron ⋆ *Choron*

This is a *sauce Béarnaise* with the addition of ¼ part of thick tomato *purée.*

▣ Hollandaise ⋆ *Hollandaise*

2 *egg yolks;* 2 *tablespoons cold water; half a small teaspoon lemon juice;* 6 *oz softened butter.*

Put the water, egg yolks, a knob of softened butter, some salt and ground pepper in a very small bowl, set in a pan of hot water, or in a *bain-marie*. Whisk very vigorously over gentle heat until the mixture is thick and frothy. Do not let the water in the pan become too hot; remove the bowl from the heat as soon as the water is too hot to dip a finger in. When the egg yolks are creamy, remove the bowl from the water and gradually add the butter divided into small pieces, still beating with the whisk. When the butter starts to blend with the eggs, replace the bowl in the water to keep it warm, but do not let it get too hot, since it curdles easily if over-heated. Add salt, pepper, and lemon to taste. (If separation does occur, add a little cold water and whisk vigorously).

26

Sauce Mousseline * *Mousseline or Foamy*

Make a *sauce Hollandaise*. At the last moment add as many tablespoons of stiffly whipped cream as eggs used for the sauce.

LA SAUCE TOMATE ET SES DÉRIVÉS * *TOMATO SAUCE AND ITS DERIVATIVES*

Sauce Tomate * *Tomato Sauce*

For 2 pints: 1 *pint tomato purée or* ½ *pint concentrated tomato paste;* 1 *oz oil or cooking fat;* 2 *oz back pork fat or pork rind;* 2 *oz carrots;* 1 *onion;* 1 *leek (white part only); a piece of celery;* 1 *sprig thyme;* 1 *bay leaf;* 2 *cloves garlic;* 1 *oz flour;* 1½ *pints brown stock or water;* 2 *lumps sugar;* 1 *oz butter.* Cooking time: 1½ hours.

Fry the pork fat, vegetables and herbs lightly in oil until they take on a slight colour. Add flour. Cook over low heat for 5 minutes, stirring with a spatula. Add the tomato *purée* or paste, water or brown stock, salt, pepper, grated nutmeg and sugar lumps. Simmer for 1¼ hours, preferably in the oven. Sieve, correct the seasoning and finish off with a nut of butter.

⊡ aux Tomates Fraîches à l'Italienne * *Fresh Tomato or Italian*

For 2 pints: 1¼ *lb tomatoes;* 4 *oz onions;* 2 *oz carrots;* 2 *oz streaky bacon; parsley;* 1½ *oz butter;* 1 *oz flour;* 1 *pint stock.* Cooking time: 1¼ hours.

Fry the carrots, onions and coarsely diced bacon in 1 ounce butter until they take on a slight colour. Sprinkle with flour and continue frying until golden brown. Add the tomatoes and mix well. Cover with water or stock. Season and add the parsley. Cook very gently for 1 hour. Sieve through a fine conical sieve. Correct the seasoning and finish off with a lump of sugar and the remaining butter. This sauce is even better if the tomatoes are first braised in the oven until all the water has evaporated.

⊡ Bolognaise * *Bolognaise*

1 *oz chopped ham or streaky bacon;* 8 *oz minced beef;* 1 *medium-sized onion;* 2 *carrots;* 1 *stick celery;* 2 *tablespoons olive oil;* 4 *oz mushrooms (optional);* 6 *tablespoons red wine;* 6 *oz tomato purée or* 2 *tablespoons concentrated tomato paste;* ½ *pint bouillon;* ½ *oz flour; marjoram; thyme or wild marjoram; nutmeg.*

Cut the onion, carrots, mushrooms and celery into very fine *julienne* strips. Fry in the oil until golden brown. Add the meat and bacon. Fry until it takes on a slight colour, then add salt and pepper. Moisten with the wine; when it has evaporated, remove the pan from the heat and add the flour. Return to the heat, stir in the tomato *purée* or paste and the *bouillon* and cook over very low heat. Add the marjoram and nutmeg, and more liquid if required. Reduce the sauce to a smooth *purée* and remove from the heat.

⊡ Provençale * *Provençale or Tomato Fondue*

For 1½ pints: 2 *lb coarsely chopped tomatoes with their seeds removed;* ¼ *pint* + 4 *tablespoons olive oil;* 2 *crushed cloves garlic;* 1 *tablespoon chopped parsley.*

Cook the tomatoes to a *purée* in boiling oil. Add salt and pepper and stir in the garlic. Cover and simmer for 20 minutes, add parsley.

LES SAUCES FROIDES ⋆ *COLD SAUCES*

Sauce Cocktail ⋆ *Cocktail*

¼ pint thick Mayonnaise; 2 tablespoons cream; 1 tablespoon tomato ketchup; 1 teaspoon cognac; 1 teaspoon sherry or Banyuls.

Mix all the ingredients together, whisking in the alcohol last. This sauce is used for cocktails of shellfish, fish, shredded chicken, etc.

▣ Mayonnaise ⋆ *Mayonnaise*

½ pint olive oil; 2 egg yolks; salt and pepper; half a small teaspoon vinegar or lemon juice.

Put the egg yolks in a small warmed china or earthenware bowl, add salt, white pepper and the vinegar. Begin beating quickly and vigorously with a small whisk. Gradually work in the oil, adding it drop by drop at first, then in a steady trickle as the sauce begins to bind, beating all the time. It does not matter whether you beat clockwise or anticlockwise, or change from one to the other. The only essential precaution is to warm the oil slightly before use; *mayonnaise* is ruined by cold oil. In winter, the oil must be brought at least to the temperature of the kitchen. When the *mayonnaise* is thick and smooth, correct the season-ing and adjust the consistency with lukewarm water. Variations may be made by flavouring the *mayonnaise* with mustard; using lemon juice instead of vinegar; adding finely chopped fresh herbs, etc. *Mayonnaise* is a basic sauce; it may also be flavoured with shellfish *purée*, anchovy, tomatoes, etc.

In spite of every care it may happen that a *mayonnaise* curdles. Place a little boiling water in another dish and little by little stir in the curdled *mayonnaise* with a whisk; it will then bind again. Alternatively, add the curdled mixture to a fresh egg yolk.

▣ Ravigote ⋆ *Ravigote*

Sauce Ravigote is a *sauce Vinaigrette* with the addition of chopped capers, parsley, chervil, tarragon and chives and a small chopped onion. It is recommended with calf's head. Nowadays it is customary to bind the *sauce Vinaigrette* with a little *mayonnaise*, which is an improvement.

▣ Rémoulade ⋆ *Rémoulade*

½ pint mustard-flavoured *mayonnaise* to which 4 level tablespoons of capers have been added. Squeeze out the capers well in a cloth to prevent the liquid from thinning the sauce.

▣ Tartare ⋆ *Tartare*

The same recipe as for *sauce Rémoulade*, but make the *mayonnaise* with one raw and one hardboiled egg yolk. Before serving add 1 level dessertspoon finely chopped chives and 1 level tablespoon finely chopped parsley or tarragon.

▣ Verte ⋆ *Green*

Blanch a mixture of chervil, tarragon, spinach and watercress in salted water, pass through a very fine sieve and mix with *Mayonnaise*.

Sauce Vinaigrette　*　*Vinaigrette*

Mix salt, pepper, oil, finely-chopped herbs and vinegar in the proportions of 1 part of vinegar to 4 of oil. Before serving beat for 5 minutes with a fork or whisk to bind the oil and vinegar, which have a tendency to separate.

If liked, to ½ pint sauce add 1 chopped hardboiled egg, 1 finely chopped shallot, some mustard and a little Worcester sauce. This sauce may also be used as a dressing.

LES BEURRES COMPOSÉES　*　*SAVOURY BUTTER*

Beurre d'Ail　*　*Garlic Butter*

3 oz peeled cloves of garlic; 4 oz butter.

Pound the garlic in a mortar, work into the butter and put through a sieve.

▣ d'Anchois　*　*Anchovy*

Crush or pass through a fine sieve 4 to 5 anchovy fillets in oil, and mix 4 ounces soft butter with the *purée*. Do not add salt, as the anchovies are salt enough.

▣ Bercy　*　*Bercy or Beef Marrow*

8 tablespoons white wine; 2 chopped shallots; 2 oz poached, finely diced beef marrow; 4 oz butter softened to a smooth spreading consistency; salt, pepper and lemon juice; 1 teaspoon chopped parsley.

Boil the wine with the shallots until reduced by half. Add the marrow and seasoning. Work in the butter and the parsley and leave in a cold place.

▣ de Cresson　*　*Watercress*

Drop a handful of watercress leaves in boiling water and remove them when the water boils up again. Cool, squeeze out thoroughly in a cloth and pass through a fine sieve. Then add 4 ounces butter. Season with salt and pepper.

▣ d'Estragon　*　*Tarragon*

8 oz butter; 3 oz tarragon leaves.
Blanch the tarragon for 1 minute. Drain, press out the water and work into the butter; sieve.

▣ de Homard　*　*Lobster*

Pound coral, liver and creamy parts of lobster. Add an equal quantity of butter and pass through a fine sieve.

▣ Maître d'Hôtel　*　*Maître d'Hôtel*

Soften 2 ounces unsalted butter without melting it; work in salt, pepper, lemon juice and 1 teaspoon chopped parsley. This butter is used for steak, kidneys, *brochettes* and some grilled fish. It should not melt until it comes into contact with the hot meat or fish.

Beurre de Kaifort * *Horseradish*

Mix 2 tablespoons of grated horseradish with 4 ounces butter. Add salt but no pepper.

▣ Marchand de Vin * *Red Wine*

8 tablespoons red wine; 1 chopped shallot; salt and pepper; 4 oz butter; 1 oz chopped parsley; 1 oz melted meat glaze.

Boil the wine with the shallot until reduced by half. Work all the ingredients together.

▣ de Moutarde * *Mustard*

Cream 3½ ounces butter with a pinch of salt and a small level teaspoon of mustard. Powdered English mustard is best.

▣ Noir * *Black*

Heat butter until black, and add some vinegar or lemon juice.

▣ Noisette * *Nut Brown*

Heat some butter till a light brown colour.

▣ Ravigote * *Ravigote*

Blanch and pound 1 shallot, some parsley, tarragon and chives. Sieve with 1 ounce butter.

▣ de Sardine * *Sardine*

The same as for Anchovy butter, using 2 sardines in oil instead of the anchovies. Add a little salt and pepper

Cold Hors d'Œuvres

ANCHOIS * ANCHOVIES

Anchovies are usually bought filleted and preserved in oil. Sometimes they are also preserved in salt; in that case remove salt thoroughly by soaking in cold milk. Wipe and separate the fillets, soaking them in oil for a few hours before serving them. This is a very simple and economical way of preparing them.

▣ Mireille * Mireille

Roll the anchovies in rings, place on thin slices of hardboiled egg and place a stoned olive in the middle of each fillet.

Anguille fumée * Smoked eel

Skin the eel and cut it into thick pieces. Bone each piece and arrange the fillets on a dish. Garnish with sprigs of parsley. Serve pieces of toast and curls of butter separately.

Artichauts farcis * Stuffed Globe Artichokes

To prepare the artichokes: cut off the tips of the leaves, trim the hearts, plunge the artichokes in boiling salted water and cook. Refresh, cut the leaves in the shape of a bowl and remove those in the centre, together with the choke.

Fill the artichoke bowls with mixed salad, such as Artichoke Salad *à la Grecque* or Manuela Rice Salad (*see recipes p.* 221 *and* 224) (*See illustration p.* 34).

▣ à la Grecque * Greek style

Cooking liquid: $\frac{1}{4}$ *pint white wine;* $\frac{1}{4}$ *pint water;* $\frac{1}{4}$ *pint olive oil; juice of* 1 *lemon;* 1 *bay leaf;* 6 *peppercorns; salt;* 8 *very small Globe artichokes.*

Remove the outer leaves from the artichokes. Cut remaining leaves short. Parboil for 10 minutes. Drain and remove the chokes. Boil up the cooking liquor for 2 minutes, then plunge the artichokes into it. Cook for 20–25 minutes, or until a leaf pulls off easily. Serve very cold with some of the cooking liquid.

31

Assiette Niçoise   *   Niçoise Platter

For 2 persons: 2 sardines; 2 skinned sliced tomatoes; 1 hardboiled egg; 1 oz tunny fish in oil; 4 anchovy fillets; 8 black olives; 4 green olives; lettuce leaves.

Make a bed of lettuce leaves on each plate, and arrange on it a sardine, tunny fish, tomato, and slices of hardboiled egg. Decorate with strips of anchovy fillet, chopped parsley and the halved olives. (*See illustration p. 34*).

Barquettes de Thon   *   Tunny fish Pastry Boats

For 6 persons: 6 oz Short or Puff pastry; 6 oz Tunny fish cream; 6 anchovy fillets.

Line small boat-shaped moulds with a thin layer of lightly salted pastry. Prick well and bake. When cold, fill with Tunny fish cream. Garnish each boat with 3 strips of anchovy fillet, arranged parallel to each other.

Tunny Fish Cream: Finely chop or sieve the tunny fish and moisten with thick *mayonnaise* as required.

CANAPÉS

Canapés are small shapes of various kinds cut from $\frac{1}{4}$ inch thick slices of bread or toast without crusts. The choice between bread and toast and the kind of butter used (Anchovy butter, Mustard or Horseradish butter, etc.) depends on personal taste and on the garnish, which is the most important part of a *canapé*.

Canapés Amiral   *   Shrimp Canapés

Spread the bread with Shrimp butter. Arrange peeled cooked shrimps on top in a regular pattern and coat lightly with clear aspic.

▣ d'Anchois   *   Anchovy

Spread bread with Anchovy butter; cover with a lattice of anchovy fillets and garnish with capers or chopped hardboiled egg.

▣ Bagration   *   Lobster

Cover the buttered bread with lettuce *julienne*, place thinly sliced cooked lobster flesh on top, coat with *mayonnaise* and garnish to taste with hardboiled eggs or lemon.

▣ de Cannes   *   Sardine

Butter some white bread, mix half a sardine without skin and bones with some butter, spread this on *canapé* and garnish with tomato or pickled onions.

▣ de Foie Gras   *   Foie Gras

Spread bread with *Foie Gras Mousse*, decorate the surface with a knife dipped in hot water and garnish with truffles.

Another Method
Cut a whole *foie gras* into slices $\frac{1}{10}$ inch thick, place on buttered bread and garnish with aspic and truffles or hardboiled egg.

▲ Œufs Mistral, p. 72
Salade de bœuf, Salade de riz Derby, Cèpes marinés. Perles de Melon, Maquereaux à la vinaigrette. ▼   33
Œufs à la mayonnaise, p. 41, 224, 37, 40, 72

34 ▲ *Salade Marguerite, Salade Orloff, Assiette niçoise, p. 222, 223, 32*

Artichauts farcis, p. 31 ▼

▲ *Mousselines de jambon, p. 40*

Hors d'œuvre de poissons de mer, p. 40 ▼   35

▲ *Salade Argenteuil, p. 41*

Tomates à l'andalouse, p. 43 ▼

Canapés au Fromage Blanc * *Curd Cheese*

Rub 4 ounces curd cheese through a fine sieve and mix with a small teaspoon of chives and 1 of caraway seeds, a pinch of salt and of paprika and a little lemon juice or vinegar. Spread thinly sliced brown or rye bread with this mixture and sprinkle with chopped chives or paprika.

▣ au Jambon * *Ham*

Roll slices of ham around a very fine slice of cucumber, cheese, cooked meat and gherkins. Place the rolls on slices of buttered bread garnished with Ham *mousse* and slices of hardboiled egg.

▣ Joinville * *Shrimp*

Fry round *canapés* in butter, cool and spread them with Shrimp butter. Roll them in chopped yolk of hardboiled egg. Place a ring of 6 peeled shrimps on top with a tiny butter rosette in the centre.

▣ à la Ménagère * *Ménagère*

Fry square *canapés* in butter. Mince some boiled beef left-overs, a hard-boiled egg, some gherkins and fine herbs. Bind the whole with fairly thick *mayonnaise*, spread *canapés* thickly with this mixture and decorate the top with a slice of tomato.

▣ à la Niçoise * *Niçoise*

Cut some round slices of white bread 1½ inches across and ½ inch thick. Fry golden brown in hot olive oil; the centre should remain soft. Cool and spread with Anchovy butter, place a small mound of well-drained tomato salad in the middle and top with a stoned olive.

▣ au Petit-Suisse * *Cream Cheese*

Blend cream cheese with a little butter, spread on buttered bread and dust one half with paprika, placing greaseproof paper over the other half to protect it.

▣ Printaniers * *Springtime*

Butter the bread and spread it with a *julienne* of lettuce with seasoned *Mayonnaise*. Place slices of hardboiled egg on top and sprinkle with chopped chives.

▣ au Saumon Fumé * *Smoked Salmon*

Butter the *canapés*, cover with slices of smoked salmon and garnish with gherkins or a hardboiled egg.

Cervelas en Vinaigrette * *Saveloy in Vinaigrette sauce*

Skin the saveloys and cut into thin slices. Pour a *sauce Vinaigrette* containing finely chopped gherkins over the slices.

Champignons et Cèpes Marinés * *Marinated Mushrooms and Boletus*

Choose small, firm mushrooms, slice or quarter them, blanch in water for

5 minutes, then pour a mustard-flavoured *Vinaigrette*, mixed with a little *mayonnaise*, on top. Marinate for 24 hours before serving. (*See illustration p. 33*).

CREVETTES * PRAWNS

Whole: Serve in an *hors d'œuvre* dish on crushed ice or hang the prawns by the tail round the rim of a glass containing sprigs of fresh parsley.

Shelled: Bind with tomato-flavoured *mayonnaise* or with Cocktail sauce to make a cocktail.

Cocktail de Crevettes ou de Homard * Shrimp or Lobster Cocktail

For 4 persons: 7 oz shelled shrimps or diced lobster meat. Cocktail sauce: 6 tablespoons thick mayonnaise; 2 tablespoons thick cream; 2 tablespoons tomato ketchup; 1 teaspoon cognac; 1 teaspoon sherry or Banyuls (dessert wine). Garnish: half a lettuce heart; salt; 4 olives with tomato stuffing; chopped parsley.

Make the Cocktail sauce by mixing all the ingredients together. Use half the sauce to bind the shrimps or lobster. Shred the lettuce finely and arrange at the bottom of chilled glasses or goblets. Sprinkle salt over. Place the shrimps or lobster on top. Coat with the rest of the sauce. Decorate the centre of each glass with a stuffed olive, or sprinkle chopped parsley over.

Crème de Thon * Cream of Tunny

Crush the tunny in a bowl with a nob of fresh butter and a little olive oil, season well and beat the *purée*, or place in the liquidiser. Arrange neatly in a dish with a garnish of sliced hardboiled eggs and sliced cooked potatoes or sprinkle with chopped hardboiled egg.

▣ Mirabeau * Mirabeau

Serve a mound of Cream of tunny in a dish. Surround with a ring of skinned sliced tomatoes and stoned olives on sticks.

Fenouil à la Grecque * Greek style Fennel

For 4 persons: $1\frac{1}{4}$–$1\frac{1}{2}$ lb fennel; $\frac{1}{4}$ pint white wine; $\frac{1}{4}$ pint water; 6 tablespoons oil; juice of 1 lemon; 1 bay leaf; 6 peppercorns; salt. Cooking time: 40–50 minutes.

Cut the fennel into quarters lengthwise, blanch for 10 minutes, then pour cold water over it to preserve the colour. Prepare the cooking liquid from the remaining ingredients, boil up for 2 minutes, add the fennel and cook for 30 to 35 minutes. When cold, serve with the cooking liquid.

Harengs Frais Marinés I * Soused Fresh Herrings I

For 4 persons: 4–5 oz gutted herrings with the heads removed; $\frac{1}{4}$ pint vinegar; $\frac{1}{4}$ pint white wine; 1 bouquet garni; 1 onion; 2 carrots; 8 peppercorns; 2 tablespoons oil; salt.

Season the herrings with salt and pepper an hour before cooking. Prepare a marinade from the vinegar, wine, *bouquet garni*, onion, carrots and peppercorns and cook for 20 minutes. Grease a deep, ovenproof dish and arrange the herrings in it. Pour the boiling marinade over the herrings and sprinkle with oil. Cover the dish with oiled paper and bake for 30–40 minutes.

Harengs Frais Marinés II   *   *Soused Fresh Herrings II*

Gut the herrings and scale. Cut off the heads and trim the tails. Lay the fish on a plate and sprinkle salt over them. Leave for 3–4 hours. Drain well. Split fish and remove backbone. Sprinkle each herring with seasoning and roll up, skin side out. Pack into a casserole, add 6 peppercorns, 2 bay leaves, and 2 finely chopped shallots. Pour over equal quantities of vinegar and water, as much as will almost cover them. Cover closely and bake in a fairly hot oven, 375°F or Gas Mark 5, for about 45 minutes. Allow to cool in the liquid. When cold, serve on lettuce, with tomato.

Herring roes are well washed and cooked in the casserole with the fish.
Mackerel may be soused in the same way.

Filets de Harengs à la Russe   *   *Kipper Fillets Russian style*

Peel and dice two raw dessert apples and place them in a dish with a little finely chopped onion, place strips of filleted kipper on top and sprinkle with white wine and oil. This is an original and savoury *hors d'œuvre*.

Herring fillets may also be served with *sauce Rémoulade* and a salad of potatoes, beet-root, celery, etc.

▣ de Harengs Saurs   *   *Filleted Smoked Salt Herrings*

Cut the fillets lengthwise into two or more pieces, according to size. Arrange in a lattice on a dish with sliced onions, sprinkle some oil and a little white wine on top.

Huîtres   *   *Oysters*

Oysters must be very fresh and opened at the last moment. Serve with lemon quarters and a sauceboat of vinegar with chopped shallots and coarsely ground pepper and with brown bread and butter.

JAMBON   *   *HAM*

Jambon en Roulades Lucullus   *   *Ham Rolls Lucullus*

For 4 persons: 8 small slices cooked ham; 3 oz purée or mousse of foie gras or chicken livers; 3 tablespoons Madeira or sherry; 1 oz butter; ¼ pint aspic.

Soften the butter and work it into a paste with the liver *purée* or *mousse*. Add the Madeira or sherry and seasoning. Spread this paste on the slices of ham and roll up. Glaze with half-set aspic jelly and set in a cool place.

▣ en Roulades Primavera   *   *Rolls Primavera*

For 4 persons: 4 slices lean cooked ham; 4 oz cooked mushrooms; 3 skinned tomatoes; 2 hardboiled eggs; ¼ pint mustard mayonnaise.

Cut up the mushrooms finely and bind with the *mayonnaise*, which should be thick and strongly flavoured with mustard. Spread the mixture on the slices of ham and roll up. Arrange in the shape of a cross on a round dish. Cut the tomatoes and eggs into rounds and arrange these alternately to fill up the spaces between the ham rolls.

Mousse ou Mousselines de Jambon * Ham Mousse or Mousselines

For 6–8 persons: 1 lb ham; ¼ pint thick cream; 2 oz tomato purée; ½ pint (approx.) sauce Béchamel; 4 oz butter; 1 pint (approx.) port-flavoured aspic; paprika.

Pound the ham finely, add the butter, cream, cold *sauce Béchamel* and tomato *purée* and work together well. Season and flavour well with paprika; add a little liquid aspic. Line a mould with aspic, leave to set and fill with the *mousse*. Complete with a coating of aspic and leave in a cold place for 1 to 2 hours. Unmould on to a round dish and garnish with chopped aspic.

Alternatively, shape the mixture into *mousselines* with a tablespoon, which should be dipped in hot water before making each one. (*See illustration p.* 35).

MELON * MELON

A good melon should be heavy, the rind should give when pressed and have an agreeable odour. It is usually served in slices or in balls, and as cold as possible, even iced. It is also served flavoured with port, Madeira or sherry. This is an excellent *hors d'œuvres*, which may also be served as dessert. (*See illustration p.* 33).

Oeufs Froids * Cold Eggs

See Cold Egg chapter on page 71.

POISSONS * SEA FISH HORS D'ŒUVRE

There are many and varied fish *hors d'œuvre*.

1. Fillets of sole on highly seasoned Tomato sauce containing thinly sliced mushrooms.

2. Fillets of hake or cod. Garnish: roughly chopped skinned tomatoes and stuffed olives.

3. Fish fillets masked with *sauce Tartare*. Garnish: shelled crayfish or scampi.

4. Fish fillets or slices. Garnish: asparagus tips. (*See illustration p.* 35).

Maquereaux à la Vinaigrette * Mackerel Vinaigrette

Boil whole or sliced mackerel in water with salt and vinegar. Drain, skin and sprinkle with *sauce Vinaigrette* mixed with fine herbs. May be served hot or cold. (*See illustration p.* 33).

Poisson en Coquille ou en Ravier * Fish Shells or Boats

For 4 persons: 8 oz left-over cooked fish or tinned fish (tunny or salmon); ¼ pint tomato-flavoured mayonnaise; 4 lettuce leaves. Garnish: olives; skinned tomatoes; hardboiled eggs.

Line the bottom of a scallop shell or boat-shaped *hors d'œuvre* dish with finely shredded lettuce. Flake the fish and bind with tomato-flavoured *mayonnaise*. Arrange this mixture on the lettuce. Garnish and decorate as desired with rounds of hardboiled egg or tomato or sliced stuffed olives. Serve fingers of toast separately.

Rougets Froids à la Niçoise * Cold Red Mullet Niçoise

For 4 persons: 4 *red mullet;* 8 *oz tomatoes;* 2 *small onions;* ¼ *pint white wine;* 1 *lemon.* Cooking time: 8–10 minutes.

Poach the red mullet in the white wine with sliced onions. Place in a dish when cold. Reduce the liquor and pour on top. Then place a fine tomato salad and the sliced onions on top of the fish and decorate with slices of lemon.

Poireaux à la Vinaigrette * Leeks Vinaigrette

For 4 persons: 2½ *lb leeks;* ½ *pint sauce Vinaigrette.* Cooking time: 1 hour.

Cut through the white part of the leeks 3 inches from the root end, tie in bundles in the same way as asparagus is prepared for cooking. Soak in hot water for 30 minutes, then cook in salted water for 20 minutes. Pour cold water over them, drain and arrange on a dish. Serve with *sauce Vinaigrette.*

Radis Noir * Black Radishes

Black radishes are hard and strong in flavour, but very good if they are peeled and sliced, then seasoned and marinated for 2 hours before use with oil and vinegar. They are also served peeled, with salt and fresh butter.

Ravier à la Danoise * Danish Salad Bowl

Place a little Potato salad in the bottom of a bowl, cover with a layer of flaked fresh or tinned salmon and coat with highly-seasoned *mayonnaise.* Edge the *mayonnaise* with chopped fine herbs.

SALADES * SALADS

Vegetable, meat or fish salads make very good *hors d'œuvre.* They provide an opportunity for giving free rein to individual imagination and taste. Personal choice takes the place of rules in this case. (*See also recipes p.* 220-224).

Salade Argenteuil * Salad Macédoine

Arrange a *macédoine* of vegetables with *mayonnaise* in a mound. Surround with cooked asparagus tips and slices of hardboiled eggs at the base. A little cooked ham may be mixed with the *macédoine.* (*See illustration p.* 36).

▣ de Betterave * Beetroot

Peel and slice a tender cooked beetroot. Season with *Vinaigrette* made with a generous amount of vinegar. The salad may be surrounded by a ring of Potato salad, but this should be added at the last moment, since beetroot stains everything with which it comes in contact.

▣ de Boeuf * Beef

Use meat from a stockpot, especially the tougher parts which are not pleasant to eat hot. Cut in very thin slices and season with *Vinaigrette,* adding some pickled gherkins, a little chopped onion and some chopped fine herbs, or tomatoes, peppers, etc. (*See illustration p.* 33).

41

Salade de Céleri Blanc * Celery

Remove the stalks from a very white and tender head of celery and cut off the leaves. Wash and scrub carefully. Cut in pieces 2 inches long and shred these, if possible lengthwise. Dry thoroughly with a cloth and soak for 1 or 2 hours beforehand in *sauce Rémoulade* mixed with fine herbs.

▣ de Céleri-Rave en Rémoulade * Celeriac in sauce Rémoulade

Cut celeriac into very fine *julienne* and scald it to make it tender and to remove its strong flavour. After draining bind with thin *mayonnaise* to which plenty of mustard and fine herbs have been added. Prepare 1 or 2 hours in advance.

We recommend scalding celeriac when it has not been cut very finely. When it is shredded as finely as tobacco it is not scalded.

▣ de Chou Blanc * White Cabbage

Finely shred a cabbage with a firm white heart and season with *Vinaigrette* and the addition of a little finely chopped onion.

▣ de Chou Rouge * Red Cabbage

Clean a firm red cabbage, remove the hard parts and shred finely. Sprinkle with fine salt and vinegar. Put into a container with a lid and place over very low heat, for about ¾ hour to soften. Drain and cool, then season with *Vinaigrette*, making allowance for the salt and vinegar already used. The salad may be surrounded with shredded peppers.

▣ de Concombre * Cucumber

Thinly peel a cucumber, halve lengthwise and carefully remove seeds and water from the inside. We suggest soaking for 1 hour in water well salted with coarse salt instead of sprinkling with fine salt. The cucumber will remain firm and crisp instead of becoming soft. Drain and press well, slice very thinly and season with oil, vinegar and fine herbs.

▣ de Pommes de Terre * Potato

Boil 1½ pounds potatoes in their jackets. Peel, slice and season while still hot with oil, vinegar, fine herbs, etc. Add ¼ pint hot *bouillon*, as the potatoes soak up the vinegar and will become dry otherwise. Serve while still slightly lukewarm. This is better than salad made from potatoes boiled in advance and seasoned when cold. The salad may be improved by using white wine instead of *bouillon*.

▣ de Volaille * Chicken

Trim poultry left-overs. Slice and mix with strips of cooked ham, sliced gherkins, fine herbs and a little chopped tarragon. Add a little salt, pepper, oil and vinegar. Mix everything thoroughly. Serve in a dish and garnish with sliced hardboiled egg.

SARDINES À L'HUILE * SARDINES IN OIL

Arrange the sardines fanwise on a long dish and surround or border them with chopped white and yolk of hardboiled egg and chopped parsley, keeping the three colours separate.

Sardines à la Tomate   *   *Sardines with Tomato Sauce*

For 4 persons: 12 *sardines in oil;* ½ *pint cold Tomato sauce.*

Arrange the sardines on a highly seasoned, cold Tomato sauce (preferably made from fresh tomatoes) flavoured with finely chopped, fresh herbs (tarragon, sage, etc.).

Saumon Fumé en Roulades   *   *Smoked Salmon Rolls*

For 4 persons: 2 *slices smoked salmon per person;* 8 *oz tunny fish in oil;* 4 *oz butter;* 10 *oz mixed diced vegetables;* ½ *pint thick mayonnaise.*

Work the tunny fish and butter to a paste and season. Spread this paste on the very thinly sliced salmon and roll up. Bind the vegetables with *mayonnaise*, and arrange on a dish in a rectangular shape. Place the salmon rolls on top. If liked, top each roll with a small, thin disc cut out of a truffle.

TOMATES GARNIES   *   STUFFED TOMATOES

Use medium-sized, evenly-shaped, firm tomatoes. Wash and remove the stalks. Cut the tomatoes in half horizontally, remove the juice and pulp carefully, season inside with salt and pepper, invert on a wire rack and leave to drain. Fill with various mixtures and garnish as desired.

Tomates à l'Andalouse   *   *Tomatoes with Onions and Peppers*

Cook 4 ounces rice in boiling salted water for 12 to 15 minutes. Drain and add a highly seasoned thin *mayonnaise* with plenty of mustard. Add some cooked and shredded green pepper and one or two tablespoons of minced Spanish onions simmered in oil without browning. Scoop out six large tomatoes and stuff with the rice mixture. Serve on a bed of lettuce leaves. (*See illustration p.* 36).

◙ Argenteuil   *   *with Asparagus and Ham*

Fill the tomatoes with a mixture of equal parts of cooked asparagus tips and cooked ham, cut into dice and bound with *mayonnaise* lightly flavoured with mustard. Coat with *mayonnaise* and decorate with rounds of gherkins.

◙ Beaulieu   *   *with Tunny Fish*

8 *large tomatoes;* 8 *oz tunny fish;* 4 *oz butter;* 1 *hardboiled egg.*

Scoop out tomatoes, season inside with salt, pepper and vinegar and stand upside down on a wire rack to drain. Make Tunny cream with tunny fish, butter, lemon juice, pepper and two tablespoons of *mayonnaise*. The *purée* should be creamy and finely crushed. Stuff the tomatoes with it and cover with egg white and yolk, chopped separately. Decorate with an olive.

◙ Dubarry   *   *with Cauliflower*

For 4 persons: 4 *tomatoes;* 1 *cauliflower weighing approx.* 1 *lb;* ¼ *pint tomato-flavoured mayonnaise; chervil or parsley.*

Blanch the cauliflower, cook lightly, and leave until cold. Place one teaspoon of *mayonnaise* in the bottom of each tomato and arrange a segment of cauliflower on it. Carefully coat with *mayonnaise*. Garnish with sprigs of chervil or parsley.

Tomates à la Russe * *with Mixed Vegetables*

Stuff with Mixed Vegetable salad bound with highly-seasoned *mayonnaise*. Place a slice of hardboiled egg on top.

▣ Sévigné * *with Chicken*

Finely dice equal quantities of cooked mushrooms and left-over cooked chicken. Bind with thick *mayonnaise*. Fill the tomatoes with this mixture, coat the top with *mayonnaise* and decorate with strips of sweet green peppers arranged to form a pattern.

Soups

Soup is served at the beginning of a meal, or following the *hors d'œuvre*—usually at dinner. There are three main types of soup:

Clear soups or *consommés*

Cream soups and soups thickened with vegetable *purée*

Unsieved vegetable soups.

CLEAR SOUPS

2 pints of soup is enough for 4 or 5 servings.

Pot-au-Feu or Bouillon

This is a basic soup served on its own or as an ingredient for a richer soup. Choose fat or lean meat according to taste. For really good *bouillon*, however, lean meat should predominate. One part of top ribs to two of silverside or clod (neck piece of beef) is a good mixture. Allow 9 ounces per person including bones. Cut up about 4 pounds of meat. Put into pan with 5 pints cold water. Boil up and skim carefully so that the *bouillon* is clear. Use only ¼ ounce salt per quart of water, add carrots, turnips, leeks and celery if available, and simmer gently without quite covering the pan, for 3 hours. Skim fat off *bouillon* before serving.

Note: We recommend skimming all fat off the *bouillon* kept for the next day, especially in hot weather, for the *bouillon* will not cool quickly enough under a layer of congealed fat and will turn sour.

Potage julienne * *Vegetable*

4 oz carrots; 2 oz turnips; 1 onion; 2 small leeks (white part only); 4 oz white cabbage or lettuce; 4 pints bouillon. Cooking time: 40 minutes.

Cut the vegetables into *julienne* strips, cover and cook them slowly in butter only, without browning, for 20 to 25 minutes. Add salt and a pinch of sugar. The fat from a *pot-au-feu* may be used instead of butter. Add the *bouillon*, after removing all fat from it, and simmer. Sprinkle with chopped chervil.

▣ au Tapioca * *Tapioca*

Pour 2 ounces of washed tapioca into 2 pints of boiling *bouillon*, stirring to prevent the tapioca from sticking together in lumps. Boil gently for 6 to 8 minutes and if the soup is not to be served at once, keep it covered, otherwise an unattractive skin will form which cannot be dissolved.

E.F.C.

D

Potage aux Pâtes   *   *Vermicelli or Pasta*

Pour 2 ounces pasta into 2 pints of *bouillon*. Boil gently for 10 to 15 minutes, depending on the thickness of the vermicelli or other pasta.

CREAM SOUPS

Cream of rice and Cream of barley form the basis of many cream soups. They also help to thicken and enrich the derivative cream soups.

Crème d'Avoine   *   *Cream of Oatmeal*

For 5–6 persons: 1¼ pints milk; 1 pint bouillon; 2 oz fine oatmeal; 2 tablespoons fresh cream or 2 oz butter.

Bring ¼ pint milk to the boil. Mix with the *bouillon* and heat. Stir oatmeal into 1 pint cold milk and pour into the boiling liquid. Cook slowly for half an hour, then skim and add cream or butter and small fried *croûtons*. May also be garnished with *juienne*, sorrel, etc.

▣ d'Orge   *   *Barley*

For 5–6 persons: Same method and proportions as for Cream of Rice. Garnish with 3 tablespoons of pearl barley boiled separately in *bouillon* for at least 45 minutes or with *croûtons* of fried bread.

▣ de Riz   *   *Rice*

For 5–6 persons: 2 oz butter; 2 oz rice flour; 2 pints veal or beef bouillon; ¼ pint milk; 1 egg yolk; 2 tablespoons cream.

Make a *roux* with butter and rice flour. Cook for 2 minutes, then add the *bouillon*. Whisk until it boils, then cook gently for about 45 minutes. Skim, add the boiled milk and season to taste. Place a yolk of egg and the cream in the soup tureen, mix and pour the boiling soup on top. Garnish with *croûtons* of fried bread.

▣ d'Asperge   *   *Asparagus*

For 6–8 persons: 1½ oz rice flour; 1¼ lb asparagus; 2 tablespoons fresh cream; ¼ pint milk; 2 egg yolks; 3 pints bouillon; 1 oz butter. Cooking time: 1 hour.

Make a *roux* with the butter and the rice flour. Cook for 2 minutes and gradually add the *bouillon*. Stir until it comes to the boil and add 1 pound green asparagus tips, previously scraped and blanched in salted water for 5 or 6 minutes. Cook over low heat for 1 hour and put through a fine sieve. Return to the heat with a little boiled milk to give a thick, creamy consistency. Thicken with the egg yolks and cream. Whisk in a little butter. Garnish with a few asparagus tips cooked in salted water to give them a good green colour.

▣ de Céleri   *   *Celery*

For 6–8 persons: 12 oz celeriac; 3 pints Cream of Rice soup; 1 oz butter 2 egg yolks; ¼ pint fresh cream. Cooking time: 40 minutes.

Peel and quarter the celeriac. Blanch well, drain, cover, and cook slowly in butter without browning for 20 to 25 minutes. Put through a sieve and finish cooking in the Cream of Rice. Bind with the egg yolks and cream. Garnish with fried *croûtons* or diced celeriac cooked separately.

Chicken Giblet Soup

For 6 persons: ¾ *lb chicken giblets; 1 large chopped onion; 2 pints chicken stock; 1 clove; 6 black peppercorns; good pinch mixed herbs; 2 teaspoons salt; 6 sticks celery, chopped; a little chopped parsley.* Cooking time: 2 hours.

Clean giblets and place in a saucepan with onion, stock, clove, peppercorns, mixed herbs and salt. Bring to the boil, cover and simmer 1½ hours or until giblets are tender. Strain, return stock to saucepan and add celery. Simmer, covered, for a further ½ hour. Cut giblets finely and add to soup. Adjust seasoning, if necessary. Reheat, and serve garnished with chopped parsley.

▣ Clamart   *   *Pea*

For 6–8 persons: 2½ *lb shelled peas; 2 oz rice flour; 1 pint boiled milk; 2 tablespoons fresh cream; 2 egg yolks; 2 pints bouillon.* Cooking time: 45 minutes.

Cook the shelled peas in an ample amount of salted water, drain and put through a nylon sieve or liquidiser of the electric mixer. Dilute the *purée* by degrees either with *bouillon* or with the cooking water from the peas and some milk. Bring to the boil and thicken with the rice flour mixed with a little cold milk. Season and sweeten slightly. Bind with the egg yolks and cream. Garnish with shredded lettuce leaves cooked separately in *bouillon*.

▣ Dubarry   *   *Cauliflower*

For 6–8 persons: 1¼ *lb cauliflower; 4 oz flour; 3 oz butter; 2 tablespoons fresh cream; ½ pint milk; 2 egg yolks; 3 pints bouillon.* Cooking time: 40 minutes.

Blanch a small cauliflower for 8 to 10 minutes. Then make a *roux* with butter and flour and add the *bouillon*. When it boils add the cauliflower and boil gently till it is tender. Then skim the soup and pass the whole through a sieve or liquidiser. Bring to the boil again with the milk, thicken with the egg yolks (optional) and the cream and garnish with small *croûtons* or florets of cauliflower.

▣ aux Huîtres   *   *Oyster*

For 4 persons: 1 *dozen (or more) oysters; juice 1 lemon; 2½ pints fish stock or water; 4 tablespoons dry white wine; 2 oz butter; 1 oz flour; salt; pepper.* Cooking time: about 10 minutes altogether.

Mix lemon juice with oysters, set aside. Add wine to fish stock, bring to boil, reduce heat, simmer 5 minutes. Melt butter in saucepan, stir in flour, cook few minutes, stirring. Gradually blend in hot stock; stir until boiling, season to taste. Just before serving add oysters and heat a few minutes until oysters are nicely plump.

▣ de Laitue   *   *Lettuce*

For 4–5 persons: lettuce; 2 pints Cream of Rice soup; ¼ pint milk; 1 egg yolk; 2 tablespoons cream.

Blanch a large handful of green lettuce leaves for 5 minutes in boiling water. Drain, cool in cold water, squeeze out and boil for 45 minutes in Cream of Rice soup. Pass the whole through a fine sieve or liquidiser, replace on the stove, add milk, season, and thicken with yolk of egg and cream (which may be replaced by a little milk and butter). Garnish with small *croûtons*, or 4 ounces of rice boiled separately.

Various vegetable cream soups may be made in the same way with left-overs of asparagus, celeriac, artichoke bottoms, turnips, chicory, etc. Always start the cooking vegetables in water and finish them in the soup.

VEGETABLE PURÈE SOUPS

Potage Crécy au Riz   *   *Carrot purée soup with Rice*

For 6–8 persons: 3 oz streaky bacon; 2 oz onions; 2 lb carrots; 4 pints bouillon; 2 oz Carolina rice; 2 oz butter; 2 tablespoons fresh cream; salt; pepper; pinch of sugar. Garnish: 1½ oz rice.

Lightly fry the diced streaky bacon and sliced onions in 1 ounce butter. Add the carrots, also sliced, then cover the saucepan and cook slowly for a few minutes at low heat. Add *bouillon* and Carolina rice. Cover and cook for 1 hour. Pass through the finest possible sieve or liquidiser. Thin with *bouillon* and bring to the boil again. Season well, add 1 ounce butter and the cream at the last moment and garnish with rice boiled in salted water.

▣ Parmentier   *   *Potato and leek*

For 5–6 persons: 3 leeks (white part only; 2½ lb potatoes; 2 oz butter; 3 tablespoons cream; bouquet garni; 2 pints water or bouillon; seasoning. Cooking time: 1 hour.

Slice the leeks finely and fry them gently in the butter until they take on a light golden colour. This will take about 10–15 minutes. Add the potatoes cut into quarters, a *bouquet garni* and enough water to cover. Then add salt and cook gently for 1 hour. Put through a fine sieve or liquidiser. Dilute to a creamy consistency with water or *bouillon*. Boil for a moment, adjust the seasoning and finish with fresh cream. Add a few *croûtons* fried in butter. A great many varieties of this soup may be obtained by varying the garnishes.

▣ Saint-Germain   *   *Split Pea*

For 8 persons: 8 oz split peas; 1 leek (green part only); 1 carrot; 2 onions; 3 oz bacon; 1 bouquet garni; 3 pints ham stock; 2 oz butter; 2 tablespoons fresh cream; seasoning; pinch of sugar. Cooking time: 1–1½ hours.

Use best quality split peas. Soak them overnight. Wash them carefully and cook in just enough ham stock to cover them well. When it comes to the boil, skim, add salt and a *mire-poix* consisting of the green part of the leek, the carrot, two large onions and the bacon, lightly cooked in butter. Now add the *bouquet garni*, cover tightly and cook slowly (preferably in the oven) for about 2 hours. Put through a fine sieve or the liquidiser, if too thick dilute with water or stock. Then boil for a moment, adjust the seasoning and stir in the cream.

▣ Soissonnais   *   *Haricot Bean*

For 8 persons: 2 pints fresh kidney beans or 10 oz dried haricot beans; 1 onion; 1 carrot; ½ pint milk; 2 oz butter; 2 tablespoons fresh cream; 3 pints bouillon. Cooking time: 1–1½ hours, depending on the type of beans used.

If dried haricot beans are used, soak overnight. Boil the beans in water with an onion and a carrot. Rub the fresh or dried haricot beans through a very fine sieve. Mix with the boiling liquor and complete with *bouillon* and milk to make the soup creamy. Bring to the boil, stirring all the time. Season, and thicken with butter and cream. Garnish with fried *croûtons*.

Tomato-Oxtail Soup

For 6–8 persons: 2 oxtails; flour; 1 oz butter; 1 pint tomato juice; 4 pints water; 1 teaspoon lemon juice; 2 to 3 oz each diced carrots, turnips, onions, and celery; 5 to 6 oz diced potatoes; 1 teaspoon salt; pepper to taste; 1 teaspoon Worcester sauce. Cooking time: 4 hours.

Cut oxtails into pieces, roll in flour. Brown slowly in hot butter, add tomato juice, water, and lemon juice. Simmer gently for approximately 3 hours or until meat is tender. Remove meat from bones, return to soup, add vegetables and seasonings, simmer further 45 minutes. Skim well.

FRENCH REGIONAL SOUPS AND FOREIGN SPECIALITIES

Cock-a-Leekie

For 4 persons: 2 pints chicken stock; 2 leeks; salt; pepper; 6 soaked prunes.

Cut the green parts from the leeks. Slit the white part and wash well. Cut into inch lengths and cut these into thin shreds lengthwise. Add to boiling stock. Simmer for 1 hour. Stone the soaked prunes and add to the soup. Simmer $\frac{1}{2}$ hour longer. Season and serve. (*Scotland*)

Kangaroo Tail Soup

2 tablespoons oil; 2 tablespoons vinegar; 1 pint red wine; 2 pints water or stock; salt; pepper; 2 bay leaves; pinch nutmeg; pinch cayenne; 1 small kangaroo tail, cut into joints; 2 onions; 2 carrots; 1 turnip; 2-3 sticks celery; 2 oz flour; $\frac{1}{4}$ pint red wine (extra). Cooking time: 3 hours.

Mix oil, vinegar, water and seasoning with wine in a large pot, and heat. Put in the prepared sectioned kangaroo tail and stand for 48 hours; add more water, if necessary, to cover. Peel and dice vegetables, add to mixture, bring to boil and simmer gently for 2-3 hours, or until meat is tender. Allow to cool, remove meat, and take meat from bones. Pass soup and vegetables through sieve or blender. Return meat to soup and reheat. Blend flour with extra wine and stir into soup, bring soup to boil and simmer gently until thickened. Serve hot.

(*Australia*).

Minestrone Milanese

For 10 persons: 12 oz potatoes; 1 onion; 8 oz cabbage; 8 oz kidney beans; 8 oz carrots; stick celery; 1 tablespoon oil; 1 oz butter; 2 oz streaky bacon; good pinch basil; 3 parsley stalks; 1 clove garlic; 6 pints bouillon or water; 4 oz rice; 2–3 oz Parmesan cheese.

Fry the sliced onion until golden-brown in the oil and butter in a stockpot. Add the vegetables diced or chopped with crushed garlic and cook over gentle heat for 30 minutes (if dried kidney beans are used, first cook them separately). Add the *bouillon* or water and boil for $1\frac{1}{4}$ hours. Add the rice. After a further 7 minutes add the chopped bacon, the basil, and parsley. Hand the Parmesan cheese separately. *Minestrone* may be served hot or cold.

(*Italy*)

Panade   *   Bread Soup

For 4 persons: $1\frac{1}{4}$ lb stale bread; 2 eggs; $\frac{1}{2}$ pint milk; 2 pints water; 2 oz butter; seasoning. Cooking time: 15–20 minutes.

Place the stale bread crusts and the water in a saucepan. Add salt and pepper and put on over low heat for the bread to absorb the water slowly. When it comes to the boil crush the bread by whisking it in the saucepan to make a smooth *purée*. Beat the eggs thoroughly in a bowl with the milk. Pour into the very hot soup, continue to whisk thoroughly and bring to the boil once more. Remove from stove, butter and season to taste. Add milk if it is too thick.

(Switzerland)

Scotch Broth

For 6–8 persons: 1 nap bone, split; or scrag end neck of mutton, or mutton shank; 2 oz barley; 1 oz marrowfat peas; 6 pints cold water; 8 oz carrot; 4 oz turnip; 8 oz parsnips; 1 onion; 2 leeks; ¼ cabbage; salt; pepper and sugar; chopped parsley. Cooking time: 3 hours.

Soak the peas overnight. Scald the barley and put it on with the peas and bone or meat and cold water. Boil up and skim. Add neatly diced vegetables, except the leek, cabbage and parsley. Season and cook slowly for 2 hours. Shred the cabbage finely. Split the leeks and cut into ½-inch pieces. Add this with the cabbage, more seasoning if required and some sugar. Simmer for another 20 minutes. Remove bone or meat. Pick off any meat. Shred this and return to pan. Add parsley to the broth and serve.

It is a good plan to make the broth sufficient for 2 days. On the second day, the broth may be better than when freshly made!

(Scotland)

Soupe aux Choux * *Cabbage Soup*

For 8 persons: 2 lb blade-bone of pork; 8 oz pickled belly of pork; 6 pints water; a good thick slice smoked Continental boiling sausage (with or without garlic); 8 oz carrots; 4 oz turnips; 8 oz leeks; 1¾ lb potatoes; 4 lb white cabbage; seasoning; 1 clove garlic (optional). Cooking time: 2 hours.

Boil the blade-bone and the belly fat as for stockpot. The meat should be washed beforehand to remove excess salt; it may even be necessary to blanch it. Boil, skim and flavour with plenty of vegetables. Boil for 1 hour, then add the quartered cabbage with the outside leaves removed. After a further 30 minutes add the sliced potatoes and raw sausage. Boil for another 25 to 30 minutes and serve. The meat may be served with the vegetables.   *(Austria)*

▣ à l'Oignon * *Onion*

For 4 persons: 1 lb onions; 3 oz butter; 2 slices bread; 1 pint milk; ½ pint bouillon; seasoning.

Cook chopped onions in butter very gently without discolouring in a covered pan, for 1 hour. Add crumbed bread, milk and *bouillon*. Continue cooking slowly for 1 hour. Sieve or use the liquidiser. Season and serve very hot.

▣ à l'Oignon, au Fromage ou "Gratinée" * *Onion with Cheese*

For 6 persons: 8 oz onions; 2 oz butter; ½ oz flour; 1½ pints water; seasoning; 2 oz gruyère cheese. Cooking time: 30 minutes.

Gently simmer the thinly sliced onions in a saucepan with the butter for 20–25 minutes. Slowly fry to a golden brown, dust with flour, brown it, add the water, pepper and salt and cook for 10 minutes. In the meantime place some very thin slices of bread in a soup tureen, sprinkle with thin flakes of *gruyère* and dabs of butter, pour the soup on top and allow to stand for 5 to 6 minutes before serving. If the soup is preferred without pieces of onion in it, it should be strained on to the bread in the tureen. This soup may also be prepared *au gratin.* Use an ovenproof soup tureen and make the soup a little thicker. Sprinkle with grated cheese, pepper generously and place in a very hot oven to brown.

Soupe au Potiron * *Pumpkin*

For 4 persons: 1¼ *lb pumpkin; 1 pint milk; 1 oz butter; 2 thick slices brown bread; seasoning; pinch sugar.* Cooking time: about 45 minutes.

Cut up the pumpkin and boil in salted water. Pass through a fine sieve together with the liquor, and add milk to give it a creamy consistency. Season and add a little sugar. Add some rather thick slices of brown bread to the soup and simmer gently for 6 minutes. Remove from heat, add butter and pour into soup tureen.

▣ aux Rognons * *Sherried Kidney Soup*

For 6–8 persons: 1 *ox kidney; 2 oz butter; 1 onion; 2 teaspoons finely chopped parsley; 4 tablespoons sherry; 3 pints brown stock; salt and pepper to taste; 1 dessertspoon flour; little water; extra parsley, finely chopped.* Cooking time: 1¾ hours.

Cut kidney into small dice, removing core. *Sauté* with finely chopped onion in hot butter until brown. Add parsley, sherry, stock, salt and pepper; simmer gently 1½ hours. Mix flour with a little water to blend, then stir into soup; simmer further 10 to 15 minutes. Serve piping hot sprinkled with chopped parsley.

▣ Savoyarde * *Special Vegetable*

For 8 persons: 7 *oz fat bacon; half a celeriac; 2 leeks; 2 turnips; 2 onions;* 3 *large potatoes; 1 pint milk; 2 oz butter; 3 pints water; 2 thick slices of bread; 2 oz grated cheese.* Cooking time: 1 hour.

Chop the bacon and fry lightly. Add the vegetables cut into small pieces, with the exception of the potatoes. Cover and cook slowly without browning for 20 minutes. Add water. Cook for 20–25 minutes. Add the potatoes, cut into thin slices, and cook. Lastly add the boiling milk and the butter. Season and pour over slices of bread sprinkled with grated cheese.

Hot Hors d'Œuvres or Entrées

Entrées or hot *hors d'œuvre*, like cold, are usually served at lunch and only occasionally at dinner when the soup course is omitted. When these preparations are served as light *entrées*, the size of the items and the amounts served are increased, and these dishes may then be served as a main part of a lunch or dinner menu. An *entrée* is very often a dish complete in itself with its own sauce and vegetables.

Allumettes aux Anchois * *Anchovy Sticks*

Roll out Puff pastry in strips 2½ to 3 inches wide and ⅛ inch thick. Take some anchovy fillets in oil and roll them in chopped hardboiled egg and parsley. Place an anchovy fillet on each strip of pastry, near the edge, and roll up the pastry to enclose the anchovy completely. Moisten the edges to seal and trim evenly. Cut one end to the shape of a fish tail and the other end to a point to make the head. Place on a baking-sheet, brush with beaten egg, score the top with a knife and bake in a hot oven, 400°F or Gas Mark 6, for 12 to 15 minutes.

Beignets de Poisson * *Fish Cakes*

An attractive way of using left-over fish (salmon, turbot, hake or cod) is to mix a little rather dry potato *purée* with an equal part of puréed or mashed fish. Add a little chopped onion cooked in butter, an egg or two according to quantity (2 eggs to the pound) and a little pepper. When the ingredients are thoroughly mixed shape into balls, flatten them, roll in flour and then in breadcrumbs, and deep fry at the last moment. Drain well on a paper napkin and serve with melted butter or a cream sauce.

BOUCHÉES * *PUFF PASTRY PATTY CASES*

For 8 persons: Order 8 patty cases from a baker or make them as follows:— Roll out 8 ounces Puff pastry ½ inch thick and cut out rounds 2 inches across with a crimp cutter. Place them on a baking sheet, sprinkled with cold water. Mark each to form the lid by pressing with a 1 inch cutter. Brush rims only lightly with egg yolk. Bake pastry in a hot oven preheated for 20 minutes, at 400°F or Gas Mark 6. Raise to 425°F or Gas Mark 7, when the pastry is put in, and after 10 minutes reduce to 375°F or Gas Mark 5. Continue baking for 15 minutes. Do not open the door during this time. Remove cases from oven and prise off lid carefully. Take away the uncooked paste from the centre, leaving only a shell.

52

▲ *Rissoles, Quiches à la lorraine, Bouchées Joinville, Ramequins, p. 59, 62, 57, 63*

Pizza, p. 62 ▼ 53

54 ▲ *Nouilles à la bernoise, p. 228*

Risotto aux cèpes, p. 229 ▼

▲ *Timbales de risotto, p. 59*

Cannelloni, p. 227 ▼

56 ▲ *Œufs brouillés à la catalane, p. 64*

Nouilles à la sauce bolognaise, p. 228 ▼

Bouchées aux Crevettes ou Joinville * *Shrimp Patties*

Round or oval patties garnished with peeled shrimps mixed with a few mushrooms to counteract the saltiness of the shrimps. Bind with well-buttered Shrimp sauce seasoned with cayenne pepper. (*See illustration p. 53*).

▣ à la Reine * *Chicken*

½ *pint white sauce or Béchamel; 8 oz diced cooked chicken; 2 oz cooked sliced mushrooms; 1 oz butter; seasoning and lemon juice.*

Mix all together. Make very hot and fill up cases, raising the mixture above the top. Replace the lids.

The patties may also be filled with various left-overs—game, fish, *gnocchi*, hardboiled eggs, etc.

Chaussons aux Oeufs * *Egg Turnovers*

For 4 persons: Puff pastry left-overs; 4 hardboiled eggs; ¼ pint Béchamel with a little tomato; 4 oz mushrooms; 1 oz butter.

Chop the eggs and mix them with the sauce, seasoning it well to counteract the slight insipidity of the eggs. Add minced mushrooms cooked in butter. Allow to cool. Roll out Puff pastry not too thick, and cut out rounds as for tartlets. Place a mound of the egg mixture on half of each round, moisten edges. Fold pastry over and press edges down firmly. Arrange on a baking sheet, brush with egg and score each patty three times with a knife tip. Bake for 18–20 minutes in a hot oven, 400°F or Gas Mark 6. Serve hot.

Croque-Monsieur * *Cheese Slices*

For 4 persons: 4 slices cooked ham; 8 slices gruyère cheese; 8 slices thin toast; 2 oz clarified butter.

Put each slice of ham between 2 slices of cheese. Sandwich between two slices lightly toasted bread. Cut out with a 1½ inch diameter round cutter. Fry on both sides in clarified butter and serve very hot.

Croquettes de Volaille * *Chicken Croquettes*

For 8 persons: 12 oz cooked chicken; 3 oz mushrooms; 1 oz boiled ham; 2 egg yolks; 1 small onion chopped; ½ lemon; ½ pint thick sauce Velouté; 1 oz butter; seasoning; egg and breadcrumbs.

Chop the onion and mushrooms and fry lightly in the butter. Add the chicken and ham finely diced, heat, bind with the thick *sauce Velouté* and boil for 5 or 6 minutes. Remove from the heat, stir in the 2 egg yolks, the juice of ½ lemon, salt and pepper and leave to cool on a buttered dish. Shape the mixture into 10 small cylinders, dip in beaten egg, roll in breadcrumbs and drop into very hot fat to fry for 5 minutes. Drain well. *Optional:* serve Tomato sauce separately.

Croûtes aux Champignons * *Mushroom Tartlets*

For 4 persons: 1 lb mushrooms; ¼ pint Béchamel; lemon juice, seasoning; 2 oz butter; bread or a 6 oz Short crust pastry flan case. Cooking time: 8–10 minutes.

Use small, very white mushrooms and cook them with butter, salt and lemon juice. Then bind with *sauce Suprême* or very creamy *Béchamel*. Simmer, dust with pepper and a pinch of cayenne, and serve either in a Short pastry flan, or on 8 individual round slices of bread, slightly scooped out and fried in butter.

Petits Pâtés Chauds * *Small Hot Patties*

Roll out Puff pastry rather more thinly than for Queen Patties and cut out using a 2 inch plain round cutter. Two rounds are needed for each patty. Place half the rounds on a moistened baking sheet and brush the edges with water. Place a small mound of well-seasoned forcemeat, possibly mixed with fine herbs, mushrooms, ham, etc., in the centre and cover with the remaining rounds, pressing down the edges well. Brush with egg, score with the tip of a small knife, bake in a very hot oven, 425°F or Gas Mark 7, for 15 minutes and serve. These patties may also be filled with forcemeat of pork, *quenelles*, fish, cheese, etc.

Pissaladière ou Tarte Niçoise * *Flan Niçoise*

For 4 persons: 6 oz Short pastry; 2 tablespoons olive oil; 6 large onions; 2 roughly chopped tomatoes; 2 oz black olives; 12 anchovy fillets. Cooking time: 30 minutes.

Slice the onions thinly. Cover and cook in olive oil without letting them brown, for 20 minutes. *Sauté* the chopped tomatoes in oil. When cooked, mix them with the onions, season and leave until cold. Line a shallow tart tin or flan ring with the Short pastry. Prick. Fill with the onion and tomato mixture, spreading it evenly, scatter stoned black olives on top and cover with the anchovy fillets arranged in a lattice pattern. Bake at 375°F or Gas Mark 5, for 30–40 minutes. Serve at once.

Les Rissoles * *Savoury Turnovers*

These small turnovers are made from Puff pastry left-overs filled with cooked meat, fish, *foie gras*, mushrooms, etc.

Roll out the pastry as for Small Hot Patties and cut out fairly large rounds with a crimp cutter. Moisten the edges with a brush. Place a teaspoon of cold filling bound with a little sauce in the centre. Fold as for Apple Turnover and fry in hot deep fat for 4 to 5 minutes. Drain and serve on a napkin garnished with fried parsley. The turnovers are served without sauce. (*See illustration p. 53*).

Soufflé de Poisson * *Fish Soufflé*

For 4 persons: 8 oz cooked fish; 2 eggs; ½ pint thick Béchamel; salt and pepper; 1 teaspoon Worcester sauce; 1 teaspoon anchovy essence; 1 teaspoon vinegar. Cooking time: 20 minutes.

Skin the cooked fish and mash with a fork if soft, otherwise pass through the mincer. Combine this *purée* with the *Béchamel*. Season well, add vinegar, essence and Worcester sauce. Heat and remove from the fire when the mixture comes to the boil. Stir in 2 egg yolks and fold in 2 stiffly beaten whites. Pour into a buttered *soufflé* dish and bake at 375°F or Gas Mark 5, for 25 minutes. Serve at once, as in the case of all *soufflés*. The same recipe may be used to make a *soufflé* from left-over poultry, ham, sweetbreads, game, etc. with appropriate seasonings.

Tarte aux Oignons * Onion Tart

For 4 persons: 6 large onions; 6 oz Short pastry; ¼ pint thin cream; 1 whole egg and 2 yolks; salt; pepper; a pinch of nutmeg; 3 oz butter. Cooking time: 30 minutes.

Slice the onions thinly; cook them slowly by the "*Etuvée*" method in as aucepan with butter, without letting them brown, then season. Line a shallow tart tin or flan ring with the Short pastry. Arrange the onions evenly on the pastry and cover with the following mixture: beat the whole egg with the yolks in a china or earthenware bowl, add salt, pepper, a small pinch of nutmeg and the cream. Strain over the onions through a fine, conical sieve. Bake, at 375°F or Gas Mark 5, for 30–40 minutes.

Timbales de Risotto * Risotto Timbales

Risotto Milanese; chopped tomato; slices of ham.

Butter some *timbale* moulds or use cups. Cut out rounds of ham the same size as the moulds. Fill the moulds with *Risotto*. Place the rounds of ham on a dish, unmould the *timbales* on them and garnish with roughly chopped skinned tomato. Serve very hot. (*See illustration p. 55*).

Vol-au-Vent Maison

8 oz sweetbreads; 8 oz cooked *breast of chicken; 6 oz mushrooms; 1 vol-au-vent case (8 oz); 2 oz carrot; 1 small onion; 1 bouquet garni; ½ pint sauce Suprême.*

Soak the sweetbreads thoroughly in cold water to keep them white, blanch, refresh and place in one pint of white *bouillon* or water. Add the carrot, onion and *bouquet garni*, cover and cook for 1 hour. When cooked, cut the sweetbreads into large dice and place in a saucepan with the breast of chicken cut up finely. Add the sliced mushrooms after cooking them in salted water flavoured with lemon. Add a little of the liquid in which the mushrooms were cooked, leave to cook for 6 to 8 minutes and bind with the *sauce Suprême*. Meanwhile heat the *vol-au-vent* case in the oven, then fill with the mixture and serve.

Cheese Dishes

BEIGNETS ★ *FRITTERS*

Beignets au Fromage ★ *Cheese Fritters*

For 4 persons: Sauce: 2 oz butter; 4 oz flour; 1 pint milk; 2 oz gruyère cheese; salt and pepper; grating of nutmeg. Batter: 4 oz flour; 3 tablespoons warm water; 4 tablespoons beer; salt; 1 egg white.

Make a Frying batter beforehand by mixing the flour with the beer, warm water and fine salt. Cover, and allow to stand for an hour. Immediately before use add the stiffly beaten egg white. In the meantime make a thick *sauce Béchamel* with the butter, flour and milk; season and let it cool before adding the cheese. Shape the fritters with a teaspoon, coat with batter and deep fry for 3 to 4 minutes in very hot oil. Serve on a napkin.

▣ Surprise ★ *Surprise Fritters*

For 4 persons: Half the quantity of sauce given above; 2 oz gruyère; 1 oz butter; 2 oz raw ham; chopped, very dry almonds. Cooking time: 3–4 minutes.

Mix the sauce with diced *gruyère*, diced ham fried in butter and the almonds. Shape into balls the size of a large plum, roll in flour and deep fry in very hot oil. Arrange on a napkin and serve very hot. Herring or anchovy fillets may also be mixed with the paste.

Croquettes au Fromage ★ *Cheese Croquettes*

For 4 persons: 1¼ lb potatoes; 4 oz gruyère; 1 egg yolk; 4 tablespoons milk; salt; pepper; nutmeg; egg and breadcrumbs. Cooking time: 2–3 minutes.

Boil the potatoes in salted water, drain and rub them through a sieve. Mix the *purée* with the egg yolk and milk. Season and combine with the *gruyère* cut in small dice. Spread on plate to cool. Shape mixture into *croquettes*, egg and crumb and deep fry in very hot oil.

Croûtes au Fromage ★ *Cheese Croûtes*

For 4 persons: 8 slices of bread ½ inch thick; 3 oz butter; 6 tablespoons white wine; 6 oz cheese (gruyère, etc.) cut into about ⅒ inch thick. Optional: rounds of tomato; very thinly sliced bacon.

Fry the bread in the butter, sprinkle with white wine and cover with the sliced cheese.

Place on a baking sheet, garnish with rounds of tomato and slices of bacon if preferred. Set in a hot oven until the cheese begins to melt. Sprinkle with paprika pepper on top, and serve very hot.

Fondue au Fromage * *Cheese Fondue*

For 4 persons: 1¼ lb cheese; ¼ pint white wine; 3 oz butter; 2 cloves of garlic; 6 tablespoons Kirsch; pepper. Cooking time: 3–4 minutes.

Good *fondue* can only be made from good cheese, preferably Emmental or fat *gruyère*. Place the thinly sliced cheese in an earthenware container if possible, after rubbing the inside with 2 cloves of garlic. Heat, and when it begins to melt moisten with white wine and stir over a low heat until the cheese has melted completely. Beat in butter in small pieces and pepper to taste. Add the Kirsch. This gives a very creamy paste. Serve in a bowl. It is eaten on pieces of bread impaled on a fork and dipped in the *fondue*.

Gâteau au Fromage * *Cheese Tart*

For 6 persons: 6 oz unsweetened Short pastry; 3 eggs; ½ pint milk; 7 oz grated fatty cheese such as gruyère.

Line a flan ring—7–8 inches—with the pastry and prick the bottom. Beat the eggs, stir in the milk and cheese, and season. Pour this mixture into the pastry case and bake in a fairly hot oven, 375°F or Gas Mark 6, for 30–40 minutes.

GNOCCHI * *GNOCCHI*

Gnocchi au Fromage * *Cheese Gnocchi*

For 4 persons: ½ pint water; 3 oz butter; 5 oz flour; 4 oz grated cheese; 4 eggs; 1 pint thin Béchamel; salt; pepper; nutmeg; melted butter. Cooking time: 30–35 minutes.

Boil the water with the butter and seasoning. Remove pan from the heat and pour in the whole of the sifted flour. Mix with a spatula. Dry this paste, which should be thick, by stirring briskly on a hot flame for 2 minutes. Leave to cool for 6–8 minutes. Add the eggs one by one, stirring each one into the mixture, and add half the cheese. Drop small balls of this mixture, the size of a cherry, into a large saucepan of boiling salted water. Simmer for 10 minutes. Drain, bind with 1 pint thin *Béchamel* and simmer for 15 minutes. Season, pour into a baking dish, sprinkle the remainder of the cheese on top. Sprinkle with melted butter and place in a moderate oven, 375°F or Gas Mark 5, so that the *gnocchi* swell while browning. Bake 15–20 minutes and serve at once, before they collapse.

▣ à la Romaine * *Roman style*

For 4 persons: 4 oz semolina; 1 pint milk; 2 oz gruyère cheese; 2 oz Parmesan cheese; 1 oz butter; breadcrumbs; 4 tablespoons bouillon; salt; pepper; 1 egg yolk. Cooking time: 8–10 minutes.

Boil the semolina in the milk, adding salt and pepper. When it is cooked, which takes approximately 15 minutes, beat in egg yolk and most of the grated cheese. Pour onto a buttered, floured baking tray. Spread ⅛ inch thick and allow to cool. Cut out small crescents with a cutter and place them in a baking dish. Sprinkle with remaining cheese mixed with breadcrumbs and *bouillon*. Pour on melted butter and brown in a very hot oven, 425°F or Gas Mark 7.

Gougère au Fromage * *Cheese Gougère*

For 4 persons: Same paste as for Gnocchi; cheese diced instead of grated; 2 oz thinly sliced gruyère cheese; ½ oz finely chopped almonds. Cooking time: 15–20 minutes.

With a bag and ½ inch plain nozzle, pipe the *Gnocchi* paste in a ring 6 inches in diameter onto a greased baking sheet. Brush with beaten egg yolk and sprinkle with the chopped almonds. Decorate with sliced cheese. Bake in a hot oven, 425°F or Gas Mark 7, for 10 minutes. Reduce to 375°F or Gas Mark 4, and continue baking for 20 minutes. Serve at once.

Omelette-Soufflé au Fromage * *Cheese Omelette Soufflé*

For 4 persons: 3 egg yolks; 5 egg whites; ½ oz butter; ½ oz flour; ¼ pint milk; 3 oz grated Parmesan; salt; pepper; nutmeg.

Melt the butter, mix in the flour, moisten with the milk, season and bring to the boil. Remove from heat, stir in the egg yolks and allow to cool. Stiffly beat the egg whites and fold them gradually and gently into the sauce with a spoon, together with the grated cheese. Pour into a buttered ovenproof dish sprinkled with cheese, leaving the centre empty (it will fill during cooking). Bake in a moderate oven, 375°F or Gas Mark 5, for 20 minutes.

Palets Prinsky * *Cheese Savouries*

For 4 persons: 5 oz flour; 2 oz butter; ½ pint water; 4 whole eggs; 3 oz grated gruyère; 1 pint Béchamel with 4 oz gruyère added; 6 oz breadcrumbs; 2 eggs beaten with 4 tablespoons oil. Cooking time: 4–5 minutes.

Prepare a *Choux* paste with the flour, butter, water and eggs. Add the 3 ounces of grated *gruyère*. Pipe in several thin, narrow strips and bake for about 25 minutes in a hot oven, 400°F or Gas Mark 6, until it is crisp, brown and dry. Make small incisions in each strip with a sharp knife to allow the steam to escape. Sandwich 2 layers of paste with a thick layer of *Béchamel*, then cut in strips as for Cream Slices, dip in cheese sauce on both sides, roll in white breadcrumbs and fry in half oil and half butter.

Pizza * *Pizza*

For 6 persons: 6 portions of Pizza pastry; 8 oz skinned tomatoes without their seeds; 7 oz mozzarella or gruyère cheese; 2 oz Parmesan cheese; 6 anchovies; 6 cloves garlic; marjoram.

Arrange the tomatoes on the pastry. Season with pepper, slice the mozzarella and arrange the slices on the tomatoes; then cover with a lattice of anchovy fillets. Add the cloves of garlic, sprinkle with Parmesan cheese, marjoram and oil. Place in a hot oven, 375°–400°F or Gas Mark 5–6, and bake for 20–30 minutes. (*See illustration p. 53*).

Quiche à la Lorraine * *Bacon and Egg Flan*

For 4 persons: 6 oz unsweetened Short pastry; 2 eggs; scant ¾ pint milk; 2 oz gruyère (optional); 3 oz bacon; salt; pepper; nutmeg. Cooking time: 25–30 minutes.

Line a flan ring with Short pastry. Prick the bottom and cover with cheese slices, and diced grilled, cooled bacon. Beat the eggs with the seasoning and add the milk. Pour into the flan. Bake for 35 minutes in a hot oven, 400°F or Gas Mark 6, and serve at once. (*See illustration p. 53*).

Ramequins * *Ramekins*

For 6 persons: 5 *oz flour;* 2 *oz butter;* ½ *pint water;* 3 *eggs and* 1 *egg yolk;* 5 *oz grated gruyère cheese;* 2 *oz very finely diced gruyère cheese.* Cooking time: 10–12 minutes.

Prepare a *Choux* paste with the flour, butter, water and eggs. Add the grated cheese. Using a forcing bag and a plain ½ inch nozzle, pipe out small puffs (the size of a small apricot) on a greased baking sheet. Brush with egg yolk. Garnish with the diced cheese. Bake in a hot oven, 375°–400°F or Gas Mark 6, and serve very hot. (*See illustration p.* 53).

Soufflé au Fromage * *Cheese Soufflé*

For 4 persons: 1 *oz butter;* 1 *oz flour;* ½ *pint milk;* 4 *egg yolks;* 3 *egg whites;* 4 *oz grated gruyère; salt; pepper; nutmeg.* Cooking time: 20–25 minutes.

Melt ½ ounce butter in a saucepan, mix it with the flour and moisten it with the milk. Add salt and pepper and bring to the boil, stirring with a whisk. When the mixture boils it should be like a thick *Béchamel.* Remove it from the heat, add remaining butter, a pinch of grated nutmeg and the egg yolks, beating briskly. Add the stiffly beaten egg whites, folding them in carefully with a metal spoon, and only then add the grated cheese. Pour the mixture into a buttered *soufflé* dish, sprinkled with cheese. Bake for 25 minutes in a hot oven, 400°F or Gas Mark 6, and serve at once in the baking dish. The *soufflé* can also be baked in small individual dishes. In this case 8 minutes baking time should be enough. If possible the oven should be hotter below than above.

Tartelettes Suisses * *Swiss Tartlets*

For 6 persons: Line 12 tartlet cases with 6 ounces Puff pastry trimmings. Make ¼ pint of thick, highly seasoned *Béchamel.* When it boils remove from heat and beat in 2 whole eggs followed by 2 *petit suisse* cheeses and 2 ounces of grated *gruyère.* Fill to within ½ inch of the top of the tartlets and bake for 10 minutes in a hot oven, 425°F or Gas Mark 7. Serve while still puffy.

Eggs

Eggs must be absolutely fresh. To test the freshness of eggs place them in a bowl of cold water. The fresh ones will sink to the bottom and lie on one side, while the doubtful ones will hover in the middle. Any that float on top should be thrown away.

HOT EGG DISHES

ŒUFS BROUILLÉS * SCRAMBLED EGGS

Butter a small saucepan well, break the whole eggs into it and season with pepper and salt. Add a tablespoon of thick cream to 3 eggs and stir lightly with a whisk while they cook (3–4 minutes). Scrambled eggs should not be overcooked or they become tough and indigestible. If they are too dry add a little butter or yolk of egg.

Oeufs Brouillés à la Catalane * Scrambled Eggs with Tomatoes and Peppers

For 4 *persons:* 8 *eggs;* 5 *oz tomatoes;* 3 *oz green peppers;* 3 *tablespoons cream;* 2 *oz butter; seasoning.*

Cut the skinned tomatoes into dice and the peppers into *julienne* strips. *Sauté* in butter. When cooked add to the eggs and cream. Continue as for basic method. (*See illustration p.* 56).

▣ aux Champignons * with Mushrooms

For 4 *persons:* 8 *eggs;* 2 *oz butter;* 4 *oz mushrooms; seasoning;* 3 *tablespoons cream.* Cooking time: 8–10 minutes.
Slice the raw mushrooms, fry them in butter till brown and combine with eggs, seasoning and cream.

▣ aux Crevettes * with Shrimps

For 4 *persons:* 8 *eggs;* 5 *oz shrimps;* 1 *oz butter;* 3 *tablespoons cream.* Cooking time: 8–10 minutes.

Fry the peeled shrimps in butter and add to eggs and cream.

Oeufs aux Croûtons * with Croûtons

For 4 persons: 8 eggs; 20 small croûtons; 6 tablespoons cream; seasoning.

Fry small white bread *croûtons*, cut in cubes, in butter without browning too much. Mix with the eggs and cream at the last moment.

▣ au Fromage * with Cheese

For 4 persons: 8 eggs; 2 oz grated cheese; 2 oz butter; seasoning; 3 oz gruyère; 6 tablespoons cream.

Add 2 ounces grated cheese to scrambled eggs, arrange on a dish and garnish with very thin slices of *gruyère*.

ŒUFS EN COCOTTE * EGGS IN A COCOTTE

These eggs are simply a variation of poached eggs, except that they are placed in a small dish, known as a *cocotte*, made of ovenproof china or earthenware. They may be poached in cream, *bouillon* or other liquid. Heat the poaching liquid allowing 1 tablespoonful for each egg and pour into the heated *cocotte*, break in the egg and put the *cocotte* in a water bath allowing the water to come half-way up each *cocotte*. Heat for 2–3 minutes with the water at simmering point. Cover and complete the cooking in a moderate oven, 375°F or Gas Mark 5. The total cooking time should take about 8 minutes. The white should be set while the yolk is still soft. Each *cocotte* is wiped dry and served on a napkin. The water bath may consist of a *sauté* pan with a lid or a roasting tin covered with a baking sheet.

Œufs en Cocotte à la Creme * Eggs in Cocotte with Cream

For 4 persons: 4 eggs; 4 tablespoons cream; seasoning.

Warm the *cocottes* and fill each with 1 tablespoon hot cream. Break one very fresh egg into each. Place *cocottes* in a pan of water, season and simmer for 2 minutes at the side of the stove. Put in the oven for 3 minutes. *Or* place in a water bath and set lightly in a warm oven, 350°F or Gas Mark 4, for 15 minutes. Serve the *cocottes* on a napkin.

▣ à la Bergère * Bergère

For 4 persons: 4 eggs; 2 oz butter; 2 oz mushrooms; 1 tablespoon chopped fine herbs.

Mix minced cooked mushrooms with the herbs and a piece of soft butter, season with salt and pepper and place in bottom of *cocottes*. Break an egg into each and cook as for the recipe for Eggs in *Cocotte* with Cream.

▣ à la Florentine * with Spinach

For 4 persons: 4 eggs; 8 oz spinach; 4 tablespoons cream; 1 oz cheese; seasoning; 1 oz butter.

Line the *cocottes* with a thin layer of spinach cooked in butter. Break an egg into each *cocotte* and add salt and pepper. Start cooking as for Eggs in *Cocotte* with Cream. When the eggs begin to set place a spoon of thick cream on top of each, sprinkle with grated cheese and brown for 1 minute in a hot oven.

65

ŒUFS À LA COQUE * *SOFTBOILED EGGS*

Boiled eggs should be at room temperature before being placed in boiling water. If they are used straight from the refrigerator they are liable to crack. Choose a lined pan large enough to hold sufficient water to cover the eggs completely.

One method is to place the eggs gently in boiling water, cover and cook for 3½–4 minutes at simmering point. The other method is to put the eggs in cold water and bring the water fairly slowly to the boil.

ŒUFS DURS * *HARDBOILED EGGS*

If hardboiled eggs are to be perfect, the following points should be observed: Do not boil longer than 8–10 minutes, according to size. If the eggs are cooked longer than necessary the white becomes tough, the yolk turns an ugly greenish colour and the whole egg gives off an unpleasant smell. The eggs must therefore be placed in boiling water, boiled briskly, and then be plunged in cold water and shelled. A frying basket is useful to boil a large number of eggs.

Oeufs Durs Aurore * *Hardboiled Aurore*

For 4 persons: 6 hardboiled eggs; ½ pint Béchamel; 2 tablespoons Tomato sauce; 2 oz grated cheese.

Prepare as for Hardboiled Eggs with *Béchamel*, keeping back 2 yolks. Place in a baking dish. Sprinkle with the chopped yolks and cheese. Brown and surround with a ribbon of Tomato sauce.

▣ à la Béchamel * *with Béchamel*

For 4 persons: 6 hardboiled eggs; ½ pint Béchamel.

Slice the eggs thinly and heat them in well-buttered and strongly seasoned *Béchamel* without letting it come to the boil.

▣ Oeufs Mornay * *Eggs Mornay*

For 4 persons: 6–8 eggs; 1 oz butter; 1 oz flour; ½ pint milk; 1 egg yolk; 1 oz grated gruyère; some breadcrumbs; seasoning. Cooking time of eggs: 2–3 minutes.

The eggs may be either softboiled, poached or hardboiled. Make a *Béchamel* with the butter, flour and milk. Cook for 5–6 minutes and thicken with the egg yolk. Arrange the eggs in a baking dish (if they are hardboiled, halve them). Cover generously with the sauce, to which some cheese has been added at the last moment. Sprinkle the remainder of the cheese, mixed with breadcrumbs, on top and brown in a very hot oven, especially if the eggs are softboiled or poached, so that they do not harden. Serve at once.

ŒUFS FRITS * *BRITISH FRIED EGGS*

Heat about ¼ pint oil in a frying pan. When it starts to smoke slide in an egg, previously broken on to a plate and lightly salted. With a spatula press the egg white, which puffs up, round the yolk to give the egg its original shape. Brown one side, then turn before the yolk has time to harden. When the white has been cooked on the other side remove the egg, drain and fry the next one. These eggs are mostly served with fried ham or bacon, and half grilled tomatoes or Tomato sauce.

ŒUFS MOLLETS * *MEDIUM BOILED EGGS*

Place the eggs in boiling water for 5–6 minutes, according to size. Then plunge them in cold water immediately to prevent them cooking further. Remove and peel them carefully. Replace in hot (not boiling) and strongly salted water until required.

All recipes using Poached eggs can be made using Medium-boiled eggs.

OMELETTES * *OMELETTES (BASIC METHOD)*

Break the eggs into a bowl, season and mix them lightly with a fork. Add ½ ounce of butter in small pats. Pour into a pan containing sizzling hot butter. Stir with a fork, especially at the edges, where the eggs cook more quickly. As soon as the eggs begin to set, stop stirring, but shake the pan from time to time to stop the omelette sticking. When the omelette is sufficiently cooked leave it without shaking for a moment to brown the underside, then roll it from one side with a fork. Knock the handle of the pan once or twice to slide the omelette on to the plate. Hold the pan in the right hand, the plate in the left and incline them both at the same time, so that the omelette automatically settles in the middle of the plate. Serve at once. It is easier to make 2 × 3 egg or 2 × 4 egg omelettes rather than 1 × 6 eggs or 1 × 8 eggs.

Omelette aux Champignons * *Mushroom Omelette*

For 4 persons: 6 eggs; 6 oz mushrooms; 1 oz butter; 2 tablespoons sauce Demi-glace. Cooking time of mushrooms: 5–6 minutes. Cooking time of eggs: 3–4 minutes over high heat.

Slice the mushrooms, *sauté* them with half the butter and bind them with two tablespoons of *sauce Demi-glace*. Fold half the mushrooms inside the omelette, serve and place the remainder of the mushrooms in an incision on top.

▣ aux Crevettes * *with Shrimps*

For 4 persons: 6 eggs; 5 oz shrimps; seasoning; 2 oz butter; 1 tablespoon Shrimp sauce.

Fill omelette with half the peeled shrimps, heated in butter, with sauce added. Garnish with remainder in an incision on top.

▣ à la Farine * *Pancake*

For 4 persons: 4 eggs; 2 oz flour; scant ½ pint cold milk; seasoning; 2 oz butter. Cooking time: 4–5 minutes.

Mix the sifted flour with the eggs and milk; season. Beat like a batter, allow to stand. Cook as for ordinary omelette. Fine herbs, boiled ham, cooked bacon, etc. may be added.

▣ au Fromage * *Cheese*

For 4 persons: 6 eggs; 2 oz butter; 2 oz grated Parmesan or gruyère; seasoning. Cooking time: 3 minutes.

Add the grated cheese to the eggs while beating them; make the omelette rather moist inside.

Omelette aux Fines Herbes * *with Fine Herbs*

For 4 persons: 6 eggs; fine herbs; seasoning; 1 oz butter.

Cooking time over high heat: 3–4 minutes.
Before beating the eggs add a suitable quantity of finely chopped parsley, chervil, tarragon and chives to them.

▣ au Lard ou au Jambon * *Bacon or Ham*

For 4 persons: 6 eggs; 3 oz lean bacon or ham; 1 oz butter; seasoning.
Cooking time of eggs: 3–4 minutes.

Dice the bacon or ham, brown in butter in the frying pan and add the eggs. It may be necessary to blanch the bacon in water for 2 minutes first to extract surplus salt.

▣ à la Lyonnaise * *with Onions*

For 4 persons: 6 eggs; 2 oz onions; 1 oz butter; seasoning; chopped parsley.
Cooking time of eggs: 3–4 minutes.

Slice the onions, cook them in butter and add the eggs mixed with the chopped parsley.

▣ Mousseline * *Mousseline or Foamy*

For 4 persons: 4 eggs; 2 tablespoons cream; 2 oz butter; seasoning.

Separate the egg yolks from the whites, mix the yolks with the cream and season with salt and pepper. Carefully fold in the stiffly beaten egg whites with a spoon. Then make in the same way as an ordinary omelette, using a large pan and a little more butter.

▣ à l'Oseille * *Sorrel*

For 4 persons: 6 eggs; 1 oz butter; seasoning; sorrel.
Cooking time over high heat: 3–4 minutes.

Finely shred a handful of sorrel, simmer in butter and add to the beaten eggs before making the omelette.

▣ Parmentier * *Potato Omelette*

For 4 persons: 6 eggs; 2 oz potatoes; 1 oz butter. Cooking time over high heat: 3–4 minutes.

Cut the potatoes in small dice and *sauté* them in butter in the frying pan. When they are done, add the eggs and make the omelette.

▣ à la Paysanne * *Paysanne*

For 4 persons: 6 eggs; 3 oz lean bacon; 2 oz potatoes; chopped fine herbs; 1 oz butter. Cooking time of eggs: 3–4 minutes.

Cook potatoes as above, add the fried, diced bacon and finally the eggs mixed with the chopped herbs.

⊡ aux Rognons * *Kidney*

For 4 persons: 6 eggs; 3 lamb's or sheep's kidneys; 1 oz butter; 2 tablespoons Madeira sauce; chopped parsley. Cooking time of kidneys: 5 minutes.

Split, skin, core and wash the kidneys, and *sauté* them quickly in very hot butter. Bind them with Madeira sauce. Fill omelette with half the kidneys and place remainder in an incision on top. Sprinkle with chopped parsley.

ŒUFS POCHÉS * *POACHED EGGS*

Boil some salted water with a dash of vinegar. Break an egg on to a plate and slide it quickly into the water. Do not put in too many eggs at once, or they will not recover their egg shape. When the water comes to the boil again, remove the pan from the heat and let the eggs stand covered for 2–3 minutes, depending on how they are to be used. Those which are to be served cold should be well cooked. As soon as the eggs are done remove them with a fish slice and plunge into hot or cold water, according to use, to rinse off the vinegar.

Oeufs Pochés Aurore * *Poached Eggs Aurore*

For 4 persons: 6–8 eggs; 8 croûtons; 1 yolk of hardboiled egg; sauce Aurore. Cooking time of eggs: 2–3 minutes.

Arrange poached eggs on *croûtons* and coat with well-buttered *sauce Aurore*. Serve sprinkled with the egg yolk rubbed through a sieve.

⊡ à la Cardinal * *Cardinal*

For 4 persons: 4–6 eggs; ½ pint sauce Cardinal (Béchamel containing cream and beaten up with Lobster butter).

Arrange poached eggs on a round dish and coat with well-buttered *sauce Cardinal*.

⊡ à l'Estragon * *with Tarragon*

For 4 persons: 4 eggs; ½ pint sauce Velouté; fresh chopped tarragon.

Arrange the poached eggs on fried *croûtons* or in *cocottes*; coat with *sauce Velouté* mixed with chopped tarragon. The eggs may be garnished with blanched tarragon leaves crossed to form stars.

⊡ à la Florentine * *with Spinach*

For 4 persons: 4 eggs; 1 lb spinach; ¾ pint sauce Mornay; 1 oz grated cheese; 1 oz breadcrumbs; 1 oz butter.

Sauté the spinach in butter and place it in the bottom of a *gratin* dish. Place well-drained poached eggs on top and coat with *sauce Mornay*. Sprinkle with cheese and breadcrumbs, dot with butter and brown in a hot oven.

⊡ au Jambon ou au Lard * *with Ham or Bacon*

For 4 persons: 6–8 eggs; 4 slices ham or bacon; 1 oz butter. Cooking time: 2–3 minutes.

Poach the eggs. Fry the ham or bacon; place a well-drained egg on each slice. Sprinkle with the fat from the pan mixed with the butter.

Oeufs pochés Joinville * *Joinville*

For 4 persons: 4 eggs; ¾ pint sauce Aurore; 12–15 peeled shrimps; 4 croûtons.

Arrange the poached eggs on fried *croûtons* and coat with *sauce Aurore* mixed with peeled shrimps.

▣ en Matelote * *en Matelote*

For 4 persons: 6 eggs; 1 pint red wine; 2 oz butter; 1 oz flour; 5 oz mushrooms; butter for cooking.

Bring the red wine to the boil and poach the eggs in it. Drain and reduce the wine after seasoning it. Bind the reduction with the butter kneaded with the flour to make a creamy sauce. A little caramel may be added to colour it brown. Arrange the eggs on fried *croûtons* and coat with the sauce mixed with diced cooked mushrooms.

▣ à la Portugaise * *Portuguese style*

For 4 persons: 4 eggs; 3 oz rice; 1 oz butter; ½ pint bouillon; 1 clove garlic; salt and pepper; 2 tablespoons diced tomato; ¼ pint sauce Mornay; 2 oz gruyère.

Melt butter in a frying pan. Add rice and stir to soften without discolouring. Pour *bouillon* over with crushed garlic. Boil up and add tomato and seasoning. Cover closely with greased paper and a lid. Cook in a fairly hot oven, 375°F or Gas Mark 5, without disturbing for 18 minutes, when no liquid should remain and the rice grains are soft but not broken. Poach the eggs.

Make a *risotto* as above and serve on a round dish. Place well drained eggs on top. Coat with *sauce Mornay*. Sprinkle grated cheese over and brown in a hot oven, 425°F or Gas Mark 7, or under the grill.

▣ Sigurd * *Sigurd*

For 4 persons: 4 poached eggs; 4 tartlet cases; 12 oz onions; 4 oz mushrooms; ¼ pint sauce Béchamel; paprika.

Arrange the eggs in small tartlet cases of Short pastry and garnish with chopped cooked onions mixed with sliced cooked mushrooms. Coat the eggs with a creamy *sauce Béchamel* highly seasoned with paprika. If desired, a mushroom top, garnished with a pinch of grated horseradish, may be placed on top.

Croustades à la Reine * *Tartlets à la Reine*

For 4 persons: 4 eggs; 4 tartlet cases; 6 oz chicken purée; ¼ pint Madeira sauce; 4 truffle slices or 4 mushroom tops.

Fill the tartlets with fine, cooked chicken *purée* bound with Madeira sauce. Place a well-drained poached egg in each, sprinkle with a little of the same sauce and decorate with a truffle slice or a mushroom top cooked in butter. Serve at once.

ŒUFS SUR LE PLAT * *FRENCH FRIED EGGS*

Small shallow copper pan with handles or small shallow ovenproof dishes with ears should be used. First, melt a little butter in the dish, heat it and break in the eggs. Then put the dish immediately into a hot oven, 400°F or Gas Mark 6, for 4–5 minutes until the eggs are just set. When serving, sprinkle a little salt and pepper on the egg whites and a little melted butter on the yolks.

Œufs sur le plat Bercy * Eggs Bercy (Fried)

For 4 persons: 4 eggs; 4 chipolatas; 1 oz butter; 2 tablespoons Tomato sauce.
Cooking time of eggs: 2–3 minutes.

Butter the dish and break the eggs into it. Between each egg place a grilled chipolata sausage. Cook in oven and pour Tomato sauce round the dish in a ring.

▣ au Beurre Noir * with Black Butter

For 4 persons: 8 eggs; 2 oz butter; 1 teaspoon vinegar or lemon juice.
Cooking time: 4–5 minutes.

Melt the butter in a pan and add the vinegar or lemon juice. Break the eggs into the pan when the butter begins to turn black; before serving sprinkle with a little black butter made separately. Add salt and pepper.

▣ aux Champignons * with Mushrooms

For 4 persons: 12 oz mushrooms; 2 oz butter; lemon juice; ¼ pint Béchamel;
¼ *pint cream; 4 eggs.* Cooking time: 15 minutes.

Take some small mushrooms, wash them and cook in butter with salt and pepper, in a covered pan. Add *Béchamel* and cream so that they are covered, simmer for 10 minutes and at the last moment add a dash of lemon juice. Pour into 4 small ovenproof dishes. Make a hollow in the centre of each and break an egg into it. Season and set the eggs in a fairly hot oven, 375°F or Gas Mark 5, for about 5 minutes.

▣ au Lard * and Bacon

For 4 persons: 8 eggs; 4 slices bacon; 1 oz butter. Cooking time of eggs:
2–3 minutes.

Fry the bacon and place in the bottom of a dish. Break the eggs on top and cook in the oven.

▣ au Parmesan * with Parmesan Cheese

For 4 persons: 8 eggs; seasoning; 3 oz Parmesan; 2 oz butter. Cooking
time: 3–4 minutes.

Butter the bottom of the dish and sprinkle it with Parmesan. Break eggs on top and sprinkle the remainder of the grated cheese over them; season, sprinkle with melted butter and cook in a very hot oven to brown the top without hardening the eggs.

COLD EGG DISHES

Cold eggs are usually poached, softboiled or hardboiled. Most cold eggs are served garnished with aspic, of which so little is needed that it is best to buy it ready-made. This aspic is usually not flavoured, and care should be taken to melt it without letting it get too hot. Flavour it with an infusion of tarragon, a little Madeira or good white wine. Then let it set again. This makes an excellent aspic jelly and is very easy to prepare.

71

ŒUFS DURS FROIDS * *COLD HARDBOILED EGGS*

Œufs Durs au Foie Gras * *Hardboiled Eggs with Foie Gras*

For 4 persons: 4 hardboiled eggs; 4 truffle slices; foie gras purée; 4 table-spoons aspic.

Place the eggs in *cocottes* and surround with a ring of *foie gras purée*. Garnish with a truffle slice and fill up *cocottes* with half-set aspic. This dish is usually made when a little *foie gras* has been left over from the day before.

▣ à la Mayonnaise * *Mayonnaise*

Slice the hardboiled eggs and arrange them attractively in a dish. Cover with light *mayonnaise* and decorate with blanched chervil or tarragon. (*See illustration p. 33*).

▣ à la Mentonnaise * *Mentonnaise*

For 4 persons: 6 hardboiled eggs; 4 oz cooked fish; 6 anchovy fillets; 6 black olives.

Halve the eggs lengthwise. Remove the yolks and work them into a paste with the fish. Rub through a sieve and bind with *mayonnaise*. Fill the whites with this mixture using a forcing bag.
Garnish: an anchovy fillet coiled round a stoned, black olive.

▣ Mistral * *Mistral*

Halve hardboiled eggs lengthwise. Place them on some skinned tomato slices, add salt and coat with *mayonnaise*. Garnish with halved, stoned olives and surround with sliced tomatoes sprinkled with chopped parsley. (*See illustration p. 33*).

▣ à la Suédoise * *Swedish style*

Cut hardboiled eggs and small, firm tomatoes into thin slices. Arrange them alternately in a dish and cover with *Vinaigrette* mixed with a little mustard. Decorate with finely sliced onion rings.

▣ à la Vinaigrette * *Vinaigrette*

For 4 persons: 8 hardboiled eggs; sauce Vinaigrette.

Slice the eggs and cover with *Vinaigrette*, or with thin, well-seasoned *mayonnaise*.

Œufs Mollets Virginia Club * *Egg Maison Virginia*

For 1–2 persons: 2 eggs boiled for 5 minutes; half a tin sweetcorn; ¼ pint thick mayonnaise; 1 tomato; 1 handful watercress (1½ oz); 1 black olive.

Drain the sweetcorn, bind with part of the thick *mayonnaise* and season. Place the two eggs on this mixture, coat with the rest of the *mayonnaise* and garnish with half a black olive. Skin the tomato, cut in two and arrange the two halves on two small bunches of watercress seasoned with oil and salt.

▲ *Bitok de poisson, p. 82*

Soles grillées, p 97 ▼   73

74 ▲ *Filets de colin à la provençale, p. 86*

Paupiettes de filets de sole au gratin, p. 99 ▼

▲ *Darnes de colin pochées, p. 84*

Croustade de filets de sole, p. 98 ▼

Œufs Pochés en Cocotte à l'Estragon * *Poached Eggs in Cocotte with Tarragon*

For 4 persons: 1 *pint aspic;* 4 *poached eggs.*

Line *cocottes* with aspic. Place a cold poached egg in each and fill up with aspic strongly flavoured with tarragon. Leave to set on ice. Turn out and place on a dish, decorating each egg with tarragon leaves.

▣ en Cocotte au Jambon * *in Cocotte with Ham*

For 4 persons: 4 *poached eggs;* 4 *oz ham;* 1 *pint aspic.*

Place a thin slice of ham at the bottom of each *cocotte* and another on top of each egg; coat with aspic. Leave to set on ice. May be turned out or served in the *cocotte*.

▣ en Cocotte à la Russe * *Russian style*

For 4 persons: 4 *poached eggs;* 1 *pint aspic;* 4 *truffle slices;* 12 *oz Russian salad.*

Line egg *cocottes* with aspic, decorate the bottom with a truffle slice and place a cold, well-drained poached egg on top. Fill up with aspic and leave to set on ice. Turn out and arrange around Russian salad piled in a dome in the middle of a round dish. Place chopped aspic between the eggs.

Fish

The nutritive value of fish is almost as high as that of meat. It is very easy to digest and very good for children, the phosphorus content being a bone-building substance.

BUYING FISH

The freshness of the fish may be recognised by sight and touch. A fresh fish is very shiny, the skin moist and even viscous, the gills bright red, the eyes prominent, not sunk in the socket. If one presses the flesh with the finger the small dent should disappear immediately. The skin over the belly must be tightly stretched. Do not buy any fish that has an unpleasant smell.

CLEANING FISH

Scale the fish, cut off the fins with scissors and remove the gills. Gut the fish by removing the intestines through the gills or through an incision in the belly. Wash well inside and out.

COURT-BOUILLON * FISH STOCK

Boiling in *court-bouillon* is the commonest way of cooking both large fish either whole or in slices, and small fish whose flesh is not too fragile, especially fresh-water fish.

Court-bouillon consists of a mixture of aromatic vegetables and herbs, water and vinegar. Sometimes white wine is used instead of vinegar, but in a larger quantity. It is made up of some sliced onions and shallots, a bunch of parsley, thyme and bay leaves, salt and pepper-corns. The amount of the ingredients depends on the quantity or size of fish to be cooked, as does the amount of water and vinegar which should be ample to cover the fish (1 part of vinegar to 16 parts of water).

Average Proportions: *To 6 pints cold water add—$\frac{1}{4}$ pint French wine vinegar; 6 oz chopped onions; 2 chopped shallots; 4 oz chopped carrots; 1 oz salt; a bouquet garni; 2 cloves; zest of 1 lemon; 12 black peppercorns.*

If wine is used—add $\frac{1}{2}$ to equal quantity wine to water.

Hot or cold fish stock may be used, according to circumstances. If it is used cold, the fish is put in at the same time as the other ingredients and the whole is put on the stove together. This is done with large fish—salmon, trout, dogfish, pike, etc.—and indeed with all fish whose cooking time is sufficiently long to allow the vegetables in the fish stock to be cooked at the same time.

When dealing with small fish or cutlets, on the other hand, the *court-bouillon* must be

78

cooked first so that the vegetables and condiments will impart their flavour to the fish. In that case the very hot fish stock is poured over the fish.

In any event, one rule must be observed—a *court-bouillon* must never be allowed to boil while the fish is cooking. It must never get hotter than simmering point, otherwise the fish will disintegrate. The only exceptions are fish cooked by the "blue" method, which should be dropped into the *court-bouillon* while it is boiling, and large shellfish, which will not cook properly below boiling point.

BRAISING

This method of cooking is used for cutlets or whole fish such as carp, salmon, trout, turbot, sturgeon and pike. Cover the bottom of a casserole, fish kettle or roasting pan with a layer of butter and on this place carrots, onions, *bouquet garni* and shallots, all lightly tossed in butter. Lay the fish on top, lard it with fat bacon and fill the pan to half the height of the fish with red or white wine, depending on the sauce to be served with the fish. Equal parts of wine and *bouillon* are sometimes used. Season with salt and peppercorns, bring to the boil on top of the stove. Then place in the oven to cook gently, basting frequently for a period, depending on the nature and size of the fish. For economy, the bacon may be replaced by greased paper or foil.

DEEP FRYING

Oil is the best fat for deep frying. The smaller the fish, the hotter the fat should be. The fat is hot enough when it smokes a very little; do not wait until it gives off blue smoke, as this means that it is burning. If you are frying large fish, do not let it brown too quickly or an outer crust will be formed, which will prevent the heat from penetrating into the centre. Nothing is more disagreeable than undercooked fish. All fish, whether fried whole or in slices, should first be dipped in salted cold milk and then rolled in flour, which will give it a crisp crust. Whole fish weighing more than 4 ounces must be scored 5 or 6 times on each side before being dipped in milk and flour. The object of this is to enable the heat to reach the centre.

When the fat is hot enough, do not put in too much fish at one time or the fat will be cooled too much and the fish will be boiled and not fried. If one only has a small amount of oil, it is best to fry the fish in two instalments over a hot flame, so that the fat, although cooled at first by the immersion of the fish, will quickly regain its former temperature.

When frying very small fish, use very hot fat and put in only a few fish at a time.

There is one fish, the burbot, which should never be either deep or shallow fried, or cooked *à la poêle* because it gives off a lot of moisture in cooking. It should be browned in a saucepan or earthenware pan.

The fish may also be dipped in batter for deep frying, or it may be brushed with egg and tossed in breadcrumbs, which must be pressed well in. Deep fried fish should be served on a napkin or on white absorbent paper.

GRILLING OR BAKING FISH IN THE OVEN

Grilling is used mainly for medium-sized fish or slices of large fish.

Grilled sole is delicious, as are small sardines and chicken turbot not weighing over 2 pounds. But the best fish for grilling are mackerel, herrings, small dogfish and red mullet. The flesh of the whiting is so fragile that it is not advisable to grill it; shad if not too large is excellent and so are cutlets of fresh salmon or tunny. The fish to be grilled should always be seasoned and floured previously, so that the fish does not stick to the metal. Cooking should not be too quick if the fish is to be done right through; to facilitate the penetration of the heat, fish weighing more than 4 ounces or so should be scored first. A metal palette knife is useful for turning fish on the grill to avoid damaging them.

When biggish sole, chicken turbot or brill are being grilled, make shallow criss-cross incisions in the black skin only; this side should be underneath when the fish is served.

Grilled fish is usually served with *Maître d'hôtel* butter, *sauce Béarnaise* or cold *sauce Tartare* which goes very well with hot grilled fish, such as eel. Failing a grill, bake the fish in a very hot oven, basting frequently with butter.

SHALLOW-FRIED FISH

This method is used only for fish weighing up to 5–9 ounces, and for cutlets of larger fish. This is the ideal method of cooking river trout and sole. Fish weighing over 3 ounces should be scored. Dip the fish in salted milk, drain and roll in flour; place in a frying pan containing browned (not black) butter. Fry gently on both sides. The fish should be golden brown and well-cooked and should be served at once. Arrange on a hot dish and sprinkle with lemon juice and the frying butter, which should be generous but not excessive. Sprinkle with chopped parsley and decorate the edges of the dish with thin half-slices of lemon, or place half a lemon on the dish.

POACHED FISH

This is the most usual way of cooking small and filleted fish to be served in a sauce. Place the fish in a buttered dish with chopped onions and shallots: moisten with red or white wine, Madeira, etc., according to recipe. Cover with oiled paper and cook in the oven without allowing to boil; the liquor is afterwards used for the sauce after boiling down (see recipes which follow).

Fish should be poached at the last moment; if kept hot for any length of time after cooking it will either become tough or crumble, according to the variety.

Sea Fish

ALOSE * SHAD

Alose Grillée * Grilled Shad

For 6 persons: 2¼ lb shad; oil; salt; 2 oz Maître d'hôtel butter. Cooking time: 40 minutes.

Score the fish, brush with oil and place on a hot grill or in a hot oven. Salt and baste several times while cooking. Turn fish over carefully when half cooked. Serve with *Maître d'hôtel* butter.

▣ à l'Oseille * with Sorrel

For 6 persons: 2¼ lb shad; 1¼ lb sorrel; 4 oz butter; ¼ pint fresh cream. Cooking time: 45 minutes–1 hour.

Grill the fish and serve on sorrel, which has been cooked separately. Alternatively it may be baked in the oven for 10–15 minutes, seasoned and placed on sorrel which has been cooked to a pulp in butter. Replace in the oven to finish baking. Pour fresh cream on top before serving.

Note: Shad can also be served in grilled cutlets or poached in fish stock.

Anguille de Mer et Congre * Sea Eel and Conger Eel

For 4 persons: 1½ lb fish. Cooking time: 15 minutes.

These two fish are members of the same family; the skin of the sea eel is browner than that of the conger eel, but the flavour is the same. It is a tasty fish, which is cooked in well-seasoned *court-bouillon*. It is usually served with Caper sauce.

BAR, MOULET, LOUP DE MER * DOGFISH, GREY MULLET, SEA BASS

The small fish belonging to this family may be grilled, deep or shallow fried or poached. The large ones are boiled in *court-bouillon* or braised and served with any suitable sauce. They may also be served cold with vinegar or *sauce Rémoulade*.

Bar ou Moulet Rôti * Baked Dogfish or Grey Mullet

For 8 persons: 3¼ lb fish; oil; 3 oz butter; sauce. Cooking time: 45–50 minutes.

The uninitiated confuse these two fish. The grey mullet is less delicate and cheaper; when boiled in fish stock it is as good as dogfish. Mullet should not be gutted.

Score, flour and oil the fish and place it on a well-heated and well-buttered dish or baking sheet, so that it will not stick. Salt lightly and place in a hot oven, baste frequently with melted butter and bake for 45–50 minutes. Serve golden brown with a sauce or *Maître d'hôtel* butter and boiled potatoes. All large fish may be baked in this way. Season often, but a little at a time, after basting.

BARBUE * BRILL

This excellent fish is cooked in the same way as turbot. If it is to be cooked whole, do not forget to scale it first.

Fillets of brill are prepared in the same way as fillets of sole. The flesh of the brill is softer than that of the turbot, but the latter is more popular.

When cooked whole in *court-bouillon* it is served on a napkin and garnished with parsley and lemon slices. Serve with *sauce Hollandaise*. It is a luxury fish and we mention it as a reminder.

Small brill and turbot of up to 2 pounds may be grilled and served with *sauce Béarnaise* or *Hollandaise* or with seasoned melted butter.

Bitok de Poisson * Fish Cakes

For 6 persons: 1¼ *lb cooked fish;* ½ *pint thick sauce Béchamel;* 3 *egg yolks.*

Flake the fish and place it in a saucepan; add the thick *sauce Béchamel*, 2 egg yolks, salt and pepper. Stir over the heat until the mixture leaves the bottom of the pan and thickens to a compact paste. Spread on a plate and leave until cold. Using a spoon, make egg-shaped cakes out of the mixture and flatten them. Dip in beaten egg, roll in breadcrumbs and fry. Decorate with strips of red pepper or tomato. *Optional:* serve Tomato or *sauce Velouté* separately. (*See illustration p.* 73).

Buisson ou Friture de Poissons Frits * Bouquet of Fried Fish

For 4 persons: 1¼ *lb small fish;* 1 *lemon; fried parsley.* Cooking time: about 3 minutes.

May be made with smelt, sand-eels or small river fish, gudgeon, etc. Clean, wash and dry the little fish, dip in milk, roll in flour and drop in very hot deep fat; if you have little fat cook a few at a time so that they are very crisp. Drain, salt and arrange in a bouquet (a cluster) with fried parsley and lemon quarters. Serve at once.

Whitebait

Whitebait are not gutted. Pick the fish over carefully, discarding damaged fish. Rinse quickly in cold water and keep on ice until required. Spread them on a cloth to dry. Dust with seasoned flour. Place them loosely in the frying basket and cook for 2 minutes in hot fat. Shake well. Reheat fat to 400°F and crisp the fish in this for 2 minutes. Drain well and season. Serve with fried parsley, cut lemon and thin brown bread and butter.

CABILLAUD, AIGLEFIN * COD, HADDOCK

These two fish belong to the same family. The flesh is lacking in firmness. It is good but so fragile that the fish can only be boiled in *court-bouillon* or fried in slices.

When boiled they are served with the usual sauces. When fried they are served with lemon, *sauce Rémoulade* or *Tartare*.

Fresh cod may also be submitted for *Morue*, salt cod, recipes for which will be found on page 90.

Baked Haddock with Rice Stuffing

$3\frac{1}{2}$-4 *lb haddock; 1 lemon; 8 oz cooked rice; 1 stick celery; 1 onion; 2 sprigs parsley; $\frac{1}{2}$ green pepper; $\frac{1}{2}$ teaspoon sage; salt; pepper; butter; lemon juice; lemon slices; parsley.* Cooking time: 50 minutes.

Remove eyes from fish, rub inside and out with cut lemon. Combine the rice with the finely chopped celery, onion, parsley and green pepper. Mix the sage, salt and pepper, well in. Stuff fish firmly with rice mixture. Place in greased baking dish or large earthenware dish. Brush with melted butter, sprinkle with lemon juice; bake in moderate oven, 350°F or Gas Mark 4, 40 to 50 minutes. Garnish with lemon slices or parsley.

Alternately, fill fish with; 4 oz soft breadcrumbs; 1 oz butter; 1 small onion; 1 stick celery; 2 sprigs parsley; salt; pepper; grated rind 1 lemon; 1 lightly beaten egg. Soften finely chopped onion and celery in heated butter, mix into breadcrumbs. Add finely chopped parsley, lemon rind; bind with egg. Fill into fish, bake as above. Cod, hake, or rock cod may be used in the above recipe.

Cabillaud Frit, Sauce Tartare * *Fried Cod with Tartare Sauce*

For 4 persons: $1\frac{1}{4}$ lb cod; 1 egg; breadcrumbs; sauce Tartare. Cooking time: 6–8 minutes.

Cut the cod into slices $\frac{4}{5}$ inch thick and egg and breadcrumb them. Fry in very hot deep fat and serve on a napkin with fried parsley. Serve *sauce Tartare* separately. The fish may also be floured instead of being egged and crumbed.

▣ Gourmet

2 tablespoons oil; 4 cod cutlets or steaks; 4 tablespoons white wine; 1 tomato, peeled and chopped; 1 clove garlic, crushed; salt; pepper; 2 bayleaves; 2 tablespoons fresh breadcrumbs; several sprigs parsley, chopped. Cooking time: 30 minutes.

Pour oil into ovenproof dish. Arrange fish pieces and tomato in dish, sprinkle with white wine, garlic, salt, pepper, bayleaves. Sprinkle breadcrumbs and parsley on top. Bake in moderate oven, 350°F or Gas Mark 4, for 25 to 30 minutes.

Laitance * *Boiled Roe*

For 4 persons: 1 cod roe, weighing about 1 lb; water; salt.

Wash roe well. Tie in muslin, or wrap in foil. Plunge into boiling salted water and cook at simmering point for 30–40 minutes. Remove muslin or foil. Slice the roe and serve with *sauce Velouté* or parsley and cut lemon.

▣ Frits * *Fried*

For 4 persons: 1 cooked cod roe, weighing about 1 lb; hot fat; 1 beaten egg or 3 tablespoons milk; 3 tablespoons seasoned flour; Tomato sauce.

Cut the cold roe in slices $\frac{1}{2}$ inch thick. Dip in seasoned flour, then beaten egg or milk and back into flour. Shake well and fry until lightly browned. Drain and serve with Tomato sauce.

Cabillaud à la Lyonnaise * *Cod with Onions*

For 4 persons: 4 slices cod, each weighing about 4–6 oz; milk; flour; 2 oz butter; 2 onions; lemon; parsley. Cooking time: 10–12 minutes.

Dip the fish in milk and seasoned flour. Fry in butter in a frying pan. Drain. Thinly slice the onions and fry them pale brown in a separate pan and cover fish with them. Garnish with a bunch of parsley and lemon.

Cabillaud Mistral   *   Mistral

For 4 persons: 1¼ *lb cod; 8 oz tomatoes; 6 oz mushrooms; ¼ pint white wine; salt; pepper; garlic; breadcrumbs.*

Cut 2 thick slices of fish, flour them and brown both sides in oil; place them in a deep baking dish. In the remaining oil fry 8 ounces peeled, chopped tomatoes, 6 ounces sliced mushrooms, a crushed clove of garlic, salt, pepper and parsley. When everything is softened add the white wine. Pour the whole over the fish, sprinkle with breadcrumbs and oil and brown in the oven for 15–20 minutes.

▣ ou Colin à la Portugaise   *   or Hake Portuguese Style

For 4 persons: 1¼ *lb cod or hake; 8 oz fresh tomatoes; 1 large onion; 1 shallot; 3 oz butter; 1 teaspoon flour; 1 pint white wine; chopped parsley.* Cooking time: 15–20 minutes.

Slice or fillet the fish and cook it in white wine. Gently fry the chopped onion pale brown in another pan with 1 ounce butter, adding the shallots and the peeled, seeded and chopped tomatoes. When the latter are soft, pour the fish liquor over the whole, reduce it, boiling briskly, for 4–5 minutes, then thicken the sauce with the remaining butter worked to a paste with the flour. Season, pour over the fish and sprinkle with chopped parsley.

CARRELETS, PLIES, LIMANDES ET FLÉTANS   *   PLAICE, DAB, LEMON SOLE AND HALIBUT

These fish are very popular. Usually they are filleted or cut into small steaks then deep fried, but sometimes they are cooked in the same way as whiting or filleted fish. If the halibut is large it is boiled in *court-bouillon,* but once cooked it is very fragile. If these fish are under 4 ounces, deep frying is the suitable cooking method.

Carrelets au Gratin   *   Plaice au Gratin

For 4 persons: 2 *plaice, each weighing about 1 lb; 4 oz mushrooms; 2 oz butter; ¼ pint white wine; tomato purée; 1 tablespoon chopped parsley; salt; pepper; 3 oz breadcrumbs.* Cooking time: 15–20 minutes.

Finely chop the raw mushrooms, brown them in a little butter and dust them lightly with flour. Add the white wine and the water, season, add a tablespoon of tomato *purée* and half of the chopped parsley, then simmer for 5 minutes. Pour over the plaice in a baking dish, and season. Sprinkle lightly with breadcrumbs and bake and brown at the same time. Serve at once sprinkled with remaining parsley. All whole fish, slices or fillets may be cooked in this way.

COLIN   *   HAKE

Colin ou Cabillaud à l'Anglaise   *   Hake or Cod à l'Anglaise

For 4 persons: 1¼ *lb hake or cod; 2 oz butter; 1 lemon.* Cooking time: 12–15 minutes.

Cook the fish in *court-bouillon* and arrange it on a napkin with a bunch of curly parsley at each end. Serve with melted butter in a sauceboat and with boiled potatoes. The potatoes and half lemons may be arranged round the fish. **Poaching time for hake steaks: 10–12 minutes.** (*See illustrations pp. 75–76*).

Colin Frit   *   *Deep Fried*

For 4 persons: 1¼ lb hake; parsley; lemon. Cooking time: 6–8 minutes.

Slice the hake fairly thinly on the slant, wash and dry the slices. Dip in milk and flour and fry in very hot oil. Serve on a napkin with lemon quarters and fried parsley.

▣ Mornay   *   *Mornay*

For 4 persons: 1¼ lb hake; 2 oz butter; 1½ oz flour; ½ pint milk; ¼ pint white wine; 2 oz breadcrumbs; 1 egg yolk; 2 oz gruyère; seasoning. Cooking time: 15–20 minutes.

Poach the fillets of hake in white wine, closely covered with greased paper. Make a very thick *Béchamel* and thin it slightly with the white wine in which the fish was cooked, after reducing it considerably over a high flame. Add the egg yolk and grated *gruyère* to this sauce. Put the fish in a baking dish, pour the sauce over, sprinkle with breadcrumbs and melted butter and brown in a hot oven.

▣ à la Sauce aux Oeufs   *   *with Egg Sauce*

For 4 persons: 1¼ lb fish; 1 pint Béchamel; 1 teaspoon made mustard; 2 hardboiled eggs; 1 tablespoon chopped parsley.

Cut the fish in thick slices. Poach in *court-bouillon* and serve on a napkin with parsley and boiled potatoes. At the same time serve the *Béchamel* mixed with the chopped eggs, mustard and chopped parsley. The sauce must be very highly seasoned.

Filets de Colin Bercy   *   *Fillets of Hake Bercy*

For 4 persons: 1¼ lb filleted hake; ¼ pint white wine; ½ pint stock: 2 oz shallots; 2 oz butter; 3 oz breadcrumbs; juice of ½ lemon; 1 oz flour; chopped parsley. Cooking time: 15 minutes.

Fillet the hake and make stock with the bones and trimmings. Toss the chopped shallots in 1 ounce butter, moisten with white wine and reduce to half. Add ½ pint stock, salt, pepper and lemon juice, chopped parsley and 1 ounce butter kneaded with the flour. Boil up stirring all the time and pour over the fish in a baking dish. Sprinkle with breadcrumbs and bake in a hot oven. Sprinkle with chopped parsley and serve.

▣ à la Florentine   *   *with Spinach*

The same method as for Hake Mornay. Before browning arrange the fish on 1 pound of leaf spinach cooked in butter.

This method can be used for all filleted fish. Hake may also be fried in cutlets or in the same way as fillets of sole.

▣ Panés   *   *Breadcrumbed*

For 4 persons: 1¼ lb hake; 1 egg; 1 oz flour; 4 oz butter; breadcrumbs; lemon. Cooking time: about 15 minutes.

Dip the fillets in salted milk, then dip them in flour, beaten egg and, lastly, breadcrumbs.

This is what is known as English style breadcrumbing or *à l'Anglaise*. Then either fry very gently in butter or cook in the oven on a well-buttered baking sheet, turning fillets after 8 minutes. Serve with *Maître d'hôtel* butter or simply with melted butter and lemon juice. Serve boiled potatoes separately.

Filets de Colin à la Provençale * *Provençale*

For 4 persons: 1¼ lb hake; ¼ pint white wine; 2 oz shallots; 2 oz onions and 1 clove garlic; 6 oz fresh tomatoes; ¼ pint oil; bay leaf; thyme; 1 tablespoon chopped parsley; 3 oz breadcrumbs.

Fillet the hake and cut the fillets into slices of about 2 ounces each. Poach them in the oven with salt, pepper, white wine, chopped shallots, bay leaf and thyme. This takes about 12 minutes. At the same time brown 2 tablespoons of chopped onions in oil, then add a clove of crushed garlic and the peeled, seeded and roughly chopped tomatoes. When they are soft moisten them with the liquor from the fish, add salt, pepper, parsley, thyme and bay leaf, boil briskly for 6–7 minutes and pour over the fish. Sprinkle with breadcrumbs and brown. If tomatoes are not in season, Tomato sauce may be used. (*See illustration p. 74*).

CONGRE * *CONGER EEL*

Congre à la Bourguignonne * *Conger Eel Bourguignonne*

For 6 persons: 2½ lb conger eel; 12 oz mushrooms; 2 oz small onions; 2 oz butter; 1 pint red wine; 1 tablespoon flour. Cooking time: 40 minutes.

First cook the small onions in 1 ounce butter and cook the mushrooms in the usual way. Cut the fish in slices ⅜ inch thick and put them in a saucepan with the onions; add the red wine, salt and pepper. Add a *bouquet garni*, cover and cook for 20–25 minutes. Add the mushrooms and cook for another 10 minutes. Then thicken the liquor with the butter kneaded with the flour.

▣ en Cocotte * *en Cocotte*

For 6 persons: 2½ lb conger eel; 2 oz fat pork or bacon; ¼ pint water; 2 oz butter; 1 onion; 2 carrots; 2 tablespoons tomato purée; 1 bouquet garni; Risotto or mashed potatoes. Cooking time: 50 minutes.

Skin the fish by sliding a small knife between skin and flesh. Lard with the fat pork or bacon and brown in butter in the *cocotte* with the sliced onions and carrots. When everything is browned add the water, season, add tomato *purée* and the *bouquet garni*. Cover and simmer in the oven for 50 minutes. Serve this delicious fish with mashed potatoes or *Risotto* of rice.

▣ à la Sauce Persil * *with Parsley Sauce*

For 5 persons: 1¾ lb fish; ¼ pint white wine; ¼ pint milk; 2 oz butter; 1 oz flour. Cooking time: 40 minutes.

Make a *court-bouillon* using white wine instead of vinegar. Simmer the fish in it, in the piece. Then make a white sauce using half milk and half the fish liquor, with a large pinch of chopped parsley. The liquor makes excellent fish soup if the *court-bouillon* is made with wine and not vinegar.

DAURADE * *SEA BREAM*

Daurade Bercy * *Sea Bream Bercy*

Same method as for Fillets of Hake Bercy. This fish is found mostly in the Mediterranean and off the African coast—occasionally off the English coast.

▣ Rôtie * *Baked*

For 4 persons: 1 sea bream, weighing about 2 lb; ¼ pint white wine; 1 rasher of fat bacon for barding; 2 oz shallot; 2 oz butter; 4 tablespoons cream. Cooking time: 25–30 minutes.

Wrap the fish in a thin rasher of fat bacon and bake, basting frequently with butter. As it cooks the bacon fat melts and by the time the fish is done it should be golden brown. Place the fish on a dish, reduce the pan residue with white wine, add the chopped shallots, boil down to half and add the butter and fresh cream. Sprinkle a little pepper over the fish and serve.

ESTURGEON * *STURGEON*

Sturgeon is cooked in exactly the same way as veal, which it also resembles in appearance when cooked. It may be braised, served as Veal *Fricandeau*, etc., accompanied by any vegetable garnish.

Fish Pie

For 4 persons: 1 lb cooked fish without skin or bone; a grating of nutmeg; ¾ pint of Velouté or Parsley sauce; 3 oz fried breadcrumbs; 1½ oz white breadcrumbs.

Flake the fish, using 2 forks. Put a layer of sauce into a fairly deep casserole, then one of fish, and a few crumbs. Repeat the layers, finishing with sauce. Completely cover the pie with fried crumbs and heat up before serving, in a fairly hot oven, 375°F or Gas Mark 5. Decorate with cut lemon.

To fry breadcrumbs: Melt 1½ ounces butter in a frying pan and when hot, add the crumbs and fry, pressing the crumbs against the sides and bottom of the pan with a tablespoon until golden brown. Season and use as required.

Another method: Scatter the crumbs in a baking tin, dot with butter and brown in the oven, stirring occasionally with a fork.

Scalloped Fish

The same recipe as for Fish Pie, using scallop shells instead of a casserole. Serve with sliced lemon.

Smoked Haddock

For 4 persons: 2 lb Finnan haddock; 2 oz butter. Cooking time: 20–30 minutes.

This is a very tasty dish for everyone who enjoys the smoky flavour.

Soak the fish in cold water for 1–2 hours. Plunge into boiling water for 5 minutes and remove skin. Drain, just cover with milk and bake in a fairly hot oven, 375°F or Gas Mark 5, for 20–30 minutes. Serve with melted butter and boiled potatoes, or with poached eggs.

HARENG * *HERRING*

Herrings are eaten in large quantities, fresh, pickled, and as kippers. When they are very fresh and fleshy, at the same time that they have roes, they constitute an excellent food.

Hareng à la Bordelaise * *Herrings Bordelaise*

Gut and wipe the herrings. Score sides, oil lightly, stuff with herbs and grill.

▣ Grillés à la Sauce Moutarde * *Grilled with Mustard Sauce*

For 4 persons: 1 *lb herrings; oil.* Cooking time: 12–15 minutes.

Gut and wipe the herrings, score on both sides, oil them and grill them. Alternatively, coat with oatmeal and fry. Serve with Mustard sauce.

▣ au Claret * *in Claret*

Score the cleaned fish, rub with mustard. Place in an ovenproof dish, pour over about 1 tablespoon tarragon vinegar. Cover with finely chopped parsley and dot with butter. Add a large glass of claret. Baste often and bake in a fairly hot oven, 375°F or Gas Mark 5, for 10 minutes. Turn over, sprinkle with breadcrumbs. Bake for a further 10 minutes.

LOTTE DE MER * *ANGLER FISH*

This economical fish is prepared in the same way as hake or cod, but it must not be deep or shallow fried since it gives off too much water during cooking. The following method is very suitable:

Filets de Lotte Dugléré * *Fillets Angler Fish Dugléré*

For 4 persons: 1¾ *lb angler fish;* 1¼ *lb fresh tomatoes;* 1 *tablespoon tomato purée;* 1 *medium-sized onion;* ¼ *pint white wine;* 2 *oz butter;* ½ *oz flour.*

Put finely chopped onion, peeled and chopped tomatoes and a little chopped parsley in the bottom of a baking dish. Place the sliced fish on top, season, add the white wine and poach in the oven. Reduce the liquor to half and bind it with the tomato *purée* and the butter kneaded with flour. Pour this sauce over the fish, sprinkle with breadcrumbs and place in a hot oven for 5 minutes.

A number of fish may be prepared in this way. The large ones should be sliced or filleted to facilitate their cooking.

MAQUEREAU * *MACKEREL*

Mackerel is one of the tastiest and cheapest sea fish. The flesh tends to be heavy and oily in texture; it is important to eat these quickly after they have been bought, and of course they should be as fresh as possible. When boiled or grilled, it is usually served with Gooseberry sauce.

Filets de Maquereaux à la Meunière * *Fillets of Mackerel Meunière*

Shallow fry in the usual way, not forgetting to score the fish if fried whole. Serve with Beurre Noisette and chopped parsley.

Filets de Maquereaux Mireille * *Mireille*

For 4 persons: 1¾ *lb mackerel; 4 oz mushrooms;* 1¼ *lb fresh tomatoes; oil;*
1 *onion;* 1 *clove of garlic;* 1 *shallot.* Cooking time: 10–12 minutes.

Fry the fish in a frying pan in very hot oil and place on a dish. In the remaining oil fry
the chopped mushrooms, onion, shallot and garlic. Brown well and pour over the fish,
sprinkle it with a little hot vinegar and surround with sliced tomatoes sautéed in oil. Sprinkle
chopped parsley over the whole. To fillet mackerel, whiting, sea bream, etc., cut off the
head, lay the fish flat on a board and hold it down with the left hand. With the right hand
slide a knife held flat along the backbone from the tail to the head.

▣ Gros, Bouillis, Sauce Persil * *Large, Boiled with Parsley Sauce*

For 4 persons: 1¾ *lb mackerel; 2 oz butter;* ½ *pint fish stock; 1 oz flour;*
1 *tablespoon chopped parsley.* Cooking time: about 20 minutes.

Boil slices of large mackerel in salted water with a dash of vinegar and some sprigs of
parsley. Make a white sauce, using the fish liquor and adding chopped parsley.

▣ Petits, Grillés à la Maître d'Hôtel * *Small, Grilled with Herb Butter*

For 4 persons: 4 mackerel, each weighing about 5–6 oz; 2 oz flour; 2 oz
butter; fine herbs. Cooking time: 10 minutes.

Flour, oil and grill the mackerel. Place on a hot dish and sprinkle with melted Herb butter.
Sprinkle with chopped parsley. Serve with Gooseberry sauce.
  If the mackerel are large, cut them open down the back and incise the bone in two places
to help cook where the fish is thickest. Leave the belly skin intact to hold the fish
together.

MERLANS * *WHITING*

Another very popular fish, with finer, more delicate flesh than the herring.
It is often used for making forcemeat.

Merlans à la Diplomate * *Stuffed Whiting*

Remove the backbone. Stuff the fish with a mixture of lightly cooked
mushrooms, tomatoes, herbs and shallots bound with *sauce Mornay*. Place in an ovenproof
dish, add a little fish stock or milk and bake in a fairly hot oven. Drain, serve coated with
sauce Mornay and cheese.

▣ Frits * *Deep Fried*

For 4 persons: 1¼ *lb whiting; milk; flour; 1 lemon; parsley.* Cooking time:
5 minutes.

Dip the whiting in milk and flour and fry in very hot deep fat. Serve with fried parsley and
lemon quarters, or *sauce Rémoulade* if preferred.

▣ Panés à la Maître d'Hôtel * *Breadcrumbed with Herb Butter*

For 4 persons: 1¼ *lb whiting; milk; flour; 1 egg; breadcrumbs; 2 oz Herb*
butter. Cooking time: 5 minutes.

Cut open the whiting down the back and carefully remove the bone. Season, dip in milk and flour, egg and breadcrumbs and deep fry. Serve on a napkin with Herb butter.

Merlans Sur le Plat ou Merlans Minute * *Minute*

For 4 persons: 1¼ *lb whiting;* ¼ *pint white wine; 4 oz butter; chopped fine herbs; breadcrumbs; 3 shallots.* Cooking time: about 20 minutes.

Sprinkle the chopped shallots over the bottom of a baking dish; place the seasoned and scored fish on top and add the white wine and herbs. Sprinkle with breadcrumbs and melted butter and put in a hot oven for 20 minutes or so.

MORUE * *SALT COD*

Salt cod must be well washed and soaked for at least 24 hours before it is cooked. During soaking the water should be changed every 3 or 4 hours. When buying salt cod, the fish should be white and the fillets thick. Fresh cod may of course be substituted in these recipes.

Morue à la Crème * *Salt Cod with Cream*

For 4 persons: 1¼ *lb salt cod;* ¼ *pint cream; 2 oz butter; flour; vinegar.* Cooking time: 20 minutes.

Soak the cod then wash well in running cold water. Flour the pieces and fry in butter very slowly to give the heat time to penetrate the centre; if it is pinkish, cook for a little longer. When the fish is done it should only be the palest brown. Place it on a dish, pour the cream into the frying pan, add a dash of vinegar and boil briskly for 2 minutes. Pepper lightly, salt if necessary and pour over the fish.

▣ à la Ménagère * *Ménagère*

For 4 persons: 1¼ *lb cod;* 1½ *lb potatoes; 1 onion; 2 oz butter; 1 oz flour;* ½ *pint milk.* Cooking time: 20 minutes.

Soak the fish for 24 hours, changing the water several times. Cut up in pieces and cook without boiling in unsalted water. When on the point of boiling, draw to one side and leave for about 10 minutes. Before cooking the fish prepare jacket potatoes and a *sauce Béchamel* with the last 3 ingredients mixed with a large, finely chopped onion cooked gently in butter without allowing it to brown. Thin the sauce with a little of the fish liquor. Peel and slice the potatoes and flake the fish on top of them, removing skin and bones. Pour the sauce over after seasoning with a little pepper.

▣ Sautée aux Tomates * *Sautéed with Tomatoes*

For 4 persons: 1¼ *lb salt cod;* 1¼ *lb tomatoes; 2 oz butter or 2 tablespoons oil; 1 clove garlic; parsley.* Cooking time: 20 minutes.

Prepare the cod as above and cut it up. Flour the pieces, put them in a frying pan in very hot butter and fry gently for 12–15 minutes. Remove the fish and place it in a dish. Into the same butter throw the peeled, seeded and coarsely chopped tomatoes. When they are done season lightly with salt and pepper, and add very finely chopped parsley and crushed and chopped garlic. Cook for a few seconds longer and pour over the fish.

RAIE * RAY OR SKATE

Raie au Beurre Noir * Skate with Black Butter

For 4 persons: 1½ lb skate; 4 oz butter; 3 tablespoons vinegar; 2 oz capers; *parsley; fish stock.* Cooking time: 15 minutes.

Unlike other fish, skate can only be prepared in a very limited number of ways; only black butter or cream go with it. The thornback, which has curved spines, is the most popular. This fish must be absolutely fresh, otherwise it gives off a smell of ammonia which makes it unfit for human consumption. Cut up the skate and simmer in fish stock without boiling. When it is done, remove the pieces with a skimming laddle and skin by scraping both sides with a knife. Arrange the pieces in a dish, add salt and pepper and sprinkle with black butter. Then pour the vinegar into the hot pan, let it boil for a few seconds and pour it over the fish. Sprinkle with chopped parsley and capers.

◙ Frite * Deep Fried

For 4 persons: 1½ lb small skates; flour; milk; parsley; 1 lemon. Cooking time: 5–7 minutes.

It is best to use very thin skate for this method. They may be fried whole, after being dipped in milk and flour, or cut up in pieces. Serve with fried parsley and lemon. They may alternatively be dipped in batter and served with Tomato sauce. Large skate may also be deep fried if cut up first.

ROUGETS * RED MULLET

In addition to the red and grey gurnard there is the true red mullet. This is an unusually good fish. Although more expensive it is often more economical, because there is very little waste, whereas the gurnard with its big head and bones is not always so advantageous. Red mullet, which is delicious, is very popular on the Côte d'Azur, where it is taken from the water, wiped, lightly floured and put straight on the grill without being gutted. In Nice it is known as the "snipe of the sea". Only the simplest recipes must be used for its preparation.

Rougets Barbecue * Barbecued Red Mullet

1 small mullet or whiting per person; salt; pepper; lemon juice; butter. Cooking time: 20 minutes.

Clean and scale fish (if using mullet, make sure all black lining is removed). Sprinkle inside of fish with salt and pepper, add squeeze of lemon juice. Arrange each fish on square of well-buttered foil, sprinkle top of each fish with salt and pepper; add knob of butter. Wrap fish neatly and securely in foil. Place on barbecue; cook, turning occasionally, approximately 20 minutes. Serve in the foil.

◙ Monte-Carlo * Monte Carlo

For 4 persons: 4 red mullet, each weighing about 6 oz; 4 slices white bread; *2 oz butter; 2 oz Anchovy butter; 2 oz Maître d'hôtel butter; Straw potatoes.* Cooking time: 6–8 minutes.

Grill the fish and place on slices of white bread, cut to the shape of the fish, fried in butter and spread with Anchovy butter. Surround with a ring of Straw potatoes and sprinkle *Maître d'hôtel* butter on top.

Rougets chauds à la Niçoise * *Niçoise*

For 4 persons: 4 red mullet; 12 oz tomatoes; oil; garlic; 4 anchovy fillets; 12 green olives. Cooking time: 8–10 minutes.

Flour the red mullet and shallow fry them in very hot oil. Arrange them in a long dish and pour over them the peeled, chopped tomatoes, sautéed in oil with a crushed clove of garlic, the anchovy fillets and stoned olives. Sprinkle with chopped parsley and place some sliced tomatoes and slices of lemon on top.

▣ à la Provençale * *Provençale*

For 4 persons: 4 red mullet, each weighing about 6 oz; 12 oz tomatoes; 2 tablespoons olive oil; parsley; breadcrumbs; garlic. Cooking time: 10–12 minutes.

Sauté the peeled and quartered tomatoes in oil and add salt, pepper, chopped parsley and crushed garlic. Also *sauté* in oil the wiped and floured red mullet. Spread half the tomatoes over the bottom of a baking dish, place the fish on top and cover with the remainder of the tomatoes. Sprinkle with breadcrumbs and cook in a hot oven, 400°F or Gas Mark 6, for about 10 minutes.

▣ Soused

2-3 lb mullet; 6 peppercorns; 2 cloves; 1 onion, sliced finely; ¾ pint white vinegar; 1 fresh red chilli, finely chopped; ¼ teaspoon cinnamon; ¼ teaspoon nutmeg; ½ teaspoon salt; ½ lemon, sliced. Cooking time 30 minutes.

Clean and scale the fish. Slit a little more than halfway through the fish and place it, flattened out, in a casserole dish. Cover with onion slices, chopped chilli, spices, seasoning, and vinegar. Cover dish and bake in moderate oven, 350°F or Gas Mark 4, for 30 minutes, or until fish is tender. Leave in liquid until cool. Remove fish and arrange on serving dish, or break into serving size pieces. Strain liquid and spoon over fish. Serve cold with salad.

Rougets-Grondins * *Gurnard*

Per person: 1 gurnard of 5–6 oz.

This fish is used mainly for *Bouillabaisse*. It may also be grilled. Score on both sides and toss in flour. Fry or grill and serve with a good sauce or *Maître d'hôtel* butter.

Roussettes à la Provençale * *Dogfish Provençale*

For 4 persons: 2 lb dogfish; ¼ pint white wine; 2 tablespoons tomato purée; 8 oz mushrooms; 1 oz butter; 2 tablespoons olive oil; 2 onions; 3 shallots; 2 cloves of garlic; parsley. Cooking time: 12–15 minutes.

Dogfish is a cheap fish, often sold skinned in the market. If not already skinned, dip in boiling water and rub with a rough cloth, slice, wash and drain. Brown the chopped onions and shallots in butter, dust well with flour, add 2 chopped cloves of garlic, the wine, tomato *purée* and a little water to make a thinnish sauce. Slice the mushrooms very thinly, brown them in a frying pan with a little oil and add them to the sauce with salt, pepper and chopped parsley, and cook for 10 minutes. Lightly brown the fish in the frying pan with a little oil and place in a baking dish. Pour the well-seasoned sauce on top, sprinkle with breadcrumbs and brown in a hot oven, 400°F or Gas Mark 6.

Friture de rivière, p. 104

Matelote de Moselle, p. 104

▲ *Anguilles au vert, p. 102*

Truites à la menuière, p. 105 ▼

▲ *Brochettes de scampi, p. 109*

Homards ou langoustes à la russe, p. 117 ▼   95

▲ *Pilaf de crevettes, p. 107*

Langoustines Château Bouscaut, p. 117 ▼

LES SOLES * *SOLE*

How to fillet a sole:

First skin the fish on both sides by making a small crosswise cut at the tail end, scrape off just enough skin to give a hold with a cloth and pull off the remainder with a single sharp jerk. Then make diagonal cuts to separate the head on the underside. Carefully slide a thin, flexible knife under one of the fillets bending it slightly so that it lies flat on the bones. Move it along bit by bit to detach the fillet, leaving no flesh on the bone, or bone on the flesh. Remove the 3 other fillets in the same way.

The bones are usually used to make a fish stock for cooking the fillets or making the sauce. It is a good idea to beat the fillets slightly with the flat of the knife to break the fibres; this prevents the fish from contracting during cooking.

When cooking a sole whole, skin it, trim the fins and tail with scissors, cut off the head and gut the fish through an opening made along the belly.

Sole Frites * *Deep Fried Sole*

For 4 persons: 4 soles, each weighing about 6–7 oz; milk; flour; seasoning; 1 *lemon; parsley.* Cooking time: 3–4 minutes.

Clean and trim the soles as above. Dip in salted cold milk for 5 minutes, then in seasoned flour, shake and fry in very hot oil until golden brown and crisp. Drain on a cloth, season and serve with lemon quarters and fried parsley. Tartare Sauce may be served as well if desired.

▣ Grillées * *Grilled*

For 4 persons: 4 soles, each weighing about 6–7 oz, or 2 soles each weighing about 8 oz; *lemon; 2 oz butter or Maître d'hôtel butter.* Cooking time: 6–8 minutes.

Score the fish lightly in a criss-cross on both sides, flour and oil, and grill, brushing with oil from time to time. Arrange on a hot dish with a border of parsley and place 3 slices of lemon on each fish. Serve melted butter or *Maître d'hôtel* butter separately. (*See illustration p.* 73).

▣ à la Meunière * *Meunière*

For 4 persons: 4 soles, each weighing about 6–7 oz; 6 oz butter; 2 oz seasoned flour; 1 *lemon; chopped parsley.* Cooking time: 6–7 minutes.

Dip the fish in milk and seasoned flour and fry in pan in 3 ounces sizzling hot butter. Fry golden brown on both sides. Check to see that the fish is properly done by raising a fillet, which should come cleanly away from the bone when fully cooked, and then place on a dish. Put the remainder of the butter in the pan and let it brown. Squeeze half a lemon over the fish, pour the butter on top and sprinkle with chopped parsley. Serve immediately with lemon quarters. Most fish may be prepared in this way.

FILETS DE SOLE * *FILLETS OF SOLE*

Filets de Sole à la Bourguignonne * *Fillets of Sole Bourguignonne*

For 4 persons: 2 soles, each weighing about 12 oz; ¾ pint good red wine; 20 *pickling onions; 6 oz mushrooms; 3 oz butter.* Cooking time of fillets: 6–8 minutes.

Poach the fillets in red wine. Cook the onions and mushrooms separately beforehand in 2 ounces butter. Reduce the cooking wine to a third and thicken with 1 ounce of butter kneaded with a tablespoon of flour. Boil up several times. Colour the sauce with a little caramel, since cooked wine is an ugly colour. Season the sauce. Surround the fillets with the onions (whole) and mushrooms and coat the whole generously with sauce.

Filets de Sole aux Champignons * with Mushrooms

For 4 persons: Same ingredients as for Fillets of sole in White Wine, plus 8 oz mushrooms; parsley; 2 oz butter; juice of ½ lemon. Cooking time: 12–15 minutes.

Same method as for Fillets of Sole in White Wine, with the addition of the mushrooms. Cook the mushrooms in butter with salt and lemon juice. Arrange the fillets in a ring on the dish with the mushrooms in the centre and coat the fillets with the sauce. Sprinkle chopped fine herbs on the mushrooms.

▣ aux Crevettes, dits Joinville * with Shrimps

For 4 persons: 8 fillets of sole; 2 shallots; 3 oz butter; 6 oz shrimps; ¼ pint white wine; chopped parsley; ½ pint sauce Hollandaise. Cooking time: 12–15 minutes.

Poach the fillets in white wine, drain and place on a long dish. Reduce the liquor and add the *sauce Hollandaise* and the shrimp *purée*, made by crushing the shells with butter and sieving. Strain the sauce through a fine sieve, season, add the peeled shrimps. To give a shrimp colour add a drop of carmine or a knife-tip of tomato *purée*. Coat fish with sauce and serve.

▣ Croustade * Vol-au-Vent

For 4 persons: 1 croustade (large vol-au-vent case); 8 fillets of sole; ¼ pint Fish fumet; 6 oz mushrooms, blanched and quartered; 6 oz shelled prawns; ½ pint sauce Velouté.

Make or buy a large puff pastry *vol-au-vent* case. Roll up the sole fillets, poach in white wine, leave until cold and cut into slices. Dice the prawns. Reduce the liquid in which the sole fillets were cooked by half and add to the sauce. Stir all the ingredients into the sauce, heat and fill the *croustade*. (*See illustration p.* 76).

▣ à la Dieppoise * Dieppe Style

For 4 persons: 8 fillets of sole; 1¾ pints mussels; ¼ pint white wine; 2 oz butter; 3–4 chopped shallots; ¼ pint White sauce; 1 tablespoon chopped parsley. Cooking time: 12 minutes.

First cook the mussels with the wine and the shallots. Strain them, leave them to stand and decant the liquor. Fold the fillets of sole in two and flatten slightly with the palm of the hand. Place them in a baking dish, dot with butter and add the mussel liquor mixed with the White sauce. Cover with greased paper and cook in a hot oven for 12 minutes without allowing to boil. Remove the mussels from their shells, keep them hot and garnish the dish with them and with chopped parsley.

▣ Gratinés à la Florentine * with Spinach and sauce Mornay

For 4 persons: 8 fillets of sole; ¼ pint white wine; 2 oz butter; 1 lb spinach; ¾ pint sauce Mornay; 3 oz grated cheese. Cooking time: 12–15 minutes.

Poach the fillets in white wine, serve on spinach sautéed in butter and coat generously with *sauce Mornay.* Sprinkle with grated cheese and brown in a hot oven, or under the grill. The spinach should be entirely covered.

Filets de Sole Mornay * *with sauce Mornay*

For 4 persons: 8 *fillets of sole;* ¼ *pint white wine;* ½ *pint sauce Mornay;* 2 *shallots;* 2 *oz grated chees*e. Cooking time: 16–18 minutes.

Poach the fillets in the wine with the chopped shallots. Reduce the liquor and add *sauce Mornay.* Coat the fillets with it, sprinkle with grated cheese and glaze in a hot oven.

▣ Murat * *(with Potatoes and Artichoke Bottoms)*

For 4 persons: 8 *fillets of sole;* 6 *oz cooked potatoes;* 3 *artichoke bottoms;* 2 *oz butter;* 1 *lemon.* Cooking time: 10–12 minutes.

Halve the fillets lengthwise, dip them in milk and flour and *sauté* them in hot butter, as for *Meunière.* When they are cooked and golden brown add some cubed potatoes, cooked separately, and 2 or 3 small diced artichoke bottoms sautéed in butter. *Sauté* the whole together for a moment and arrange in a mound, sprinkling with lemon juice and *Noisette* butter. Sprinkle with chopped parsley.

▣ Orly * *Orly*

For 4 persons: 1¼ *lb fillets of sole; chopped parsley; lemon juice;* ½ *pint Tomato sauce; Frying batter.* Cooking time: 4–5 minutes.

Halve the fillets lengthwise and macerate in lemon juice with salt, pepper and chopped parsley. Dip in batter, deep fry in oil and serve with lemon, parsley and with Tomato sauce handed separately.

Paupiettes au Gratin * *Stuffed and Gratinated*

For 6 persons: 3 *sole, each weighing about* 12 *oz;* 8 *oz Quenelle forcemeat;* 1 *pint sauce Mornay;* 12 *crayfish tails;* ¼ *pint white wine:* 12 *thin slices of truffle.* Cooking time: 12 minutes.

Wash and dry the sole fillets and beat them lightly to flatten. Spread a layer of forcemeat on the skin side and roll up, starting from the tail end. Tie in position with two loops of string. Arrange the fish olives in a buttered saucepan and poach in white wine. Butter a *gratin* dish. Arrange the fish in it, garnish each fillet with a crayfish tail and a thin slice of truffle. Reduce the cooking liquid, add to the *sauce Mornay,* pour over the fish olives and gratinate in the oven. (*See illustration p.* 74).

▣ au Vin Blanc * *in White Wine*

For 4 persons: 2 *sole, each weighing about* 14 *oz, or* 8 *fillets;* ¼ *pint white wine;* 2 *oz butter;* ¾ *pint plain White sauce;* 1 *egg yolk;* 3 *shallots;* ½ *lemon.* Cooking time: 12–15 minutes.

Fold the fillets of sole in two and beat gently with a wooden spoon or palette knife. Place in a buttered baking dish, season with salt, pepper and chopped shallots, just cover with white wine, cover with buttered paper and place in a hot oven for 12 minutes, but do not allow to boil. In the meantime make a plain White sauce, keeping it rather thick. Beat in egg yolk and seasoning. When the fish is cooked drain off the liquor into a fairly large saucepan and boil briskly until reduced to about 4 tablespoons; add the White sauce, which should be thinned, but bear in mind that sauces served with fish should always be creamy. Butter and season to taste, sharpen with lemon juice and coat fish with the sauce.

THON* *TUNNY*

Thon à la Bordelaise * *Tunny Bordelaise*

For 4 persons: 1¼ *lb tunny;* 4 *oz mushrooms;* 4 *tablespoons white wine;*
8 *oz tomatoes;* 1 *large onion;* 2 *shallots;* 2 *oz butter;* 2 *tablespoons oil; parsley;* ½ *pint sauce
Demi-glace.* Cooking time: 35–40 minutes.

Brown the slice of tunny in half oil and half butter; add the chopped onion, sliced shallots
and peeled and quartered tomatoes. Add the wine and *sauce Demi-glace.* Season, cover and
braise for half an hour. Arrange the tunny on a dish, reduce the liquor and add to it the
sliced mushrooms sautéed in remaining butter. Pour the sauce over the fish and sprinkle
with chopped parsley.

▣ Grillé * *Grilled*

For 4 persons: 1¼ *lb tunny.* Cooking time: 8–10 minutes.

Fresh tunny is a delicious, economical and very nourishing fish. It is bought in slices ⅘ inch
thick. Season with salt and pepper, brush with oil, and grill under a high heat, basting with
oil from time to time. To see if sliced grilled fish is done, insert the tip of a knife in the backbone and move it gently from side to side. When the fish is cooked the bone can be loosened
quite easily. Serve with melted butter and boiled potatoes or with *sauce Tartare.*

▣ à la Ménagère * *Ménagère*

For 4 persons: 1¼ *lb tunny;* 8 *oz tomatoes or mushrooms;* ¼ *pint red wine;*
2 *oz butter;* 1 *onion;* 1 *tablespoon lemon juice;* 3 *tablespoons tomato purée.*

Place a thick slice of tunny in a saucepan of water and blanch for 8–10 minutes to remove
the oil from the flesh. Drain, and dry, brown both sides in butter, and place on a plate.
Add a chopped onion to the butter which remains, brown it, dust with flour, cook for a
moment and then add the wine, ½ pint water and lemon juice. Add the concentrated tomato
purée. Replace the fish in this sauce. When it boils cover the pan and leave to simmer slowly
for an hour. Add mushrooms or tomatoes sautéed in butter, according to season. Serve
fish with sauce poured over.

TURBOT * *TURBOT*

This is a luxury fish which the housewife will only serve on rare occasions.
Clean the turbot very carefully through the gills and through an opening in the belly on
the dark side. Wash thoroughly and leave to soak in running cold water for several hours.
Place in a large saucepan, or fish kettle if available. Cover well with salted cold water, but
do not add any other seasoning, vegetables, etc., which might detract from the delicate
flavour of the fish. It is, however, permissible to add ¼ pint milk to keep the flesh as white
as possible. Do not boil but simmer very gently. A turbot of 5 pounds should be cooked
at this temperature for about 20 minutes. For turbot steaks 12–15 minutes are enough.
Serve with *sauce Hollandaise* or simply with melted butter.

Turbotin Grillé * *Grilled Chicken Turbot*

Small or chicken turbot, not weighing more than about 3 pounds, may be
grilled after scoring on both sides. Serve with melted or *Maître d'hôtel* butter or any sauce
suitable for fish. Serve boiled potatoes separately. *Sauce Béarnaise* is an excellent accompaniment to grilled fish. Cooking time: 30–35 minutes. For grilling methods see the beginning of the section on fish.

Filets de Turbot   *   *Fillets of Turbot*

Like brill, turbot may be cooked and served as fillets. In this case all garnishes and sauces for fillets of sole may be used. Cooking time: 8–10 minutes.

POISSONS DE MER FROIDS   *   *COLD SEA FISH*

Bar à la Grecque   *   *Bass Greek style*

For 4 persons: 1 bass, weighing 2 lb; court-bouillon; 2 tomatoes; 12 stoned black olives. For the Mussel salad à la Grecque: 4 oz mussels; 8 oz blanched mushrooms; 4 oz sliced tomatoes; 2 oz blanched button onions; 2 oz artichoke hearts; juice of 1 lemon; olive oil; salt and pepper.

Cook fish in *court-bouillon* and leave until cold. Cut into pieces and decorate each with slices of tomato and 1 black olive. Prepare Mussel salad *à la Grecque* by tossing all ingredients together. Arrange the fish on the salad. (*See illustration p.* 75).

Colin Froid à la Russe   *   *Russian Style Cold Hake*

For 4 persons: 1¼ lb hake; Russian salad; mayonnaise; anchovy fillets.

Any good fish left-overs can be served in this way. Remove skin and bones, arrange on a long dish with a little Russian salad at each end and decorate with very thick *mayonnaise* piped through a forcing bag. Complete with a few anchovy fillets.

Fresh-Water Fish

ANGUILLE * *EEL*

Anguille Grillée Tartare * *Eel Tartare*

For 4 persons: 1¼ *lb eel;* ½ *pint red wine;* 1 *onion;* 1 *shallot;* 1 *clove of garlic;* 1 *bouquet garni; breadcrumbs;* 1 *egg white; parsley; sauce Tartare.* Cooking time: 22–25 minutes.

Cook the eel in red wine, as for Matelote of Eels (see *p.* 104). Wipe the pieces, egg and breadcrumb them, and deep fry. Serve on a napkin with fried parsley and *sauce Tartare* served separately.

▣ en Matelote à la Bourguignonne * *Matelote of Eel Bourguignonne*

For 4 persons: 1¼ *lb eel;* 1 *onion;* 1 *shallot;* 1 *clove of garlic;* ½ *pint red wine;* 1 *bouquet garni;* 1 *liqueur glass brandy;* 2 *oz butter;* 20 *button onions;* 4 *oz mushrooms.* Cooking time: 20 minutes.

Put some sliced onions and shallots, a crushed clove of garlic, a *bouquet garni*, salt and pepper in a saucepan. Place the eel on top after skinning, slicing and cutting into pieces the length of a finger. Put the pan on the stove and flame the eel with a glass of liqueur brandy (optional). Cover with red wine and cook for 20 minutes. Remove the pieces of eel and keep them hot. Add the cooked mushrooms and the onions which should have been glazed separately. Reduce the liquor slightly and thicken with 2 ounces butter kneaded with ¾ ounce flour. The sauce should be creamy, but not too thick. Add a little caramel to brown the sauce, since the wine gives it an ugly mauvish colour. Simmer for a moment and place in a deep dish or timbale. To improve the presentation the dish may be decorated with *croûtons* of fried bread and crayfish.

▣ au Vert * *au Vert*

For 6–8 persons: 2 *eels, each weighing about* 2–2½ *lb;* 3 *oz butter;* 8 *oz sorrel;* 1 *small handful parsley and chervil;* 1 *sprig each savory and sage;* 6 *oz carrots cut into julienne strips (optional);* ¼ *pint white wine;* 3 *egg yolks; juice of* 1 *lemon;* 1 *small level teaspoon cornflour or potato flour.* Cooking time: 25 minutes.

Cut the eels into thick pieces after skinning, gutting and washing them. Heat the butter and drop the eels into it. Cover with a fairly thick layer of finely chopped sorrel, chervil, parsley, savory and sage. Leave to cook slowly for 5 minutes without adding any further ingredients, then pour in white wine with water to cover. Add seasoning and cook for 20–25 minutes. Place the egg yolks in a bowl with the juice of 1 lemon, the cornflour or potato flour, and thin with a little cooking liquid from the eels. Add to the sauce to bind it without letting it boil. Remove the eels, arrange in an earthenware dish and pour all the sauce over them. Leave until cold. Garnish with the carrot *julienne* if liked. This dish is eaten cold or luke-warm. (*See illustration p. 94*). (*Belgium*)

BROCHET * *PIKE*

Brochet au Beurre Blanc * *Pike with White Butter*

The pike is poached in fish stock, skinned and served with White butter sauce, in which the quality of the butter is the main factor for success.

▣ en Blanquette * *Blanquette*

For 4 persons: 1¾ *lb pike; 2 oz butter; ½ oz flour; ½ pint white wine; 4 oz mushrooms; 20 button onions; 2 egg yolks; ¼ pint thick cream.* Cooking time: 30–35 minutes.

Cut the pike in fairly thick slices and brown them in butter. Sprinkle with flour, cover with the wine and an equal amount of water, add the mushrooms and small onions, cook slowly and season well. Thicken at the last moment with the egg yolks and cream.

▣ au Court-Bouillon * *in Court-Bouillon*

For 6 persons: 1 *pike, weighing about* 2¾ *lb; ½ pint court-bouillon; 4 oz butter or ½ pint White sauce; 2 tablespoons capers.* Cooking time: 40–45 minutes.

Use enough *court-bouillon* for the fish to be completely covered in the fish kettle. Scale and gut the fish and place it in the cold *court-bouillon*. Poach without boiling. Drain, skin, place on a folded napkin to absorb the moisture and serve with white melted butter or White sauce with capers. Left-overs may be served cold with *mayonnaise* or in shells gratinated with *sauce Mornay*.

▣ en Fricassée * *Fricassée*

For 6 persons: 2½ *lb pike; 2 oz butter; ½ oz flour; 6 oz mushrooms; 20 button onions; ½ pint white wine; scant 2 egg yolks; ½ pint thick cream.* Cooking time: 30–35 minutes.

Cut the pike in fairly thick slices and brown them in butter. Sprinkle with flour, add the wine and a little water, the mushrooms and the onions. Heat to boiling point for a few minutes then simmer until cooked. Season well. At the last moment thicken with the egg yolks and cream.

Brocheton au Bleu * *Small Pike au Bleu*

For 4 persons: 4 *small pike, each weighing about 6 oz; court-bouillon.* Cooking time: 3–4 minutes.

For this recipe it is essential that the fish should be killed only at the last moment. Scale, gut and cover with boiling *court-bouillon* and boil for 3–4 minutes. The *court-bouillon* should be well-seasoned and boiled beforehand. Serve with boiled potatoes and melted butter.

Carpe à la Marinière * *Carp Marinière*

For 8 persons: 4½ *lb carp; 2 oz butter; ½ pint white wine; 2 shallots; 12 oz mushrooms; parsley; 2 oz breadcrumbs; 8 gudgeon; 1 lemon.* Cooking time: about 25 minutes.

Scale and clean the carp, and put it in a deep baking dish surrounded by the mushrooms.

Season and add the wine and enough water almost to cover the fish. Surround with the shallots, chopped parsley and the butter kneaded with breadcrumbs and bake in a hot oven. When serving, sprinkle the fish with lemon juice and place 8 fried gudgeon around; they must not be immersed in the sauce.

Petite Friture de Rivière * Deep Fried Small River Fish

Gudgeon and roach are deep fried, as explained at the beginning of the chapter, i.e. dipped in cold, salted milk and flour. The slightly larger fish may be shallow fried. The fat must be very hot; do not cool it by frying too many fish at once. Fry them at the last moment, serve immediately with fried parsley and lemon. (*See illustration p. 93*)

Matelote de Moselle * Matelote Moselle

For 6 persons: 8 oz eel; 8 oz carp; 8 oz pike; 8 oz tench; ¼ pint fresh cream; 2 egg yolks; 6 chopped shallots; 2 cloves garlic, finely chopped; 6 oz button mushroom caps; 8 oz small onions; 2 tablespoons cognac; 1¼ pints white wine; 1 bouquet garni; 3 oz butter; 12 small, heart-shaped croûtons. Cooking time: 25–30 minutes.

Scale, gut and wipe the fish and cut into pieces. Fry the shallots lightly in 1 ounce butter. Add the eel. Meanwhile, poach the mushrooms with 1 ounce butter and lemon juice. Flame the eel in cognac and add the white wine, stirring to detach the juices and particles from the pan. Add the remaining fish, the mushroom stock, garlic, *bouquet garni* and shallots tossed in butter. Season and cook slowly for 15–18 minutes. Remove the fish and keep hot, covered with buttered paper. Cook the stock until the small onions are soft, then bind with 1 ounce butter worked to a paste with ¾ ounce flour. Mix well and remove from the heat. Bind with the egg yolks and cream. Adjust the seasoning. Add the mushrooms, mask the fish with sauce and garnish with the *croûtons*. (*See illustration p. 93*).

Pauchouse Bourguignonne * Pauchouse

For 8 persons: 3½ lb fresh-water fish; 16 lardoons; 12 oz mushrooms; 24 button onions; 6 cloves of garlic; 1 bouquet garni; croûtons; 2 tablespoons cognac; 2 oz butter; 1 oz flour; 1 pint white wine. Cooking time: 25–30 minutes.

A speciality of Burgundy, this is a white wine *matelote*. Use tench, carp, small pike, eels, perch, trout, etc. Clean, scale and wipe the fish, cut in pieces and place in a *sauté* pan with seasoning, the lardoons, onions, mushroom caps, whole cloves of garlic and the *bouquet garni*. Add the white wine, place over brisk heat and set alight with cognac the moment it comes to the boil (in the days of wood fires this happened spontaneously by contact with the flames). Cook for 25–30 minutes. Remove fish. Make a blond *Roux* with the butter and flour. Whisk in the fish liquor and when boiling remove the garlic and *bouquet garni*. Add fish, and simmer in the sauce. Serve with *croûtons* of bread rubbed with garlic and fried in butter.

On the Atlantic coast there is a similar dish known as *chaudrée*, but it is not necessarily made with fresh-water fish.

Salmon Mousse

For 4 persons: 6 oz cooked salmon (fresh or canned); ½ pint aspic; ¾ pint thick cream; seasoning; 1 teaspoon anchovy essence; small piece of cucumber; 2 egg whites.

Flake and chop the fish. Whisk the aspic until frothy and lightly whisk the cream. Add salmon to aspic and then pour into the cream, with 1 tablespoon chopped cucumber. Season to taste and stir until almost setting. Quickly fold in the stiffly whipped whites and pour into a prepared *soufflé* case or glass dish. When quite set, after removing the paper band, garnish with some sliced cucumber. Lobster, crab or any highly flavoured fish may be used instead of salmon.

To prepare the soufflé case: Tie a band of greaseproof paper round the outside of the case, having the paper band 2 inches higher than the case.

Tanches à la Lorraine   *   *Tench Lorraine*

For 4 persons: 4 tench, each weighing about 6–7 oz; ½ pint white wine; 2 egg yolks; scant ¼ pint cream; 2 oz butter; 2 oz parsley; 2 onions; 8 shallots; thyme; bay leaf; ½ lemon. Cooking time: 20–25 minutes.

Scale, clean and wipe the tench. Place on a bed of parsley, stalks removed, sliced onions, shallots, thyme, bay leaf, salt and peppercorns. Add the wine and ¼ pint water. Cook slowly, drain the fish, and strain the liquor. Reduce the liquor to half, and add the cream. Simmer for 15 minutes. Thicken with egg yolks, remove from heat and beat in the butter in small pats. Place the fish in a baking dish, pour the sauce on top and sprinkle with the chopped shallots, and chopped parsley. Place in a hot oven, 400°F or Gas Mark 6, for 5 minutes and serve sprinkled with a little lemon juice.

TRUITES   *   *TROUT*

Truites à la Crème   *   *Trout with Cream*

For 6 persons: 6 trout; each weighing about 6–7 oz; seasoning; thyme; parsley; marjoram; ½ pint thick cream; 1 lemon; 2 oz breadcrumbs; 1 oz butter. Cooking time: 15 minutes.

Place the trout in a baking dish with salt, pepper, fine herbs and lemon juice moistened only with a little water. Cover and cook in a fairly hot oven, then drain off the liquor into a saucepan. Stir in the thick cream, boil the whole down to half, pour over the trout, sprinkle with breadcrumbs, dot with butter and brown in the oven.

▣ à la Meunière   *   *Meunière*

Same method as for Sole *à la Meunière*.
Trout may also be prepared in the same way as Plaice *au Gratin*, or with red wine, like Fillets of Sole. (*See illustration p. 94*).

▣ de Rivière au Bleu   *   *River Trout au Bleu*

For 4 persons: 4 trout, each weighing about 5–6 oz; court-bouillon; 2 oz butter or ¼ pint sauce Hollandaise. Cooking time: 4–5 minutes.

This is a simple and very good way of cooking river trout. Like blue poached pike, the trout must not be killed until a moment before cooking. Make and cook beforehand a *court-bouillon* with vinegar and condiments, sufficient to cover the fish. Hold the fish in a cloth so that it does not slip, and knock the head against a table or stone to kill it. Clean quickly, but do not scale, since it is the slimy covering of the skin which gives the blue look. Pat carefully with a cloth and drop into briskly boiling *court-bouillon* and poach for 4–5 minutes. Drain and place in a dish with a little of the liquor. Serve with melted butter and lemon quarters or with *sauce Hollandaise.*

Saumonée au Court-bouillon   *   *Sea Trout in Court-bouillon*

This is a very expensive fish. With char, it is certainly one of the best fresh-

105

water fish. When hot, serve with any fine sauce which will bring out the delicacy of its flavour—*Mousseline, Hollandaise,* Shrimp, *Chivry,* etc. When cold, it may be decorated attractively and served with eggs, shrimps, tarragon, parsley and tomatoes.

LES POISSONS D'EAU DOUCE FROIDS * *COLD FRESH-WATER FISH*

Truite en Gelée * *Trout in Aspic*

For 8 persons: 8 river trout, each weighing about 6 oz; court-bouillon; 6 crayfish; aspic; parsley; 2 hardboiled eggs; 1 tomato; 2 truffles; mayonnaise.

Wash and clean the trout and arrange them in a ring by tying head to tail with string. Poach slowly in *court-bouillon* and leave to cool. In the same *court-bouillon* boil 5 or 6 crayfish. Drain and dry the fish and place on a long dish decorated with curly parsley. Place the crayfish at one end and surround the dish with half eggs decorated with thin slices of tomato and truffle. Coat the whole well with cold, almost setting, aspic. Serve *mayonnaise* separately.

Tranches de Truite Saumonée en Bellevue * *Sea Trout Steaks Bellevue*

For 8 persons: 1 *sea trout, or* 1 *cut of salmon weighing* 3½ *lb;* 8 *hardboiled eggs;* ¾ *pint mayonnaise;* 16 *prawn or scampi tails;* 1 *small cucumber;* 1 *tomato;* 1 *small truffle.* Cooking time: 15 minutes.

Cut the fish into 8 steaks and cook in a *court-bouillon.* Drain and divide each steak into two. Remove the skin and trim. Arrange on a dish. Decorate each half steak with a thin slice of tomato, cucumber and truffle. Cut each hardboiled egg into two, remove the yolk, put through a sieve, season and work into half the *mayonnaise.* Fill the egg whites with this paste, using a forcing bag with a fluted pipe. Garnish the eggs with the prawn tails. Serve the remaining *mayonnaise* separately.

Shellfish and Seafood

CRABES * CRAB

Crabes ou Tourteaux Mornay * Crab Mornay

For 4 persons: 4 crabs, each weighing about 1 lb; 2 oz grated cheese; ½ pint sauce Mornay; 1 oz butter; 1 oz breadcrumbs; parsley. Cooking time: 15–20 minutes.

Plunge live crabs into boiling salted water (4 ounces salt per gallon) and boil closely covered for 20 minutes. Leave until cold, then remove claws and legs. Crack them and pick out the flesh. Flake. Detach the undershells and discard the apron, stomach sac and grey spongy fingers. Remove all soft flesh from the shells and mix this with the white flesh from the claws and legs. Scrub the hard shells and pack the seasoned crabmeat into them. Coat with sauce and sprinkle with cheese and breadcrumbs. Dot with butter, and brown in a fairly hot oven, 375°F or Gas Mark 5, or under the grill. May also be served cold, coated with *mayonnaise*. Sprinkle chopped parsley over.

CREVETTES * SHRIMPS

Live shrimps should be thrown into well-salted boiling water. Then immerse a piece of red-hot iron, such as a poker, in the water. Fishermen treat shrimps in this way to improve the colour of the shells.

Pilaf de Crevettes * Shrimp Pilaf

For 4 persons: 1½ lb cooked shrimps; 8 oz rice; ½ pint Curry or Shrimp sauce; 3 oz butter; 1 pint bouillon. Cooking time: 17–18 minutes.

Shell the cooked shrimps while cooking the rice, as follows: fry the rice slightly in 2 ounces butter and add the *bouillon*; cover closely and boil without disturbing for 17–18 minutes. The rice should then be dry. Mix in some dabs of butter carefully with a fork. Bind the shrimps with sauce and keep them warm. Arrange the rice in a ring with the shrimps in the middle. Dublin Bay prawns, crayfish and crabs may be prepared in the same way. (*See illustration p. 96*).

ECREVISSES * CRAYFISH

Ecrevisses à la Bordelaise * Crayfish Bordeaux Style

For 4 persons: 16 live crayfish; ¼ pint white wine; ¼ pint sauce Velouté; 3 tablespoons brandy; 2 onions; 2 carrots; 3 oz butter; 2 shallots; a small piece of meat glaze; 1 tablespoon chopped parsley.

Brown a *mirepoix* of carrots, onions and shallots in 2 ounces butter and throw in the live

107

washed crayfish. *Sauté* on a hot flame until the shell turns red. Flame with the brandy and add the white wine and *sauce Velouté* and cook for 10 minutes. Place the crayfish in a dish. Reduce the liquor with the meat glaze, remove from heat, add 1 ounce of butter and pour over the crayfish. Sprinkle with chopped parsley.

▣ au Court-bouillon ou à la Nage * *Boiled*

For 4 persons: 16 *crayfish;* 2 *onions;* 2 *carrots;* 2 *shallots; parsley; thyme; bay leaf;* ½ *pint white wine; seasoning;* 1 *level tablespoon salt;* 6 *peppercorns; parsley stems.* Cooking time: 10–12 minutes.

Slice the onions, shallots and carrots; make and boil a *court-bouillon* with thyme, bay leaf, salt, peppercorns and parsley. Boil until the vegetables are cooked, then add the white wine. Wash the crayfish and remove the intestinal tract by pinching the middle section of the tail level with the flesh and pulling it; the tract will come out easily with it. Throw the crayfish into the stock, cover and boil for 10–12 minutes, according to size. Pour into a dish and serve in the liquor in which it was cooked.

HOMARD * *LOBSTER*

Homard Fra Diavolo * *Lobster Fra Diavolo*

For 3 persons: 1½ *lb boiled lobster;* 4 *oz Creole Rice;* 14 *oz roughly chopped tomatoes;* 1 *oz butter;* 1 *oz chopped parsley;* 1 *large clove crushed garlic; approx.* ¼ *pint olive oil; pepper; a little powdered marjoram.*

Cut the lobster in half lengthwise and arrange in a shallow, ovenproof dish. Remove stomach sac and intestinal cord. Warm for a short time in the oven. Meanwhile *sauté* the chopped tomatoes and the garlic in olive oil, add the chopped parsley and the marjoram and pour over the lobster. Garnish with sprigs of parsley and wedges of lemon. Serve Creole Rice separately.

▣ Newburg * *Newburg*

For 4 persons: 1 *boiled lobster;* 4 *tablespoons melted butter and* 1 *tablespoon olive oil;* 3 *tablespoons brandy;* 2 *tablespoons Madeira;* ½ *pint cream;* 2 *egg yolks; pinch salt and cayenne.*

Split lobster in half lengthwise. Remove meat from shells and cut into scallops. Heat in melted butter and oil. Moisten with half the brandy and Madeira and warm. Serve heaped in a hot dish. Coat with a liaison, made by mixing together the cream, yolks and remaining brandy, and heating it gently until it thickens.

▣ Thermidor * *Thermidor*

For 4 persons: 1 *boiled lobster;* 1 *oz butter* + 1 *tablespoon olive oil;* ¼ *pint Plain White sauce; for the Bercy reduction:* 1½ *oz butter;* 1 *shallot finely chopped;* 1 *tablespoon white wine; pinch salt.*
1 *teaspoon "made" mustard; seasoning;* 1 *egg yolk;* 1 *oz grated Parmesan cheese; clarified butter; chopped parsley.*

To make the Bercy reduction: Cook shallot in 1 ounce butter to soften. Add wine and salt. Boil to reduce to ½ quantity. Beat in ½ ounce butter. Remove lobster meat from shells, split in half lengthwise. Discard sac. Cut flesh into scallops and heat up in butter and oil, with the soft parts. Do not re-cook. Strain *Bercy* reduction into White sauce. Add egg yolk, mustard and seasoning. Heat up and add to hot lobster. Mix carefully and fill up shells.

Sprinkle cheese over. Brush with clarified butter and either salamander or grill for about 10 minutes. Sprinkle chopped parsley over and serve with watercress.

LANGOUSTINES * *DUBLIN BAY PRAWNS*

Dublin Bay prawns are treated in exactly the same way as crayfish. The shelled tails may also be served with Rice *Pilaff*.

Langoustines en Brochettes au Curry * *Curried Brochettes of Prawns*

For 2 persons: 8 scampi or 6 shelled raw Dublin Bay prawns; 6–8 very thin slices bacon; 7 oz Rice à la Grecque; 1 level tablespoon curry powder; 1 oz butter.

Wash the shellfish well and clean the tails thoroughly. Wrap them in the bacon and impale on small skewers. Melt the butter and add a little curry powder. *Sauté* the shellfish in the butter; when they are cooked, arrange on the rice. (*See illustration p.* 95).

◙ Frits * *Fried*

For 4 persons: 1 lb frozen scampi; 2 tablespoons seasoned flour; egg and breadcrumbs; quarters of lemon; ¼ pint sauce Tartare; brown bread and butter.

Thaw out scampi in cold water. Drain well and dry in a cloth. Toss in seasoned flour. Coat with egg and crumbs. Fry in hot fat for 5–7 minutes. Drain well and serve with brown bread and butter, lemon and *sauce Tartare*.

Seafood

Bigorneaux * *Winkles*

Boil in white wine for 5 minutes and eat cold, using small snail forks to extract the winkles from their shells.

Calmars à la Basquaise * *Basque Style Calamary (Ink Fish)*

For 4 persons: 2 lb calamary; 2 tablespoons oil; 1 onion; 2 cloves of garlic; spices; 1 pint white wine; croûtons. Cooking time: about 1 hour 20 minutes.

Calamary are a kind of octopus known on the Basque Coast as chipirones. They are also popular in Italy and known as Inkfish, and highly esteemed by gourmets. Remove bone and intestines and keep the sepia (black fluid), or part of it, in a bowl. Cut the body and tentacles into pieces. Toss some chopped onion, a little garlic and some fine herbs in oil, add the calamary and brown the whole for 10–12 minutes. Add enough white wine just to cover. Simmer gently for a good hour after seasoning well with salt, pepper and spices. Before serving, mix the black sepia with 3 tablespoons water and pour into the saucepan to thicken the sauce. Serve with bread *croûtons* fried in oil.

Clovisses * *Venus' Shells*

Venus' shells are found mainly on the Atlantic coasts and distinguished by an oval regular shining shell, reddish outside and white inside. They are eaten a great deal in England and America in particular. Venus' shells may be swallowed like oysters if shelled and free of sand. They may be eaten with *mayonnaise*. In that case, open them on the stove, remove from shells and wash, then bind with well-seasoned *mayonnaise*.

Coques * *Cockles*

After washing, open them on the stove. They may be eaten as they are, or with vinegar, mixed with a little fine pepper and chopped shallots.

COQUILLES SAINT-JACQUES * *SCALLOPS*

Like all shellfish, they must be fresh, heavy and firm. They are a very popular *entrée*.

Coquilles à la Diable * *Devilled scallops*

For 4 persons: 4 scallops; 2 oz butter; 1 onion; 2 oz breadcrumbs; 1 tablespoon chopped parsley; 2 oz white bread without crusts; mustard; ¼ pint Béchamel; seasoning; Worcester sauce.

Wash, and put the scallops in the oven until they open, then remove from shells. Throw away the black part, and wash scallops thoroughly. Chop them and mix with chopped onion previously cooked in butter, white bread, dipped in milk, well-squeezed and crumbled, chopped parsley, salt, pepper, the *Béchamel*, a pinch of mustard and a few drops of Worcester sauce. Fill the shells with this mixture, sprinkle with breadcrumbs and brown in the oven.

Cocquilles à la Duchesse * *Duchess*

Prepare in the same way as Scallops *à la Parisienne*, but with a forcing bag make a border of mashed potatoes mixed with egg yolk and a little butter around the edge of each shell.

▣ à la Parisienne * *Parisian style*

For 4 persons: 4 scallops; 6 oz mushrooms; generous ¼ pint white wine; 1 onion; 1 shallot; 2 oz butter; 1 oz flour; 3–4 tablespoons milk; 2 oz gruyère; 2 oz breadcrumbs.

Wash and place the scallops on the stove or in the oven until they open. Remove the flesh and keep the hollow half of the shell. Wash carefully in several changes of water, since they tend to be sandy. Cook the scallops in a fish stock of white wine, chopped onion and shallot, *bouquet garni*, salt and pepper, for 10–15 minutes. Cook the mushrooms separately. Make a fairly thick sauce with the butter and the flour, adding the strained liquor from the scallops and the milk. Cook the sauce for a few minutes. Slice white part of scallop, cut off the black beard and discard and dice the coral. Add the cut-up scallops and mushrooms to the sauce. Season well. Stir over heat for 5 minutes, draw aside and add the grated *gruyère*. Fill the well-cleaned scallop shells with the mixture, sprinkle with cheese and breadcrumbs and brown. Serve very hot.

Huîtres * *Oysters*

Oysters must be very fresh. Open them at the last minute and serve with quarters of lemon and a sauceboat of vinegar with chopped shallots and coarsely ground pepper. Slices of buttered rye bread are recommended as an accompaniment.

MOULES * *MUSSELS*

Mussels are delicious. They must be fresh and firmly attached to the shell. It is wiser not to eat them from June to September. Always discard the weed under the black tongue. Before use wash thoroughly in frequent changes of water. Scrub with a hard brush and remove any seaweed adhering to them. Mussels should not be overcooked; the whole cooking process takes only 5–6 minutes.

Moules à la Créole * *Creole Mussels*

Boil 2 ounces of well washed rice in salted water for not more than 16–17 minutes: drain, rinse and dry. Boil 2 pints of shelled mussels with a little white wine and onions: reduce liquid considerably, adding a little curry powder. Pour this liquid over the mussels and rice, add oil and vinegar and serve chilled.

▣ à l'Italienne * *Italian*

For 4 persons: 3½ pints mussels; pepper; thyme; parsley; 6–8 fresh tomatoes; saffron, if liked; 2 oz fresh butter.

Place the scrubbed washed mussels in a saucepan and cook them dry, without any liquid, only adding a little pepper, thyme and parsley. Shake the pan frequently. When the shells are wide open, drain the juice, let it stand, then decant it and replace on the stove with a *purée* of fresh tomatoes. Reduce over a high flame with fresh butter; a pinch of saffron may be added if desired. Serve this sauce separately at the same time as the shelled mussels.

Moules à la Marinière * *Marinière*

For 4 persons: 3½ pints mussels; ¼ pint white wine; 2 oz butter; 2 shallots; 1 *tablespoon chopped parsley; thyme.*

Wash and brush the mussels, wash again in several changes of cold water, brushing them at the same time, without letting them soak, otherwise they will open and lose their sea water. Boil them in a large saucepan with pepper (but no salt), parsley, thyme, and chopped shallots. Add the wine, cover, and boil briskly until the shells are wide open. Remove them from the liquor; if they are cooked too long they will become hard and shrivelled. Pour off the liquor into another pan, add fresh butter and parsley. Boil briskly until reduced to half, add the mussels which should have been shelled and cleaned. Heat without boiling and serve at once.

◙ à la Poulette * *Poulette*

For 4 persons: Same ingredients as for Marinière, plus 1 oz butter; 1 oz flour; generous ¼ pint cream; 1 egg yolk; 7 oz Créole Rice.

Prepare mussels as for *Marinière* and decant the liquor. Make a *Roux* with the butter and flour, add the liquor and then the cream. Add the egg yolk and re-heat but do not boil, whisking briskly all the time. Remove from heat immediately, season and add the chopped parsley and shelled mussels. Serve Creole Rice separately.

Pilaf de Moules à l'Orientale * *Pilaf of Mussels Orientale*

For 4 persons: 3½ pints mussels cooked à la Marinière; 7 oz Pilaf Rice; curry or saffron; 2 oz butter; 1 oz flour.

Cook the *Pilaf* Rice and the mussels. Make a *sauce Velouté* with the butter, flour and mussel liquor. Add a large pinch of curry powder or saffron, according to taste. Bind the mussels with this sauce and place them in the centre of a rice ring.

Ormeaux à la Ménagère * *Ormers Ménagère*

For 4 persons: 8 ormers (mollusc known as the ear shell); 2 tablespoons oil; 2 oz butter; 1 egg white; 1 egg; breadcrumbs. Cooking time: 8–10 minutes.

Ear-shells are popular in Chinese Restaurants. This snail is dry and tough, but leaves a pleasant taste in the mouth. Remove from the shells raw, beat fairly hard with a heavy implement and egg and breadcrumb. Cook gently in a frying pan with butter and oil. Serve with *Maître d'hôtel* butter, with a slice of hardboiled egg on each.

Oursins * *Sea Urchins*

Sea urchins are popular along the Mediterranean seaboard. Cut a lid off them with scissors. Eat them with a small spoon or by dipping fingers of bread into them.

Praires * *Clams (Prairie Oyster)*

Clams are popular in America. They are mostly eaten raw as *hors d'œuvre*, but may be served hot, as follows: open them on the stove, like mussels, then place in each

▲   *Turban de bœuf à la gelée, p. 137*

Bœuf froid à la niçoise, p. 137   ▼

114 ▲ *Ris de veau à la jardinière, p. 145*

Tournedos Château Figeac, p. 131 ▼

▲ *Quasi ou longe de veau, p. 145*

Foie de veau à l'anglaise, p. 141 ▼

▲ *Medaillons de veau Véronèse, p. 142*

Jarret de veau ou osso bucco, p. 142 ▼

a little butter mixed with finely chopped shallots and chopped parsley. Add the juice of a lemon, sprinkle with breadcrumbs and put in the oven for a few minutes.

Supions Frits * *Deep Fried Squid*

These delicious little calamaries are served chiefly in the south of France. First remove the cuttle bone and ink pouch. Wash, dry and flour, and deep fry in very hot fat. Half cover the pan to avoid splashes. Serve at once while very crisp.

CRUSTACÉS FROIDS * *COLD CRUSTACEANS AND SHELL-FISH*

HOMARD OU LANGOUSTE * *LOBSTER OR ROCK LOBSTER*

Homard ou Langouste à la Mayonnaise * *Lobster or Rock Lobster*

Boil in strongly salted water, 20 minutes for a lobster weighing 1 pound, 35 minutes for a lobster of 2 pounds. Drain, break open the shell and leave to cool, head down, so that the water which penetrated during cooking will drain out. Halve lengthways with a strong knife, remove stomach sac and intestinal cord and serve on a napkin surrounded with parsley. Hand *mayonnaise* separately.

▣ à la Russe * *Russian style*

For 4 persons: 2 boiled lobsters, each weighing 1 lb; 1 lb diced mixed vegetables; ½ pint mayonnaise; 4 hardboiled eggs; 1 truffle; 1 lettuce.

Split each lobster in half lengthwise. Remove sac and cord, and arrange on a bed of lettuce. Bind the mixed vegetables with the *mayonnaise* and arrange on the upper part of the lobsters. Garnish with rounds of hardboiled egg and truffle cutouts. Serve *mayonnaise* separately. (*See illustration p. 95*).

Langouste en Bellevue * *Rock Lobster (or Crawfish) Bellevue*

For 4 persons: 1 rock lobster, weighing about 2 lb 6 oz; 1 lb macédoine; 3 hardboiled eggs; 3 fresh tomatoes; 1 lettuce; mayonnaise.

Boil and drain the rock lobster as for Lobster. Cut the membranes under the tail with scissors in such a way that the whole of the flesh of the tail comes out in a piece, without breaking or damaging the shell. Place a bed of lettuce leaves on a large fish platter and put the shell on it, tail well spread out. Cut the flesh into nice slices and arrange them down the middle of the shell so that they overlap, from the feelers to the tail. Place a thin slice of truffle on each and brush with oil so that everything looks fresh. On each side of the shell arrange a mound of vegetable *macédoine* mixed with *mayonnaise* and decorate with sliced hardboiled eggs and tomatoes. Serve *mayonnaise* separately.

Langoustines Château Bouscaut * *Dublin Bay Prawns Château Bouscaut*

For 6 persons: 15 Dublin Bay prawns; 15 large prawns; 24 stoned black olives; generous ¼ pint mayonnaise; 1 lb Russian salad thickened with aspic; sprigs of parsley.

Cook the Dublin Bay prawns and the prawns in a *court-bouillon* and shell them when cold.

117

Divide each prawn into two. Fill the Russian salad thickened with aspic into a mould and leave until cold. Unmould. Arrange the Dublin Bay prawns and the prawns in a ring on the Russian salad and garnish with the olives, *mayonnaise* and parsley. (*See illustration p.* 96).

Moules à la Mayonnaise   *   *Mussels Mayonnaise*

For 4 persons: 3½ pints mussels; scant ½ pint white wine; scant ½ pint mayonnaise; 8 oz boiled potatoes.

Boil the mussels with the wine and shell them. Strain the liquor through a cloth and boil it down considerably. When the mussels are cold, bind them with lightly salted *mayonnaise* well seasoned with mustard and mixed with 2 tablespoons of the reduced liquor. Arrange the mussels in a small round or oval dish and surround them with a ring of potatoes seasoned with a little oil and vinegar.

Tourteau à la Russe   *   *Russian style Crab*

For 6 persons: 1 crab, weighing about 4 lb; 6 oz macédoine of vegetables; ½ pint mayonnaise; 2 hardboiled eggs; chervil; tarragon.

Boil the crab in salted water in the same way as for Crab Mornay. Open the shell, including claws, and remove all flesh and edible parts. Flake with 2 forks. Mix with a salad of *macédoine* of vegetables. Bind with highly-seasoned *mayonnaise* and replace in the washed, dried shell. Coat the whole with *mayonnaise* and decorate the top with tarragon, chervil, hardboiled egg, etc.

LES GRENOUILLES   *   *FROGS' LEGS*

Frogs' legs are sold impaled on skewers. It is important that they are always perfectly fresh as they go bad very quickly. To prepare: wash thoroughly and cut off the feet with scissors, before use.

Les Grenouilles en Beignets   *   *Frogs' Legs Fritters*

Allow a dozen frogs' legs per person for an *entrée*. Soak the legs for a little while with salt, pepper, chopped parsley and a few drops of vinegar before cooking. Dry at the last moment, dip in Frying batter and deep fry for 5 minutes in very hot fat. Serve in a mound with parsley.

▣ Sautées Fines Herbes   *   *Sautéed with Fine Herbs*

Cut off the feet with scissors and *sauté* the legs in very hot butter in a frying pan with chopped shallots and a pinch of garlic. Place on a dish, reduce the butter, etc. remaining in the pan, together with white wine, sprinkle with chopped fine herbs and serve with lemon quarters.

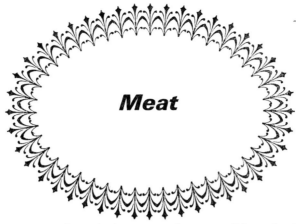

Meat

The prime cuts of meat come from the least muscular parts of the animal so the most tender portions of meat—the prime cuts—are found on either side of the backbone. Muscles which are more actively employed, such as leg muscles, have more and stronger connective tissue and are therefore the tougher cuts of meat which require long, slow cooking to soften the fibres.

It is useful to know something of the cuts most suitable for roasting, grilling, stewing and braising. For grills and roasts the prime cuts should be used—fillet, loin or rump steak. Ribs also make an excellent joint. The second category, which includes chuck steak, silverside, brisket, top and back rib and the thin flank, lend themselves to braising or pot roasting. However, the top of sirloin, or thin flank, from prime cattle will make excellent juicy steaks.

The other parts, such as leg and shin, sticking, clod, shoulder steak and skirt are also used for various kinds of stew, casseroles and goulash.

Brisket, silverside and top side are usually used for boiling.

Where there is no waste (*entrecôte*, fillet steak, roasts, etc.) allow 5 ounces per person as a minimum.

For braising meat sold with bones, and where the meat tends to shrink because of the long cooking period, allow at least 5 to 6 ounces per person. Stews can be re-heated or eaten cold, whereas *entrecôte* or an underdone joint cannot be reheated. It is, therefore, possible to buy a larger quantity of the cheaper cuts and make enough for two meals. The stockpot also takes more meat, because it is usual to make enough *bouillon* at a time for two days.

LE BŒUF * VARIOUS BEEF DISHES

Aiguillette de Bœuf Braisée * Braised Aitchbone of Beef

For 6 persons: 2 lb aitchbone; ¾ pint white wine; 8 oz carrot; 2 onions; 1 stalk celery; 3 oz fat bacon; 2 oz cooking fat; seasoning; bouquet garni; sauce Demi-glace. Cooking time: about 2½ hours.

Aitchbone lies below the rump. You could use silverside, brisket or flank for this dish.
Lard the meat with fat bacon and brown it in cooking fat with the sliced onions, carrots and celery. Drain off fat, and add white wine. Reduce this to half, then add enough slightly thickened *sauce Demi-glace* to well cover the vegetable foundation. Season and add the *bouquet garni.* Cover meat closely with a greased paper. Put on lid and stew gently for 1 hour. Add more *Demi-glace* if necessary and continue cooking in a fairly hot oven, 375°F or Gas Mark 5, for 1½ hours or until the meat is tender. Remove meat. Strain sauce and skim off surface fat. Reduce sauce if necessary and pour over meat. Serve and garnish to taste with *Risotto,* carrots and peas, or Braised cabbage.

119

Bœuf à la Bourguignonne   *   *Beef Bourguignonne*

For 4 persons: 1½ *lb beef; 2 cloves garlic; 2 oz cooking fat; 2 oz butter;*
¼ *pint red wine; 4 oz lean bacon; 20 shallots; 8 oz mushrooms; thyme; bay leaf; parsley;*
1 *tablespoon tomato purée; 1 tablespoon flour; 1 pint bouillon.* Cooking time: 3 hours.

Use any of the cheaper cuts of beef and cut it in fairly large cubes. Brown the meat in hot
fat. When it is brown, sprinkle with flour and add 2 cloves of chopped garlic. When the
flour is brown add the red wine with *bouillon*. Bring to the boil. Add salt, pepper and a
bouquet garni. Fry the bacon in butter with the shallots and add to the beef. Cover closely
and cook very slowly for 3 hours. Add the mushrooms whole or in halves and the tomato
purée 10 minutes before serving. Skim fat off sauce and serve with boiled potatoes.

▣ en Daube   *   *Marinated and Stewed*

For 6 persons: 2 *lb topside, silverside or brisket;* ½ *bottle red wine; 4 table-*
spoons *oil; 4 oz fat bacon; 2 onions; 3 carrots; 3 tablespoons tomato purée; 2 cloves garlic;*
1 *level dessertspoon flour; bouquet garni.* Cooking time: 2 hours.

Leave meat whole or cube it. If whole, lard with the fat bacon; if in cubes, thread a piece
of the fat bacon through each cube. Put the meat in a braising pan with the sliced onions
and carrots, garlic cloves, the *bouquet garni*, salt and pepper, and pour the oil and red
wine over. Marinate for 4 hours, turning the meat occasionally, then cook slowly in a
hermetically sealed casserole for at least 2 hours. At the end of 1 hour add tomato *purée*.
When tender, skim off the fat and thicken the sauce with a little flour mixed with cold water.
Serve at once with the well-reduced sauce.

▣ à la Mode   *   *à la Mode*

For 6 persons: 2 *lb aitchbone, rump or topside; 4 oz fat bacon; 2 oz lard;*
2 *tablespoons brandy;* ½ *bottle white wine; 1 calf's foot, skinned and boned;* 1¼ *lb small
whole carrots; 8 oz shallots.* Cooking time: 3 hours.

Lard the meat with fat bacon, then season and brown it all over in lard. Add shallots and
brown lightly. Drain off the surplus fat, flame the beef with brandy, add the white wine,
and enough water to cover the meat. Surround the meat with some bacon rinds and a
calf's foot, which should have been blanched for 5 minutes and then cooled. Season, colour
the gravy with caramel, cover and cook gently for 1½ hours. Add carrots and continue
cooking until all is tender. Skim off fat, and remove meat. Arrange vegetables and sliced
calf's foot round the meat in a dish. Reduce the gravy over a hot flame until fairly concentrated, then pour round the meat.

▣ Sauté à la Lyonnaise   *   *Sautéed Lyonnaise*

For 4 persons: 1½ *lb beefsteak, entrecôte or rump;* ¾ *lb onions; white wine;*
4 *oz butter.* Cooking time: 15 minutes.

Slice the onions finely and *sauté* in 3 ounces butter. Beat sliced beef lightly, *sauté* separately
in remaining butter. Sprinkle with a little white wine and top with the onions to serve.

Australian Meat Pie

To make 10–12 *pies: Pie Base: 8 oz plain flour;* ½ *teaspoon salt;* ¼ *pint water;*
2 *oz beef dripping. Pie Tops:* 12 *oz Puff pastry; egg to glaze. Filling:* 1–1½ *lb coarsely minced
beef; 1 teaspoon salt; pepper;* ½ *pint beef stock; good pinch nutmeg;* 1½ *oz plain flour; extra*
¼ *pint stock; parisienne essence (gravy browning).* Cooking time: about 40 minutes altogether.

Sift flour and salt into basin. Place water and dripping in saucepan. Heat gently to melt dripping, but do not reduce liquid quantity. Pour hot liquid into well in centre of flour. Mix with a knife to begin with and when cool enough use hands. Knead on lightly floured board until free of cracks. Roll out and line bases of small pie tins. (Use saucer to cut circles.) Fill centre with prepared filling.

Place the minced beef in the bottom of a heavy saucepan and place over moderate heat. The beef should contain enough of its own fat to brown in, without adding any excess oil. When meat is well-browned, drain off any liquid, then add stock, salt, pepper, and nutmeg. Bring to the boil, then simmer for a few minutes. Mix the flour with the extra stock until smooth. Take pan from heat and cool slightly, then stir in flour mixture. Bring back to boil, stirring continuously, until well thickened. Cook a further few minutes. Add sufficient parisienne essence to give a rich brown colouring.

Roll out pastry on lightly floured board, and cut with saucer to make rounds for tops. Wet edges of pastry bases, and gently press tops into place. Pierce centre with pointed knife for steam to escape. Brush well with egg glaze. Place in hot oven, 400°F or Gas Mark 6, for approximately 10 minutes, until browned, then reduce heat to moderate 350°F or Gas Mark 4, and cook further 5 minutes.

Boulettes de Bœuf en Sauce Piquante * *Small Beef Balls in Piquant Sauce*

For 6 persons: 8 oz cooked beef; 8 oz sausage meat; 1 oz lard; 1 onion; fine herbs; 4 oz white bread; 1 shallot; 1 clove of garlic; ½ pint Tomato sauce; 1 oz butter; 2 tablespoons oil. Cooking time: 10–15 minutes.

Mince the beef and mix it with the sausage meat and a piece of dry bread, dipped in *bouillon*, squeezed out and crumbled. Add salt, pepper, chopped shallot, crushed chopped garlic, and chopped onion cooked in lard. Form into small balls, flatten slightly, roll in flour and fry in butter and oil. Serve *sauce Piquante* or Tomato sauce separately.

Carbonade of Beef with Beer

For 4 persons: 1¼ lb rump or thin flank; 1 oz butter; ½ pint Demi-glace; ¾ lb onions; ½ pint beer; 2 oz lard; 1 bouquet garni. Cooking time: 2 hours.

Sauté thickish slices or cubes of steak in butter in a frying pan. Place them in a casserole on a thick layer of sliced onions lightly sautéed in lard. Cover with another layer of onions, season and add the beer. Add a *bouquet garni* and the *Demi-glace*. Cover and cook slowly in the oven for at least 2 hours. Skim off fat and serve with boiled potatoes.

Golden Meat Puffs

For 4 persons: 1 lb cold cooked beef, cut into thin strips; juice of 2 lemons; 1 teaspoon salt; pinch pepper; oil for frying; Tomato sauce. Batter: 4 oz plain flour; ½ teaspoon salt; 6 tablespoons beer; 4 tablespoons warm water; 1 teaspoon brandy; 2 egg whites. Cooking time: 5–10 minutes.

Make batter, sift flour with salt, add beer, water, and brandy, beat well. Just before using batter, beat egg whites stiffly and fold in. Combine lemon juice, salt and pepper, pour over meat, let stand 1 hour. Drain, dip in batter, and cook meat strips in hot oil until nicely brown. Serve hot with hot Tomato sauce.

Old Fashioned Shepherd's Pie

For 4 persons: 1 *large onion, finely chopped;* 2 *oz butter;* 1 *lb cold cooked beef, minced or finely chopped;* ½ *oz flour;* ½ *pint beef stock;* 2 *teaspoons Worcester sauce; salt; pepper; grated lemon rind;* ½ *teaspoon finely chopped herbs;* 6 *large potatoes;* ¼ *pint milk;* 2 *oz butter;* 1 *egg yolk.* Cooking time: 30 minutes.

Heat butter in pan, *sauté* onion until golden, add beef, *sauté* for a few minutes. Stir in flour and add beef stock slowly, stirring all the time, until mixture boils and thickens. Add sauce, salt, pepper, lemon rind and mixed herbs and combine well. Take off heat and keep warm. Peel, chop potatoes and cook them in boiling salted water until tender, drain and mash them with milk and butter. Place the meat mixture in a well-greased oven-proof dish, and top with mashed potato, spread in a rounded shape. Brush with beaten egg yolk, and bake in hot oven, 400°F or Gas Mark 6, for 20 minutes, or until potato topping is golden brown. Serve immediately.

Savoury Meat Crescents

For 4 persons: 8 *oz Puff pastry;* 1 *lb cold cooked beef, chopped finely;* ½ *oz flour;* ¼ *pint beef stock;* 2 *oz chopped celery;* 2 *oz chopped onion;* 2 *oz chopped green pepper;* 2 *oz butter; salt; pepper;* 1 *oz chopped parsley;* 1 *oz chopped green olives;* 1 *beaten egg mixed with* 3 *tablespoons milk; breadcrumbs; oil for frying; parsley.* Cooking time: 15 minutes altogether.

Sauté celery, onion, and green pepper in hot butter in pan until soft. Stir in flour, add stock slowly, stirring continuously. Bring to boil and stir until mixture thickens. Add cooked meat, olives, parsley, and season well with salt and pepper. Roll out pastry very thinly, and cut into rounds about 3 inches in diameter. Spoon a little filling into each, glaze edges with egg and milk mixture. Fold in halves, pressing edges down securely. Brush with egg and milk mixture, coat with breadcrumbs. Deep fry in hot oil until golden brown. Drain and serve hot, sprinkled with parsley.

BEEFSTEAK   *   *BEEFSTEAK*

Steaks may be cut from various parts of the animal. Beefsteak is generally cut from the fillet, sirloin or rump.

Porterhouse steak is a very large, thick piece of upper cut of sirloin. When cooked on the bone it is known as T-bone steak in America.

Fillet steak is cut from the lower part of the fillet.

Tournedos are cut in small rounds from the thin end of the fillet.

Châteaubriand is a thick steak (2 inches or more) cut from the middle of the fillet.

Filets Mignons are cut from the flat tongue-like piece at the thin end of the fillet. They are divided in two lengthwise.

Entrecôte is a medium-sized, thin steak cut from the meat between the ribs, or from the sirloin or rump.

Note: Weight of portion depends on the type of meal being served—an 8 ounce steak is not too much as an average helping for a man, at an informal meal.

122

A steak weighing 6–8 ounces is enough for one or two, depending on the number of courses. Cook it for 4–5 minutes on each side to keep it rare, either by frying it in a little butter or oil, or by grilling. When it is sufficiently cooked on one side, beads of blood begin to pearl on the surface of the uncooked side. Turn the steak at this point with palette knives. Season the cooked side with salt and pepper. Do not season the other side until you place it on the serving dish. Then serve at once with *Maître d'hôtel* butter and watercress. Garnish as desired.

All the recipes for *entrecôte* apply to beefsteak.

Barbecued Beef on Skewers

For 4 persons: 2 lb rump steak; 1 large onion, finely chopped; salt; pepper; 1 teaspoon Worcester sauce; 2 tablespoons oil; 2 tablespoons red wine; 1 teaspoon dry mustard; 2 crushed cloves garlic. Cooking time: 15-25 minutes.

Cut beef into 1-inch squares, put into earthenware or glass bowl. Combine finely chopped onion with all remaining ingredients, pour over steak and toss; let stand for several hours or overnight. Next day arrange on skewers, alternating steak squares with any of the following: mushroom caps, tomato wedges, wedges of green or red pepper, or bacon cubes. Grill on hot greased barbecue grill, or under hot grill, turning often and basting occasionally with any leftover marinade, until cooked to taste.

Beefsteak Grillé, Sauce Tartare * Fried Steak with Sauce Tartare

Cut the steak in thick slices. Beat lightly. Flour them and fry in butter and oil. Dust with pepper and salt and brown well. Serve with *Tartare sauce*. Cooking time: 10 minutes.

▣ Haché * Mince Patties

For 4 persons: 1¼ lb beef; 2 oz butter; 1 egg yolk; flour; salt and pepper. Cooking time: 10–15 minutes.

Mince the beef twice. Season with salt and pepper and combine with a beaten egg yolk. Shape into balls. Flatten into round cakes, using a little flour for coating. Fry in butter. Sliced onions, fried in butter, may be placed on top or Sour cream sauce poured over.

Carpetbag Steak

For 4 persons: Piece of rump steak about 2½ inches thick, and weighing about 1 lb; about 20 oysters; salt; pepper; butter. Cooking time: 10-20 minutes, depending on personal taste.

Make pocket in steak with sharp knife. Dust pocket with salt and pepper, fill with oysters. Sew edges of pocket together or fasten with small skewers. Brush surface of steak with melted butter and cook under hot, preheated grill until cooked according to taste. Cut into serving pieces, transfer to hot dish, season with salt and pepper and dot with butter. Serve at once. *(Australia)*

Châteaubriand * Châteaubriand Steak

For 4 persons: 1 thick slice of beef from the centre of the fillet, weighing about 1½ lb. Cooking time: about 15–20 minutes.

A *châteaubriand* must be grilled, and as it is thick it should not be browned first. Trim, then oil the meat before and several times during cooking; add a little salt at a time, 2 or 3 times. The steak must be served with *sauce Béarnaise*, and surrounded by *Soufflé* potatoes.

ENTRECÔTE * *ENTRECOTE STEAK*

Entrecôte et Beefsteak Grillés * *Grilled Steak*

For 4 persons: 1½ lb steak for grilling. Cooking time: 6–8 minutes.

Have the steaks cut from one of the prime cuts of beef. Trim and flatten them. Oil the meat on both sides, place on a hot grill. Serve with *Maître d'hôtel* butter and Chipped potatoes. Turn frequently during cooking, and season with salt and milled pepper.

▣ à la Béarnaise * *Entrecôte Béarnaise*

Serve the grilled entrecôte with watercress, Chipped potatoes and *sauce Béarnaise.*

▣ à la Bordelaise * *Bordelaise*

Place even-sized slices of ox marrow, poached in salted water, on the grilled meat and serve *sauce Bordelaise* separately or pour it on top.

▣ à la Lyonnaise * *Lyonnaise*

For 4 persons: 1½ lb entrecôte; ¾ lb onions; 2 oz butter; ¼ pint white wine; 2 tablespoons meat gravy or bouillon. Cooking time: 30–40 minutes.

Sauté the trimmed *entrecôte* in a frying pan. Toss thinly sliced onions in butter; when they are golden brown, add 1 or 2 tablespoons of gravy from a joint (or use *bouillon*), a dash of vinegar, salt, ground pepper and white wine. Reduce slightly, pour over the *entrecôte* and sprinkle with chopped parsley.

▣ à la Maître d'Hôtel * *Maître d'hôtel*

For 6 persons: 2 entrecôte steaks, each weighing about 1 lb to 1¼ lb; 4 oz Maître d'hôtel butter; watercress. Cooking time: 12–15 minutes.

Grill the steaks and arrange on a long dish. Garnish them with *Maître d'hôtel* butter and surround with watercress.

▣ à la Marchand de Vin * *with Red Wine*

For 6 persons: 2 entrecôte steaks, each weighing about 1 lb to 1¼ lb; scant ½ pint red wine; 4 oz chopped shallots; 6 oz butter; lemon juice; chopped parsley. Cooking time: 12–15 minutes.

Wipe steaks. Trim off fat and skin. *Sauté* the steaks in 4 ounces butter. Pour off butter and add the red wine to loosen the crusty sediment. Add the shallots and seasoning, and cook to soften shallots only. Thicken the sauce with remaining butter, adding a small piece at a time and beating it in before adding the next. Add the lemon juice and parsley and pour over the steaks.

Entrecôte Mirabeau * *Mirabeau*

For 6 persons: 2 *entrecôte steaks, each weighing about* 1 *lb to* 1¼ *lb;* 24 *stuffed olives;* 15 *strips anchovy fillets;* 1 *oz Anchovy butter; watercress.* Cooking time: 12–15 minutes.

Grill the steaks and spread with Anchovy butter. Arrange the strips of anchovy in a lattice pattern on top and place half an olive in each division. Garnish with olives and a small bunch of watercress.

▣ à la Niçoise * *Niçoise*

For 4 persons: 1 *entrecôte steak weighing about* 1½ *lb;* 4 *tomatoes;* ¾ *lb potatoes;* 3 *oz butter;* 2 *cloves of garlic;* 1 *tablespoon chopped parsley; seasoning.* Cooking time: 30–40 minutes.

Lightly beat the steak and *sauté* in 2 ounces butter. Season when half cooked. Halve each tomato and squeeze gently to remove seeds and pulp. Season the shells and fill up with a little butter, chopped parsley and finely chopped garlic. Bake on a greased tin covered with greased paper in a fairly hot oven, 375°F or Gas Mark 5, until tender—about 5 minutes. Fry the Straw potatoes. Serve the meat with the tomatoes at one end of the dish and the potatoes at the other.

FILET DE BŒUF RÔTI * *ROAST FILLET OF BEEF*

A fillet should always be larded; insert strips of fat bacon using a larding needle, through the fillet. The joint may be cut from the thick or middle of the fillet. The cooking time will vary slightly according to thickness, 12 minutes per pound is usual. To be tender and appetising it should be pink inside; do not overcook. Serve with its own gravy and various garnishes.

Filet de Bœuf au Madère * *Fillet of Beef with Madeira*

For 6 persons: 2 *lb fillet of beef;* 4 *oz butter; scant* ¼ *pint Madeira;* 8 *oz mushrooms;* 1 *onion;* 1 *carrot;* ½ *pint sauce Demi-glace; tomato purée.* Cooking time: 40 minutes.

Brown the fillet in 2 ounces butter with a sliced onion and carrot in a casserole. Add the Madeira and *sauce Demi-glace*. Season, add 1 tablespoon tomato *purée*, cover and cook in the oven, 400°F or Gas Mark 6. The meat should not be covered by the sauce. When about to serve skim the fat off the sauce and add the mushrooms sautéed in remaining butter. The meat will be pink, less underdone than a roast, but tender.

Emincé de Filet de Bœuf à la Crème * *Sliced Fillet of Beef with Cream*

For 4 persons: 1¼ *lb fillet;* ¼ *pint thick cream;* 2 *oz butter; lemon; fine herbs.* Cooking time: 2–3 minutes.

This may be made using the thin tip of the fillet (*mignon*), or some other tender cut of beef.

Slice the beef thinly and toss into a frying pan of very hot butter to brown and stiffen. Pour in thick cream immediately, add salt, pepper, chopped fine herbs and the juice of half a lemon. Boil up once and serve immediately.

Filet de Bœuf Champignons   *   Mushrooms

For 4 persons: 4 pieces fillet steak; 6 shallots, finely chopped; 4 oz mushrooms, finely sliced; 2 cloves garlic, crushed; 4 oz butter; 2 tablespoons brandy; ¼ teaspoon Worcester sauce; ¼ pint cream; pepper; salt. Cooking time: 5-10 minutes.

Pound steaks with mallet, heat butter in frying pan, and brown steaks quickly on both sides. Add brandy and light, *sauté* for a minute, then remove steaks to a warm plate. Add shallots, garlic, and mushrooms to pan and *sauté* until tender. Stir in Worcester sauce, cream, and add pepper and salt to taste. Pour hot sauce over steaks to serve.

Faux Filet Grillé à la Bûcheronne   *   Grilled Rump Steak Bûcheronne

For 4 persons: 1½ lb sliced rump steak; 6 oz butter; 1¼ lb mushrooms (boletus); 2 tablespoons thick cream; 2 oz lean bacon; ¾ lb cooked potatoes. Cooking time: 20–30 minutes.

While frying the meat, *sauté* the mushrooms in 2 ounces butter until done. Dice the potatoes and bacon finely and fry them in remaining butter; brown well. Mix the mushrooms with the cream. Arrange the meat with the mushrooms on top and surround by the potatoes. The potatoes may be fried in deep fat.

Fondue Bourguignonne   *   Fondue Bourguignonne

For 6 persons: 2 lb top sirloin or top rump; a variety of cold sauces (such as Aurora; Mustard; Curry; Rémoulade; Vinaigrette or Mayonnaise; etc.); approx. 1 pint oil.

Cut the raw meat into cubes of about half an inch. Heat the oil to smoking point and pour into a small pan which is placed in the centre of the table on a spirit lamp or electric hotplate. Impale a piece of beef on the end of a thin wooden stick. Dip in the boiling oil for a few moments, then remove, transfer to a fork and dip into one of the sauces arranged in separate dishes. It is very important not to use a fork to dip the meat into the oil, to avoid painful burns on the lips.

Glazed Pickled Beef

For 4-6 persons: Piece of pickled silverside (about 2 to 3 lb); water; onion, (stuck with cloves); peppercorns; bay leaf; quartered carrots; 3 oz brown sugar; ½ oz dry mustard; sherry. Cooking time: 1½-2 hours.

If meat is very salty, wash and soak in cold water 2 to 3 hours. Then place in large saucepan with sufficient warm water to cover, add onion, carrot, and seasoning. Bring slowly to boiling point, then reduce to simmer. Skim well, cover, and simmer till tender, allowing approximately 35 minutes per pound. When cooked, allow to cool in cooking liquid. Remove from saucepan, drain and dry. Place meat in baking dish. Combine brown sugar and mustard, mix to a stiff paste with sherry. Spread this mixture over beef, and bake in a moderate oven, 350°F or Gas Mark 4, for 20 to 30 minutes, or until meat is well-glazed. Spoon glaze over meat as it melts. Serve hot or cold.

Hungarian Goulash

For 6 persons: 2¼ lb rump; 8 oz onions; 2 oz lard; 1¼ lb tomatoes; 3 tablespoons tomato purée; paprika; pinch of marjoram and cumin. Cooking time: 2–3 hours.

Cut the meat in fairly large cubes. Brown the chopped onions in lard, add the beef, stir and cover the pan so that the meat gives off its juice. After a quarter of an hour add the tomato *purée*, ¼ pint water and the chopped tomatoes. Season with salt, marjoram, cumin, plenty of paprika, and a *bouquet garni*, cover and cook slowly for 2–3 hours. Serve in a deep dish, garnished with boiled or buttered potatoes.

Langue de Bœuf, sauce Madère   *   *Ox Tongue with Madeira sauce*

Ox tongue may be used fresh or pickled. Pickled is preferred, as it has more flavour and cooks more easily and in a rather shorter time.

Whether fresh or pickled, wash the tongue thoroughly and soak in salted water for 1 hour before cooking. Rinse and truss by passing a metal skewer under the tip and into the root.

Put a pickled tongue in cold water, unsalted, and a fresh tongue into boiling water with 2 tablespoons salt added. Flavour both with an onion stuck with cloves, a crushed clove of garlic and a *bouquet garni*. Boil up slowly and simmer until tender, i.e. the little bones in the root are easily pulled out. An average sized tongue—3½–4 pounds—takes 3½–4 hours, rather less if the tongue is pickled. When tender, skin carefully, beginning under the tip; remove the small bones in the root using 2 forks, and trim the root. Reheat tongue in the liquor and serve with various vegetables—French or haricot beans, green peas and carrots, mashed potatoes, etc. Serve also a piquant sauce, such as Caper or Madeira.

Miroton   *   *Boiled Beef with Sauce*

For 4 persons: 1¼ *lb boiled beef; 8 oz onions; 1 oz butter; 1 pint bouillon; white wine; 2 level tablespoons flour.*

Gently brown the sliced onions in butter, stir in the flour and let it colour; add the *bouillon* and boil up. Season and add the cold sliced beef. Simmer for 15 minutes and sprinkle a little white wine on top before serving.

Mixed Grill

For 4 persons: 4 small tournedos; 4 small veal fillets; 4 small slices of calf's liver; 4 chipolata sausages; 4 small lamb cutlets; 4 rashers of bacon; 4 half-tomatoes; 4 large mushrooms; Chipped potatoes; 2 oz Maître d'hôtel butter.

This dish consists of a variety of grilled meats attractively arranged on a round platter. But of course other grilled meat may be included, such as calf's kidneys, fillet of pork etc.

Paupiettes de Bœuf à l'Orientale   *   *Oriental Style Beef Olives*

For 4 persons: 1¼ lb rumpsteak; 2 oz ham; 2 oz butter; 6 oz mushrooms; 4 tomatoes; 2 onions; 6 oz cooked rice; 2 oz cooking fat; 1 tablespoon tomato purée; 6 tablespoons white wine; 1 carrot; 1 clove of garlic; 2 oz flour; 1 pint bouillon; bouquet garni. Cooking time: 2 hours.

Cut 8 slices of beef about 3 × 5 inches and beat out lightly. Spread with the following mixture: finely mince the onion, ham, mushroom stalks and brown them in 1 ounce butter. Season the beef, spread the minced, browned mixture on it, then roll up each slice, tying it at both ends and in the middle. Brown the beef olives gently in cooking fat with sliced onions and carrot. When browned add the *bouillon*, the tomato *purée*, the *bouquet garni* and the garlic. Stir until boiling, add the wine, cover and cook. When done, remove the string and arrange on the rice which has been boiled and kept hot. Place a mushroom cap cooked in butter on each olive and garnish with halved, grilled tomatoes. Strain the gravy and pour it over the meat.

Pointe de Bœuf Braisée à la Bourgeoise   *
Braised Beef Bourgeoise

For 4 persons: 2 lb aitchbone of beef; 4 heads of celery; 1¼ lb potatoes; 1 clove of garlic; 1 tablespoon chopped parsley; 4 tomatoes; 1 oz butter. Cooking time: 2½–3 hours.

Prepare and braise meat as for Braised Aitchbone of Beef (*p.* 119). Slice the beef and pour its own gravy over it and garnish with the lower part of 4 heads of braised celery, boiled potatoes, sprinkled with parsley, and a small mound of diced, peeled tomatoes sautéed in butter with a crushed clove of garlic.

Pointe de Culotte de Bœuf à l'Anglaise   *   *Boiled*
Topside of Beef

For 6 persons: 2½–3 lb topside or brisket of beef; 1¼ lb carrots; 8 oz turnips; 1–2 sticks celery; 2 leeks; 1 onion; bay leaf; seasoning; water. Cooking time: about 1½ hours.

Prepare the fresh vegetables. Put all ingredients in a pan and add water to come half way up the sides of the meat. Heat to boiling point. Skim. Simmer until tender. Additional vegetables may be added during the last hour or cooked separately. Serve the meat sliced and surround with vegetables. Use some of the liquor as a sauce or keep it for soup.

Queue de Bœuf en Hochepot   *   *Stewed Oxtail*

For 4 persons: 1 oxtail, weighing about 1½ lb; 8 chipolata sausages; 2 pig's feet, each cut into 4 pieces; 1 pig's ear; water; salt; 1 small cabbage; 12 shallots, or small onions; 12 turnips, olive shaped; 12 small carrots. Cooking time: 4 hours.

Buy the tail jointed. Scald well, dry and cut into pieces. Remove most of the fat from the root end. Scald the feet and the ear. Put the tail into a pan with the feet and the ear. Cover with cold water and add salt—1 teaspoonful to 2 pints water. Boil up and skim. Simmer for 3 hours. Add the root vegetables and quartered cabbage. Simmer for 1 hour longer. Grill the sausages. Serve the vegetables in the middle of a large dish. Arrange the tail around them, with the sausages, the feet and the ear cut into fine strips. Thicken ½ pint of the gravy with ½ ounce flour, blended with cold water. Boil up and pour round tail. Serve with boiled potatoes. Remaining gravy may be used for soup.

Roast Beef

For 6 persons: 2 lb rump, sirloin or rib cut thick; 2 onions; 2 carrots; 2 oz lard; seasoning; ¼ pint white wine; ¼ pint bouillon. Cooking time: 2 hours.

The joint may be roasted uncovered in the oven or pot roasted, with a lid on the pan. Cover the joint with thinly sliced kidney fat, to prevent dryness. Sprinkle salt in the roasting tin. Add lard and heat to smoking point. Brown the meat all over and roast for 10 minutes at 400°F or Gas Mark 6. Add vegetables cut in large pieces. Continue cooking until the beef is tender. Remove from pan and keep hot. Pour off surplus fat. Add wine and *bouillon* to the pan and reduce quickly by half. Season. Slice the meat thinly and strain the gravy over it.

Roast Beef Garnished with Vegetables

For 8 persons: 3 lb rolled beef or ribs of beef; 3 oz lard; 1 cauliflower; 8 small onions; 12 small carrots; seasoning. Cooking time: about 2 hours.

Sprinkle salt in *sauté* pan and add lard. Heat to smoking point and put in the beef. Brown it quickly all over. Transfer to a roasting tin, cover, and cook beef in a fairly hot oven, 375°F or Gas Mark 5, for 1 hour. Add carrots and sliced onions and continue cooking for ½ hour. Add cauliflower broken into florets, with a sprinkling of salt. Cook for ½ hour longer. Check for readiness by plunging a skewer into the thickest part—some blood should show at the puncture, as the beef should be served underdone. Serve the beef with the vegetables around it, or separately, with the gravy in a sauceboat.

To make the Gravy: Pour off excess fat. Add ¾ pint *bouillon* (or water). Reduce by fast boiling by one third. Check seasoning, and strain. Roast Beef is excellent served cold.

Roast Meat Loaf

For 6 persons: 2 eggs; ¼ pint milk; 2 oz raw rolled oats; 1 teaspoon salt; ½ teaspoon dried herbs; ¼ teaspoon pepper; 1 oz butter; 1 onion, coarsely chopped; 1½ lb minced steak; 1 lb sausage meat. Glaze: ¼ pint tomato sauce; few drops chilli sauce; 1 oz brown sugar; ¼ teaspoon dried mustard; ¼ teaspoon meat extract. Cooking time: 1¼ hours.

In large bowl, beat eggs lightly with fork. Stir in milk, oats, salt, herbs, and pepper; set aside. In hot butter in frying pan, *sauté* onion until tender, then add to egg mixture with meat; mix well until combined. Line 9 × 5 × 3 inch loaf tin with waxed paper. Turn meat mixture into tin, packing down well; refrigerate, covered, at least 2 hours. Run spatula around edge of meat loaf to loosen. Carefully turn out into shallow baking tin, keeping original shape as much as possible; bake in a moderate oven 30 minutes. Meanwhile make glaze: in a small bowl, combine all ingredients, mixing well. Brush top and sides of meat loaf with glaze. Bake further 45 minutes, brushing several times with glaze. Remove to hot plate and serve.

Rognons de Bœuf au Madère et aux Champignons
* *Ox Kidneys and Mushrooms with Madeira*

For 4 persons: 1½ lb ox kidney; 1 level tablespoon flour; 8 oz mushrooms; pinch sugar; ¾ pint bouillon; 4 oz butter; 4 tablespoons Madeira; 1 tablespoon tomato purée. Cooking time: 1 hour.

Remove skin, core and fat from the kidney. Slice thinly and *sauté* in 3 ounces very hot butter with sugar added over a high flame to close the pores, so that they do not lose their blood. Add the sliced mushrooms after sautéing them separately in remaining butter. Sprinkle with flour, and brown lightly, add Madeira, *bouillon* and the tomato *purée*, season, and boil up. Simmer until kidney is tender—1 hour—stirring frequently. Sprinkle with chopped parsley and serve at once with 6 ounces Boiled Macaroni (*p. 227*).

Note: Sheep kidneys are also good stewed. Split each kidney, skin and core. Cook as for ox kidney, allowing ½ hour.

Steak, Kidney and Mushroom Pie

For 6 persons: 2 sheep's kidneys; 2 lb round (rump) steak; seasoned flour; 2 oz butter; 2 chopped onions; 1 pint beef stock or bouillon; ½ bay leaf; 4 oz sliced mushrooms; 12 oz flaky or puff pastry; egg yolk for glazing. Cooking time: 2½ hours altogether.

Skin, core, and dice kidneys, cut steak into 1-inch cubes; toss in seasoned flour. Heat butter in saucepan, *sauté* onions until transparent, add steak and kidney, and cook until browned on all sides. Add stock, bay leaf and mushrooms, and simmer, covered, 1 to 1½ hours or until meat is almost tender. Adjust seasoning if necessary. Pour into pie dish, place pie funnel in centre of dish. Leave to cool. Roll out pastry to oblong just larger than pie dish. Cut thin strips from ends and fit around moistened edge of dish. Brush pastry rim with water and place remaining pastry on top of pie. Press edges together, trim off excess pastry, using sharp knife. Make 2 slits in centre to allow steam to escape. Glaze with beaten egg yolk. Stand dish on baking sheet, bake in hot oven 400°F or Gas Mark 6, for 20 to 25 minute, reduce heat to 375°F or Gas Mark 5, and bake further 25 to 30 minutes or until pastry is golden brown.

South Pacific Curry

For 4 persons: Meatballs: 1½ *lb lean minced beef;* 2 *oz shredded cabbage; pinch ground ginger;* 1 *large onion;* 1 *clove garlic; pinch ground cloves;* 1 *green pepper;* 2 *teaspoons curry powder;* 1 *teaspoon lemon juice; salt; seasoned flour; oil or fat for frying.* Cooking time: 30 minutes altogether.

Mince or finely chop onion, garlic, and green pepper. Mix together cabbage, ginger, cloves, curry powder, and meat. Season with salt, add lemon juice, and minced ingredients. Roll into balls, dust with seasoned flour. Brown balls in heated fat or oil. Drain, put aside.

Curry: 2 *oz butter;* 2 *sliced onions;* 1 *crushed clove garlic;* ½ *teaspoon ground ginger;* ½ *teaspoon turmeric;* ¼ *oz curry powder;* ¼ *teaspoon cayenne pepper; pinch cinnamon;* 2 *large tomatoes, skinned and sliced thickly;* 1 *small diced potato;* 8 *oz pineapple cubes;* ½ *pint coconut milk; salt; hot fluffy cooked rice.*
Heat butter in pan, add onion and garlic, *sauté* until light brown in colour. Add ginger, turmeric, curry powder, cayenne pepper, and cinnamon. Stir well, cook three minutes. Add sliced tomatoes, potato, and pineapple. Cook gently 5 minutes, stirring continuously. Add coconut milk and salt to taste; add meat balls. Cover, simmer gently about 15 to 20 minutes. Do not stir but shake pan lightly from time to time. Serve with hot fluffy rice.

Coconut milk: Pour ¾ pint water over 1¼ ounces of coconut in saucepan. Bring to the boil, turn off heat, stand a few minutes. Strain, press out liquid with a spoon.

TOURNEDOS * *TOURNEDOS*

Tournedos are cut from the fillet, they are 1¼–1½ inches thick, each weighing about 4 ounces. They are trimmed to a round shape and tied.

Tournedos à la Béarnaise * *Tournedos Béarnaise*

For 4 persons: 4 *slices fillet of beef, each weighing about 6 oz; oil; seasoning;* 4 *croûtons of toasted bread;* 1 *lb potatoes;* 4 *tablespoons sauce Béarnaise.* Cooking time: 4–5 minutes each side, according to the thickness.

Beat *tournedos* lightly. Season and marinate in oil for 10 minutes. Grill and arrange on *croûtons*. Garnish each with a tablespoon of *sauce Béarnaise*, and serve with Fondant potatoes. The *tournedos* must be served underdone.

▣ à la Chasseur * *Chasseur*

For 4 persons: 4 *slices fillet of beef, each weighing about 6 oz;* 8 *mushroom caps; scant* ¼ *pint white wine;* ½ *pint sauce Chasseur;* 1 *oz butter;* 1 *tablespoon oil;* 4 *croûtons;* 1 *tablespoon chopped parsley.* Cooking time: 4–5 minutes each side, according to size.

Sauté the *tournedos* in half butter and half oil. Keep hot and fry the *croûtons*, and grill the mushroom caps. Add the wine to the frying residue and reduce. Add to sauce Chasseur. Place *tournedos* on *croûtons*. Coat with *sauce Chasseur* and serve sprinkled with chopped parsley. Garnish with mushroom caps.

Tournedos Château Figeac * *Château Figeac*

For 4 persons: 4 tournedos; 4 cooked artichoke bottoms; 8 oz cooked asparagus tips; 8 oz small carrots; 12 mushroom caps; ½ pint sauce Bordelaise. Cooking time: 4–5 minutes, each side.

Sauté or grill the *tournedos*, mask with *sauce Bordelaise*. Garnish with the heated artichoke bottoms filled with asparagus tips and with the boiled carrots. Top each *tournedos* with three mushroom caps. Serve *Château* potatoes separately. (*See illustration p.* 114).

▣ Clamart * *Garnished with Peas*

For 4 persons: 4 slices fillet of beef, each weighing about 6 oz; 4 cooked artichoke bottoms; ½ pint green peas; 4 croûtons; 2 oz butter; seasoning. Cooking time: 6 minutes.

Sauté the *tournedos* in butter and fry the *croûtons*. Heat up artichoke bottoms and fill with peas, cooked *à la Française*. Serve *tournedos* on fried *croûtons*, sprinkle with the frying butter. Garnish with artichoke bottoms and green peas. Serve with *Noisette* potatoes and Madeira sauce.

▣ à l'Estragon * *with Tarragon*

For 4 persons: 4 slices fillet of beef, each weighing about 6 oz; tarragon; 2 oz butter; ¼ pint tomato juice; ¼ pint bouillon; 4 fried croûtons. Cooking time: 6 minutes.

Sauté the *tournedos* in butter, place on *croûtons* and arrange 3 or 4 blanched tarragon leaves in a cross on each. Add tomato juice to pan with *bouillon*. Reduce to a third. Coat *tournedos* with tomato-flavoured gravy cooked with a large pinch of chopped tarragon. Serve Roast potatoes or Chipped potatoes separately.

▣ Marie-Louise * *Marie-Louise*

For 4 persons: 4 tournedos; 2 oz butter; 4 cooked artichoke bottoms; 4 fried croûtons; 8 oz onion purée; ½ pint Demi-glace; 4 mushrooms; 8 oz Duchesse potatoes.

Sauté the *tournedos* and the mushrooms in butter. Heat artichoke bottoms and onion *purée*. Fry the *croûtons*. Place *tournedos* on *croûtons* and coat with light *Demi-glace*. Place on each an artichoke bottom filled with onion *purée* and decorated with a cooked mushroom cap. Surround with Duchesse potatoes.

▣ à la Portugaise * *Portuguese style*

For 4 persons: 4 tournedos, each weighing about 6 oz; 4 fried croûtons; 2 tomatoes; 2–3 tablespoons Tomato sauce; 8 oz mushrooms; ¼ pint white wine; 8 oz Fondant potatoes.

Sauté the *tournedos* in butter and place them on *croûtons*. Reduce the residue in the pan with the wine and Tomato sauce and pour over the *tournedos*. Place a half tomato stuffed with sautéed mushrooms on each *tournedos* and arrange a mound of Fondant potatoes in the middle.

Tripes à la Lyonnaise * *Tripe Lyonnaise*

For 4 persons: 1¼ lb cooked tripe; 3 oz lard; 1 oz flour; 8 oz onions; scant ¼ pint white wine; 3 tablespoons tomato purée; vinegar; seasoning; bouquet garni. Cooking time: 2–3 hours.

Pre-cooked tripe from the butcher must be used for this recipe, as raw tripe takes at least 8 hours cooking. Slice the tripe thinly and brown in 2 ounces of lard in a casserole; dust with flour, let it colour and add the wine and tomato *purée.* Add enough water to cover the tripe. Season with salt, pepper and *bouquet garni.* Brown the onions in 1 ounce lard in a frying pan and add to the tripe. Cook gently for 2–3 hours, stirring from time to time to prevent sticking. Skim fat off sauce and serve with a dash of vinegar and chopped parsley.

▣ à la mode de Caen * *Caen style*

For 8 persons: 4 lb tripe; 1 cow's heel; 8 oz kidney fat; 1 large bouquet garni; 4 tablespoons brandy; 3 onions; 3 carrots; the white of 4 leeks; 4 cloves; 6 peppercorns. Cooking time: 10–12 hours.

If the tripe is to be good it is necessary to prepare a large quantity. It keeps well and may be reheated without loss of flavour. Soak the tripe in running water for several hours. Blanch, cool, and cut up. Place half in an earthenware ovenproof dish with the sliced onions, quartered carrots, the *bouquet garni* and leeks. Add 6 peppercorns and 4 cloves in a muslin bag, the chopped up fat and the quartered cow's heel. Place the remainder of the tripe on top and add salt. Add the brandy and enough water to cover the tripe completely. Do not use white wine or cider, this would turn the sauce black. Seal the dish hermetically with dough or use foil and a close-fitting lid. Start at low heat and leave in a moderate oven, 350°F or Gas Mark 4, for 12 hours. When the tripe is cooked skim the fat off the sauce and serve boiling hot.

LE BŒUF FROID * *COLD BEEF*

Beefsteak Tartare

For 2 persons: 8 oz rump or fillet steak; salt and pepper; 2 egg yolks; onion rings; chopped capers; chopped parsley.

Remove fat and sinews from the steak. Mince the meat twice. Add salt and pepper. Divide into 2 equal portions. Shape each into a round flat cake. Make a hollow nest in the middle of each—put ½ an eggshell containing a raw egg yolk in this nest. Garnish with onion rings, chopped capers and chopped parsley.

Bœuf à la mode en Gelée * *Beef à la mode in Aspic*

For 6 persons: Same ingredients as for Beef à la mode; 1 calf's foot; 4 oz fresh pork rinds.

Prepare in the same way as Beef *à la mode*, adding the calf's foot and pork rinds. When everything is cooked, drain the meat, calf's foot, rinds, carrots and onions. Decorate the bottom of a bowl with the carrots and onions. Place the beef in the middle and surround

▲ *Côtelettes d'agneau, sauce peperonata, p. 152*

Mutton chops, p. 151 ▼ 133

134 ▲ *Côtelettes de porc aux pommes, p. 155*

Gigot d'agneau à la boulangère, p. 153 ▼

▲ *Médaillons de porc à la hongroise. p. 156*

Jambon braisé, p. 159 135

▲ *Côtelette de porc glacée, p. 155*

Choucroute garnie, p. 199 ▼

with the remaining vegetables. The calf's foot may be added, but it must be sliced, as it is hard when cold. Skim the fat off the gravy when it is cold, strain it through a cloth and pour it over everything. Leave to set and turn out the next day.

The same dish may be made with veal.

Bœuf à la Niçoise * Niçoise

For 4 persons: About 1 lb cold roast or boiled beef without bones; cooked French beans or other vegetables; 3 tomatoes; 2 hardboiled eggs; gherkins.

Make a salad of French beans, to which may be added cauliflower sprigs, or any other leftover vegetables. Dress this salad on a round dish, carve the meat in thin slices and lay on top of salad, surround with slices of very firm skinned tomatoes and cover the whole with a *sauce Vinaigrette* with a pinch of mustard. Decorate the meat with sliced hardboiled eggs, tomatoes and gherkins. (*See illustration p.* 113).

Salade de Bœuf * Beef Salad

In addition to these recipes, beef may also be served with salad accompanied by *mayonnaise, Tartare sauce,* etc. Recipes will be found in the *hors d'œuvre* section.

Turban de Bœuf à la Gelée * Turban of Beef in Aspic

For 4 persons: 1 lb boiled beef; ½ pint aspic; 2 hardboiled eggs; fine herbs; 4 oz boiled ham; 2 gherkins; 1 skinned tomato; potato and French bean salad; ¼ pint mayonnaise.

Cut the beef and the ham in match-like strips. Chop the hardboiled eggs and gherkins and mix everything with cold aspic on the point of setting. Pour into a *savarin* mould and put in a cold place to set. Turn out and fill the centre with Potato salad and French beans bound with *mayonnaise*. Decorate with a sliced tomato. (*See illustration p.* 113).

LANGUE DE BŒUF * OX TONGUE

Dressed Tongue

1 boiled tongue; Glaze; cold aspic; Maître d'hôtel butter; lettuce; tomato.

Cook the tongue as directed on p. 125. Skin the tongue while hot. Remove the root bones. Set the tongue on a board, and fix it to the board by pushing a skewer through the root and into the board. Push another skewer into the board in front of the tip so that the tongue is arched.

When cold, trim the root end; remove the skewers and brush the tongue with glaze, then coat with cold aspic. Decorate with *Maître d'hôtel* butter and serve on lettuce with sliced tomato round. Fasten a frill round the root end.

▣ Pressed

When skinned and trimmed, curl the tongue round and pack into a round tin—it must be a tight fit. Weight it down. Turn out when cold and finish with glaze etc. Serve on lettuce.

LE VEAU * VEAL

Blanquette de Veau * White Stew of Veal

For 4–6 persons: 2 lb stewing (shoulder) veal; 20 button onions: 3 medium carrots; 8 oz mushrooms; 3 oz butter; 1½ oz flour; 4 tablespoons cream; 1 egg yolk; chopped parsley; seasoning. Cooking time: 1½ hours.

Cut up the veal into convenient sized pieces and put it into a saucepan with cold water to cover. After it has boiled for 5–6 minutes, hold the saucepan under the cold tap and cool and rinse the meat well. Cover with fresh water, salt, *bouquet garni*, sliced carrots and onions. Replace lid and cook gently for 1¼ hours or until the veal is quite tender. Make a white *roux* with 2 ounces butter and the flour. Whisk in 1 pint of the strained liquor. Make into a creamy sauce, cook it for 15 minutes, beat in egg yolk and add the mushrooms cooked in remaining butter and cream. Combine sauce and veal and simmer gently for 1–2 minutes. Correct seasoning. Serve the veal and vegetables on a hot dish, with the mushrooms on top. Strain the sauce over, and scatter with chopped parsley.

Cervelles de Veau au Beurre Noir * Calf's Brains in Black Butter

For 4 persons: 2 lb brains; 1 pint bouillon; 2 oz butter. Cooking time: 20 minutes.

Soak the brains for several hours, changing the water several times. Skin and cook in *bouillon*. Drain, serve and sprinkle with Black butter.

The brains may also be deep-fried and served with Tomato sauce or White sauce mixed with some *mayonnaise*.

▣ Beignets * Fritters

For 4 persons: 2 lb cooked brains; Frying batter; fried parsley; sliced lemon; Tomato sauce or White sauce with mayonnaise.

Cut brains into neat pieces. Dip in batter and fry them in hot deep fat until golden brown. Cool fat slightly and fry parsley. Drain and season. Serve with lemon and sauce.

Cœurs de Veaux * Calf's Heart Sautéed

For 4 persons: 2 hearts; 2 oz butter; 8 slices lean bacon; 1 oz flour; seasoning; 1½ lb boiled potatoes; ½ pint sauce Chasseur; chopped parsley. Cooking time: 20 minutes.

Cut hearts into thin slices. Fry bacon rashers, remove and keep warm. Add butter to bacon fat. Toss heart slices in seasoned flour and *sauté* in the fats. Serve garnished with bacon. Sprinkle with the fats used for cooking and some chopped parsley. Serve *sauce Chasseur* and boiled potatoes.

CÔTELETTES DE VEAU * VEAL CUTLETS

Côtelettes de Veau à la Bonne Femme * Veal Cutlets Bonne femme

For 4 persons: 4 veal cutlets; 1 tablespoon flour; 2 oz butter; 2 oz lean bacon; 15 button onions; ¾ lb new potatoes; ¼ pint bouillon; seasoning. Cooking time: 20 minutes.

Take some fairly thick cutlets. Beat well, salt and pepper them and flour both sides. *Sauté* in hot butter for 10 minutes over moderate heat (the butter must not turn black). Cover with button onions glazed separately, diced potatoes cooked in butter and fried cubes of lean bacon. Add *bouillon*. Cover and simmer until tender. Serve cutlets with vegetables, and pour sauce round.

▣ Côtelettes en Cocotte à la Crème　*　*in Cream*

For 4 persons: 4 cutlets; 2 oz butter; ¼ pint cream; Fondant potatoes; seasoning. Cooking time: 20 minutes.

Beat cutlets, season them and toss in flour. Cook the cutlets in butter in a casserole over a moderate flame so that they do not turn too brown. When tender, pour in the cream and bring it to simmering point, add salt and pepper and serve in the casserole. Serve with Fondant potatoes.

▣ en Cocotte à la Ménagère　*　*Ménagère*

For 4 persons: 4 cutlets; 2 oz butter; 15–20 glazed button onions; 8 oz carrots; ¾ lb potatoes; scant ¼ pint white wine. Cooking time: 40 minutes.

Sauté the cutlets in butter in an earthenware casserole. Add the onions, the carrots and the potatoes. Add the wine, cover and leave to cook gently.

▣ Grillées　*　*Grilled*

For 4 persons: 4 cutlets; seasoning; 1 tablespoon flour; 2 oz butter; green peas. Cooking time: 15–20 minutes.

Salt, pepper and roll the cutlets in flour. Brush with melted butter and place on a rather hot grill. Cook slowly, turning and buttering frequently to prevent the surface from drying out. Serve with *Maître d'hôtel* butter and a garnish of green peas.

▣ Pojarski　*　*Pojarski*

For 4 persons: 1¼ lb fillet of veal; 2 onions; 6 oz butter; 2 oz white bread; 1 egg; paprika; ½ pint Sour cream sauce; breadcrumbs. Cooking time: 12 minutes.

Remove all sinews from the meat, mince twice and mix with chopped onions cooked until soft in 2 ounces butter, seasoning, and stale bread soaked in milk, squeezed out and crumbled. Season and shape into 8 cutlets. Push a piece of macaroni into each cutlet to represent a cutlet bone. Egg and breadcrumb, and fry quickly in very hot butter. Arrange in a circle on a round dish, and decorate with a cutlet frill. Serve with a garnish of vegetables and *sauce Smitane* (Sour cream sauce).

▣ Sautées　*　*Sautéed with Sherry*

For 4 persons: 4 veal chops; salt and pepper; 1-2 oz butter; ½ oz finely chopped chives; 4 tablespoons sherry; about ¼ pint cream; 4 oz thinly sliced mushrooms; little extra butter. Cooking time: 25 minutes.

Season chops with salt and pepper, *sauté* gently in melted butter. When cooked (they should take approximately 20 minutes, depending on size and thickness of the chops), transfer to heated dish, sprinkle with chives; keep warm. Stir cream and sherry into pan juices, and add mushrooms which have been sautéed gently in another pan in a little butter. Cook about 5 minutes, but do not allow to boil. Season to taste and pour over chops; serve at once.

139

Côtelettes de Veau Sautées aux Fines Herbes   *
Sautéed with Fine Herbs

For 4 persons: 4 cutlets; 3 oz butter; scant ¼ pint white wine; 1 teaspoon fine herbs. Cooking time: 15–20 minutes.

Salt, pepper and flour cutlets on both sides. Fry in 2 ounces very hot butter. Place on a dish, put remaining butter, wine and chopped fine herbs in the pan, boil up briskly and pour over the meat.

Emincé de Veau à la Crème   *   *Sliced Veal in Cream Sauce*

For 6 persons: 1¾ lb fillet of veal cut into very thin slices; 1 tablespoon flour; 1 chopped onion; 6 tablespoons white wine; 3 oz butter; 1 teaspoon meat glaze; ¼ pint fresh cream; lemon juice; 8 oz mushrooms. Cooking time: 8–10 minutes.

Beat the veal until it is parchment thin. Season with salt and pepper, coat with flour and score on both sides. *Sauté* quickly in very hot butter, keeping the veal underdone, then drain. Fry the onion in butter in the same pan until it takes colour lightly and add the white wine. Scrape the pan with a wooden spoon to detach the juices, reduce the wine by a third, add the meat glaze and cream and boil up for a moment only, to keep the sauce fairly thin. Adjust the seasoning and add a few drops of lemon juice and the meat. Heat until the meat begins to cook, then transfer to a deep dish. Add finely sliced, cooked mushrooms if desired. Serve very hot.

▣ à la Piémontaise   *   *Piémontaise*

For 4 persons: 1 lb fillet of veal; seasoning; 1 tablespoon flour; 3 oz butter; 8 oz rice; 1 tablespoon tomato purée; 8 oz mushrooms; ½ pint sauce Béchamel. Cooking time: 8 minutes.

Cut the veal into 4 slices and beat lightly. Season and toss in flour. Score on both sides. Make a *Risotto*, adding tomato *purée* to flavour and colour. Fry the veal quickly in butter. Fry the mushrooms and season them. Shape the *Risotto* into a ring in a round dish. Add veal and mushrooms to *sauce Béchamel*. Heat up and fill the ring with this mixture.

ESCALOPES DE VEAU   *   *ESCALOPES OF VEAL*

Escalopes de Veau à l'Anglaise   *   *Breadcrumbed Escalope of Veal*

For 4 persons: 4 escalopes, each weighing about 4½ oz; 1 egg white; 2 tablespoons olive oil; breadcrumbs; 2 oz butter. Cooking time: 8 minutes.

Season the veal, which should be cut thin. Beat well, flour, dip in egg white beaten with an equal part of oil and roll in the breadcrumbs. Pat crumbs in thoroughly and score fillets on both sides. Then fry in butter, not too briskly, to avoid burning the bread before the meat is cooked. Serve sprinkled with lemon juice and the cooking butter. Never pour sauces or other liquids over breadcrumbed meat, since the aim of breadcrumbing is to give a crisp surface. Serve with various vegetables.

▣ à la Chasseur   *   *Chasseur*

For 4 persons: 4 escalopes, each weighing about 4½–5 oz; 8 oz mushrooms; 2 chopped shallots; ¼ pint white wine; chopped parsley; ¼ pint sauce Demi-glace. Cooking time: 12–15 minutes.

Beat *escalopes* well, then *sauté* and brown in butter and oil. Add the wine, season, cover and cook gently. In the meantime, clean and slice the mushrooms, reserving 4 whole mushrooms for garnish; brown them in butter and oil, add shallots, parsley and sauce, pour the whole over the *escalopes* and simmer for a few minutes. Arrange the meat in a ring with the mushrooms in the middle and a mushroom cap on each *escalope*.

Escalopes de Veau Cordon Bleu * with Ham and Cheese

For 6 persons: 12 veal escalopes, each weighing about 2 oz; 6 slices ham, *each weighing about ½ oz; 6 slices gruyère cheese each weighing about ½ oz; 2 eggs; breadcrumbs; flour; 4 oz cooked spaghetti, tossed in butter; 2 oz clarified butter.* Cooking time: about 15 minutes.

Flatten and season the *escalopes*. Sandwich them in pairs with a slice of ham and a slice of cheese, coat with flour, dip in beaten egg and then in breadcrumbs, patting the breadcrumbs well in. Fry on one side and then on the other in clarified butter until golden-brown. Serve *spaghetti* down middle of hot serving dish, and arrange *escalopes* overlapping on top.

▣ à la Viennoise * Viennoise

For 4 persons: 4 escalopes, each weighing about 4–5 oz; seasoned flour; *egg and breadcrumbs; 3 oz butter + 1 tablespoon oil for frying.* Cooking time: 6 minutes. *Garnish:* 4 slices lemon; 4 stoned olives; 4 anchovy fillets; 2 tablespoons chopped parsley; 1 hardboiled egg, yolk and white sieved separately; 2 tablespoons chopped capers; 1 **oz** *Noisette butter; juice of 1 lemon.*

Beat *escalopes* until parchment thin, then toss in flour and coat with egg and breadcrumbs, patting the crumbs well in. Score on both sides. Fry in hot butter and oil for 3 minutes on each side. Place a stoned olive, with anchovy wrapped round it, on each slice of lemon, and top each *escalope* with this. Arrange lines of white of egg, parsley, yolk of egg and capers round the dish in this order. Lay the *escalopes* down the middle. Add lemon juice to sizzling *Noisette* butter and pour over the veal.

Foie de Veau à l'Anglaise * Calf's Liver and Bacon

For 4 persons: 4 slices calf's liver, each weighing about 4 oz; 1 tablespoon *seasoned flour; 8 slices lean bacon; 3 oz butter.* Cooking time: 2 minutes each side.

Remove skin and tubes from the liver and flatten with a knife. Scrape the bacon slightly and fry in the frying pan, then remove it and keep warm. Leave the bacon fat in the pan, add butter and quickly *sauté* the liver, after first flouring it lightly. Serve garnished with the bacon. Sprinkle with the butter used in cooking. Serve boiled potatoes separately. (*See illustration p.* 115).

Fricandeau à l'Oseille * Veal Fricandeau with Sorrel

For 4 persons: 1¼ lb topside or fillet of veal; 1 oz lardoons; 1 oz bacon; 1 *onion; 2 carrots; 1 bouquet garni; ½ pint bouillon; 2 lb sorrel.* Cooking time: 1½ hours.

Take a large, thick slice of veal, trim and lard it. Place the meat in a roasting pan lined with the bacon in strips, sliced onions and carrots, and the *bouquet garni*. Cover closely with greased paper and the lid. Cook on the stove until the vegetables colour and add enough *bouillon* or some rather fat brown gravy, to cover the vegetables. Season and place in the oven. Braise in a fairly hot oven, 375°F or Gas Mark 5, basting frequently to glaze the meat well, and adding more *bouillon* as required. Cook the sorrel as indicated on *p*. 205. Serve meat on a layer of sorrel which has been mixed with cream. Pour the well-reduced gravy, with the fat skimmed off, on top. The sorrel may be replaced by any other vegetable or by mushrooms (8 ounces). Mushrooms should be shredded and cooked in a little *bouillon* with a knob of butter added. Spinach and peas are also suitable.

Jarret de Veau ou Osso Bucco   *   *Knuckle of Veal or Osso Bucco*

For 4 persons: 4 slices knuckle of veal about 2 inches thick; 2 oz butter or lard; 4 tablespoons oil; 2 carrots; 1 head of celery; half an onion; parsley; zest of 1 lemon; 2 tablespoons concentrated tomato paste; about 1¾ pints bouillon; ½ pint white wine; 1 clove garlic. Cooking time: 1½–2 hours.

Coat the slices of veal in flour and fry lightly in the oil and butter. Add the finely diced carrots, onion and celery and brown. Moisten with the white wine. Add the tomato paste, season and reduce. Add *bouillon* to come half-way up the meat. When the meat is tender add the parsley, lemon zest and finely chopped garlic. Serve mashed potatoes separately. (*See illustration p.* 116).

Langue de Veau à la Duchesse   *   *Calf's Tongue Duchess*

For 6 persons: 1 pickled tongue; 2 oz lard or butter; 1 lb potatoes; 1 pint sauce Demi-glace; 2 tablespoons tomato purée; ¼ pint white wine; 2 onions; 3 carrots; 2 shallots; fine herbs; 2 gherkins. Cooking time: 2–3 hours.

Soak tongue and wash well. Blanch, cool and scrape it to remove the white skin. Cut the onions, carrots and shallots into small, very regular dice and brown in the fat together with the tongue. When the vegetables have coloured add the wine and *sauce Demi-glace*, strongly flavoured with tomato; season, cover closely and braise gently for 2–3 hours or until tender. Skim fat off sauce, add 1 or 2 diced gherkins and a pinch of chopped fine herbs. Skin tongue and remove bones at the root. Slice the tongue and place it in the middle of a long dish edged with a border of Duchess potatoes browned in the oven. Pour sauce over tongue without straining.

Médaillons de Veau Véronèse   *   *Veal Medallions Véronèse*

For 4 persons: 8 medallions of veal (slices cut from the choicest part of the fillet); 1 tablespoon seasoned flour; 2 oz butter; 4 oz sliced ham; 4 black olives; 8 oz roughly chopped tomatoes; ¾ lb green noodles. Cooking time: 10 minutes.

Boil the noodles in salted water for 20 minutes. Rinse well in boiling water. Drain and add a knob of butter. Coat medallions with flour and *sauté* in butter until well browned on both sides. Cut out small rounds of ham, using a knife or cutter and fry them lightly in butter. Place one on each medallion. Arrange the medallions on the cooked noodles, which have been kept hot and buttered. Top each medallion with a spoonful of chopped tomato and sprinkle with *Noisette* butter (butter cooked to a nut-brown colour). Garnish with half an olive (*See illustration p.* 116).

Nids d'Hirondelles   *   *Swallows' Nests*

For 4 persons: 4 escalopes of veal, each weighing about 4 oz; 4 very thin slices ham; 2 tablespoons chopped onions; 4 hardboiled eggs; parsley; flour; butter; 2 carrots; 8 small onions; 2 tablespoons white wine; ¼ pint bouillon; 1 teaspoon flour; 12 oz Potato purée. Cooking time: 1¼ hours.

Use thin escalopes, and beat well to flatten. Season, cover with a little chopped onion cooked in butter, and chopped parsley. Place a slice of ham on each, then a hardboiled egg. Tie up and roll in flour. Brown in butter with sliced carrots and small onions, add wine and braise in a warm oven for 1 hour, adding the *bouillon* gradually and basting frequently. After cooking, allow to rest for a few minutes, then remove the string and cut each roll in half. Pipe potato *purée* in the form of nests with half a veal roll in each. Thicken the sauce with flour, 2 teaspoons flour per ¼ pint sauce. Serve the sauce separately.

NOIX DE VEAU * *FILLET OF VEAL*

As a large piece of fillet of veal is often difficult to obtain in one piece, you may substitute loin, shoulder or leg of veal in the following 3 recipes.

Noix de Veau en Casserole à la Grand'Mère *
Casseroled Veal

For 6 persons: 2 lb of veal; 3 oz dripping; 25 small shallots; 6 oz lean bacon; 1 bouquet garni; 2 tablespoons tomato purée; 1¼ lb chestnuts; ½ pint bouillon. Cooking time: about 1½ hours.

Brown the meat and shallots in dripping, surround with the bacon cut in strips and peeled chestnuts. Add the *bouillon*, salt, pepper, a *bouquet garni* and 1 or 2 tablespoons of tomato *purée;* cover closely and cook in a moderate oven.

To peel chestnuts: Either boil chestnuts for 10 minutes, then remove outer shell and brown skin. Or slit chestnut shells and put nuts into a moderately hot oven, 375°F or Gas Mark 5, until they crack, when shells are easily removed.

▣ Judic * *Judic*

For 6 persons: 2 lb of veal; 3 oz dripping or butter; 4 oz onions; 8 oz carrots; 2 oz bacon; seasoning; bouquet garni; ½ pint bouillon. Garnish: 3 Braised lettuces; 6 Stuffed tomatoes; 3 lb Château potatoes; ¼ pint Madeira sauce. Cooking time: 1½ hours.

Brown the trimmed meat with the sliced onion, carrots and bacon in dripping in a casserole. Cover closely and sweat for 5 minutes. Add *bouillon*, seasoning and *bouquet garni*. Replace lid and cook until tender. Remove meat and keep hot. Strain the gravy and thicken with flour—1 teaspoon for each ¼ pint gravy. Pour into a sauceboat. Serve the meat, surrounded by Braised lettuces, coated with Madeira sauce, and Stuffed tomatoes. Serve potatoes separately.

▣ Rôtie, Champignons * *Roast, with Mushrooms*

For 6–8 persons: 1 fillet veal weighing about 3–4 lb; ½ oz prepared mustard; 1 oz finely chopped parsley; 2 oz softened butter; 1 onion, sliced; 1 piece celery, sliced; 1 carrot sliced; ½ pint chicken or veal stock; ½ lb mushrooms, sliced and sautéed in a little extra butter; extra ½ teaspoon mustard; salt; pepper. Cooking time: 1¾–2 hours.

Make a paste of the mustard, parsley, and butter. Spread over the veal. Place in a baking dish with the onion, carrot, and celery. Add stock, cook in hot oven, 400°F of Gas Mark 6, for 20 minutes, then reduce heat to 350°F or Gas Mark 4, and continue cooking, allowing 25 minutes per pound cooking time; baste frequently. Remove meat to serving dish and keep warm. Skim fat from pan juices and reduce slightly over moderate heat—there should be about ½ pint liquid remaining; strain and return to pan. Add the mushrooms, extra mustard, salt and pepper, reheat; slice meat and spoon sauce over.

Noix de Veau Rôtie, Pommes Paille   *   *Roast Veal with Straw Potatoes*

For 6 persons: 2 lb of veal, in a thick piece; 1 onion; 1 carrot; ¼ pint bouillon; 6 tomatoes; 1½ lb Straw potatoes; chopped parsley; 2 oz butter. Cooking time: 1½ hours.

Season the meat, put it into a roasting pan, sprinkle with melted butter and brown all over rather quickly. Add the sliced onion and carrot. Brown them, then add the *bouillon*, cover the pan with another roasting pan, and cook in the oven, 400°F or Gas Mark 6, basting frequently. Score the tomatoes in the shape of a cross to a depth of about ⅖ inch, salt them and add to the meat after 1 hour 20 minutes. To check whether the meat is done, push a trussing needle deeply into it. When withdrawn, a bead of clear liquid should appear. Remove the meat and the tomatoes, skim off the fat and thin the gravy with a little *bouillon*. Strain, heat and thicken with flour. Serve separately.

Slice the meat thinly and garnish the dish with Straw potatoes and the tomatoes, sprinkled with a little butter and chopped parsley.

Paupiettes de Veau Braisées   *   *Braised Veal Birds or Olives*

For 4 persons: 4 escalopes, each weighing about 4 oz; 4 oz Pork forcemeat; 1 oz butter; 1 onion; 2 carrots (4 oz); bouillon; 4 bacon rashers. Cooking time: 1 hour.

Veal birds are made with very thin *escalopes*. Season and cover with a thin layer of Pork forcemeat sprinkled with fine herbs, roll up, wrap in bacon, and tie with string. Brown quickly in butter with sliced onions and carrots. When everything is well browned fill pan half-way with *bouillon*. Cover with oiled paper and cook in a fairly hot oven, 375°F or Gas Mark 5, basting frequently. When tender, remove bacon and string. Skim fat carefully off gravy before serving and accompany with green peas, spinach *Risotto*, or Duchess potatoes.

▣ Braisées à la Grecque   *   *Braised Veal Olives Greek style*

For 4 persons: 4 escalopes, each weighing about 4 oz; 1 onion; breadcrumbs; 4 oz ham; tomato purée; 6 oz Risotto; 2 oz butter. Cooking time: 45–50 minutes.

Season and flatten thin *escalopes*. Spread with finely chopped onion cooked in butter, a little crumbled dry white bread, and chopped parsley. Then place a very thin slice of ham on each *escalope*, roll up and tie both ends. Braise as above with tomato-flavoured gravy, remove string and serve on *Risotto*.

Pieds de Veau Vinaigrette   *   *Calf's Feet Vinaigrette*

For 4 persons: 4 lb calf's feet; bouillon; 2 onions; 1 carrot; half a lemon; 1 hardboiled egg; ¼ pint Vinaigrette dressing; fine herbs. Cooking time: 3½ hours.

Bone the calf's feet and put into cold water and boil for 5 minutes. Cool and rinse thoroughly under the cold tap; drain and rub with half a lemon. Cook in *bouillon* with an onion and carrot for 3 hours. Cut into fine strips while hot, and combine with *sauce Vinaigrette* so that they remain soft. Add to the *Vinaigrette* a chopped hardboiled egg, finely chopped herbs and 1 or 2 tablespoons of the liquor. Eat hot or cold.

Poitrine de Veau Farcie   *   *Stuffed Breast of Veal*

For 8 persons: 3 lb breast of veal; 1 lb sausage meat, mixed with 2 chopped onions cooked in butter and chopped fine herbs; 3 oz bread; bouillon; 1 egg; 2 carrots; 2 onions; 1 oz lard. Cooking time: 2 hours.

Bone the breast and make a slit in the underside to form a pocket. Bind the sausage meat with an egg and white bread dipped in *bouillon*. Fill the breast with this stuffing and sew up the opening. Lightly brown sliced carrots and onions. Add veal and when brown cover vegetables with *bouillon*. Braise closely covered in a hot oven, 400°F or Gas Mark 6. Skim off fat and serve breast sliced and sprinkled with the gravy. Garnish with carrot and turnip cut into strips and cooked separately; serve also mashed potatoes. Vegetables used as braise foundation are never used as garnish. Stuffed breast is also excellent cold.

Quasi ou Longe de Veau en Casserole   *
Casseroled Loin of Veal

For 4 persons: 2 lb loin or boned shoulder; 2 oz cooking fat; 2 onions; 2 carrots; seasoning. Cooking time: about 1½ hours.

Brown the meat in the casserole with butter or good cooking fat, adding sliced onions and carrots and a seasoning of salt and pepper. Add only ¼ pint of water and seal the casserole hermetically. Cook in a fairly hot oven, 375°F or Gas Mark 5, until the meat may easily be pierced with a skewer. Very little liquid is needed to start with as the meat will cook in its own juice. A garnish, such as small onions, carrots, potatoes, artichoke bottoms, etc., may be cooked round the meat. Rice or a similar garnish is cooked separately. (*See illustration p.* 115).

To seal hermetically: Make a flour and water dough. Work up until smooth and pack round join of lid to casserole.

Ragoût de Veau aux Légumes   *   *Stewed Veal with Vegetables*

For 4 persons: 1½ lb shoulder or breast of veal; 2 oz butter; 1 pint bouillon; 20 button onions; 1¼ lb carrots, celeriac or turnips; 2 tomatoes; ¾ lb green peas; ¼ pint cream; ½ oz flour. Cooking time: about 2 hours.

Cut up the meat and toss it in butter without letting it colour. Dredge with flour, add the *bouillon*, season, cover and cook for ¾ hour. Prepare a garnish of diced vegetables and green peas. Mix the vegetables with the meat, cover well, and cook for ¾ hour. Place in a dish and thicken the sauce with flour mixed with fresh cream.

RIS DE VEAU   *   SWEETBREADS

General preparation before cooking is as follows:—

Wash well and soak for 1 hour in cold water. Wash again and put on to boil in cold water. Boil up and blanch for 5 minutes. Dip in cold water to stiffen, and rinse. Remove gristly parts, fat and loose skin. Wrap in muslin and press between 2 plates for 1 hour—this breaks the fibres and prevents shrinkage during cooking.

Ris de Veau Braisé à la Jardinière   *   *Braised Veal Sweetbreads with Vegetables*

For 4 persons: 1¼ lb sweetbreads; 4 fried bread croûtons; 2 oz butter; bouquet garni; 1 onion; 2 carrots; 2 oz bacon; ¾ pint bouillon. Garnish: 1½ lb mixed vegetables. Cooking time: 1 hour.

Prepare sweetbreads as above. Braise for 30–40 minutes on a bed of roughly cut vegetables and chopped bacon as for *Fricandeau* with Sorrel (*p*. 141). While they cook, prepare a gar-nish—carrots, turnips, French beans, green peas. All these vegetables, properly trimmed, cooked separately, then tossed in butter, are placed in mounds around the sweetbreads, which are arranged on fried *croûtons* in the middle of the dish and sprinkled with their own gravy. The dish may be improved by decorating it with sliced truffles and grilled mush-rooms. (*See illustration p*. 114).

Ris de Veau à la Crème   *   *with Cream*

For 4 persons: 1 lb blanched sweetbreads; seasoning; 2 oz butter; 1 table-spoon flour; scant ½ pint cream; 6 oz mushrooms; half a lemon; 2 tablespoons brandy. Cooking time: 20 minutes.

Slice prepared sweetbreads. Season, flour and fry in butter on both sides for about 8 minutes. Slice mushrooms and cook in 1 tablespoon cream and ½ ounce butter until tender. Place sweetbreads on a dish, pour cream into the pan wth lemon juice and brandy and reduce to half; add cooked mushrooms, boil up again once or twice and pour over sweetbreads.

ROGNONS DE VEAU   *   *CALF'S KIDNEYS*

Rognons de Veau à l'Anglaise   *   *Calf's Kidneys à l'Anglaise*

For 4 persons: 2 kidneys; 2 oz butter; breadcrumbs; 1 egg; parsley; half a lemon. Cooking time: 6–8 minutes.

Remove the core and most of the kidney fat. Halve kidneys, wash and dry. Season, dip in flour and in beaten egg mixed with a little oil. Roll in fine breadcrumbs and press the crumbs well in. Place them in a lightly greased, heated baking dish and cook in a very hot oven, or grill them 3–4 minutes on each side, basting with butter. Serve with *Maître d'hôtel* butter.

▣ Sautés   *   *Sautéed*

For 4 persons: 2 kidneys; 8 oz mushrooms; fine herbs; 2 oz butter; scant ¼ pint white wine or Madeira. Cooking time: 4–6 minutes.

Slice the kidneys thinly and *sauté* them in butter in a frying pan over a brisk flame. Very finely sliced mushrooms may be sautéed with the kidneys or separately. At the last moment reduce with white wine or Madeira. Serve sprinkled with chopped fine herbs. Kidneys are usually served with Rice *Pilaff* (*p*. 229).

Roulade de Veau   *   *Stuffed Rolled Veal*

For 8 persons: 2 lb veal; 2 oz dripping; 2 onions; 2 carrots; bouquet garni. Stuffing: 4 oz bread; 2 onions; 2 shallots; 1 oz butter; fine herbs; 1¼ lb sausage meat; ¼ pint tomato-flavoured gravy. Cooking time: about 2 hours.

This is a very popular dish for large families. The best cuts to use are boned shoulder or breast. Flatten the meat well. Mix the bread, dipped in *bouillon* or milk, the chopped onions and shallots cooked in butter, the chopped fine herbs and sausage meat and season. Spread this stuffing over the meat and roll. Tie up, not too tightly, brown in dripping and cook gently for 2 hours in a casserole with onions, sliced carrots and a little tomato-flavoured gravy. When tender, remove string. Serve with a vegetable and the sauce with the fat skim-med off. The left-overs may be sliced and eaten cold with gherkins and salad.

Sauté de Veau Marengo   *   *Sautéed Veal Marengo* (*or with Mushrooms*)

For 4 persons: 1¼ *lb shoulder of veal; 2 onions; flour; 1 clove of garlic;* ¼ *pint white wine; 2 oz butter; oil; 1 bouquet garni; chopped parsley; 2 tablespoons tomato* purée; *bouillon; 4 oz mushrooms; croûtons.* Cooking time: about 2 hours.

Cut up the meat and brown well in butter mixed with an equal quantity of oil. When it is well browned, add the chopped onions. Let them colour, too, add a shaking of flour and the crushed garlic. Add the wine and tomato *purée* to make the sauce, which may be thinned with a little *bouillon*. Season, add the *bouquet garni* and cook for 1½ hours. Add the mushrooms and allow another half hour or so to finish cooking. Carefully skim fat off sauce and serve with heart-shaped bread *croûtons*, fried in oil. Sprinkle chopped parsley over and serve.

Tendrons de Veau à la Paysanne   *   *Tendrons of Veal Paysanne*

For 4 persons: 4 *slices breast of veal, weighing about* 1½ *lb; 1 oz lard; 2 carrots; a* ¼ *turnip; 2 onions; 2 tomatoes; 8 medium-sized potatoes; 3 tablespoons white wine; salt; pepper;* ½ *pint bouillon.* Cooking time: about 1½ hours.

Tendrons are pieces of breast of veal cut 1–2 fingers wide along the whole width of the breast. They are delicious when cooked in the oven for a long time in a covered dish. Brown the tendrons in lard in the frying pan after seasoning. Place in a deep baking dish on top of and surrounded by a generous garnish of sliced or diced vegetables. Add the wine and when the wine boils away, the hot *bouillon* and 2 tablespoons tomato *purée* or peeled tomatoes. Cover and cook in the oven for 1½ hours, basting the meat frequently with the gravy. If there is not enough gravy add a little water. Serve the tendrons on the vegetables to which may be added potatoes, beans or peas, cooked separately. Skim fat off gravy, which should be well boiled down, and pour it over the tendrons.

LE VEAU FROID   *   *COLD VEAL*

Côtes de Veau à la Printanière en Gelée   *   *Veal Cutlets in Aspic*

For 4 persons: 4 *grilled cutlets, each weighing about 4 oz;* 1¼ *lb boiled new carrots; 20 boiled button onions; 1 pint aspic; parsley.*

Pour ¼ inch cold aspic into a scalded sponge sandwich tin. When set, place in the cold trimmed cutlets, and pack the carrots and onions—cooked green peas might be included—round them. Almost cover with aspic and when set, fill up with aspic to completely cover the cutlets and vegetables. Refrigerate until set. Dip tin in hot water, and turn out. Serve on a large flat dish and garnish neatly with sprigs of parsley.

Tête de Veau Vinaigrette   *   *Calf's Head Vinaigrette*

For 4 persons: 2 *lb boned calf's head; half a lemon; 1 onion; 2 carrots; 1 bouquet garni;* ¼ *pint white wine; sauce Vinaigrette.* Cooking time: 2–3 hours.

Wash the head and steep in cold salted water for 2–3 hours. Blanch the calf's head and put it on the stove in plenty of cold salted water. Boil for 5 minutes and rinse under the cold tap. Drain, rub with the half lemon, and cut in square pieces. Cook in plenty of white stock, mixed, while still cold, with a large handful of flour. Add the wine, onion, carrots and peppercorns. Cover and cook over moderate heat until tender. The head should be well done. The tongue is cooked with the head, while the brains are cooked separately. Skin and slice the tongue and serve very hot with the head and brains. Steamed potatoes and *sauce Vinaigrette* are handed separately. Chopped parsley, finely chopped onion and chopped capers are other usual accompaniments.

Veau à la Suédoise * *Veal Swedish style*

For 4 persons: 1 lb left-over veal; half a celeriac; 2 dessert apples; 2 tomatoes; 1 hardboiled egg; Tartare sauce and mayonnaise.

Slice the veal and cover with thick *sauce Tartare*. Dress in a ring round a salad of celeriac and apples, thinly sliced and bound with *mayonnaise*. Decorate with sliced skinned tomatoes and hardboiled egg.

Veal Tartare

For 4 persons: 6 slices cold cooked veal; prepared mustard; fine breadcrumbs; 1 egg; oil or melted butter; ½ oz each finely chopped shallots and gherkins; scant ½ pint mayonnaise. Cooking time: 5-10 minutes.

Spread veal slices with prepared mustard, dip in beaten egg and then in crumbs. *Sauté* in hot oil or butter until lightly browned on both sides. Drain well, serve piping hot with tartare sauce, made by combining the shallots, gherkins, and mayonnaise.

LE MOUTON * *MUTTON*

Mutton and lamb are excellent and very nutritious. The best-flavoured meat comes from sheep whose pasture is close to the sea.

The leg, saddle, shoulder (i.e. the boned saddle), and loin are the best cuts. The liver, heart, kidneys and brains are also popular.

The cutlets and chops are cut from the ribs and loin. In the recipes which follow we have used the term cutlet but, of course, a chop could be used instead. Usually one lamb cutlet and one chop per person is allowed.

Cassoulet à la Ménagère * *Haricot Bean Stew*

For 4 persons: 2 lb shoulder of mutton; 2 oz cooking fat; 8 oz haricot beans; a knuckle of pork; 4 oz fresh pork rinds; lard; 3 cloves; 3 onions; 2 carrots; 2 cloves of garlic; 1 pint bouillon; 2 tablespoons tomato purée. Cooking time: 1½–2 hours.

Soak the beans in cold water for 4–5 hours, then put them on to cook with cold water, an onion stuck with cloves, 2 cloves of garlic, the rinds and knuckle of pork. Cook very gently for about an hour so that the beans are done but do not break. Cut the mutton in large pieces and brown in cooking fat. When the meat is well browned add the chopped onions. Season, cover and moisten from time to time with good *bouillon*, add the tomato *purée* and simmer gently for 1 hour. When the beans are almost done add them to the meat with the sliced carrots and the diced rinds. Cook for another half hour or so. The *cassoulet* may be served in the dish in which it is cooked. If liked, sprinkle with breadcrumbs and brown in the oven before serving.

148

Crown Roast of Lamb

For 6-8 persons: 14-16 *lamb rib cutlets, in piece; 1 oz flour; ½ pint vegetable or chicken stock; pepper; salt. Stuffing: 2 oz sliced celery; 1 oz finely chopped onions; 3 oz butter; 6 oz soft breadcrumbs; 1 egg; 1 tablespoon water; 4 oz finely chopped fresh mint; ¼ teaspoon mixed dried herbs; salt; pepper.* Cooking time: 2½ hours.

Ask butcher to prepare cutlets without cutting through sections, and have the skin removed. Tie ribs together in a circle, bones to the outside, to resemble a crown. Fill cavity with prepared stuffing. *Stuffing: Sauté* celery and onion in butter until soft and golden. Add crumbs, the egg beaten with water, mint, herbs, salt and pepper. Mix with fork, pack lightly into centre of roast. Place in well-greased baking dish; cover ends of chops with pieces of raw potato to prevent burning. Bake in moderate oven, 350°F or Gas Mark 4, for 2 to 2½ hours. Pour off fat from baking dish, leaving about 2 tablespoons, stir in 1 ounce flour, mix well in, then add stock. Bring gently to the boil and simmer for a few minutes to make rich brown gravy. Add pepper and salt to taste.

Daube of Mutton Provençale

For 6 persons: 3 *lb shoulder of mutton; 6 oz fat bacon; 3 carrots; 3 onions; garlic; lean bacon; 3 sheep's trotters; oil; 1 bottle red wine; 4 oz pork rinds; 6 fresh tomatoes; seasoning; 1 bouquet garni.* Cooking time: 5 hours.

Bone the mutton and cut it in cubes, lard each one with fat bacon and marinate for 24 hours in the wine with a little oil, the chopped onions, chopped carrots and *bouquet garni.* Place the meat in a casserole with a chopped onion and clove of garlic, some pieces of lean bacon, the boned sheep's trotters and some small pieces of rind, all well blanched. Add seasoning and the *bouquet garni.* Strain the marinade over the meat and add some quartered tomatoes. Seal hermetically and cook slowly in the oven for 5 hours. Skim off fat before serving in the casserole.

GIGOT DE MOUTON * *LEG OF MUTTON*

Boiled Leg of Mutton

For 8 persons: 1 *leg of mutton, weighing about 6–7 lb; 3 lb altogether of new carrots, turnips, small onions, French beans; 1 pint Caper sauce.* Cooking time: 2½–3 hours.

Trim the leg, wrap in a napkin and tie up, place in a large stewpan of salted boiling water and simmer slowly. Three-quarters of an hour before meat is cooked, in the same stewpan, and also wrapped in a cloth, cook the carrots, turnips, small onions and French beans. Surround the joint with this vegetable garnish, together with boiled potatoes, cooked separately. Serve with Caper sauce, made with the stock from the mutton. This dish is mainly served in the spring with new season's vegetables.

▣ à la Bretonne * *Breton style*

For 10 persons: 1 *leg of mutton, weighing about 7–9 lb; 1 pint or 1 lb haricot beans; 3 onions; 3 cloves of garlic; 3 tablespoons tomato purée; 2 oz dripping.* Cooking time: 2½–3 hours.

Cut the cloves of garlic in two and insert in incisions in the meat. Roast the mutton in a hot oven, 400°F or Gas Mark 6—or at a gentle "sizzle", basting occasionally. Brown the chopped onions with a little fat from the joint, add the tomato *purée,* thinned with a little *bouillon.*

Add the cooked haricot or flageolet beans (*p.* 204). The beans may be served round the joint or separately, decorated with a little parsley.

Gigot de Mouton Rôti * *Roast*

For 8–10 persons: 1 leg of mutton, weighing about 7–9 lb; 3 cloves of garlic;
2 *oz dripping.* Cooking time: 2½–3 hours.

Trim the joint, cut off the end of the bone and season. Insert the garlic in incisions near the knuckle and roast the joint in the oven, 400°F or Gas Mark 6, allowing 20 minutes per pound. Baste from time to time and do not add anything except dripping and some fine salt —above all no water. Surround with the bone and trimmings. These will help to make the gravy when the joint has been removed from the roasting tin. To test for readiness, plunge a skewer into the thickest part; no blood should be visible when it is withdrawn.

To make the Gravy: Strain off surplus fat, leaving the sediment in the tin. Stir in 2 teaspoons flour and rub over pan to collect sediment. Add ½ pint *bouillon* and stir until boiling. Boil fast to reduce slightly. Correct seasoning and strain.

Pré-Salé

Pré-Salé is a description of origin and means "salty meadows by the seashore", meaning the pastures of the Breton coast. The grass is supposed to give a specially good flavour to the lamb and mutton.

Roast the mutton as above. Half an hour before it is ready put some breadcrumbs mixed with melted butter over the surface and baste well. The resulting crust resembles the knobbly skin of the sheep from the salt meadows.

Haricot de Mouton * *Haricot Mutton*

For 4 persons: Same ingredients as for Navarin of mutton, (p. 153) but replace the turnips and carrots by 1 lb haricot or flageolet beans.

When the meat is almost done, skim the fat off the sauce and add the previously cooked beans. Simmer them with the mutton for a few minutes. Serve in a hot dish with parsley sprinkled over.

Langues de Mouton * *Sheep's Tongues*

For 4 persons: 8–12 sheep's tongues; salt; carrots; onions; bouquet garni;
bouillon.

Soak tongues in cold water for 1 hour. Wash. Simmer for 1½ hours in sufficient slightly salted water to cover. Drain and cool slightly. Skin and trim root end. Serve on a *purée* of vegetables with one of the following sauces poured round: Tomato (*p.* 27), Piquant (*p.* 22), Onion (*p.* 25).

▣ Braisées * *Braised*

Cook as above for ½ hour. Cool, and trim. Melt 1 ounce dripping in a pan, add some diced carrot, 1 sliced onion, 1 stick celery and a *bouquet garni*. Fry until golden brown. Add the tongues, 1 tablespoon tomato *purée*, seasoning and 1 pint brown stock. Boil up, skim and cover closely. Put into a hot oven, 400°F or Gas Mark 6, and braise for 1½ hours or until tender. Skin the tongues, and serve on creamed potatoes, *Risotto*, chestnut *purée*, or celeriac, etc. Reduce sauce slightly and strain over the tongues.

Langues de Mouton Frites * *Fried Sheep's Tongues*

Cook as above, skin and trim. Slice lengthwise, coat with egg and breadcrumbs, *sauté* in butter until nicely browned and serve with vegetables and Tomato sauce.

Mutton Chops

For 4 persons: 4 chops, each weighing 6–7 oz; 1 oz Maître d'hôtel butter; Worcester sauce. Cooking time: 12–15 minutes.

Skin the chops and beat out lightly. Season. Grill or *sauté* in butter until tender—turning frequently during cooking. Garnish with *Maître d'hôtel* butter and sprinkle with a few drops of Worcester sauce. Serve also Chipped potatoes and a chosen vegetable. (*See illustration p. 133*).

Pieds de Mouton à la Poulette * *Sheep's Trotters with Poulette Sauce*

For 4 persons: 4–6 sheep's trotters; 1 onion stuck with cloves; 1 carrot; 6 oz mushrooms; lemon juice; chopped parsley; bouquet garni; seasoning; scant ¼ pint vinegar; 1 pint sauce Poulette or 1 pint cream. Cooking time: 3–4 hours.

Halve and bone the trotters, carefully remove the tuft of hair in the middle, flame and wash them. Bone and blanch. Put them in a large pan of cold water which has been mixed with a handful of flour. Add an onion stuck with a clove, carrot, *bouquet garni*, salt, pepper and vinegar. Cook gently for 3–4 hours. Drain and simmer in a *sauce Poulette*, adding a few cooked mushrooms, lemon juice and parsley. The trotters may be simmered in fresh cream instead of sauce for a few minutes.

When about to serve, remove from heat, thicken cream with 3 egg yolks. Do not boil again. Add lemon juice and parsley.

Poitrine de Mouton Tartare * *Breast of Mutton with Tartare Sauce*

Boil the breast of mutton in Cabbage soup (*p.* 50). Drain, bone and cool under pressure. Cut up into diamond-shaped pieces. Brush with melted butter. Dust with dried mustard and breadcrumbs. Sprinkle with oil or fat and grill. Serve piping hot with *Tartare sauce* and mashed potatoes.

Incidentally, the Cabbage soup is excellent after the meat has been boiled in it.

The breast may be braised or cooked in *bouillon* instead of Cabbage soup.

Rognons de Mouton en Brochettes * *Sheep's Kidneys on Skewers*

For 4 persons: 4 kidneys; Maître d'hôtel butter; watercress. Cooking time: 5–6 minutes.

Wash the kidneys. Cut them open lengthwise without splitting them entirely, skin and core them, and keep them open by impaling them on a skewer. Sprinkle with butter and salt and grill them. Serve them topped with a nut of *Maître d'hôtel* butter, and surrounded by watercress.

The kidneys may also be breadcrumbed by rolling them in melted butter and breadcrumbs.

Rognons de Mouton Sautés Turbigo * *Sautéed Sheep's Kidneys Turbigo*

For 4 persons: 8 sheep's kidneys; 8 chipolatas; 4 croûtons; 3 oz butter; 1 tablespoon flour; 4 oz mushrooms; 16 shallots; ½ pint sauce Demi-glace; 2 tablespoons bouillon; 1 tablespoon tomato purée; 4 tablespoons white wine; chopped parsley; lemon juice.

Skin and core the kidneys. Wash them and halve them lengthwise; toss in flour. Melt butter and when hot fry the *croûtons*. Drain and keep hot. Fry the kidneys and chipolatas in the remaining fat. Cook the mushrooms in *bouillon*, with ½ ounce butter and a squeeze of lemon juice added. When everything is tender, arrange 2 kidneys on each *croûton* with a chipolata on top of each kidney. Add wine and chopped, sautéed shallots to the butter in the pan. Heat up and stir in the sauce *Demi-glace* and tomato *purée*. Boil up and add parsley and lemon juice to sharpen. Arrange the kidneys round a hot dish and pour the sauce over them. Mound the mushrooms in the centre and serve very hot.

L'AGNEAU * *LAMB*

CÔTELETTES D'AGNEAU * *LAMB CUTLETS*

Côtelettes d'Agneau Braisées Champvallon * *Braised Lamb Cutlets with Onion and Potatoes*

For 4 persons: 8 cutlets; 3 large onions; 2 cloves garlic; 1½ lb potatoes; seasoning; 1 pint bouillon; chopped parsley. Cooking time: 2 hours.

Sauté the cutlets in the frying pan; place them in a deep baking dish on a bed of raw sliced potatoes, sliced onions, crushed garlic and seasoning. Cover with sliced potatoes and onions; season and cover entirely with *bouillon*. Put on the lid, boil up and cook in a moderate oven, 350°F or Gas Mark 4, for 1½ hours. Serve in the baking dish in which they were cooked, with chopped parsley sprinkled over.

▣ Grillées * *Grilled*

Lamb cutlets are grilled in accordance with the principles indicated at the beginning of the section which deals with cooking methods in general. If there is no grill, *sauté* them in a frying pan in lard or oil. It is difficult to give a cooking time, since this varies with the thickness of the cutlet. Usually, a cutlet weighing 4–5 ounces will take 4 minutes on one side and 3–4 minutes on the other; the thinner they are, the more quickly should the surface be browned. They are usually served underdone and each topped with *Maître d'hôtel* butter. Garnish: French beans, Straw potatoes, fennel with Parmesan cheese, cress.

▣ au Riz, Sauce Peperonata * *with Rice and Pepper Sauce*

For 4 persons: 8 oz rice; 2 oz grated cheese; 4 lamb cutlets; 2 oz butter. Cooking time: 4 minutes on each side. *Pepper sauce: 4 tablespoons oil; 4 tablespoons chopped onions; 2 cloves garlic; 3 green peppers; 1¼ lb very ripe tomatoes; ¼ pint bouillon. Garnish: 4 sliced cooked tomatoes or 1 lb shelled peas, buttered; 8 oz mushrooms.*

Boil the rice in the usual way. Trim and season the cutlets and *sauté* them in hot butter. Serve cutlets on rice with cheese added. Garnish with peas and mushrooms at both ends of dish or mounds of sliced tomatoes down one side.

This recipe for Pepper sauce goes particularly well with lamb cutlets.

Pepper Sauce: Toss the onions in oil without letting them colour, add the crushed garlic and shredded peppers. Dip the tomatoes into boiling water for a second, take them out and peel them. Halve them, squeeze them to remove the seeds, dice them, add them to the peppers, season with salt, add the *bouillon* and simmer with the lid on for 30–40 minutes. (*See illustration p.* 133).

Gigot d'Agneau à la Boulangère * *Baked Leg of Lamb Boulangère*

For 8–10 *persons:* 1 *leg of lamb, weighing about* 6–7 *lb;* 1¼ *lb potatoes;* 3 *large onions;* 4 *cloves of garlic; mint sauce.* Cooking time: 2½–3 hours.

Trim the joint and cut off end of shank. Halve the garlic cloves and insert them into the lamb. Rub salt over the surface. Roast the joint: when it is half done surround with sliced onions and thinly sliced potatoes. Sprinkle with salt. Finish cooking together, basting frequently. There will be no gravy, since the potatoes absorb it all, so make a little separately, with the shank bones and trimmings. Slice and arrange on the potatoes, and serve with mint sauce. Leg of lamb is excellent cold, so a whole leg may be cooked for only 4–6 people and the remainder eaten at another meal. (*See illustration p.* 134).

▣ Creole * *Creole*

For 6 *persons:* 1 *medium-sized leg of lamb;* ½ *teaspoon chilli sauce (to taste);* 1 *tablespoon Worcester sauce;* 1 *tablespoon vinegar;* 2 *tablespoons oil; salt; pepper;* ½ *pint stock;* 2 *onions, finely chopped;* 1 *clove garlic, crushed;* ¼ *pint extra stock.*

Place meat in baking dish. Combine remaining ingredients, except extra stock, and pour over meat. Roast in a hot oven, 400°F or Gas Mark 6, for 20 minutes, then turn oven down to moderate, 350°F or Gas Mark 4, and continue roasting until meat is well-browned and tender, allowing approximately 25 to 30 minutes per pound. Baste frequently. Transfer cooked lamb to serving dish. Skim fat from sauce, check seasoning. Add extra stock, bring to boil, stirring. Serve with the lamb.

Navarin d'Agneau ou Ragoût de Mouton * *Lamb Stew*

For 4 *persons:* 1¾ *lb stewing lamb or mutton;* 2 *tablespoons flour;* 1 *clove garlic;* 2 *tablespoons tomato purée;* 1 *bouquet garni;* 20 *small onions;* 2 *oz dripping;* 1¼ *lb carrots and turnips;* 1¼ *lb new potatoes; parsley.* Cooking time: about 2 hours.

Trim the meat (shoulder, breast or best end) and cut it into large cubes and brown well over a hot flame in very hot fat. Pour off most of the fat and dredge the meat with flour, brown it well and add a clove of crushed garlic. Moisten with water, add tomato *purée*, salt, pepper and *bouquet garni*. Darken the sauce a little with caramel, cover and cook slowly for 1 hour. Add the onions, carrots and turnips, all well browned in the excess fat in a frying pan with a pinch of sugar to caramelise the vegetables. Cook slowly for 45 minutes. Remove all fat from the gravy, add new potatoes or small potatoes which will not break. Finish cooking over a low flame or in the oven so that the meat and vegetables are done at the same time. Skim fat off again if necessary and serve sprinkled with chopped parsley.

Ris d'Agneau * *Lamb's Sweetbreads*

These are prepared and cooked in the same way as Calf's Sweetbreads (*p.* 145), and are used to fill *bouchées* or *vol-au-vent* cases.

Summer Lamb Salad

For 6 persons: 1 *boned and rolled shoulder of lamb;* 4 *oz rolled oats or soft breadcrumbs;* 1 *egg;* ½ *oz chopped parsley;* 1 *onion, finely chopped;* 1 *teaspoon grated lemon rind;* ½ *oz chopped gherkins;* 1 *large tomato, peeled and chopped;* ¼ *teaspoon Oregano; salt; pepper.* Cooking time: 1½-2 hours.

Unroll meat carefully onto flat board. Combine remaining ingredients in bowl, mix well together. Spread evenly on meat, re-roll. Secure with fine string, wrap in greased aluminium foil. Bake in moderate oven, 350°F or Gas Mark 4, for 1½ to 2 hours. Remove foil for last 40 minutes' cooking time. Cool and place in refrigerator. Cover a large platter with crisp salad greens. Arrange the thinly sliced meat over the greens. Garnish with celery, cucumber, tomato wedges, radishes, pineapple rings.

LE PORC * *PORK*

Andouillettes à la Lyonnaise * *Pork Sausages with Onions*

For 4 persons: 1½ *lb sausages;* 2 *large onions;* 1 *tablespoon vinegar; oil and butter.* Cooking time: 10–12 minutes.

Shred and stew the onions in butter. Cut the sausages into ½ inch thick slices and fry in equal quantities of oil and butter. Add the onions and fry all together. Sprinkle with vinegar and chopped parsley and arrange piled up in a dish. Serve with mashed potatoes.

▣ Farcie * *Stuffed*

For 3 persons: 6 *pork sausages;* 3 *rashers bacon;* 2 *oz soft breadcrumbs;* 1 *small grated carrot;* 1 *small grated onion;* ½ *tablespoon each of chopped parsley and celery;* ½ *teaspoon mixed dry herbs;* ½ *teaspoon salt;* 1 *teaspoon melted butter;* 1 *egg yolk or* 1 *tablespoon milk;* 1 *oz fat for frying.* Cooking time: 40-45 minutes.

Parboil sausages 5 minutes, drain. Combine breadcrumbs, carrot, onion, parsley, celery, herbs, salt and butter. Bind with beaten egg yolk or milk. Cut slit along centre of each sausage and fill with stuffing. Wrap half rasher of bacon around each sausage, secure with toothpick or small skewer. Melt fat in baking dish. Place sausages in dish, bake in moderate oven, 350°F or Gas Mark 4, for 40 to 45 minutes, then remove to hot plate. Make gravy in baking dish and serve with sausages.

Barbecued Spareribs

For 6 persons: 4 *lb pork spareribs;* 2 *teaspoons dry mustard;* 1 *teaspoon Worcester sauce; salt; pepper;* 2 *tablespoons oil; good* ½ *pint tomato ketchup;* ½ *teaspoon Tabasco sauce.*

Cut ribs into serving portions. Combine remaining ingredients, pour over ribs. Let stand at least 2 hours, then drain; bake in moderately hot oven, 375°F of Gas Mark 5, until ribs are well-browned and crisp, basting frequently with marinade.

Boudin aux Pommes de Reinette * *Black Pudding Sausages with Dessert Apples*

Peel, core and slice some dessert apples. Let them cook very gently in butter, grill or sauté the sausages and serve them on the apples.

Carré de Porc * *Loin of Pork*

The loin consists of all the cutlets. The joint is chined for easier carving. Roast the loin in the same way as the fillet and garnish with various vegetables, e.g. mashed potatoes, puréed peas, spinach etc. Always cook pork thoroughly; it might be harmful if underdone. Cold pork is just as popular, and more digestible, than hot pork.

Côtelettes de Porc Glacées * *Glazed Pork Cutlets*

For 4 persons: 2 pork cutlets; a dash of white wine. Cooking time: 18–20 minutes.

It is better to take 2 thick cutlets of 10–12 ounces each rather than 4 of 6 ounces each, as the meat will be more tender. Beat well on both sides. Salt and flour lightly and fry very slowly in lard, turning frequently while cooking. Place on a hot dish. Pour off the fat from the frying pan and keep it for further use; reduce the pan residue with white wine and pour over the cutlets. Serve with *Château* potatoes, grilled tomatoes and green peas. (*See illustration p.* 136).

CÔTES DE PORC * *PORK CHOPS*

Côtes de Porc aux Pommes * *Pork Chops with Apples*

For 4 persons: 4 pork chops, each weighing about 6 oz; 2 apples (pippins); ½ pint gravy; 2 oz butter. Cooking time: 15 minutes.

Trim the chops, season and *sauté* in butter. Add the gravy to detach the juices, reduce and pour over the chops. Peel, halve and core the apples. Divide into even slices without cutting them through completely. Bake quickly in a very hot oven, making sure they do not get too soft. Place half an apple on each chop without detaching the slices. Sprinkle brown sugar over and set in the oven or under the grill for a moment to brown. Before sautéing, pork chops are often tossed in flour and coated with egg and breadcrumbs. (*See illustration p.* 134).

▣ à la Normande * *with Apples and Cream*

For 6 persons: 6 pork chops; 2 oz butter; ½ pint cream; the juice of 1 lemon; 2 lb cooking apples.

Cut off excess fat from the chops. Season chops and fry in butter, cook slowly until pork is well-done. Transfer chops to a serving dish and keep warm. Reduce the pan residue with cream, season with lemon juice and pour over the chops. Serve with warm Apple sauce. The chops can also be garnished with apples peeled, cored, cut in eighths and cooked in butter.

Filet de Porc Rôti, Garni * *Roast Garnished Fillet of Pork*

For 4 persons: 2 fillets of pork, each weighing about 1 lb; 1 clove garlic; 1 onion; 1 carrot; scant ¼ pint white wine; scant ¼ pint bouillon; 4 tartlet cases filled with green peas and carrot balls or dice; 4 tomatoes. Cooking time: 45 minutes.

Season the fillets with pepper and salt, rub with garlic, sprinkle with melted lard and put on to roast with the sliced onion and carrot. Roast at 450°F or Gas Mark 8, for 15 minutes. Then reduce to 375°F or Gas Mark 5, so that they will be done inside without burning on top. Baste with the fat from time to time. After 30 minutes add the tomatoes, which may

155

be cooked at the same time as the joint. Boil peas and carrots separately, adding a pinch of sugar to both. When done, remove the meat and tomatoes; pour off all the fat, add the wine, boil it down, add the *bouillon*, allow to boil for a moment, strain and serve separately. Slice the meat thinly. Garnish the tomatoes with a little fresh butter and chopped parsley. Arrange the tomatoes and filled tartlet cases round the meat.

Médaillons de Porc à la Hongroise * Pork Medallions Hungarian Style

For 4 persons: 8 medallions of pork cut from the fillet, each weighing about 2 oz; 1 red pepper and 1 green pepper cut into julienne strips; 1 finely sliced onion; 2 large tomatoes, skinned and roughly chopped; 1 tablespoon white wine; ½ pint Cream sauce; paprika; garlic salt; 2 oz butter. Cooking time: 4 minutes for each side.

Season the pork with the garlic salt. *Sauté* in the butter and keep hot. Fry the peppers and onions lightly in the same butter; when half cooked add the tomatoes. Add the white wine, stir to detach the juices from the pan and finish cooking over low heat. Place the medallions on the serving dish, spread the garnish on top, mask with sauce and sprinkle lightly with paprika. Serve *tarhonya* (Hungarian paste speciality) separately. (*See illustration p.* 135).

Pieds de Porc au Madère * Pig's Feet with Madeira Sauce

For 4 persons: 2 pig's feet; thyme; bay leaf; pepper; cloves; ¼ pint white wine; ½ pint Madeira sauce; 1 tablespoon tomato purée. Cooking time: 3–4 hours.

If possible use feet which have been salted for several days. Wash, boil in water for about 1 hour, rinse in cold water and halve. Heat a spoonful of lard in a casserole, add the feet, a bay leaf, a sprig of thyme, 3 or 4 peppercorns and 2 cloves. Simmer for a few moments, add white wine, ½ pint water and a tablespoon of tomato *purée*. The feet should be covered with liquid. Seal hermetically and cook for at least 2 hours in a moderate oven. If the liquid boils away too much, add a little hot water. In the meantime make a good Madeira sauce. Drain the feet, place in sauce and simmer in it for about 30 minutes. Serve with sautéed or boiled potatoes.

Pork in Black Bean Sauce

For 2 persons: 10 oz lean pork; salt and pepper; 2 teaspoons black bean paste (black beans can be bought from Chinese food stores. Take amount of beans required, wash well in hot water to remove excess salt, then mash to paste in small bowl with wooden spoon); oil for frying; 1 leek; 1 green pepper; 1 small red pepper, or chilli; 3 teaspoons chicken stock. Cooking time: 20-30 minutes.

Cut pork into thin strips, 1 inch long. Toss in salt, pepper, and 1 teaspoon black bean paste. Heat oil in frying pan and *sauté* the meat quickly over a good heat. Add chopped leek, diced pepper and chilli, remaining black bean paste, and stock. Serve hot.

Potée Paysanne * Farmer's Pork Dish

For 6 persons: 2¾ lb salt hand (or belly) of pork; 1 lb thickly sliced lean bacon; 1 sausage; cabbage; potatoes; carrots; onions. Cooking time: 2–3 hours.

Soak the pork for about 2 hours. Put the pork in a pan and cover with cold water. Bring to the boil, skim, cover and simmer. After 1½ hours add the vegetables, and after another ½ hour some potatoes, the bacon and the raw sausage. When everything is well done serve the sliced meat on the vegetables. The stock makes an excellent soup.

Ragoût de Porc   *   *Pork Stew*

Same recipe as for Haricot Mutton (*p.* 150). It is also served with mixed vegetables, haricot beans cooked beforehand, potato *purée*, rice, etc.

Roast Pork

For 4 persons: 1¾–2¼ *lb pork;* 2 *oz lard;* 1 *onion;* 1 *carrot;* ¼ *pint white wine.* Cooking time: allow 30–35 minutes per pound.

Buy a piece of loin, scored and jointed, or use leg, hand or spare rib. Brown the meat in lard with a sliced onion and a sliced carrot, cover and cook in a fairly hot oven, 375°F or Gas Mark 5. The bones should be put in with the meat to make a good gravy. Remove the meat when it is thoroughly cooked, pour off three-quarters of the fat and reduce with white wine. Slice the joint and pour the gravy over it. Serve with Apple sauce and mashed potatoes.

▣ with Baked Apples or Apple Sauce

For 6-8 persons: 1 *small leg of pork or fillet from leg weighing about* 4 *lb; salt; ground ginger; oil.*

Ask butcher to score pork rind well. Place roast in well-greased baking dish. Rub skin with generous amount of salt and a little ground ginger. (The salt will ensure a good crackling). Roast in a hot oven, 400°F or Gas Mark 6, for 20 minutes, then reduce heat to 350°F or Gas Mark 4, and continue cooking until meat is well-browned and tender, allowing 25 to 30 minutes per pound cooking time. Make a thin gravy with the pan drippings, and serve pork with gravy and baked apples or apple sauce.

BAKED APPLES: Wash medium-sized apples well, remove cores. With a sharp knife cut through the skin round the centre of the apple—this prevents them bursting during cooking. Place apples in lightly greased baking dish, fill centres with sultanas and a little sugar. Put 3-4 tablespoons water in baking dish. Bake in a fairly hot oven, 375°F or Gas Mark 5, approximately 30 minutes, or until tender when tested with a skewer.

APPLE SAUCE: 1 *pint stewed apple pulp; juice* ½ *lemon;* ½ *teaspoon cinnamon; sugar to taste;* 1 *oz butter;* 1 *teaspoon finely chopped preserved ginger.*

Pass apple through sieve or blender. Place in saucepan with lemon juice, cinnamon, sugar, butter. Heat gently, stirring, and add ginger. Serve hot.

Roulades de Porc Parmentier   *   *Stuffed Pork Rolls*

For 4 persons: 8 *slices of pork, each weighing about* 3 *oz;* 1 *teaspoon fine herbs;* 1 *onion;* 4 *oz sausage meat;* 3 *tablespoons white wine;* 3 *oz butter;* 1½ *lb potatoes;* 1 *tablespoon tomato purée.* Cooking time: 1½ hours.

Have thin, large slices cut from a lean fillet of pork, flatten them, season, and spread each one with seasoned sausage meat mixed with a finely chopped onion and fine herbs. Roll and tie firmly at each end. Brown well in butter, add white wine, cover and cook gently for 1½ hours. In the meantime gently sweat the peeled, diced potatoes in butter; salt and shake frequently during cooking. Remove string from meat, place on a dish, surround with the potatoes and pour the gravy, combined with a tablespoon of tomato *purée*, on top.

157

Saucisses Grillées aux Choux * Baked Sausages with Cabbage

Prick the sausages, moisten them with a little water and put them in a very hot oven. When they are brown arrange on shredded cabbage sautéed in the fat from the sausages. Cooking time: 15 minutes.

Sweet and Sour Pork

For 6 persons: 2-2½ *lb lean pork;* 10 *oz drained, canned pineapple pieces;* 1 *medium cucumber or 6 gherkins;* 1 *red pepper or canned pimento;* 2 *onions;* ½ *bunch shallots; cornflour; oil for frying;* 4 *oz mushrooms; boiled rice. Sauce:* 1 *egg yolk;* 1 *oz sugar;* 1 *table-spoon soy sauce;* ¼ *teaspoon salt;* ½ *tablespoon tomato sauce;* 6 *oz reserved pineapple juice;* ½ *tablespoon cornflour;* 1 *tablespoon sherry;* 4 *tablespoons vinegar; salt; pepper.* Cooking time: about 1 hour, altogether.

Mix together sugar, soy sauce, salt, sherry, and egg yolk; stir well. Cut meat into bite-sized pieces, place in soy sauce mixture. Stir well until coated with marinade. Cover, leave 1 hour, stir occasionally. Slice onions, chop shallots diagonally. Core and remove seeds from pepper, cut into thin strips. Slice mushrooms, cut cucumber into chunky strips. Fry onion in a little hot oil until transparent. Add pepper and shallots, cook further 3 to 4 minutes. Add mushrooms, cook until softened. Stir in pineapple pieces and cucumber. Keep hot. Drain meat from marinade, reserve liquid. Toss meat in cornflour. Heat oil, cook meat until golden brown and cooked through; drain well. Add meat to vegetables, keep hot. Blend the cornflour with reserved pineapple juice. Add vinegar, tomato sauce, stir into remaining marinade. Bring up to the boil, stirring continuously, season. Pour sauce over meat and vegetables, stir to coat evenly. Serve hot on a bed of boiled rice.

LE PORC FROID * COLD PORK

Pâté de Foie Genre Charcutier * Liver Pâté (Charcutier)

For 6 persons: 1¼ *lb pig's liver;* 1¼ *lb fat bacon;* 2 *eggs;* 10 *oz lard;* 3 *onions;* 2 *shallots;* 1 *clove garlic; about* 3 *oz flour; thyme; bay leaf; pig's caul (or pieces of bacon fat).* Cooking time: 2 hours.

Pass the liver, bacon, lard, onions, shallots and garlic twice through the mincer or liquidiser. Season with salt and pepper and combine with 2 whole eggs, flour, thyme and bay leaf, making a homogeneous paste. Spread a piece of caul (or bacon fat) over the inside of a *terrine* and fill with the paste. Cover with caul or bacon fat, close *terrine*, place in a baking tin of water and cook for about 2 hours in a moderate oven. The water in the tin should be boiling all the time; if it evaporates, fill up with boiling water. Leave to cool. Serve in slices. Only remove pig's caul from the part to be eaten. This excellent *pâté* is almost as good as *pâté de foie gras.*

Rillettes * Rillettes or Preserved Pork in Pots

For 6 persons: 2¼ *lb lean pork;* 2¼ *lb green fat bacon; salt; pepper; bouquet garni.* Cooking time: 4 hours.

Dice the meat and bacon finely and place in heavy saucepan. Add salt, pepper and *bouquet garni.* Cook for 4 hours over low heat, stirring frequently with a wooden spoon. When the meat is cooked to shreds, put into small earthenware pots. Cover with strong paper and tie. Some goose meat may also be mixed with the pork.

JAMBON ★ *HAM*

Cuisson d'un Jambon ★ *To Cook a Ham*

Soak the ham in cold water overnight. Scrape well and bring to the boil slowly in plenty of cold water. As soon as the water boils, draw to the side of the stove and keep just at simmering point until it is cooked, allowing 20 minutes per pound. A whole ham takes about 3 hours—a half ham requires about the same time.

When the ham is to be served cold, cool it in the liquor, then drain to finish cooling. Remove skin. Dab surface with soft paper to remove surplus fat. Roll in fine crumbs and stick in a few cloves.

If the ham is to be served hot, drain, skin, trim off part of the fat and braise it in wine. Place it in a roasting pan, pour over ½ pint of Madeira or white wine, sprinkle lightly with brown sugar and bake in the oven for 30 minutes, basting frequently. It should be golden brown, like any other roast. Skim the fat off the gravy, reduce to a third and add to ½ pint *sauce Demi-glace.* Hot ham may be served with various garnishes, such as spinach, green peas, mixed vegetables, mushrooms, etc.

Baked with Pineapple

For 20 persons: 1 uncooked ham weighing about 10 to 12 lb; water; 1 lb brown sugar; 6 green apples, peeled, cored, and quartered; 1 tablespoon dried mustard; 3 oz brown sugar (extra); dry sherry; 1 large can (1 lb 13 oz) pineapple rings, drained; glacé cherries.

Soak ham at least 12 hours in water to cover; change water from time to time. Drain well, place in large pot with water to cover. Add brown sugar and apples, cover and bring slowly to the point just below boiling, then simmer, without allowing liquid to boil, until ham is cooked. Allow 30 minutes per pound cooking time. Allow ham to cool in cooking liquor. Drain ham, peel off skin; trim away any excess fat. Combine mustard and extra brown sugar, mix to thick paste with sherry; spread over ham. Arrange pineapple slices over ham, securing with toothpicks, add cherries. Sprinkle with a little extra brown sugar; bake in moderate oven, 350°F or Gas Mark 4, about 20 minutes or until pineapple is well glazed and lightly browned.

▣ Braised

Boil the ham, then drain, remove the skin and some of the fat and place in ½ pint wine, Madeira, or champagne. Lightly dredge with brown sugar to glaze. Cover closely and cook in a hot oven, 425°F or Gas Mark 7, for 30 minutes. When cooked the ham should be as brown as a real roast. Remove the fat from the wine and add the latter to ½ pint *sauce Demi-glace.* Serve the ham hot with a garnish such as spinach, peas, mixed vegetables, mushrooms, truffles, etc. (*See illustration p.* 135).

Ham-Asparagus Rolls

For 4 persons: 8 thick slices of ham; 2 10½ oz cans of asparagus spears; 2 oz flour; 2 oz butter; 1 pint milk; salt; pepper; 4 oz grated cheese. Cooking time: 10 minutes.

Drain asparagus spears well. Take 4 or 5 spears and roll slice of ham around them, continue with all ham slices. Melt butter in pan over low heat, remove from heat, stir in flour. Work together until smooth. Return to low heat, stir for a few minutes until mixture bubbles. Gradually stir in milk off the heat, then return to heat and cook, stirring constantly, until sauce comes to boil, then simmer for another 3 minutes. Add grated cheese and stir until melted; season to taste. Pour over ham-asparagus rolls.

Ham Rissoles

For 4 persons: 1 lb minced, cooked ham; butter or oil for frying; 1 small finely chopped onion; ½ finely chopped green pepper; 2 finely chopped sticks celery; 2 large potatoes, cooked and mashed; 1 teaspoon Worcester sauce; salt and pepper; flour. Cooking time: 10 minutes.

Heat a little butter or oil in frying pan and cook the onion, green pepper, and celery over gentle heat until tender, stirring occasionally. Mash potato without any liquid so that it is very dry. Mix vegetables with ham, potatoes, and Worcester sauce. Season to taste; refrigerate. Form into 8 round cakes, about ½ inch thick; coat lightly with flour. Cook in lightly greased frying pan or on griddle until golden on both sides and heated through.

Stuffed Ham Slices

For 3 persons: 1 oz butter; 4 oz chopped mushrooms; 1 chopped onion; 1 teaspoon prepared mustard; 1½ oz fresh breadcrumbs; 2 tablespoons chicken stock; 6 thin slices ham. Cooking time: 40 minutes altogether.

Heat the butter in saucepan. Add onion, *sauté* until transparent, add mushrooms, mustard, breadcrumbs, and sufficient chicken stock to moisten. Spread this mixture on ham slices and fold slices in half. Wrap each one in aluminium foil and bake in moderate oven, 350°F or Gas Mark 4, for 25 to 30 minutes. Remove from foil to serve.

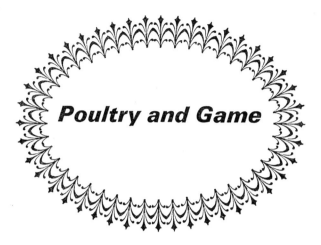

Poultry and Game

Poultry includes not only chicken, geese, ducks, turkeys and guinea fowl, but all birds reared for domestic consumption.

When choosing young poultry, certain considerations—indications of the freshness and the quality of the bird—should be borne in mind. The legs will be smooth, the feet should be supple and the beak and breastbone pliable. A good test is to press the breastbone —in a young bird this should bend easily. Fresh birds have firm, pleasant smelling flesh and clear prominent eyes. The main types of chicken available include:—

Boiling fowl which the French call *Poularde*. Boiling fowl which weigh between 3–4 pounds and may be poached, steamed or casseroled. The older, tough, boiling fowl should really only be used for stocks, soups and forcemeats.

Frying or small roasting chickens may be large, spring chickens, cockerels or pullets. Nowadays this type of chicken is usually a product of broiler farms, and they are killed when they are about 3 months old.

TO DRAW POULTRY

Pick out any quills with a pointed knife. Singe bird over a flame to remove any hairs and odd feathers. Rub over with a coarse cloth. Remove sinews from legs and cut these off at the drumstick. Cut the neck skin lengthwise on the underside. Take hold of the neck and twist it off as near the body as possible. Remove crop and windpipe, and cut off the head, leaving a long neck skin. Loosen everything with the forefinger. Make an incision below the tail. Cut out the vent carefully. Loosen everything with the forefinger. Grip the gizzard and pull it out with the rest of the intestines, including the heart and the liver, with the gall. Detach the lungs. Wipe out with a damp cloth. Split the gizzard and discard the inside bag. Cut gall bladder from liver. Wash the giblets—neck, heart squeezed to remove blood, liver, and gizzard, and use to make stock. The legs and feet, scalded, with outside skin removed, may be used for stock with the giblets.

JOINTING A CHICKEN

A spring chicken is cut in four, whereas a larger bird will give 2–4 pieces of white meat from the breast in addition to the wings and the drumsticks.

LES POULETS ET POULARDES * *CHICKEN AND BOILING FOWL*

Chicken Curry

For 6 persons: 1 *chicken, weighing about 4 lb; 2 tablespoons oil; 2 onions;* 1 *tablespoon curry powder;* $\frac{1}{4}$ *pint coconut milk; scant* $\frac{1}{2}$ *pint chicken stock;* $\frac{1}{4}$ *pint cream;* 12 *oz rice.* Cooking time: 30–40 minutes.

Joint the chicken, remove skin and *sauté* in oil with the finely sliced onions and the curry powder. Gradually pour in the chicken stock and strained coconut milk to cover. Add a *bouquet garni*, cover and cook for 30 minutes. Reduce the cooking stock and bind with the cream. Serve Rice *à l'Indienne* separately.

To prepare coconut milk: soak 2 tablespoons dessicated coconut in $\frac{1}{4}$ pint of milk for 20 minutes. Strain.

◙ Chicken Croquettes

For 36: 8 *oz cooked chicken;* 1$\frac{1}{2}$ *oz butter;* 1 *oz plain flour;* $\frac{1}{2}$ *pint stock; salt; pepper; breadcrumbs;* 1 *egg.* Cooking time: about 15 minutes.

Melt butter in saucepan, stir in flour off the heat then cook *roux* for a few minutes, stirring constantly. Remove pan from heat and gradually add stock. Stir over gentle heat until mixture boils, then simmer for 2 minutes. Season well. Cut chicken into small dice and mix into sauce. Cool. When mixture is cold, form into cylinder shapes about 3 inches in length, using wet hands. Roll in breadcrumbs, then dip in slightly beaten egg and roll in breadcrumbs again. Deep fry in hot oil. When golden, remove and drain. Serve hot.

◙ Coq au Vin à la Dijonnaise * *Chicken in Wine Dijonnaise*

For 4 persons: 1 *chicken, weighing about 2–2$\frac{1}{2}$ lb;* 1 *bottle red wine;* 6 *oz ean bacon;* 20 *small onions; flour; nutmeg;* 2 *oz butter; chopped parsley.* Cooking time: 50–60 minutes.

Cut up the chicken, skin and flour the pieces. Brown them in butter in a casserole; add the onions and the bacon cut in strips. When everything is browned add a bottle of good quality red burgundy. Bring to the boil. Season with salt, pepper, *bouquet garni* and a grating of nutmeg. Cover and cook gently. Skim fat off sauce and reduce or thicken at the last moment with chicken blood, as for jugged hare. Sprinkle with chopped parsley and serve in the casserole after checking the seasoning.

◙ Poule au Riz * *Boiled Chicken with Rice*

For 8 persons: 1 *boiling fowl, weighing about 5 lb;* 12 *oz rice;* 2 *oz butter;* 1 *egg yolk;* 2 *sliced onions;* 2 *sliced carrots;* 2 *chopped leeks.* Cooking time: 2–3 hours, according to quality. *Sauce:* 3 *oz butter;* 2 *oz flour;* 1 *pint chicken stock;* 1 *egg yolk;* 2 *tablespoons cream; squeeze lemon juice; seasoning.*

Place the fowl in a pan and add stock or water to come three-quarters of the way up the bird. Add the sliced onions, carrots, leeks, seasoning and a *bouquet garni*. Cover the saucepan with a tight-fitting lid. Bring to the boil and simmer gently for 1$\frac{1}{2}$–2 hours. When it is tender, strain the stock. Toss the rice in butter, add chicken stock (3 parts of stock to 1 of rice), cover closely and cook gently for 18 minutes. In the meantime make the white sauce as instructed below. Carve the fowl and arrange it on the rice. Coat with sauce. Alternately, leave the fowl whole and serve the sauce separately. *For the sauce:* Melt 2 ounces butter, add flour and cook for 2 minutes without colouring. Whisk in stock with lemon juice and seasoning and continue whisking until boiling. Mix egg yolk and cream, and stir in the boiling stock. Reheat without boiling. Add remaining 1 ounce butter in small pieces, beating one piece in before adding the next. (*See illustration p.* 170).

Poulet au Blanc * *White Stew of Chicken*

For 6 persons: 1 *chicken, weighing about 3 lb;* 1 *onion stuck with a clove;* 1 *carrot;* 8 *oz mushrooms;* 2 *leeks;* 1 *bouquet garni;* ¾ *pint white sauce, made as above.* Cooking time: 35–45 minutes.

Cut up the chicken and put it in a casserole with an onion stuck with a clove, a quartered carrot, 8 leeks, *bouquet garni,* salt and peppercorns, and add enough water or stock to cover the chicken. Cook for 30 minutes, or until tender. Skim fat off stock, strain it and use three-quarters pint of it to make a white sauce. Thicken this with 1 egg yolk and 2–3 tablespoons cream, replace the chicken in it with mushrooms cooked separately and simmer for 4–5 minutes.

▣ Chicken in Cream Sauce

For 4 persons: ½ *green pepper;* 1 *oz butter;* 4 *oz sliced mushrooms;* 1 *tablespoon grated onion;* 1½ *lb diced, cooked chicken;* ½ *oz flour; salt;* ½ *pint milk or cream;* ½ *pint chicken stock;* 3 *egg yolks;* 1 *tablespoon lemon juice;* ⅓ *teaspoon paprika;* ½ *teaspoon celery salt;* 2 *tablespoons dry sherry.* Cooking time: about 15 minutes.

Remove pith and seeds from green pepper; blanch in boiling water 5 minutes. Drain and chop finely. Heat butter in saucepan, add green pepper, mushrooms, and grated onion. *Sauté* a few minutes. Sprinkle in flour and salt. Cook, stirring constantly for 2 minutes. Gradually blend milk or cream and stock; add chicken. Stir over gentle heat until sauce thickens, simmer 3 minutes. Stir a little of the sauce into the beaten egg yolks, then return mixture to the saucepan. Add lemon juice, paprika, and celery salt. Reheat gently, stirring, but do not allow to boil. Just before serving, stir in sherry.

▣ de Grain en Cocotte à la Bonne Femme *
Casserole Bonne Femme

For 4 persons: 1 *spring chicken, weighing about 3 lb;* 25 *button onions;* 25 *lardoons lean bacon;* 8 *oz mushrooms;* 2 *oz butter; bouillon. Garnish: Carrots and cubed potatoes, cooked separately.* Cooking time: 40–45 minutes.

Brown the whole trussed chicken in butter, in the casserole, on both sides. Add a little good *bouillon* and surround with the onions and the bacon, previously fried in butter. Season, cover and cook in the oven for 15 minutes. Add the raw mushrooms and continue cooking until all is tender. Remove trussing thread from chicken, carve it, replace it in the casserole in its original shape and serve surrounded by the garnish. (*See illustration p.* 162).

▣ en Cocotte à la Paysanne * *Peasant Style*
Casserole

For 4 persons: 1 *chicken, weighing about 3 lb; carrots; small onions; turnips;* 25–30 *lardoons lean bacon.* Cooking time: 40–45 minutes.

Same method as preceding recipe. Toss the diced vegetables in butter before adding them to the casserole. *To make gravy:* Reduce the liquid in the casserole with white wine and *bouillon* after browning the chicken. Serve in the casserole on the vegetables.

Poulet en Fricassée * *Fricassée of Chicken*

For 6 persons: 1 chicken, weighing about 3 lb; seasoned flour; 2 oz butter; 2 tablespoons oil; 15 small onions or shallots; ¼ pint white wine; 8 oz mushrooms; bouquet garni; 2 egg yolks; 3 tablespoons cream; 1 tablespoon chopped parsley; seasoning. Cooking time: 45–50 minutes.

Cut up the chicken. Toss the joints in seasoned flour and *sauté* in butter and oil, to colour without browning. Dredge lightly with flour. Add wine and enough water to cover the chicken. Stir until boiling. Season and add onions and *bouquet garni*. Cover closely and cook for 40 minutes. Add mushrooms and continue cooking until all is tender. Arrange chicken joints on hot dish. Thicken sauce with egg yolks mixed with cream. Coat the chicken and sprinkle chopped parsley over.

▣ Marengo * *Marengo*

For 6 persons: 1 chicken, weighing about 3 lb; seasoned flour; 2 oz butter; 2 tablespoons oil; 1 large onion; ¼ pint white wine; 3 tablespoons tomato purée; 1 clove garlic; bouquet garni; seasoning; bouillon; 8 oz mushrooms; chopped parsley. Garnish: 6 fried croûtons; 6 fried eggs; 6 crayfish, cooked in court bouillon.

Joint the chicken. Toss in flour and brown lightly in butter and oil. Fry the onion lightly. Add wine and reduce to half before adding the tomato *purée*, crushed garlic, *bouquet garni* and seasoning. Add *bouillon* to cover chicken. Cover closely and cook for 25 minutes. Add raw sliced mushrooms and cook for 15 minutes. Serve chicken on a hot dish, remove *bouquet garni* from gravy and skim off surface fat. Pour the gravy over the chicken. Surround with fried *croûtons*, fried eggs and crayfish. Sprinkle chopped parsley over.

▣ Rôti * *Roast*

For 4 persons: 1 chicken, weighing about 3 lb; 2 oz dripping; seasoning; 1 dessertspoon cornflour; ½ pint giblet stock. Accompaniments: ½ pint Bread sauce; ½ pint gravy; 4 potatoes, cut for Game chips; watercress. Cooking time: 45–50 minutes.

A roasting chicken should be 6–7 months old and very tender. *To test for this:* Press the tip of the breastbone. This should be pliable and bend easily.

Rub the chicken over with salt and season the inside. Truss it and put into a roasting tin on its side. Baste with hot dripping. Cover with greased paper and roast in a hot oven, 400°F or Gas Mark 6, for about 30 minutes. Turn and continue roasting for 20 minutes. Test for readiness by piercing the thigh with a skewer. The liquid oozing out should be clear. If blood shows, cook for longer. When tender, remove the chicken and pull out trussing string. Keep the bird hot while making the gravy. Serve with gravy, Bread sauce, Game chips and watercress.

To make the gravy: Pour off the fat, leaving the sediment in the tin. Sprinkle cornflour over. Stir in the stock and boil up, stirring all the time. Correct the seasoning and strain into a sauceboat.

▣ Sauté Bercy * *Sautéed Bercy*

For 5 persons: 1 chicken, weighing about 3 lb; seasoned flour; 3 oz butter; 2 tablespoons oil; 4 finely chopped shallots; scant ½ pint white wine; scant ½ pint Demi-glace; 4 oz chipolatas; 8 oz mushrooms; lemon juice; chopped parsley. Cooking time: 35–45 minutes.

Joint the chicken, toss in seasoned flour and *sauté* in 2 ounces butter and oil until tender.

164

Arrange in serving dish and keep hot. Toss the shallots in the *sauté* pan, add wine and reduce to half. Stir in *Demi-glace*, a squeeze of lemon juice and the sliced mushrooms with chipolatas. Cook for 10 minutes. Remove from heat and add 1 ounce butter. Pour this over the chicken and sprinkle with parsley. The *Demi-glace* may be replaced by some meat extract to give a slightly stronger flavour.

Poulet Sauté à la Chasseur   *   *Sautéed Chasseur*

For 5 persons: 1 chicken, weighing about 3 lb; seasoned flour; 2 oz butter; 2 oz oil; ½ pint sauce Chasseur; ¼ pint white wine; croûtons; chopped parsley. Cooking time: 25 minutes.

Cut up the chicken. Toss in seasoned flour and *sauté* in butter and oil. When browned, turn, cover closely and cook in a hot oven, 400°F or Gas Mark 6, until tender. Meanwhile make the *sauce Chasseur*. When the chicken is tender, pile it on a round dish. Pour off fat. Add wine and reduce to half. Add this reduction to the *sauce Chasseur* and coat the chicken with it. Sprinkle with parsley and garnish with fried *croûtons*.

▣ Sauté Parmentier   *   *Sautéed Parmentier*

For 5 persons: 1 chicken, weighing about 3 lb; 1¼ lb potatoes; ½ pint Demi-glace; 2 oz butter; 2 tablespoons oil; ¼ pint white wine; 1 onion; chopped parsley. Cooking time: 30–35 minutes.

Cook in the same way as Chicken Sauté Bercy. Blanch the diced potatoes, cook them in extra butter and add finely chopped onion when they are two-thirds done. Arrange the chicken in a pyramid, surround with the potatoes. Pour fat from *sauté* pan, add white wine, and reduce. Add the *Demi-glace*, remove from heat and add a good pat of butter. Pour over chicken and sprinkle with chopped parsley.

▣ Sauté à la Portugaise   *   *Sautéed Portuguese style*

For 4 persons: 1 chicken, weighing about 3 lb; generous ¼ pint white wine; 8 tomato halves stuffed with 4 oz mushrooms; 4 tomatoes; 2 oz sliced mushrooms; 2 cloves garlic. Cooking time: 30–35 minutes.

Cook in the same way as Chicken Marengo. Arrange the chicken on a dish. Reduce the liquor in the pan with white wine, add the peeled, seeded and diced tomatoes, sautéed in butter, with sliced mushrooms and crushed cloves of garlic. Pour over the chicken and surround with tomato halves filled with cooked chopped mushrooms and baked until tender. Sprinkle chopped parsley over everything. Whole braised tomatoes may replace the stuffed tomatoes.

Foies de Poulet Sautés   *   *Sautéed Chicken Livers*

For 4 persons: 2 oz butter; 2 finely chopped onions; 1 lb chicken livers; seasoned flour; 2 oz extra butter; ½ lb sliced mushrooms; ½ oz flour; 1 pint chicken stock; salt; pepper; little grated nutmeg; ¼ pint sour cream; 6 tablespoons dry sherry; 2 bacon rashers. Cooking time: 15-20 minutes.

Heat butter in frying pan, *sauté* onions until transparent. Cut livers into 2 or 3 pieces, discarding any gall-bladders; toss in seasoned flour. *Sauté* until tender in frying pan with onions. In another pan, *sauté* mushrooms in melted extra butter until tender. Sprinkle flour over chicken livers and cook, stirring, 2 or 3 minutes. Draw aside, gradually stir in stock. Slowly bring to boil, stirring constantly. Add mushrooms, salt, pepper, nutmeg, sour cream, and sherry. Simmer 3 minutes. Fry bacon until crisp; crumble. Turn chicken livers into serving dish, sprinkle with bacon.

Pilaf de Poulet à l'Orientale * *Oriental Chicken Pilaf*

For 4 persons: 1 spring chicken; 8 oz rice; 1 onion; 2 tablespoons oil; 2 oz butter; 3 tomatoes; 1 pint bouillon; 2 peppers; saffron; bouquet garni. Cooking time: 30–35 minutes.

Cut the chicken into fairly small pieces. Brown them in butter and oil with a chopped onion. When the chicken has coloured add 8 ounces rice and fry together; add the *bouillon*, peeled, seeded and quartered tomatoes, salt, pepper, saffron, *bouquet garni* and 2 finely shredded peppers and cook covered for half an hour. Serve in a *timbale* or deep dish.

A chicken *pilaf* may also be prepared by cooking the chicken alone, as for a White Stew of Chicken, and the *pilaf* rice separately; the rice is then served in a ring with the chicken in the middle.

Risotto de foie de poulet * *Chicken Liver Risotto*

For 4 persons: ½ lb chicken livers; 2 finely chopped onions; 4 oz butter; 12 oz long grain rice; 3 sliced sticks celery; about 1¼ pints chicken stock; salt; pepper; 2 oz grated Parmesan cheese. Cooking time: 40-45 minutes.

Heat the butter in large saucepan. Add onion and celery, *sauté* 10 minutes, stirring occasionally. Cut chicken livers into quarters, discarding gall bladders. Add to pan, cook further five minutes. Stir in well-rinsed rice, stir over heat 5 minutes. Add stock, bring to boil; reduce heat and simmer, covered, until rice is tender and liquid absorbed (about 20 to 25 minutes). Stir in Parmesan cheese, adjust seasoning.

Savoury Chicken Puffs

For 50: 1 16 oz can condensed cream of chicken soup; ½ pint water; 2½ oz plain flour; 4 oz butter; ¼ oz gelatine; 1 tablespoon extra water; 4 oz minced cooked chicken; ¼ oz chopped parsley; salt; pepper; beaten egg; browned breadcrumbs; oil for frying. Cooking time: 5-10 minutes.

Mix soup and water. Melt butter in saucepan, stir in flour, cook for a few minutes, then remove from heat and stir in soup. Stir over low heat until boiling and smooth. Remove from heat, add gelatine dissolved in extra water, chicken and parsley, and season well with salt and pepper. Chill overnight. Form into small balls, roll in breadcrumbs, dip in beaten egg, roll in breadcrumbs again. Deep fry in hot oil until golden, serve hot.

CANARD * DUCK

Canard aux Cerises * *with Cherries*

For 6 persons: 1 duck weighing about 4–5 lb; salt and pepper; ½ teaspoon dried rosemary; ¼ pint oil; 3 tablespoons honey; duck giblets; 1 bayleaf; 1 onion; 4 peppercorns; ½ pint water; 16 oz can cherries; ½ oz arrowroot; watercress or parsley to garnish. Cooking time: about 2½ hours altogether.

Rub duck with salt and sprinkle with pepper and rosemary. Heat oil in large saucepan, brown bird on all sides. Transfer contents of saucepan to baking dish, brush duck with warmed honey. Roast in moderate oven 350°F or Gas Mark 4, for 30 minutes, basting occasionally. Prick skin to release excess fat. Place giblets in saucepan with bayleaf, onion, peppercorns and water. Simmer gently until reduced slightly; strain. Add ¼ pint of syrup from the can of cherries, simmer again until ½ pint remains. Blend arrowroot with 2 table-spoons water, add to sauce, stir over heat until thickened. Drain fat from duck, place bird in deep casserole. Spoon over sauce, cover and return to warm oven, 325°F or Gas Mark 3, for 1½ hours or until duck is tender. Add drained cherries to casserole 10 minutes before end of cooking time. Arrange duck on serving dish, spoon sauce over. Arrange cherries on either side, garnish with watercress or parsley.

Canard avec Sauce à l'Abricot   *   *with Apricot Sauce*

For 6 persons: 1 *duck weighing about 5 lb; melted butter or fat; little melted honey; 16 oz can apricots; juice 1 lemon; water; ½ oz arrowroot or cornflour; nut of butter; 4 tablespoons brandy.*

Place duck in baking dish, brush with melted butter and honey. Roast in hot oven, 400°F or Gas Mark 6, for 15 minutes, then reduce heat to moderate, 350°F or Gas Mark 4, and cook until tender, allowing 25 to 30 minutes per pound cooking time. After first 30 minutes, prick skin gently with fork or skewer to release excess fat. Baste and turn bird occasionally. Keep hot. Drain apricots, reserving syrup. To the syrup add lemon juice and sufficient cold water to make ½ pint. Blend arrowroot or cornflour with 2 tablespoons cold water, add to apricot mixture and cook, stirring, over low heat until sauce has thickened. Add butter and apricot halves. Cook until heated through, then add brandy. Place duck on warm serving dish, arrange apricot halves around it, spoon sauce over.

▣ aux Olives   *   *with Olives*

For 4–5 persons: 1 *duck, weighing about 3–4 lb; 2 oz butter; 2 sliced onions; 2 sliced carrots; 2 oz chopped bacon rashers; bouquet garni; ¼ pint bouillon; ¼ pint white wine; ½ pint sauce Demi-glace; 15 olives.* Cooking time: 45–60 minutes.

Truss the duck and brown in the butter. Remove, and brown the vegetables and bacon. Add *bouquet garni* and lay the bird on the vegetable foundation. Cover closely and sweat for 5 minutes. Add *bouillon*, replace lid and braise in a hot oven, 400°F or Gas Mark 6, for 45 minutes or until tender. Remove from pan and draw out trussing string. Add wine to pan. Reduce slightly and add the sauce *Demi-glace*. Boil up for 3 minutes. Pass through a sieve and skim off surface fat. Return to pan with duck. Stone the olives, scald them and add to pan. Heat up and serve the duck with the olives round it. The sauce may be poured round the duck, or served separately to allow for easy carving.

▣ à l'Orange   *   *with Orange*

For 4 persons: 1 *duck, weighing about 3–4 lb; 5 oranges; ½ pint thin brown sauce; 3 tablespoons curaçao.* Cooking time: 45–60 minutes.

Braise the duck as for preceding recipe. When it is ready, pour fat off sauce and strain it, add the juice of 2 oranges, curaçao and the finely shredded zest of 3 oranges, blanched for 3 minutes in boiling water. Do not let the sauce boil again. Carve the duck, pour sauce over it and garnish all round with orange segments from which all seeds and white skin have been removed, and the remaining orange cut in thin slices with fluted edges. (*See illustration p. 169*).

Canard aux Petits Pois * Duck with Green Peas

For 6 persons: 1 *duck, weighing about 4–6 lb;* 2 *oz butter; seasoning; bouquet garni;* 6 *oz lean bacon;* 20 *button onions;* 1 *pint bouillon;* 8 *oz fresh green peas.* Cooking time: 45–60 minutes.

Brown the duck with butter, onions and strips of lean bacon; pour off most of the liquid. Remove the duck, dredge onions and bacon with a tablespoon of flour, brown and add *bouillon.* Replace the duck. Add seasoning and a *bouquet garni* and bring to the boil. Add the peas at the same time or up to 15 minutes later, according to their age, so that everything is ready at the same time. Serve duck with onions and peas round it. Thin down the sauce if necessary, remove *bouquet garni* and serve sauce separately.

Salmis de Canard * Salmi of Duck

For 4 persons: 1 *duck, weighing about 3–4 lb;* 8 *oz fat bacon;* 1 *onion;* 2 *tablespoons oil;* 1 *shallot; garlic; thyme; bayleaf; parsley;* ¼ *pint white wine;* ¼ *pint red wine;* 4 *tablespoons Madeira;* ½ *pint brown sauce. Garnish:* ½ *lb cooked mushrooms; some heart-shaped croûtons fried in butter.* Cooking time: 45–60 minutes.

Roast the duck, with fat bacon, keeping it slightly underdone. In the meantime make the following sauce: brown the chopped onion with the oil; when it has coloured add a shallot and, one minute later, a crushed clove of garlic, a sprig of thyme and bay leaf and 3 sprigs of parsley. Boil up, add the red and white wine, and allow to boil away completely; at this point add the brown sauce and let it simmer. Cut up the duck into 2 legs, 2 wings and 5 or 6 slices of breast and keep the pieces hot with a little Madeira without allowing it to boil (very important). Pound the carcase to a fine *purée* and add to the sauce; bring just to the boil and strain sauce over duck. Add some cooked mushrooms; do not boil or the meat will turn hard. Arrange in a mound. Surround with fried *croûtons.*

Caneton Rôti * Roast Duckling

Use the same method as for Roast Chicken (*p.* 164), but there is no need to add butter if the bird is fat. Allow 15–20 minutes roasting time per pound, in a moderate oven, 350°F or Gas Mark 4. Pour off most of the fat before making the gravy.

DINDE * TURKEY

Turkey is drawn and singed in the same way as chicken. Care must be taken to break the legs, and remove the strong muscles, as this makes the legs much more tender. Truss the turkey and roast after seasoning inside and out. Allow 12–15 minutes cooking time per pound for a large turkey and 20–25 minutes per pound for a smaller bird.

Dinde aux Marrons * Turkey with Chestnuts

For 10 persons: 1 *turkey, weighing about 10–12 lb;* 1½ *lb sausage meat; nutmeg;* 2 *shallots;* 1 *lb cooked chestnuts.* Cooking time: 2–2½ hours.

Draw the leg sinews from the turkey, and cut off the feet. Mix sausage meat thoroughly with finely chopped shallots and season with salt, pepper and grated nutmeg. Combine this mixture with the skinned chestnuts cooked in water, taking care not to break them. Fill the turkey with this stuffing, sew up the opening and truss. Cover breast with fat bacon or kidney fat. Roast in a fairly hot oven, 375°F or Gas Mark 5, until tender. Remove trussing

▲ *Poulet de grain en cocotte à la bonne femme, p. 163*

Canard à l'orange, p. 167 ▼

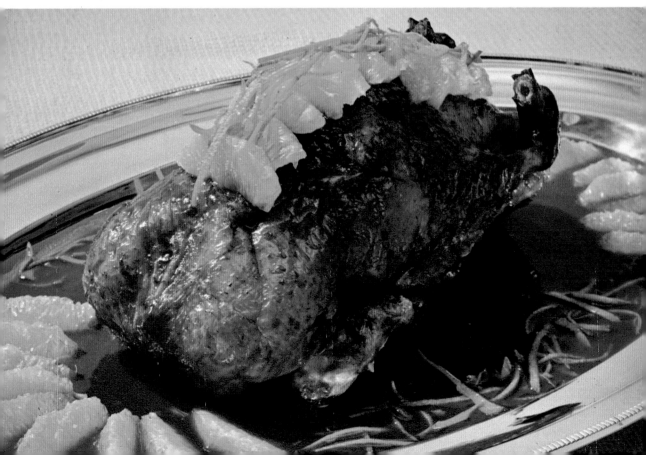

▲ *Poule au riz, p. 162*

Râble de lièvre aux champignons, p. 178 ▼

▲ *Perdreaux à la vigneronne, p. 181*

Pâté de veau en croûte, p. 183 ▼   171

172 ▲ *Perdreau aux choux, p. 180*

Selle de chevreuil, p. 175 ▼

string and serve with the following accompaniments: sausages, Bread sauce, gravy, Cranberry sauce, bacon rolls, and a green vegetable.

Pilaf de Dinde   *   Turkey Pilaff

For 4 persons: 1 large onion, chopped; 4 oz butter; 12 oz uncooked long-grain rice; salt; pepper; 1 bay leaf; 1 lb cooked, diced turkey; about 1½ pints chicken or turkey stock; 2 oz chopped walnuts. Cooking time: 20-25 minutes.

Melt butter in large heavy saucepan, add onion, *sauté* until golden. Add rice, salt and pepper continue to cook, stirring until rice turns golden. Add turkey, bay leaf and stock, cover; simmer 20 minutes or until rice is tender and stock absorbed. Toss lightly with chopped nuts, serve at once.

OIE   *   GOOSE

Oie à la Choucroûte   *   Goose with Sauerkraut

For 4–6 persons: 1 goose, weighing about 6 lb; 2 lb of sauerkraut; 1½ lb sausage meat; 1 lb lean bacon; seasoning. Cooking time: about 2 hours.

Stuff the goose with the sausage meat, truss and roast in a casserole. Braise the sauerkraut with the bacon until part cooked, then bury the goose in the sauerkraut and complete the cooking.

▣ Farcie aux Marrons   *   Stuffed with Chestnuts

For 8–10 persons: 1 goose, weighing about 6 lb; 2¼ lb chestnuts. Cooking time: 1¾–2 hours.

Slit the chestnuts at the thick end and bake until tender. Peel and let them cool, before inserting them in the goose; they may be mixed with the chopped liver. Truss the goose and roast it.

▣ Rôtie   *   Roast

Roast without butter or fat. Start off in a fairly hot oven, 375°F or Gas Mark 5. After 15 minutes prick the skin with a fork to allow the fat to run out. To see if it is done, prick where the leg joins the body; if it is cooked right through, a drop of liquid as clear as water will run out. Serve with Sage and onion stuffing, gravy, Apple sauce and green peas.

LES PIGEONS ET PINTADES   *   PIGEONS AND GUINEA FOWLS

Pigeons are cooked in the same way as ducks. See recipes for Duck with green peas or olives. They must be cooked for at least 25 minutes; even very young squabs require this cooking time.

Farcis à l'Anglaise   *   Stuffed

For 4 persons: 2 young pigeons; 2 oz bread; 2 oz beef suet; 3 oz butter; 3 oz fat bacon; 2 onions; 1 egg; spices. Cooking time: 35–40 minutes.

Chop the onions and brown them in butter: chop the suet, dip a small piece of bread in *bouillon* and squeeze it out, crumble it and mix suet, bread, onion, a whole egg, salt, pepper, thyme, parsley and sage, chopped very fine. Stuff the pigeons, sew up the opening, truss and bard with fat bacon on the breast. Roast in a hot oven, 400°F or Gas Mark 6, basting occasionally with butter. Serve on a fried *croûton* or thick toast. Accompaniments usually include Bread sauce, gravy, salad, Chipped potatoes and fried crumbs.

PINTADE * *GUINEA FOWL*

Guinea fowl is prepared in the same way as pheasant. If roasted, it must be basted constantly, since the flesh is rather dry. They usually take about ¾ of an hour to roast. Guinea fowl must be young, they are not to be recommended if over one year old.

LA VOLAILLE FROIDE * *COLD POULTRY*

Confit d'Oie * *Preserved Goose*

Cut each goose into quarters, salt and pickle them for 24 hours, then wipe them and poach gently for about 2 hours in the goose fat that has collected. Do not let the fat get too hot; it should merely simmer, otherwise the goose will be fried instead of poached. The goose quarters are cooked when you can prick them with a needle without any blood running out. Drain and remove the bones. Place the pieces of goose in sterilised earthenware or stone jars and cover completely with the fat used in cooking, after carefully decanting it to remove the juices from the goose. Top with melted lard to a depth of ½ inch. Tie down and store in a cool place. Preserved goose will keep for a very long time. Store it in several small jars which can be used up quickly once they are opened, rather than in large ones in which the goose may spoil if left open for any length of time.

Poulet Froid à la Gelée * *Chicken in Aspic*

For 5 persons: 1 chicken, weighing about 3–4 lb; 2 pints aspic jelly; 3–4 tablespoons Madeira.

Making aspic is too laborious a job for the housewife and we therefore recommend buying it ready-made. Melt it gently, following instructions on the packet and allowing for Madeira or port, and let it cool. Cut up a cold roast chicken and arrange tastefully in a deep dish; cover with aspic at the moment the latter is beginning to set. With skill it is possible to carve the chicken and replace it in its original shape in a *pâté terrine* and then cover it with aspic. The Madeira may be replaced by a pinch of fresh tarragon leaves infused in the hot aspic.

CHEVREUIL * *VENISON*

Buck venison is considered to be the finest. The haunch and saddle are roasted in the oven or on the spit. The shoulder may also be roasted, but it is better to jug it, like hare (see below). Lard the joint and remove all sinews. Marinate for 2–3 days in red wine with 2 onions stuck with cloves, 2 sliced carrots, a *bouquet garni* and some peppercorns. Drain the meat and roast in a hot oven, 400°F or Gas Mark 6, about 20 minutes to the pound and 20 minutes over. Serve with a garnish of vegetables and *sauce Poivrade* or Venison. Alternatively, wrap up in a flour and water paste and enclose the whole in foil. Roast as above. Break off the paste 20 minutes before serving. Dredge the joint with flour, baste with butter and crisp in a hot oven.

Côtelettes de Chevreuil * *Venison Cutlets*

For 4 persons: 8 cutlets.

Marinate the cutlets for 24 hours and cook in very hot butter after drying carefully. They may be garnished in a number of ways—with chestnut or lentil *purée*, mushrooms, etc. Serve with a light game sauce, such as *sauce Chasseur*.

Gigue de Chevreuil Marie-Stuart * *Leg of Venison Mary Stuart*

For 8–10 persons: 1 leg of venison, weighing about $4\frac{1}{2}$ lb; $1\frac{1}{4}$ lb chestnuts; 8 oz Gratin forcemeat; 3 egg yolks; $1\frac{1}{4}$ pints sauce Poivrade. Cooking time: about $1\frac{1}{2}$-$1\frac{3}{4}$ hours.

Marinate the leg of venison with oil and white wine with some chopped shallots added. Darn lardoons through on the outer surface (or enclose in paste) and roast in a hot oven. Garnish with *croquettes* prepared as follows: make a chestnut *purée*, mix with the *Gratin* forcemeat, bind over the heat with the egg yolks, leave until cold, form into pear-shaped *croquettes*, dip in egg and breadcrumbs and fry. Serve *sauce Poivrade* separately.

Selle de Chevreuil * *Saddle of Venison*

For 8 persons: 1 saddle of venison, weighing about $4\frac{1}{2}$ lb; 10 apples (use very firm ones); 1 small jar redcurrant jelly; 1 pint sauce Poivrade. Cooking time: $1\frac{1}{2}$-$1\frac{3}{4}$ hours.

Darn lardoons of pork fat through the outer surface of the saddle of venison and marinate in red wine containing a *bouquet garni*. Roast in a hot oven. Garnish with peeled, cored apples cut into small keg shapes and poached in water lightly flavoured with lemon. Keep the apples rather firm. When serving, place a little redcurrant jelly in the hollowed-out centre of each apple. (*See illustration p.* 172).

LAPIN * *RABBIT*

There are two kinds of rabbit, the wild rabbit, which is classed as game, and the domestic or hutch rabbit. The wild rabbit is cooked in the same way as hare, jugged, as a loaf, *pâté*, etc. It may also be cooked in the same way as the domestic rabbit, sautéed, or *Chasseur* style as a stew. It may also be stuffed whole and braised.

Lapin de Garenne à la Jeanneton * *Rabbit Jeanneton*

For 8 persons: 2 wild rabbits, each weighing about 2 lb; 2 oz butter; 2 tablespoons oil; 3 chopped shallots; a clove of garlic; 8 oz tomatoes; 1 pint white wine; 1 pint water; salt; pepper; bouquet garni; sprig of thyme. Garnish: 1 oz butter; 1 lb fried sliced onions; fried croûtons; chopped parsley. Cooking time: $1\frac{1}{2}$-2 hours.

Prepare the rabbit, joint it and fry lightly in a *sauté* pan in butter and oil until golden. Add shallots, crushed garlic and the tomatoes, peeled, seeded and coarsley chopped. Simmer for 10 minutes, half cover with equal parts of wine and water. Season, add a *bouquet garni* and the thyme. Cover closely and simmer for $1\frac{1}{4}$ hours, or until tender. Remove rabbit joints, reduce the sauce and strain it. Add butter in small pieces, beating each piece well in. Serve the rabbit, coated with sauce and garnished with mounds of fried onion rings, fried *croûtons* and some chopped parsley.

Lapin Sauce Soubise　*　*Rabbit with Onion Sauce*

For 4-6 persons: 1 *large or 2 small rabbits;* 1½ *pints chicken stock or water; juice* ½ *lemon;* 2 *onions; bouquet garni of thyme, parsley and bay leaf;* 12 *small white onions;* 3 *oz butter;* 1 *oz plain flour;* 2 *egg yolks;* 4 *tablespoons milk;* 1 *oz chopped parsley; salt; pepper.* Cooking time: 1¼-1½ hours.

Soak rabbit in salted water; drain, joint into pieces. Place in saucepan, cover with chicken stock or water, add lemon juice. Put in the whole 2 onions, and *bouquet garni.* Bring to boil, skim well. Cover, simmer for an hour or until tender. Remove from heat, take out rabbit, strain liquid into basin and reserve. (You should have about 1 pint liquid). Heat 2 ounces of the butter in saucepan, *sauté* the small white onions for about 8 minutes, without browning. Remove from pan. Add remaining butter to melt in pan, mix in flour, stir over heat 1 minute. Slowly add rabbit stock, stirring continuously so that sauce is smooth and free from lumps; simmer 5 minutes. Combine egg yolks and milk with a little of the hot sauce, mix well, then return all to saucepan and stir well. Add rabbit, onions, chopped parsley, and reheat, stirring, but do not allow to boil. Taste, adjust seasoning before serving.

▣ Sauté à la Chasseur　*　*Sautéed Chasseur*

For 4 persons: 1 *rabbit, weighing about* 2½ *lb;* 2 *oz lard; flour;* ½ *pint white wine;* ½ *pint water;* 8 *oz mushrooms;* 3 *shallots;* 2 *tablespoons tomato purée; seasoning; bouquet garni.* Cooking time: 1½-2 hours.

Cut up the rabbit and *sauté* in a casserole with a little very hot lard. Brown well, dredge with flour, add 2 or 3 chopped shallots and, when the flour is brown, add white wine and water. Add salt, pepper, *bouquet garni* and tomato *purée.* Cook at low heat for 1½ hours, add sliced mushrooms browned in oil. Skim off fat and serve sprinkled with chopped parsley.

Gibelotte de Lapin 1　*　*Rabbit Stew 1*

For 6 persons: 1 *rabbit, weighing about* 3 *lb;* 25 *button onions;* 2 *oz butter;* 25 *strips lean bacon;* 2 *lb potatoes;* 2 *cloves garlic;* ½ *pint water;* ½ *pint red wine.* Cooking time: about 1½-2 hours.

Brown as above, dredge with flour, add a little garlic instead of shallots, then red wine, water and seasonings. After three-quarters of an hour's cooking add button onions and strips of lean bacon, both browned in butter. Cook for another 20 minutes, then add some new potatoes and cook until all is tender. If the sauce is not brown enough, add a few drops of caramel.

▣ Gibelotte de Lapin II　*　*Rabbit Stew II*

For 4 persons: 1 *large rabbit; salted water;* 1 *large onion;* 1 *oz fat;* 1 *oz plain flour;* ½ *teaspoon pepper; little salt;* 1 *pint stock or water;* 3 *rashers bacon, rind removed;* 1 *carrot;* 1 *white turnip;* 1 *stick celery;* ½ *teaspoon grated lemon rind; pinch nutmeg; finely chopped parsley.* Cooking time: about 2 hours.

Joint rabbit into pieces, wash in salted water; dry well. Peel onion, slice thinly. Heat fat in saucepan and fry rabbit pieces till brown; lift out. Add onion to pan, cook lightly, mix in flour, pepper and salt, and allow to brown. Pour over the stock, stir over heat until sauce boils and thickens. Add rabbit and finely chopped bacon. Peel vegetables, cut into strips or rings, add to saucepan with lemon rind and nutmeg. Cover, simmer gently about 1½ hours or until rabbit is tender. Add more liquid if required. Serve hot, sprinkled with parsley.

Lapereau Farci * *Stuffed Rabbit*

For 4 persons: 1 *large rabbit;* 2 *large tomatoes;* 1 *teaspoon grated lemon rind;* 3 *oz soft breadcrumbs;* 1 *teaspoon chopped parsley;* ½ *teaspoon dried thyme;* 1 *chopped shallot;* 1 *oz melted butter;* 1 *small egg; salt and pepper;* 2 *bacon rashers;* 3 *oz fat;* ¼ *pint stock.* Cooking time: 1½-1¾ hours.

Soak rabbit in salted water for several hours. Prepare stuffing. Chop skinned tomatoes, mix with lemon rind, breadcrumbs, parsley, thyme, shallot, and melted butter. Season lightly, mix in egg. Drain rabbit, dry, stuff with mixture, and truss. Melt fat in baking pan, brown rabbit all over. Top with bacon rashers, add stock. Bake rabbit in moderate oven, 350°F or Gas Mark 4, basting occasionally with liquid, until tender, about 1¼ hours. Remove bacon for last 10 minutes of cooking. Serve hot with gravy made from pan juices, adding the crumbled bacon.

▣ à la Ménagère * *with Sausagemeat*

For 6 persons: 1 *young rabbit, weighing about* 3 *lb;* 12 *oz sausage meat;* 1 *lean slice bacon;* 1 *lean slice smoked ham; the rabbit's liver;* 4 *onions;* 2 *oz bread;* 1 *clove garlic;* 2 *carrots;* 1 *bouquet garni;* ½ *pint white wine; some bouillon.* Cooking time:1½-2 hours.

Mince the liver, bacon and ham with 1 or 2 onions; mix with the sausage meat, a piece of bread soaked in cold *bouillon*, a clove of garlic, thyme, and bay leaf, all well crushed. Fill the rabbit with this stuffing and sew up the belly; brown in a braising pan with some bacon, the onions and carrots. Add white wine and *bouillon* to come three-quarters of the way up the rabbit. Season, cover and cook. If liked, thicken the sauce with blood and strain after skimming off fat. Red wine may be used instead of white.

LIÈVRE * HARE

You can tell young hare by the slightly pointed muzzle; on an older animal it is blunt. Also, if you feel between the two bones underneath the forepaws, there is a small lump, like a pea, which disappears with age. The ears are more pointed in a young hare. The traditional method of cooking hare is to jug it.

Civet de Lièvre * *Jugged Hare*

For 4 persons: 1 *hare, weighing about* 3 *lb;* 20 *button onions;* 2 *oz dripping; flour;* 1 *clove garlic;* 4 *oz lean bacon;* 8 *oz mushrooms;* 3 *tablespoons brandy;* 1 *bottle good red wine;* 1 *tablespoon tomato purée; spices; blood if possible.* Cooking time: 2½-3 hours.

Paunch and cut up the hare. Keep as much of the blood as possible, add some vinegar to prevent it clotting. Marinate the hare in red wine with the 2 sliced onions and carrots. Dry and brown over a high flame in a casserole with a little fat. Sprinkle with flour and brown this. Add the brandy and set it alight; add a clove of crushed garlic and 2 minutes later add the wine from the marinade and an equal quantity of water. Add salt, pepper, a blade of mace, a few cloves, *bouquet garni* and tomato *purée*. Cover and cook for 1 hour, then add the onions, browned in butter, and the bacon, cut in strips and browned. Cook for another hour, then skim some of the fat off the sauce and add 8 ounces very clean raw mushrooms. When everything is quite tender, mix the hare's blood with some spoonfuls of sauce and pour into the pan. Stir, boil up once and serve. Garnish with forcemeat balls made with the liver, heart and kidneys and decorate with *glacé* cherries. If you have no hare's blood, ox blood may be used instead. To make the sauce richer, ¼ pint of fresh cream may be added before serving.

Râble de Lièvre à l'Aigre-doux   *   *Sweet-Sour Saddle of Hare*

Same method as below. Add a level teaspoon of redcurrant jelly and a little pepper to the sauce. Serve with unsweetened *purée* of cooking apples with a little lemon juice.

▣ aux Champignons   *   *with Mushrooms*

For 3–4 persons: 1 saddle of hare, weighing about 2 lb; ¼ pint cream; 1½ lb button mushrooms; 2 oz pork fat; 2 oz larding bacon. Cooking time: 1 hour.

Darn thin lardoons through the outer surface of the saddle of hare and leave for 24 hours in a marinade using ½ pint of white wine, 3–4 tablespoons cognac, finely sliced shallots, thyme, bay leaf and pepper. Cover with the pork fat. Roast in a hot oven, 425°F or Gas Mark 7, for 45 minutes. Remove from the oven when cooked. Rinse out the pan with the marinade, reduce by three quarters, strain through a fine, conical sieve and return to the pan. Add the cream and cook for a few minutes to bind. Pour this over the saddle and roast for 5 minutes at 350°F or Gas Mark 4. Arrange the saddle of hare on a serving dish and mask with the sauce. Garnish with the mushrooms, finely sliced and sautéed in butter. Serve with stewed redcurrants in a sauce-boat. (*See illustration p.* 170).

SANGLIER ET MARCASSIN   *   *BOAR AND YOUNG BOAR*

Same recipes as for Venison.

Feathered Game

Bécasses ou Bécassines Flambées   *   *Flambéed*
Woodcock or Snipe

For 4 persons: 4 snipe; 8 tablespoons champagne; 4 tablespoons champagne brandy. Cooking time: 15 minutes.

Do not draw the snipe; roast in a hot oven, 425°F or Gas Mark 7, for 10 minutes only. Cut each bird into 4 pieces and keep hot for a few minutes. During this time pour off cooking fat and reduce the residue with champagne. Crush the entrails in this, chop up the carcase and put in a press to extract the blood; mix it with the entrails. Season, pour over snipe, pour on a dash of brandy, set alight and serve at once.

Blackcock and Grey Hen

These are a variety of grouse and are trussed and cooked in the same way. Cooking time: 30–35 minutes. These birds, like pheasants, must be well hung. They are not very popular, being rather an acquired taste.

Cailles à la Turque   *   *Quails Turkish style*

For 4 persons: 4 quails or fieldfares; 4 oz butter; salt and pepper. Risotto: 6 oz rice; ¾ pint bouillon; 2 oz butter; 2 aubergines; 1 tablespoon oil; extra butter; 3 tablespoons thick Tomato sauce. Cooking time: 12 minutes.

Fry the rice in butter for 6 minutes, add seasoning, *bouillon* and aubergines, neatly diced. Cover closely and cook for 12 minutes. Draw the birds, season insides and truss. Brown in butter, then cook quickly until tender. Add oil to rice, and serve in a deep dish or *timbale* with the quails on top. Pour over a little Tomato sauce reduced with the residue of the pan in which the quails were browned.

Capercailzie

For 8–12 persons. This is the largest of Scottish game birds. It is sometimes called the Wood grouse or Wild turkey. It should be hung for at least 4 days. This gives added flavour and makes the flesh more tender. Hang by the head and undrawn. Blood should drop from the beak when the bird is ready for cooking.

Roast Capercailzie is prepared and cooked like Pheasant (see below). Put it into a very hot oven, 450°F or Gas Mark 8, for 10 minutes. Reduce to 350°F or Gas Mark 4 and cook at a very gentle "sizzle" for about 1 hour, although this varies depending on the age and size.

Accompaniments include Gravy, Bread sauce, fried crumbs, Chipped potatoes and a French salad.

Faisan Rôti * *Roast Pheasant*

For 6–8 persons: Cooking time: young bird, 30 minutes: older birds, 40 minutes.

Hang pheasant by the head in a cold place, without plucking or drawing, as soon as you return from the shoot. Hang for a week or longer depending on weather. Then pluck, clean, truss, bard with fat bacon, salt the inside and insert a small piece of rump steak. Roast for 30–40 minutes in a hot oven, 400°F or Gas Mark 6, or on the spit with butter and fine salt, basting frequently. The gravy is made as for chicken. Serve on a *croûte* of fried bread with a bunch of watercress. The usual accompaniments include fried crumbs, Bread sauce, Chipped potatoes and salad.

Failing a spit, it may be roasted in a casserole (*see Chicken, p.* 161).

▣ Salmis * *Salmi*

For 8 persons: 2 *young pheasants;* 2 *tablespoons oil;* 1 *tablespoon tomato purée;* 1 *onion;* 1 *shallot; garlic;* 4 *tablespoons red wine;* 4 *tablespoons white wine; flour;* 6 *oz mushrooms;* 6 *croûtons of fried bread.* Cooking time: 40 minutes.

Salmis is only good when made from young game. Make gravy by cutting the neck, head, pinions and gizzard into very small pieces, brown with a little fat or oil and add a large glass of water; cook slowly with salt and pepper. Roast the pheasants for 30 minutes, so that they are slightly underdone, and make the sauce: brown the chopped onion in oil; when it yellows, add the shallot and, after 1 minute, a crushed clove of garlic, a sprig of thyme, a bay leaf and 3 sprigs of parsley. Boil up, add the red and white wine and reduce to a quarter of original quantity. Add the prepared gravy and the tomato *purée*, thicken lightly with 1 ounce butter kneaded with a large pinch of flour, and cook slowly. Carve the pheasants, removing the legs and wings, and detaching breasts from carcase. Skin each piece, divide legs into 2 and breast into 5 or 6 slices. Keep the pieces hot in a little sauce without boiling (very important). Chop the carcase to a fine *purée*, add the sauce, just bring to the boil, strain, add some cooked mushrooms and do not allow to boil as this would make the meat hard. Replace the pheasant in its original shape, or arrange pieces in a mound, pour sauce on top, and surround with heart-shaped *croûtons* fried in oil.

Roast Grouse

For 4 persons: 2 *birds.*

Use only young birds for roasting, and serve them slightly underdone. Truss and roast in the same way as Pheasant for about 35 minutes, replacing the rump steak inside with 1 ounce butter seasoned with salt, pepper and lemon juice, which help to keep the bird juicy. Roast at 400°F or Gas Mark 6, basting occasionally with butter. When almost ready, remove barding bacon, dredge with flour and baste, to give a frothy finish. Serve each bird on a fried *croûte* with watercress. Accompaniments include Gravy, Bread sauce, fried crumbs, Chipped potatoes, salad and cranberry jelly. If liked, the fried *croûte* may be spread with a paste made by pounding the parboiled liver with some butter and seasoning. Place *croûte* under bird five minutes before serving. Old grouse should be served braised or in a casserole with *sauce Salmis*. Cook in a warm oven, 350°F or Gas Mark 4. The cooking time depends on the age, but is usually 1–1½ hours.

Perdreaux aux Choux * *Partridge with Cabbage*

For 4 persons: 4 *trussed partridges;* 4 *oz butter;* 1 *large cabbage; Giblet gravy;* 2 *frankfurters;* 8 *oz lean bacon; carrot; onion; bouquet garni; seasoning.* Cooking time: 1½–2 hours.

Blanch the cabbage in boiling water, drain, and press out as much water as possible. Braise in fat in a casserole with the partridge, first browned in butter, embedded in it. Also add the sliced frankfurters and de-salted bacon. Add a sliced carrot, a sliced onion, a *bouquet garni* and 6 peppercorns. Seal the casserole hermetically and braise in a warm oven, 350°F or Gas Mark 4, for about 1½ hours. If the bird is not tough remove it as soon as it is done; check up from time to time. Let the cabbage and sausage braise until tender. Place half the cabbage in a hollow dish, lay the halved partridges on top surrounded by bacon, sausage and sliced carrots. Cover with remaining cabbage. Pour gravy made from the giblets on top, or serve birds on top of cabbage. The same recipe may be used for Pheasant. (*See illustration p.* 172).

Perdreaux Rôtis * *Roast Partridge*

Same method as for Roast pheasant. Cooking time: 20 minutes. Accompaniments as for Roast Pheasant.

▣ à la Vigneronne * *with Grapes*

For 3 persons: 3 partridges; 6 slices pork fat for barding; 6 croûtons; ¾ lb peeled grapes without their pips; 3 oz butter; ¼ pint white wine; ½ pint game stock. Cooking time: 18 minutes.

Bard and truss the partridges. Roast in butter in a hot oven, 400°F or Gas Mark 6. Heat the grapes in their own juice. Arrange the partridges on fried *croûtons*. Drain off the butter used in cooking and rinse out the pan with white wine. Reduce, add the game stock, boil rapidly for a moment and strain. Trim the slices of pork fat used for barding, cover the partridges with them and garnish with the grapes. Serve mashed potatoes and the gravy separately. (*See illustration p.* 171).

Wild Duck in Port

For 4 persons: 2 wild duck, cleaned and singed; 2 onions, chopped; 2 bay leaves; 2 cloves; ½ teaspoon thyme; salt and pepper; port wine; 10 small white onions; ½ oz butter; 2 tablespoons oil. Cooking time: 2 hours.

Place cleaned ducks in bowl, add spices and seasonings and chopped onion, pour over enough port wine to cover; stand for 48 hours. Heat oil in heavy pot, add drained, dried ducks, *sauté* until browned a little on all sides, then add marinade and simmer gently for about 2 hours. *Sauté* the small onions in heated butter separately, then add to ducks about half an hour before ready. The sauce should be thick when ducks are tender; if not thick enough, remove ducks and keep warm, and cook sauce over fast heat until it reduces and thickens.

Pâtés and Terrines

Pâtés and *terrines* are made in the same way, but the former require a dough, the recipe for which will be found on *p.* 233, in the chapter on Pastry, Doughs and Basic Mixtures.

Pâtés with a crust are baked in special tins which are made in a variety of shapes. The most practical ones have a hinged side, which makes it much easier to remove the baked *pâté*. It is very easy to make long *pâtés*, known as *Pâté pantin*, without a mould.

LES PÂTÉS * *PÂTÉS (PIES)*

Pâté de Foie de poulet * *Chicken Liver Pâté*

1 medium-sized onion; 1½ oz butter; 4 tablespoons dry sherry; 1 lb minced lean pork; 1 lb grated pork fat; 1 lb minced veal; 1 lb chicken livers; pinch each ground cloves, grated nutmeg, and ground ginger; 3 beaten eggs; 2 teaspoons salt; ½ teaspoon pepper; ¼ pint cream; 2 oz flour; 1½ tablespoons brandy; 2 crushed cloves garlic; 1¼ oz powdered aspic jelly; pimento and black olives to decorate. Cooking time: about 2 hours.

Place chicken livers in saucepan and just cover with water. Bring to boil, simmer five minutes, drain and mince. Grate onion, heat butter and *sauté* onion until transparent. Stir in sherry, continue cooking until sherry has almost evaporated. Combine minced chicken livers, pork veal, and grated fat. Add remaining ingredients (except aspic jelly and decorations) and onion mixture; beat well. Fill into ovenproof dish with 4 pint capacity or 2 2-pint dishes. Stand in baking dish containing hot water. Bake in moderate oven 1 to 2 hours or until mixture shrinks from sides of dish and juices no longer look pink; drain off fat. Weigh down *pâté* and leave to cool. Turn out when cool; wash dish. Mix aspic jelly into 1 pint boiling water, stir until powder has completely dissolved. Pour enough into the base of the dish to raise the top of the *pâté* level with top of dish; refrigerate until set. Place *pâté* in dish on top of set aspic, spoon more of the aspic, which should have almost reached setting point, down the sides of the dish and spread thinly over top of *pâté*. Refrigerate until set. Before serving decorate top with pimento cut into decorative shapes, and slices of black olive.

▣ de Lapin * *Rabbit*

For 4 persons: 1 young rabbit; seasoning; grating of nutmeg; ¼ pint brandy or Madeira; 4 oz fat bacon; 1 lb Pork forcemeat; 1 lb Pie pastry. Cooking time: 1½–2 hours.

Soak the rabbit for 1 hour in cold salted water. Rinse and dry. Bone the back and legs and take out the sinews. Season with salt, pepper and nutmeg, and macerate in brandy or Madeira for ½ hour. Put a layer of forcemeat into the *pâté* tin, then the rabbit pieces mixed with strips of fat bacon. Finish by spreading remaining forcemeat on top. Moisten with stock. Roll the pastry out to the size of the tin. Cut a band from it about $\frac{1}{2}$ inch wide. Moisten rim of pie dish with water and lay the band on this. Moisten. Roll out remaining pastry to fit top. Lay on top and press down. Trim. Make a hole in the centre. Brush top with beaten egg. Decorate with leaves made from trimmings. Bake at 375°F or Gas Mark 5. When ready, if necessary fill up *pâté* with boiling seasoned *bouillon*.

Pâté Pantin   *   *Pantin*

This is made using the same quantities as for Rabbit *Pâté*. It is a long *pâté* made without a tin. Make the dough rather firm and roll it out in a rectangle about $\frac{1}{3}$ inch thick. In the middle place lengthwise layers of Pork forcemeat or sausage meat alternating with the main filling—rabbit, veal, poultry, lean pork, etc., beginning and finishing with a layer of forcemeat. Fold up the two sides over the filling, then the two ends, moistening the edges so that they stick well. Turn the *pâté* upside down on the baking sheet and on top place a thin piece of dough, the same shape as the *pâté* but smaller, to make a decorative lid. The lid may be decorated with small leaves of dough trimmings. Brush all over with beaten egg, score the lid with a knife and make a hole about $\frac{1}{5}$ inch across in the centre for the steam to escape, otherwise the dough will crack. Bake in a moderate oven, 375°F or Gas Mark 5, for 1–1$\frac{1}{2}$ hours for a *pâté* weighing about 3 pounds.

▣ de Veau en Croûte   *   *Veal in a Pastry Crust*

For 6 persons: 1 lb Pie pastry; 12 oz Pork forcemeat or sausage meat; $\frac{1}{2}$ lb lean veal; spices; 2 tablespoons brandy; 2 slices cooked tongue or boiled ham, each weighing about 2 oz. Cooking time: about 1$\frac{1}{2}$ hours.

Line the buttered tin with about three-quarters of the dough, keeping the rest for the lid, and prick the bottom 3 or 4 times with a skewer. Season the forcemeat with $\frac{1}{4}$ ounce salt, pepper and spices and mix with the brandy after soaking the cut up veal in it for 1 hour. Place half the forcemeat in the bottom of the tin, cover it with a slice of ham, spread the veal on top and cover it with a second slice of ham. Add the remainder of the forcemeat and place a small sprig of thyme and a small piece of bay leaf on top; these will give a pleasant aroma to the *pâté*. Cover with the remainder of the dough and decorate. Make a small hole in the middle to allow the steam to escape and brush with egg. Place in a fairly hot oven, 375°F or Gas Mark 5, and bake for 50–60 minutes. The *pâté* is done when clear juice comes out through the hole on top. *Pâtés* are served cold, and made one or even two days before, especially in winter. (*See illustration p.* 171).

LES TERRINES   *   *TERRINES*

Terrines have the same filling as *pâtés*. The dish must always be lined with very thin slices of fat bacon before being filled with alternate layers of forcemeat and meat. Cover the top with more bacon, place a little thyme and bay leaf on top and seal lid with a simple flour and water paste. To cook, put the *terrine* in a dish containing about 1$\frac{1}{2}$ inches boiling water and place in an oven hot enough for the water to continue boiling. To check if the *terrine* is done, remove the lid after 40–50 minutes; the melted fat on top should be quite clear. Cool under a weight of about 2 pounds to compress the filling as it cools. All *terrines* are treated in the same way.

Terrine de Foie de Porc   *   *Pig's Liver Terrine*

For 6 persons: 1¼ lb pig's liver; 8 oz fat bacon; 1 onion; parsley; 4 table-spoons brandy; 3 eggs; 4 oz bread without crusts.

Trim and chop the liver and bacon. Add onion, chopped parsley and some stale bread dipped in milk and well squeezed out. Season with 1 ounce salt, ground pepper, spices and brandy; combine with 3 whole eggs. Line and fill a *terrine* as above. Cover, place in a tin of water and cook for about 1½ hours. Half an hour after removing from oven, place a 2 pound weight on a board on the *terrine*, as described above.

To keep *terrines* for several months, turn out when cold and carefully remove all gravy and fat from the outside. Wash the *terrine* dish, replace the *pâté* mixture and cover completely with melted lard. Allow to set, cover with parchment paper, and replace lid. Stick a strip of paper all round the crack to close it as hermetically as possible; close the small hole in the lid. If stored in a cool, dry place, *terrines* will keep for as long as 6 months or even longer. The lard, which is removed from the *terrine* before it is served, may be used for cooking.

◻ de Veau   *   *Veal*

¾ lb silverside of veal; ¾ lb fresh pork; ½ lb green fat bacon; 2 onions; 1 shallot; 1 clove garlic; ¼ pint white wine. Cooking time: 1½ hours.

An excellent dish which may be prepared the night before. Dice the veal, pork and bacon fairly small. Combine the pieces with sliced onion, chopped shallot and garlic; season and fill a *terrine* with the mixture. Add the wine and seal the *terrine* hermetically. Boil up once and cook in a moderate oven, 375°F or Gas Mark 5, for 1½ hours. Put in a cool place. Serve very cold.

Re-Heated Food

Re-heated or left-over food has always had rather a bad connotation and people tend to think that is dull and tasteless. However, with a little imagination and the use of well-flavoured vegetables, spices and sauces, left-over dishes can be tasty and quick to prepare.

It is very important when using left-over cooked meat, fish or poultry to heat it very thoroughly by bringing it to boiling point and then reducing the heat so that the food simmers for 10–15 minutes.

Below is a large selection of recipes for dishes using left-over fish, meat and poultry. Many people nowadays prefer to cook enough meat for 2 days so that they can use half one day and half the next, for an attractive left-over dish, which saves a great deal of time and effort.

Additional recipes may be found in the chapters on *hors d'œuvres, entrées,* cold meats and salads. Left-over food is also used to make rissoles, fish or meat cakes, savoury pancakes, hash and *croquettes.*

LE POISSON * *FISH*

Kedgeree * *Kedgeree*

For 4 persons: 12 oz cooked fish, either salt, white or smoked; 6 oz boiled rice; 1–2 hardboiled eggs; 1 raw egg; 2 oz butter; seasoning; grating of nutmeg; chopped parsley; cut lemon.

Flake the fish, discarding skin and bones. Melt butter, add rice, fish, chopped hardboiled eggs, seasonings and beaten egg. Mix with a fork and heat thoroughly. Mound on a hot dish, sprinkle chopped parsley over. Serve with lemon.

Poisson Froid à la Mayonnaise * *Fish with Mayonnaise*

Remove the skin and bones from the cold, cooked fish and flake it. Add 2 or 3 tablespoons of vinegar, some finely diced gherkins and 5 or 6 tablespoons of *mayonnaise.* Arrange this mixture on a dish in the shape of a fish and coat with very firm *mayonnaise.* Decorate with skinned tomato slices, some capers and some radishes cut into rosettes, and crisp lettuce leaves.

LE BŒUF * BEEF

Fricadelles ou Boulettes * Fried Beef Balls

For 6–8 persons: 1¼ *lb cooked beef;* 1 *onion;* 8 *oz potatoes;* 1 *egg;* ½ *pint Tomato or Piquant sauce.*

Mince the beef finely and mix with fried minced onion, chopped fine herbs, potato *purée* and a raw egg; season well. Divide the mixture into portions the size of a large egg; roll on a floured board, flatten, fry in a very little hot fat and serve with Tomato or Piquant sauce.

Hachis Parmentier * Minced Beef Parmentier

For 6 persons: 1¼ *lb beef;* 4 *oz onions;* 1 *oz fat;* ¼ *pint white wine;* 1 *pint bouillon;* 2 *tablespoons tomato purée;* 1 *lb potatoes.*

Mince the beef. Chop and lightly brown the onions, in fat. Dust with flour and add the wine and *bouillon.* Add the mince and the tomato *purée.* Season well, simmer gently for 45 minutes, stirring from time to time. While the mince is cooking, make a potato *purée* mixed with *bouillon* instead of milk. Place the mince at the bottom of a baking dish, cover entirely with the potato *purée* and brown in a very hot oven. After 8–10 minutes, when the potatoes have a crust, brush top with a little melted butter and beaten egg yolk to give it a good colour.

Langue en Tranches Tartare * Sliced Tongue Tartare

Slice the remains of an ox tongue ¼ inch thick, flour, egg and breadcrumb, and shallow fry in butter and oil. Serve hot with cold *Tartare sauce.*

LE VEAU * VEAL

Cassolette Suzanne * Cassolette Suzanne

For 4 persons: ¾–1 *lb veal left-overs;* 1¼ *lb spinach;* 2 *oz butter;* 6 *oz cooked mushrooms;* 1 *pint Béchamel.*

If the left-overs are not enough to provide a meal in themselves, it is still possible to turn them into an excellent and sufficient *entrée.* Blanch, drain and cool the spinach, squeeze out and *sauté* in butter without chopping. Divide among a number of small china *cocottes* or scallop shells, place coarsely minced veal or sweetbreads mixed with chopped mushrooms and *Béchamel,* on top. Season and heat in the oven. Coat with *Béchamel* and garnish each one with a cooked mushroom cap.

This recipe can, of course, also be used for other kinds of meat (alone or mixed) and poultry.

Coquilles de Veau Mornay * Scalloped Veal Mornay

For 4 persons: 8–12 *oz veal left-overs;* 8 *oz cooked mushrooms;* ½ *pint Béchamel;* 2 *oz grated cheese; breadcrumbs.*

Thinly slice left-over veal and mushrooms; combine the well-seasoned *Béchamel* with 1 ounce grated cheese. Place a little *Béchamel* in a scallop shell, the meat on top and coat

186

with the same sauce. Sprinkle with grated cheese and breadcrumbs. Brown in a hot oven, 400°F or Gas Mark 6. The shells may be edged with a border of Duchess potatoes piped through a forcing bag and fluted nozzle.

Croquettes de Veau * *Veal Croquettes*

For 4 persons: 8 oz cooked veal; 4 oz cooked mushrooms; 1 egg yolk; 4 table-spoons Béchamel; breadcrumbs; ½ pint Tomato sauce. Cooking time: 3–4 minutes.

Cut meat into very small dice. Bind with some thick *Béchamel*, add chopped mushrooms and yolk of egg, salt and pepper and stir the mixture over heat until it leaves the sides of the pan. Spread on a plate. Allow to cool, then divide into egg-sized pieces, shape into rolls with a little flour, egg and breadcrumb and, at the very last moment, deep fry in very hot fat for 3 or 4 minutes. Serve with Tomato sauce.

LE MOUTON ET L'AGNEAU * *MUTTON AND LAMB*

Emincé de Mouton aux Cèpes * *Sliced Mutton with Boletus Mushrooms*

For 4 persons: 1 lb mutton left-overs; 4 oz boletus or mushrooms; 2 oz butter; 1 onion; 2 shallots; ½ pint white wine; ½ pint bouillon; 2 tablespoons tomato purée; chopped parsley. Cooking time: 6–8 minutes.

Slice the remains of a leg or shoulder of mutton thinly, carefully removing any skin or hard parts. Brown the chopped onions and shallots with the sliced boletus in butter. Sprinkle with a tablespoon of flour and let it brown while stirring with a spatula. Add the white wine, reduce to half, add the *bouillon* and tomato *purée*. Cook for 2–3 minutes, move the saucepan to the side of the stove, add the sliced mutton and cook thoroughly for 4–5 minutes. Pour on to a hot dish and sprinkle with chopped parsley.

Hachis de Mouton * *Minced Mutton*

For 4 persons: 1¼ lb cooked meat; 1 onion; croûtons of fried bread; 2 shallots; parsley; salt; pepper; bouillon.

Finely mince the meat with the shallots and parsley, and season with salt and pepper. Chop the onion very finely and cook it very gently in butter without letting it colour. Add the mince and 2 tablespoons *bouillon*. Heat gently, When everything is well-heated, place the mince on a dish and surround with *croûtons*. Tomato sauce may be served separately.

LA VOLAILLE * *POULTRY*

Poulet en Aspic * *Chicken in Aspic*

Trim some cooked chicken left-overs and cut in thin slices or strips. Also cut up a little ham, 2 hardboiled eggs and some gherkins. Fill a bowl with this mixture, pour on some cold aspic and let it set. Turn out and edge with fresh parsley.

Cassolettes de Poulet Joconde * *Cassolettes of Chicken Jaconde*

Place a thin layer of asparagus tip salad or minced cooked mushrooms in the bottom of some small china *cocottes*. Cover with minced chicken, coat with *mayonnaise* and top with a slice of skinned tomato covered with a slice of hardboiled egg.

LE GIBIER * *GAME*

Canapés Saint-Hubert * *Canapés Saint-Hubert*

Mince the cooked game, put it in a saucepan, moisten with Madeira, stir in *sauce Demi-glace* and reduce to the consistency of a *purée*. Fry slices of bread without crusts in butter and mound with the game *purée*. Decorate with a slice of truffle or a button mushroom cap. Serve very hot.

Selle de Chevreuil * *Saddle of Venison*

Slice up the left-over fillet, glaze with jelly and serve with *chanterelle* salad.

▲　*Tomates farcies au fenouil, p. 224*

Roulades de choux farcis, p. 199 ▼

▲ *Assortiment de pommes de terre, pp. 213-217*

Jardinière de légumes, pp. 195-219 ▼

▲ *Courgettes farcies à l'orientale, p. 202*

Fonds d'artichauts au gratin, p. 194 ▼

▲ *Salade de saison, p. 220*

Tomates farcies à la piémontaise, p. 211 ▼

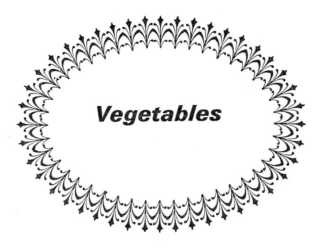

Vegetables

ARTICHAUTS * *ARTICHOKES*

Artichauts Mireille * *Artichokes Mireille*

For 4 persons: 4–6 globe artichokes, according to size; 3 tablespoons olive oil; 12 small onions; 4 tomatoes; scant ¼ pint bouillon. Cooking time: 30–40 minutes.

Use very small artichokes, trim the stalk, remove outer leaves. Trim tips of remaining leaves and cook in a saucepan with the head downwards in *bouillon*, olive oil, salt, peppercorns and small onions. Add 4 peeled, quartered tomatoes and cover. Cook fairly briskly until tender. Serve with onions and tomatoes, preferably cold, rather as an *hors d'œuvre* or a vegetable.

▣ Farcis à la Barigoule * *Barigoule*

For 4 persons: 4 large globe artichokes; 4 oz mushrooms; few rashers bacon; 1 tablespoon oil; 2 tablespoons white wine; 2 oz ham; 3 tablespoons tomato purée; seasoning; 2 shallots. Cooking time: ¾–1 hour.

Chop the mushrooms and brown them in oil. Add chopped ham, 2 tablespoons of the thick tomato *purée*, salt, pepper, fine herbs and chopped shallots. Trim tops of artichoke leaves, trim bottom, drop in boiling salted water and keep them underdone. Cool, remove middle leaves and choke. Fill the artichokes with the mushroom mixture, cover with a strip of bacon and tie it on with string. Place artichokes in a casserole containing the very hot oil, add white wine and remaining tomato *purée*. Cover with oiled paper and bake in a moderate oven, 350°F or Gas Mark 4, for 35–40 minutes. Remove string and serve with gravy after skimming off fat; reduce it if necessary.

▣ Sauce Blanche ou Vinaigrette * *with White or Vinaigrette Sauce*

For 4 persons: 4–6 globe artichokes. Cooking time: ¾–1 hour.

Trim the tops off the leaves, trim the bottoms and wash them, then cook in boiling salted water with a little sugar added until the leaves pull out easily. Cool a little, drain. Remove choke and arrange on napkins. Serve with hot white sauce, such as *sauce Hollandaise* or *Mousseline*, or with *Vinaigrette*.

193

Fonds d'Artichauts * *Artichoke Bottoms*

For 4 persons: 4–6 artichokes. Cooking time: 25 minutes.

Peel the artichoke bottoms raw, cut off the leaves and rub bottoms with lemon. Boil in salted water with lemon juice after mixing it with 1 or 2 tablespoons of flour while still cold. When done, cool and remove the choke. If the artichokes are cooked with the leaves still on, pieces of the bottom will come away with the leaves.

Cooked fonds d'artichauts or artichoke bottoms may be bought in tins, ready for use.

▣ Clamart * *with Peas*

For 4 persons: 8 artichokes; ¾ lb green peas; 2 oz butter.

Prepare the artichoke bottoms as above and garnish with peas. When about to serve sprinkle with *Noisette* butter.

▣ au Gratin * *au Gratin*

For 6 persons: 6 large or 12 small cooked artichoke bottoms; 1 lb cooked asparagus tips or cooked cauliflower; ¾ pint sauce Mornay; 1 oz melted butter; 2 oz grated Parmesan cheese.

Heat the asparagus or cauliflower in butter and season. Fill the artichoke bottoms with the vegetable and mask with the *sauce Mornay*. Sprinkle with the Parmesan cheese and a little melted butter. Gratinate in a hot oven or under the grill. (*See illustration p.* 191).

Quartiers d'Artichauts Sauce Lyonnaise ou Italienne * *Artichokes with Lyonnaise or Italian Sauce*

For 4 persons: 4–6 artichokes. Cooking time: 25 minutes.

Trim artichoke stalks and leaves. Quarter the artichokes and cook them in boiling salted water and sugar. Remove choke, drain, brown a little over heat with oil, then place on a dish and pour *sauce Lyonnaise* or Italian over them.

ASPERGES * *ASPARAGUS*

Use asparagus as fresh as possible. Scrape the asparagus from the head downwards. Trim the stalks to equal lengths. Wash well and tie in bundles. Cook in boiling salted water, standing on the stalks with the heads up, until tender. Cooking time: 20–30 minutes.

Asperges à la Flamande * *Asparagus Flemish style*

For 4 persons: 2 lb asparagus; 2 hardboiled eggs; 8 oz melted butter. Cooking time: 18–25 minutes.

Allow half a hardboiled egg to each person. It should be sieved and mixed with melted butter and served with asparagus cooked as above.

▣ à la Milanaise * *Milanaise*

For 4 persons: 2 lb asparagus; 8 oz butter; gruyère.

Cook asparagus as above, and arrange with half the tips at either end. Sprinkle with grated *gruyére* and pour plenty of *Noisette* butter over them. Put in a hot oven for 3 minutes to brown.

Asperges Sauce Hollandaise * *with Sauce Hollandaise*

For 4 persons: 2 lb asparagus.

Wash, trim, tie in bundles and cook as directed. Serve on a folded table napkin, or in an asparagus dish, with *sauce Hollandaise* in a sauceboat. Other suitable sauces are: *Mousseline* and Butter. Melted butter is also suitable.

◙ Vinaigrette * *with Vinaigrette*

Cook as above and serve the asparagus lukewarm, with *sauce Vinaigrette* separately.

Pointes d'Asperges à la Crème * *Asparagus Tips with Cream*

For 4 persons: 2 lb asparagus; ½ pint sauce Béchamel; 1 egg yolk; 1 tablespoon cream. Cooking time: 20 minutes.

Prepare and cook the asparagus as directed above. Cut off the tender part of the asparagus tips and discard the stalks. Add cream to a light *Béchamel*, season with salt and a little sugar. Thicken this sauce with an egg yolk. Add the tips and reheat carefully. Serve in a deep dish. The tips may also be served with butter like peas; the two vegetables are sometimes also mixed. An excellent cream soup may also be made with asparagus tips.

AUBERGINES * *AUBERGINES*

Aubergines Farcies * *Stuffed Aubergines*

For 4 persons: 4 aubergines; 4 oz chopped mushrooms; 2 oz butter; breadcrumbs; garlic; fine herbs. Cooking time: 6–7 minutes.

Halve the aubergines lengthwise without peeling. Incise the flesh $\frac{1}{10}$ inch deep all round the edge and make some incisions in the centre. Salt and leave to drain for 15 minutes. Deep fry in oil. When tender, drain and scoop out flesh without damaging skin. Chop the flesh with a trace of garlic and fine herbs, and mix with the mushrooms fried in butter. Fill the skins with this mixture, sprinkle with breadcrumbs and butter and brown. Serve very hot.

◙ Farcies Boston * *Boston Stuffed*

For 4 persons: 3 aubergines; ¼ pint sauce Béchamel; ¼ pint cream; 1 egg; 2 oz grated gruyère. Cooking time in the oven: 7–8 minutes.

Cook the aubergines as above, chop the flesh, mix it with several spoonfuls creamy *Béchamel*, season, mix with a whole egg and most of the grated *gruyère*. Fill the skins with this mixture. Place on a long dish, sprinkle with cheese and brown in a hot oven for 7–8 minutes. When serving, pour some spoonfuls of hot, salted double cream on top. Do not use garlic.

◙ Frites * *Deep Fried*

For 4 persons: 4 aubergines. Cooking time: 5 minutes.

Peel and slice the aubergines ¼ inch thick. Salt and leave to drain. Dry, flour singly and drop in very hot oil. Serve at once, for they turn soft very quickly.

Aubergines à la Meunière * *Fried*

For 4 persons: 2–3 aubergines, according to size, each giving 5 slices;
2 oz butter; 1 lemon. Cooking time: 4–5 minutes.

Peel the aubergines, slice lengthways and sprinkle with fine salt. Leave to drain for 20–30
minutes, then dry, flour, and fry in butter on both sides in a frying pan. Serve on a long dish
sprinkled with lemon juice and with 2 ounces *Noisette* butter poured over.

▣ à la Provençale * *Provençale*

For 4 persons: 4 aubergines; 4 tomatoes; 1 clove garlic; flour; chopped
parsley. Cooking time: 15 minutes.

Peel and slice, salt and drain the aubergines. Then flour and *sauté* with a little very hot
oil. In the meantime, in another pan, *sauté* peeled, seeded and quartered tomatoes. When
the two vegetables are done, mix them in a pan with a pinch of crushed garlic, *sauté* together
for a few minutes, pour into a dish and sprinkle with parsley.

CAROTTES * *CARROTS*

Carottes Chantilly * *Carrots Chantilly*

For 4 persons: 1½ lb young carrots; 1 lb shelled peas; 2 oz butter; ¼ pint
thick cream; seasoning; sugar.

Peel carrots and, if small, keep whole; otherwise cut into 2-inch lengths and quarter these
lengthwise if thick. Cook carrots and peas in separate pans in boiling salted water. When
tender, drain and add seasoning and a good pinch of sugar to both. Toss gently. Add cream
to carrots and heat up, without boiling. Serve in a circle in a hot shallow casserole, with
the peas mounded in the centre.

▣ à la Crème * *with Cream*

For 4 persons: 1½ lb carrots; butter; ¼ pint cream; chopped parsley. Cooking
time: 30 minutes.

Boil the carrots in salted water, whole if they are new, sliced if they are bigger. Drain, fry
them in butter in a frying or *sauté* pan and pour thick, very fresh cream over them. Serve
with parsley sprinkled over.

▣ Glacées * *Glazed*

For 4 persons: 1½ lb new carrots; bouillon; 1 level teaspoon sugar; 2 oz
butter.

Choose new, round carrots if possible, or cut up and trim larger ones. Put on to cook
with enough *bouillon* to cover them; add salt, sugar and a little butter. Cook gently without
a lid until all the moisture has evaporated and the carrots are left with a glazed surface.
These carrots are used mainly as a garnish.

▣ Panachées * *with Potatoes*

For 4 persons: 1 lb carrots; 1½ lb potatoes; 2 oz butter; chopped parsley.
Cooking time: 30 minutes.

Slice the carrots, cook them in salted water and when nearly done add some sliced potatoes, which should finish cooking at the same time. Drain, butter generously and add parsley. The combination of these two vegetables is a particularly good one.

Carottes Vichy * Vichy

For 4 persons: 1½ lb carrots; 2 oz butter; salt; bouillon; 1 oz sugar; chopped parsley. Cooking time: 30 minutes.

Scrape some good, sweet carrots and slice them very thinly. Put them in a fairly large *sauté* pan with a generous lump of fresh butter, a little salt and a teaspoon of sugar, and cover with cold *bouillon*. Boil briskly without a lid until the *bouillon* has evaporated and you can hear the carrots sizzling in the butter. Serve at once with chopped parsley.

CÉLERI * CELERY
Céleri en Branches au Jus * Celery Braised with Gravy

For 4 persons: 2 heads of celery; 2 onions; 1 carrot; seasoning; ½ pint rich bouillon; ¼ pint gravy. Cooking time: 1½ hours.

Clean some nice celery heads, removing the green leaves, cut in 2 or 4, scrape the top and wash carefully. Blanch 15 minutes in boiling water, cool, and put into a casserole with sliced carrots and onions and seasoning. Add the *bouillon*, cook for a good hour, drain, place in a vegetable dish and pour some hot, good veal gravy, specially kept for this purpose, on top.

▣ à la Milanaise * Milanaise

For 4 persons: 2 heads of celery; 2 oz grated Parmesan cheese; chopped parsley; 1 oz butter. Cooking time: 1⅓ hours.

Clean the celery well and trim the root end to a point. Cut the stalks into halves or quarters and wash. Drain and cut each stalk into 1 inch lengths. Tie in bundles. Cook in salted water until tender and drain. Remove string, sprinkle with Parmesan cheese and melted butter, and chopped parsley. Fried eggs often accompany this dish.

CÉLERI-RAVE * CELERIAC
Céleri-Rave en Beignets * Celeriac Fritters

For 4 persons: 2 lb celeriac; butter or oil; Tomato sauce. Cooking time: 35 minutes.

Peel and cut the celeriac into ½ inch slices crosswise and cook in salted water with some lemon juice until almost done. Drain, flour, egg and breadcrumb, either whole or cut in quarters. Deep fry and serve with a light Tomato sauce.

▣ à la Ménagère * Ménagère

For 4 persons: 2 celeriac; 2 onions; 2 carrots; bouillon; 8 oz tomatoes. Cooking time: 35–40 minutes.

Peel and blanch the celeriac, then cut in 2–inch pieces and add to a casserole in which you have lightly browned 1 or 2 onions and the same number of carrots; add peeled and quartered tomatoes. Season and add a little *bouillon* or gravy. Celery may be cooked with a piece of casserole veal after being blanched. It is excellent cooked in the veal gravy in this way. Celeriac is good either as a vegetable or as a meat garnish.

Céleri-Rave au Parmesan * *Celeriac with Parmesan*

For 4 persons: 2 *lb celeriac;* 1 *pint Mornay sauce; Parmesan cheese.* Cooking time: about 35 minutes.

Peel and cut the celeriac into 2-inch pieces. Cook in boiling, salted water with lemon juice. Drain and coat with *sauce Mornay* made with Parmesan instead of *gruyère,* and brown.

Chokoes au Gratin

For 4 persons: 1 *or* 2 *small young chokoes for each person; salted water;* salt; pepper; ½ *pint Béchamel sauce;* 2 *oz grated cheddar cheese.* Cooking time: 20-30 minutes.

Cook the chokoes whole in boiling salted water until just tender, about 10 to 20 minutes, depending on size; do not overcook. Drain the chokoes and split them, season with salt and pepper. Place them in an ovenproof dish, pour the Béchamel sauce over, and sprinkle grated cheese on top. Place in fairly hot oven, 375°F or Gas Mark 5, until cheese is melted and golden brown. *(Australia)*

CHICORÉE * *ENDIVE*

Many people confuse chicory and endive, since the French call *endive* what we generally call chicory, and vice versa. It will probably be helpful to give a description of the two main types and to separate the recipes for each vegetable under their French names. The endive referred to in the following recipes is the green curly-leaved salad variety, which sometimes has a slightly bitter taste.

Chicorée à la Crème * *Endive with Cream*

For 4 persons: 2¼ *lb endives;* 1 *escarole (Bavarian endive);* 1 *oz butter;* ¾ *oz* flour; ¼ *pint Béchamel;* ½ *pint bouillon.* Cooking time: 1½ hours.

Wash and cook the green part of the endives slowly in salted water; the green of an escarole may be added to them. When they are done (the cooking takes a long time) rinse well and squeeze by hand, then chop the endives. Make a light *roux* with the butter and flour, place endives in this and add some fat *bouillon.* Season, cover and braise in a moderate oven for 45 minutes. Change to another pan, for the endives should have browned, then add *Béchamel* and a little cream. Check the seasoning, simmer for a few moments and serve surrounded by *croûtons* of fried bread.

▣ Cuite * *with Béchamel Sauce*

For 4 persons: 2½ *lb endives;* ½ *pint Béchamel;* 2 *oz butter.* Cooking time: 1½ hours.

Clean the endives, keeping the white part for salad. Cook in salted water; when very tender drain, rinse and squeeze by hand. Chop and bind with plenty of *Béchamel* and simmer in this for a moment. Season with salt, pepper and grated nutmeg. This may serve as a vegetable or as a garnish for meat.

CHOUX * *CABBAGE*

The brassica or cabbage family is very large, ranging from Brussels sprouts through green and red cabbage, cauliflower and broccoli to the kohlrabi. All are delicious and lend themselves to a number of different recipes.

Choucroute * *Sauerkraut*

Choose firm, white cabbages. Discard bruised and broken leaves, and cut the cabbage into quarters. Cut out the centre stalk, then wash and drain well. Slice finely. Pack into a jar in layers, sprinkling coarse salt between. Use ¼ pound salt to 12 pounds cabbage. Press down well and cover the top with cabbage leaves. Place a weighted board on top—to keep the cabbage covered with the brine which forms. Keep in a warm place. Fermentation is complete in 4–6 weeks, when the sauerkraut is ready for use.

Garnie * *Garnished*

For 4 persons: 2½ lb sauerkraut; 6 oz fat bacon rinds; 1 boiling sausage; 4 oz lean bacon; 2 onions; 2 carrots; 2 cloves; lard or ham fat; potatoes; 1 smoked knuckle of ham; ½ pint dry white wine or bouillon. Cooking time: 2–3 hours.

Sauerkraut may be bought ready-made, or use the recipe above. Wash in plenty of water and squeeze out by hand. Place the bacon rinds in the bottom of a casserole and half the sauerkraut on top. In the middle of the sauerkraut place a piece of lean bacon, a sausage, and the meat to be served at the same time—knuckle, duck, goose, etc., then add the seasoning—an onion stuck with cloves, carrots, salt and peppercorns. Cover with the remainder of the sauerkraut, and *bouillon* or wine and plenty of lard, good dripping or goose fat. Seal hermetically with greased paper and a lid and braise very slowly in the oven. Serve with the meat and with boiled potatoes. (*See illustration p.* 136).

Chou Rouge Farci * *Stuffed Cabbage*

For 4 persons: 1 cabbage, weighing about 4 lb; 1 lb sausage meat; 4 oz soft breadcrumbs; 1 onion; 1 whole egg; 1 piece of barding bacon; 1 pint sauce Demi-glace. Cooking time: 1½ hours.

Trim a medium-sized cabbage. Soak well in salted water and rinse. Remove the heart and keep it for other purposes; place the hollowed cabbage in boiling salted water and blanch for 10 minutes. Drain and fill with the following forcemeat: sausage meat, bread, a whole egg, chopped onions, fine herbs, garlic and seasoning. Surround the cabbage with the bacon, tie it on, and braise in a casserole, in sauce, for at least 1 hour. (*See illustration p.* 189).
Cabbage leaves may be separated and each filled with forcemeat if this is preferred.

Petits Choux Farcis (Dolmas) * *Stuffed Cabbage Leaves or Dolmas*

For 4 persons: 1 lb cabbage; ¼ lb forcemeat (as for Stuffed Cabbage); bacon; vegetables; ½ pint gravy; 2 tablespoons Tomato sauce; lemon juice and sliced lemon. Cooking time: 40–50 minutes.

These stuffed cabbage leaves look most attractive. Put a portion of forcemeat on each leaf, blanched beforehand, and press leaves in a cloth to give them a rounded shape. Place in a dish with fat bacon and sliced vegetables. First cook for 5 minutes without liquid, then add tomato-flavoured gravy. Cover with paper and bake in a moderate oven for a good hour. Serve in the cooking liquor, greatly boiled down, sprinkle with lemon juice and put a lemon slice on each cabbage. In this way they are lighter and more digestible.

Chou Rouge à la Flamande * *Flemish Red Cabbage*

For 4 persons: 2 lb red cabbage; 8 oz dessert apples; ground cinnamon; 1 tablespoon vinegar; 4 oz lard; 1 tablespoon icing sugar. Cooking time: 1½–2 hours.

Remove any damaged leaves. Quarter the cabbage. Remove stalk and large ribs, wash well and cut into *julienne* strips. Season with salt, pepper and a pinch of cinnamon and add the vinegar. Stir and place in a casserole with plenty of lard or butter. Seal hermetically and cook in a moderate oven for at least 1 hour. Now add the apples—peeled, seeded, cut in smallish quarters and dredged with sugar. Spread evenly among the cabbage. Cook for another ½ hour. Serve in casserole or vegetable dish.

Chou Rouge au Vin Rouge * *Red Cabbage with Red Wine*

For 4 persons: 2 lb red cabbage; 4 oz chopped onions; 6 oz lean bacon; 1 oz lard; 1 pint red wine; 2 oz flour; seasoning. Cooking time: 2½ hours.

Remove any damaged leaves from cabbage, and wash it well. Quarter it, cut out stalk and thick ribs, re-wash carefully and cut in coarse *julienne* strips. Cut the bacon in strips and brown in the lard with the onions. Add flour to make a *roux*. Put in the cabbage, season with salt and pepper, and stir up well. Cover and cook on the stove for a good half hour. At the end of this time bring the wine to the boil and set it alight, pour it over the cabbage immediately and cook it in the oven for at least another 2 hours. Serve in a vegetable dish after checking the seasoning.

Choux Verts à l'Anglaise * *Buttered Green Cabbage*

For 4 persons: 2 lb cabbage; butter; pepper. Cooking time: 15–20 minutes.

Halve cabbage, cut out stalk and wash well in salted water. Shred finely and boil cabbage in salted water. Drain and add some butter, shake well. Add salt and ground pepper. Serve in a vegetable dish.

▣ Braisés * *Braised*

For 4 persons: 2 lb cabbage; 1 onion; 3 cloves; 1 carrot; bouquet garni; bacon or ham fat; bouillon. Cooking time: 1½–2 hours.

Quarter the cabbage. Soak in salted water. Rinse and remove stalk and large ribs, blanch well and drain. Garnish the bottom of a casserole with bacon trimmings or ham fat, an onion stuck with cloves, carrot and *bouquet garni*. Place the cabbage on top with a piece of lean bacon or ham in the middle if desired, and half cover with rather fat *bouillon*. Season, cover with greased paper and a lid and braise in the oven for at least 1½ hours. In principle the cabbage is ready when it has absorbed all the *bouillon*.

▣ au Gratin * *au Gratin*

For 4 persons: 2 lb cabbage; scant ½ pint Béchamel; 2 oz grated cheese; butter; breadcrumbs. Cooking time: 1–1½ hours.

Boil the washed cabbage in salted water until done, rinse and drain, squeeze out and chop finely. Combine with the *Béchamel*, season and heat, remove from stove and add three-quarters of the grated cheese. Pour into a baking dish. Sprinkle with remaining cheese, breadcrumbs and butter, and brown.

Choux Brocolis * *Buttered Broccoli*

For 4-6 persons: 1½ lb broccoli; 2 oz butter; pepper; salt; juice ½ lemon. Cooking time: 15 minutes.

Wash broccoli, trim off ends of stalks and coarse leaves. Cut a deep cross in base of very thick stalks to facilitate cooking. Place in saucepan with small amount of boiling, salted water; boil about 15 minutes or until tender. Drain, add salt, pepper, butter and lemon juice, toss lightly. Serve at once.

Choux de Bruxelles Glacés   *   *Buttered Brussels Sprouts*

For 4-6 persons: 1½ *lb Brussels sprouts; 2 oz butter; 1 tablespoon lemon juice; salt; pepper.* Cooking time: 15 minutes.

Remove any wilted outer leaves from sprouts, remove hard end of stem. Cut a cross in base of stems to ensure even cooking. Wash thoroughly. Cook in a little boiling salted water until tender, about 15 minutes. Drain well. Heat butter until it begins to brown. Add lemon juice, salt and pepper, then add sprouts, toss lightly. Serve at once.

▣ Sautés   *   *Sautéed*

For 4 persons: 2 lb Brussels sprouts; 2 oz butter. Cooking time: 25 minutes.

Trim and wash the sprouts thoroughly. Soak in cold salted water and rinse. Cook until tender in boiling salted water. Drain and put in hot butter. *Sauté* until lightly browned.

CHOU-FLEUR   *   *CAULIFLOWER*

For 4 persons: 2 lb cauliflower. Cooking time: 20–25 minutes.

Trim the cauliflower, leaving some of the tender leaves round the flower; also trim the stalk. The cauliflower may be left whole or divided into florets. Soak in cold salted water for some time, then rinse well. Blanch cauliflower for 5 minutes. Drain off water. Replace with boiling water. Sprinkle salt over and cook until tender. Drain and serve with *sauce Hollandaise* or *sauce Mousseline* or melted butter.

▣ au Gratin   *   *au Gratin*

For 4 persons: 2 lb cooked cauliflower; ¾ *pint sauce Mornay; 2 oz butter; 1 oz breadcrumbs.* Cooking time: 6–8 minutes in the oven.

Place the cooked and well-drained cauliflower in a baking dish. Coat generously with *sauce Mornay,* sprinkle with cheese, breadcrumbs and melted butter, and brown.

▣ à la Polonaise   *   *Polonaise*

For 4 persons: 2 lb cooked cauliflower; 1 hardboiled egg; white bread; 3 oz butter; chopped parsley. Cooking time: 20–25 minutes.

Drain the cooked cauliflower and toss it lightly in butter without breaking it. Place on a dish in its natural shape, if possible, then fry a large handful of finely crumbled dry white bread in plenty of butter. When it is golden brown, pour over the cauliflower and sprinkle top with chopped hardboiled egg and parsley.
This excellent recipe is particularly suitable when the cauliflower is not white enough to be presented in its natural state. In culinary language these fried breadcrumbs are called a *Polonaise.*

Choux-Raves ou Rutabagas   *   *Kohlrabi*

A turnip-rooted cabbage. Both the root and the green tip are used.

For 4 persons: 2 lb kohlrabi. Cooking time: 35–40 minutes.

Kohlrabi may be prepared in the same way as celeriac. In eastern France it is made into excellent sauerkraut.

Concombres à la Crème   *   *Creamed Cucumbers*

For 4-6 persons: 2 large green cucumbers; ½ pint Béchamel sauce; chopped parsley or chives; salt and pepper; salted water; 4 tablespoons cream. Cooking time: 5-10 minutes.

Peel cucumbers, split in 2 lengthwise. Cut each half cucumber into 4 pieces, cook in boiling salted water until just tender, about 5 minutes. Heat Béchamel sauce, add salt, pepper, parsley or chives, and cream. Fold in drained cucumber, heat gently before serving.

Côtes de Bette au Gratin   *   *Gratinated Mid-Ribs of Swiss Chard*

For 4 persons: 2 lb mid-ribs of Swiss chard; ½ pint thick sauce Béchamel; 1 oz butter; 2 oz grated Parmesan cheese. Cooking time: 30 minutes.

Clean the Swiss chard, removing the green part of the leaves. Scrape the mid-ribs, cut into small pieces about 1 inch long and cook in salted water for 15 minutes. Butter a *gratin* dish, cover the base with *sauce Béchamel*, arrange the mid-ribs on top and cover over with the rest of the sauce. Sprinkle with Parmesan cheese and melted butter and gratinate in a hot oven for 15 minutes.

Courge   *   *Boiled Acorn or Baby Squash*

For 4 persons: 1 or 2 baby squash per person, depending on size; salt; pepper; butter. Cooking time: 15-20 minutes.

Trim stems, but do not peel squash. Cook whole, in boiling salted water, about 15 to 20 minutes, or until tender. Drain well, split in half if desired, or serve whole. Season with salt and pepper and place a generous knob of butter on top of each squash.

COURGETTES   *   *COURGETTES*

Prepare in the same way as aubergines. (*See pp.* 195–197).

Courgettes Farcies à l'Orientale   *   *Courgettes Stuffed Oriental Style*

For 6 persons: 3 courgettes, peeled, cut into two lengthwise and blanched; 6 oz cooked rice; 6 oz peeled quartered tomatoes; 8 oz cooked minced meat; soft breadcrumbs; 2 oz butter; ¾ pint Tomato sauce. Cooking time: about 15 minutes.

Scoop out the centres of the *courgettes*, using a teaspoon. Chop the pulp and mix with the cooked rice, tomatoes and minced meat. Fill the *courgettes* with this mixture, sprinkle with soft breadcrumbs, dot with butter and gratinate. Pour Tomato sauce round and serve. (*See illustration p.* 191).

ENDIVES   *   *CHICORY*

The following recipes refer to the vegetables with long heads looking rather like thin white cos lettuces. Chicory heads are kept white by growing them in darkness. Prepare by removing outer leaves, trimming the tops if necessary and washing in plenty of water, to remove sand and grit. Then tie the heads with pieces of cotton. If you do not like the rather bitter taste of chicory, blanch the heads in boiling water.

Endives Braisées   * *Braised Chicory*

For 4 persons: 2 lb chicory; 2 oz butter; 1 lemon; ½ pint Demi-glace. Cooking time: about 1 hour.

Remove any damaged outer leaves and simmer for 15 minutes in salted water. Remove, drain well and place in a flat casserole. Season with pepper, the juice of 1 lemon and pour over enough *Demi-glace* to cover the chicory. Cover with buttered greaseproof paper, replace the lid and cook slowly in a warm oven, 325°F or Gas Mark 2, till done.

▣ à la Flamande   * *Flemish style*

For 4 persons: 2 lb chicory; 2 oz butter; 1 lemon. Cooking time: 1 hour.

Chicory may be blanched in water until almost cooked and then finished in butter or brown sauce. For those who like cooked chicory, we recommend the following recipe. Scrape the root but do not cut it off, and remove damaged leaves. Wash well and drain. Place a sizeable lump of butter in a large *sauté* pan and when it is hot, but not browned, place the chicory in it side by side in 2 rows. Salt and sprinkle generously with lemon juice and a very little water. Cover with buttered paper and place in the oven like this until it has lost all its moisture and starts to turn yellow in the butter. Arrange in a vegetable dish and pour on a light brown sauce or good gravy. Chicory may also be fried—same method as above—but replace the brown sauce by *Noisette* butter.

▣ au Jambon Gratinées   * *with Ham au Gratin*

For 4 persons: 4 heads of braised chicory; 4 slices cooked ham; ½ pint sauce Béchamel; 2 oz grated gruyère. Cooking time of chicory: about 1 hour.

When cooking the chicory change the water twice to remove the bitter flavour. Drain and roll each head in a slice of cooked ham. Cover with *Béchamel* mixed with cheese and brown in the oven.

ÉPINARDS   * *SPINACH*

Epinards en branches à l'Anglaise   * *Buttered Spinach*

For 4 persons: 2 lb spinach; 2 oz butter; salt; pinch of sugar. Cooking time: 10 minutes.

The excellent spinach obtainable in spring is delicious prepared in this way. Pick out each leaf to remove centre stalk and thick ribs. Wash thoroughly in several waters. Lift dripping wet into a dry pan. Add seasoning and a pinch of sugar. Cook with the lid on the pan until tender. Drain well or rinse in cold water and squeeze out by hand. *Sauté* in hot butter for a few minutes and serve.

▣ à la Crème   * *with Cream*

For 4 persons: 2 lb spinach; 2 tablespoons cream; croûtons; 2 oz butter; 2 tablespoons Béchamel. Cooking time: 10 minutes.

As this spinach is puréed or chopped, only remove the big stalks. Cook as above and, after rinsing and squeezing, pass through a sieve or chop and fry slightly in very hot butter. Bind with *Béchamel*. Salt and sugar lightly. Mound in a vegetable dish as soon as done and pour on 2–3 tablespoons of thick cream and decorate with some fried *croûtons*.

Épinards Purées aux Œufs * Puréed with Eggs

For 4 persons: 2 lb spinach; ½ pint Cream sauce; 1 oz butter; 4 eggs; fleurons.

Clean and wash spinach well and remove stalks; cook as above. Rinse quickly in cold water. Drain, squeeze out by hand, rub through a sieve, combine with *Noisette* butter and Cream sauce, and season. Mound in a hot dish and surround with *fleurons*. To garnish, quarter hardboiled eggs and remove and sieve the yolks. Sprinkle sieved yolks in the centre, sprinkle with a little salt and chopped parsley, and surround with the whites to resemble a daisy.

FENOUIL OU ANETH * FENNEL

This is a comparatively little-known vegetable. It originally came from the east, and it is grown and eaten more in the south than in the north of France. It makes a delicious *hors d'œuvre* when prepared *à la Grecque* (see *Hors d'œuvre*); it may also be blanched, braised or used to garnish meat. It looks not unlike celery, but has a very marked aniseed flavour.

Fenouil à la Provençale * Fennel Provençale

For 4 persons: 3 fennel roots; 1¼ lb tomatoes; garlic; ¼ pint bouillon; 2 onions. Cooking time: 1 hour.

Clean fennel roots; remove the hard, fibrous outer stems; then quarter and blanch in water for 15 minutes. Drain and place in a casserole with sliced onions, chopped garlic and the quartered tomatoes. Add *bouillon* and cover; braise in a moderate oven for 1 hour. Serve in the casserole.

Fèves * Broad Beans

For 4 persons: 1 lb broad beans; 1 oz butter; 4 tablespoons cream; seasoning. Cooking time: 30–40 minutes.

Broad beans must not be shelled until the last moment before cooking. Cook them in boiling salted water. Drain when tender. Toss in butter and add cream. They may also be prepared in the same way but sieved after cooking and served as a *purée*. Serve hot.

HARICOTS * HARICOT BEANS

Haricots Blancs à la Bretonne * White Haricot Beans Bretonne

For 4 persons: 1 lb haricot beans; ½ lb onions; butter; 2 tablespoons tomato purée. Cooking time: 35 minutes for fresh beans; 1½ hours for dried ones.

"String" the beans. Cook them, starting them in boiling water if fresh, in cold water if dried, after soaking for 6–8 hours. Brown some chopped onions with butter or good fat, add tomato *purée* and then the beans and simmer together for a few minutes. May be served either as a vegetable or as a garnish with leg of mutton, sprinkled with chopped parsley.

▣ Flageolets * Flageolet Beans

For 4 persons: 2 lb fresh beans; butter; cream. Cooking time: 25 minutes.

Flageolet beans are prepared in the same way as Haricot Beans, with butter, cream, or *à la Bretonne*.

Haricots Rouges au Vin * Red Haricot Beans with Wine

For 4 persons: 2 lb fresh beans; 1 onion; 1 oz dripping; flour; ¼ pint red wine; bacon; ham. Cooking time: 35 minutes.

Cook the red haricot beans in the same way as the white ones. Brown a chopped onion in hot dripping, dredge with flour and add red wine. Cook for 10 minutes, add the beans and let them simmer in the sauce for a moment. These beans may be served with lean bacon or diced ham.

▣ Verts * French Beans

To retain the colour of green vegetables—beans, peas, cabbage, etc.—boil in salted water with the lid off.

▣ Verts à la Crème * with Cream

For 4 persons: 2 lb French beans; salt; 2 oz butter; cream or Béchamel. Cooking time: 18–20 minutes.

Top and tail the beans and remove the "string". If large, cut in half lengthwise. Boil in salted water, *sauté* in butter and moisten either with cream or with light *Béchamel*.

▣ Verts à la Maître d'Hôtel * Maître d'Hôtel

For 4 persons: 2 lb French beans; ¼ pint Béchamel or 2 oz butter. Cooking time: 18–20 minutes.

Wash, "string", top and tail the beans. Boil in salted water, drain and bind with a light *Béchamel* or toss in butter. Sprinkle chopped parsley over and serve.

▣ Verts à la Portugaise * Portuguese style

For 4 persons: 2 lb French beans; 4 oz fat unsmoked bacon; 8 oz tomatoes; salt; fat bouillon. Cooking time: 45 minutes.

Place the prepared raw beans in a saucepan with the finely diced bacon, add peeled, chopped tomatoes, salt, pepper, and ¼ pint *bouillon*. Cook for rather a long time with the lid on and serve with chopped parsley sprinkled over. The beans will not keep their colour but they taste delicious.

Laitues Braisées * Braised Lettuce

For 4 persons: 2 lettuces; 2 oz sliced lean bacon; 2 oz onions; 1 carrot; ½ pint bouillon or gravy. Cooking time: 40–50 minutes.

Choose large lettuces with a firm heart; remove damaged leaves, and wash carefully. Throw into boiling, salted water for 15–20 minutes, then rinse under the tap, drain and squeeze well by hand. Halve, salt, pepper, and place in a baking dish on a bed of bacon, lard and sliced carrot and onions. Press close together and place on the stove until the vegetables at the bottom brown a little. Add the *bouillon*, cover with greased paper and a lid, and place in the oven, 375°F or Gas Mark 5, until the lettuce is almost dry. Serve and pour some reduced gravy on top.

Lentilles à la Lorraine * *Lentils Lorraine*

For 4 persons: ½ lb lentils; 2 oz bacon; 2 oz butter; 1 onion; seasoning; a clove of garlic. Cooking time: about 2 hours.

Soak the lentils overnight. Cook them in boiling salted water until tender. Lightly brown finely chopped onion in 1 ounce butter with the finely shredded bacon. Add cooked lentils with a little of the liquor in which they were cooked. Thicken with remaining butter kneaded with some flour. Add the crushed clove of garlic. Adjust the seasoning and serve.

Maïs en Epis * *Corn on the Cob*

Corn cobs should be young, fresh and plump. Remove the outer leaves, and put into boiling, salted water and cook until tender. The time will vary according to the size and age of the cob, allow 12 minutes for fresh young cobs and up to 30 minutes for older cobs. Do not overcook, otherwise they turn hard and yellow. Drain well, skewer and serve with plenty of hot butter, pepper and salt.

MARRONS * *CHESTNUTS*

Marrons Braisés * *Braised Chestnuts*

For 4 persons: as a vegetable, 1½ lb chestnuts; as a garnish, 1 lb. Cooking time: 40 minutes.

To avoid crushing chestnuts which one wants to keep whole, cut all round the shell of each one with a sharp knife. Place in a strainer and dip into fat hot enough to fry them. Leave until half cooked, then drain and peel, holding them with a cloth; the two halves of the shell will come away at the same time. Wipe and finish cooking either with good gravy or some light brown sauce.

If the chestnuts are to be used to stuff a goose or a turkey, proceed in the same way but cook until fully done, either in the fat or in the oven.

▣ Purée de Marrons * *Chestnut Purée*

Peel the chestnuts. Scald to remove the inside skin and cook until done in salted water with a piece of celeriac for flavour. Drain, rub through a sieve and add a little milk or *bouillon* to make the mixture soft.

NAVETS * *TURNIPS*

Navets à la Crème * *Turnips with Béchamel*

For 4 persons: 2 lb turnips; 2 oz butter; 1 pint Béchamel. Cooking time: 30 minutes.

Peel the turnips. New turnips are quartered, old ones sliced. Cook in salted water until tender, and drain. Toss in butter. Serve in a vegetable dish, and coat with *Béchamel*.

▣ Farcis * *Stuffed*

For 4 persons: 2 lb small round turnips; 6 oz sausage meat; 1 pint bouillon or gravy; breadcrumbs. Cooking time: 45 minutes.

Use white turnips with a purple collar; peel and scoop them out with a vegetable cutter. Blanch for 8–10 minutes, drain and stuff with any meat filling—minced meat, sausage meat, etc. Place in a deep dish, half-fill with fat *bouillon*, sprinkle with breadcrumbs and finish cooking in the oven, browning on top. Turnips prepared in this way are usually used as a garnish.

Navets Glacés * *Glazed*

For 4 persons: 2 lb turnips; 1 oz butter; 2 level teaspoons salt; sugar. Cooking time: 30 minutes.

Peel and slice the turnips, put in a saucepan with enough water or *bouillon* to cover them, and season. Add a teaspoon of sugar, salt and butter. Simmer for 20–30 minutes without covering until all the liquid has boiled away. Serve when they are cooked, dry and shiny.

OIGNONS * *ONIONS*

Oignons Amandine * *Onions Amandine*

For 4 persons: 2 oz butter; 2 oz blanched, shredded almonds; 1 oz brown sugar; 1 crushed clove garlic; salt and pepper; little dry white wine or stock; 8 medium-sized onions, peeled. Cooking time: 1 hour.

Melt butter, stir in almonds and sugar. Add garlic, seasoning, wine or stock. Put in onions, stir until well coated. Transfer to greased casserole, cover, bake in moderate oven, 350°F or Gas Mark 4, for 1 hour, shaking pan occasionally. Serve from casserole.

▣ Frits * *Deep Fried*

For 6 persons: 4 large onions; flour; egg white.

Peel the onions and cut into rings. Dip first in flour then in beaten white of egg and then in flour once more. Fry, a few rings at a time, in very hot deep fat, until they are crisp and golden. Drain well on absorbent paper and serve hot.

▣ Glacés * *Glazed*

For 4 persons: 1 lb small onions; bouillon; 3 oz butter; 1 dessertspoon sugar.

Peel the onions. Put them into a pan with enough *bouillon* to almost cover. Add the butter and sugar. Cover and cook until tender, and the liquor has almost completely evaporated.

Oseille * *Sorrel*

For 4 persons: As a vegetable: 2 lb sorrel. As a garnish: 1 lb; 4 oz butter; 1½ *oz flour; seasoning;* ¾ *pint bouillon; pinch sugar;* ½ *pint sauce Béchamel; 2 egg yolks.* Cooking time: 30–40 minutes.

Wash the sorrel in several waters. Drain and slice. Cook until tender in a little salted water. Drain well. Make a *roux* with 2 ounces butter and the flour. Whisk in *bouillon* and whisk until boiling. Season and add sugar. Add the sorrel. Cover and braise in the oven, 375°F or Gas Mark 5. When tender, sieve and return to pan with *Béchamel*. Boil up. Stir in beaten yolks to thicken. Heat up but do not boil. Beat in remaining butter in small pats. Serve in a hot dish.

Persil Frits * *Fried Parsley*

Wash parsley and pick over the heads, removing superfluous stalks. Dry well. Plunge into hot fat (using a frying basket for easy handling). Fry until the spluttering stops. Drain quickly. Season. Shake in soft paper and serve at once.

POIREAUX * *LEEKS*

Poireaux Braisés * *Braised Leeks*

Remove the root and cut away the leaves to within 1½ inches of the white part of 12 large leeks. Halve them and wash very thoroughly under running water. Blanch for 2 minutes. Make a slightly browned *roux* with a tablespoon of butter and the same amount of flour, and add leeks to it. Add ¼ pint gravy and cover with buttered paper, Braise for 1 hour in a fairly hot oven, 375°F or Gas Mark 5. Serve leeks in a hot dish. Beat ½ ounce butter into sauce. Add a squeeze of lemon juice and pour this over the leeks.

▣ en Branches * *Boiled*

For 4 persons: 2¾ lb leeks; ½ pint Béchamel, Mousseline or other sauce. Cooking time: 30–40 minutes.

Prepare the leeks as above, cut them lengthways and tie in small bundles after washing in plenty of water. Steep in hot water for 30 minutes, changing the water twice to remove the strong flavour. Cook in boiling salted water until tender, and serve like asparagus accompanied by similar sauces.

PETITS POIS * *PEAS*

Petits Pois à l'Anglaise * *Green Peas*

For 4 persons: 2 pints shelled peas; 2 oz butter; 1 teaspoon sugar. Cooking time: 15 minutes.

Cook the peas in boiling, salted water, with a sprig of mint added. Do not boil too briskly or the skins will break. Use plenty of water and leave the lid off the pan so that they stay green. Drain thoroughly, replace in the saucepan on the stove to dry them slightly, then add a good lump of fresh butter, salt and sugar, and serve. Shake the pan gently while drying the peas so that the peas absorb the butter.

▣ à la Bonne-Femme ou à la Ménagère * *Green Peas Ménagère*

For 4 persons: 2 pints peas; 4 oz lean beacon; 1 oz butter; small onions; bouillon; 1 lettuce; 1 tablespoon flour. Cooking time: 30 minutes.

Brown the bacon strips in butter, together with 1 chopped onion or several small whole spring onions. When everything is brown, sprinkle with flour, cook this *roux* for a moment and then moisten with *bouillon* as though preparing a very light sauce. Add the shelled peas and lettuce. Season lightly because of the bacon and cook until tender.

▣ à la Française * *à la Française*

For 4 persons: 2 pints shelled peas; lettuce leaves; 1 dozen small onions; 2 oz butter; 1 teaspoon sugar; fine herbs; ¼ pint water. Cooking time: 15–20 minutes.

Put the peas in a saucepan with 1 ounce butter and salt, sugar, small onions, and a few finely shredded lettuce leaves. Cover with water, add a bunch of parsley and chervil—no thyme or bay leaf. Cook gently with lid on for 15–20 minutes, according to size and quality. Remove parsley and chervil. Add remaining butter. Toss gently and serve.

Petits pois à la Menthe * *with Mint*

For 4 persons: 2 pints peas; 1 bunch mint; 2 oz butter; pinch sugar. Cooking time: 15–20 minutes.

Cook the peas gently in plenty of boiling, salted water with a bunch of mint added. Drain when tender, add butter and sugar. Serve with a few blanched mint leaves on top.

Purée de Pois Cassés * *Split Pea Purée*

For 4 persons: ½ lb split peas; 8 small onions; 2 carrots; seasoning; 2 oz butter; lardoons of fat bacon. Cooking time: 2 hours.

After soaking the peas overnight put them on to cook in just enough water to cover them. Add onions and carrots and some lardoons sautéed in butter. Cook gently with the lid on for 2 hours. Strain the thick *purée*. Re-heat, without boiling, with seasoning and butter.

POIVRONS * *PEPPERS*

Poivrons Farcis au Gras * *Stuffed Peppers*

For 5 persons: 5 peppers; 1¼ lb pork sausage meat; 1 clove garlic; 2 shallots; parsley; 3 oz breadcrumbs; fine herbs; 1 egg; 2 tablespoons oil; ½ pint Tomato sauce. Cooking time: 30–40 minutes.

Remove the stalks and seeds from the peppers. Chop garlic, parsley, and shallot, then add to the sausage meat. Mix in some breadcrumbs and bind with an egg. Fill the peppers, sprinkle with breadcrumbs and moisten with a few drops of oil or melted butter. Bake in the oven in a lightly oiled dish with about ¼ pint *bouillon* added. Arrange on a dish, with Tomato sauce, seasoned with a trace of garlic, poured round.

▣ Farcis au Riz * *Stuffed with Rice*

For 5 persons: 5 peppers; 4 oz rice; 5 tomatoes; 2 tablespoons olive oil; ½ pint Tomato, Demi-glace or cream sauce. Cooking time of rice: 10 minutes; of stuffed peppers: 1 hour.

Use one tablespoon of rice per pepper. Cut off the stalks of peppers and remove the seeds through the hole. Wash the rice in cold water and boil it for 10 minutes. Strain and add to it the pulp of 5 tomatoes, fine herbs, salt, pepper and the olive oil. Stuff the peppers and bake in the oven for 1 hour. Only use the sweet peppers from the south, which are green, yellow or red, and fairly large. Pour sauce round.

Ratatouille Niçoise * *Ratatouille Niçoise*

For 6 persons: 2 onions, finely sliced; 2 tablespoons oil; 1 lb courgettes; 1¼ lb roughly chopped, skinned tomatoes without their seeds; 1¾ lb sliced aubergines; 2 peppers cut into fine strips; 2 cloves garlic; seasoning; bouquet garni. Cooking time: 30 minutes.

Fry the onions lightly in oil, add tomatoes, the diced *courgettes*, aubergines, peppers, whole cloves of garlic and *bouquet garni*. Season. Cook until all the liquid has evaporated.

Salsifis * *Salsify*

For 4 persons: 3 lb salsify; flour; 3 tablespoons vinegar. Cooking time: 1 hour.

Peeling, preparing and cooking this vegetable puts off many housewives who do **not** always have the time for the long preliminaries. Mostly, salsify is scraped with a knife, until white, or use a small vegetable paring knife, which is quicker. As the salsify are peeled, plunge into cold water and vinegar to prevent them turning reddish. Keep the tops, which make an excellent salad. To cook, whisk a large handful of flour in 8 pints of water, add salt, and vinegar. Place the salsify, cut up lengthwise if too large, in this and boil with the lid off, since the floured water will boil over like milk. If the salsify is cooked the day before, leave it in the liquor or it will turn black.

Salsifis Frits * Deep Fried

For 4 persons: 2 lb salsify; parsley; lemon juice; ½ pint Frying batter.

Make a Frying batter, drain the cooked salsify, and cut into short lengths. Place in a bowl with salt, pepper, chopped parsley and lemon juice and macerate for 30 minutes. Then dip in batter one by one and drop in very hot fat, oil if possible. When they are golden brown and the batter is crisp, drain on a cloth and serve at once, garnished with fried parsley.

▣ Sautés * Sautéed

For 4 persons: 2 lb salsify; 4 oz butter; chopped parsley. Cooking time: 1 hour.

Drain the salsify and stew slowly in a covered frying pan with plenty of hot butter until slightly yellow, season to taste and sprinkle with chopped parsley.

▣ au Velouté * Sauce Velouté

For 4 persons: 2 lb salsify; 1 pint sauce Velouté. Cooking time: 15 minutes.

Make a *sauce Velouté* with ordinary *bouillon*, but without egg yolks, and simmer the cooked salsify in it. Season with salt, pepper and lemon juice. Serve with chopped parsley.

TOMATES * TOMATOES

Tomates à l'Avignonnaise * Tomatoes Avignonnaise

For 4 persons: 6 tomatoes; 2 aubergines; butter; garlic; parsley. Cooking time: 25 minutes.

Sauté halved tomatoes in oil and combine with sliced aubergines, sautéed separately. Season with crushed chopped garlic and chopped parsley.

▣ à la Bonne Femme * Bonne Femme

For 4 persons: 4 oz cooked veal; 8 tomato halves; 2 shallots; fine herbs; 1 egg; breadcrumbs; ½ pint Tomato sauce; bread. Cooking time: 20 minutes.

Mince the meat and combine with ⅓ its own volume of bread, dipped in milk or *bouillon*, and well squeezed out. Season with chopped shallots and fine herbs; add the egg. Scoop out some tomatoes, season them and fill with the mixture; sprinkle with breadcrumbs and melted butter. Place in a hot oven for a good quarter of an hour. Serve with Tomato sauce poured round.

Tomates Farcies * Stuffed

For 4 persons: 8–10 *tomatoes; 4 oz cooked meat; 2 oz raw sausage meat; salt; pepper; garlic; breadcrumbs; oil; chopped parsley; bouillon;* ½ *pint Tomato or Demi-glace sauce.* Cooking time: 20 minutes.

Finely mince some left-over cooked meat, mix with half its weight of raw sausage meat add chopped garlic, season with salt, pepper and chopped parsley and, if it is too dry, moisten with *bouillon.* Fill the scooped-out and seasoned tomatoes with the mince. Place on a greased tin. Sprinkle with breadcrumbs and oil, cover with a greased paper and bake in a fairly hot oven, 375°F or Gas Mark 5, for about 20 minutes until tomatoes are cooked. Serve with a light Tomato sauce.

The tomatoes may also be stuffed without meat, either with chopped mushrooms, or simply with crumbled bread, garlic and fine herbs, or with fried, chopped aubergine flesh. The tomatoes should be firm and not too large if they are to stay intact.

▣ Farcies à la Piémontaise * Piémontaise

For 4 persons: 8–10 *tomatoes; 2 oz Risotto Piémontaise;* ½ *pint sauce Demi-glace; 1 oz cheese.* Cooking time: 15 minutes.

Make a tomato-flavoured *Risotto (see p.* 230). Halve the tomatoes, scoop them out and fill with the rice, mixed at the last moment with grated cheese. Place on a greased ovenproof dish. Sprinkle with breadcrumbs and oil or butter, and brown in a fairly hot oven, 375°F or Gas Mark 5, for a good 15 minutes. Serve with sauce poured round. (*See illustration p.* 192).

▣ Farcies à la Provençale * Provençale

For 4 persons: 8 *tomatoes; breadcrumbs; parsley; garlic.* Cooking time: 15 minutes.

Halve the tomatoes, scoop them out and fill with a mixture of dry, crumbled bread, parsley, and chopped garlic. The garlic flavour should predominate. Sprinkle generously with oil and bake in a fairly hot oven, 375°F or Gas Mark 5. Serve hot or cold.

▣ Sautées Grillées * Sautéed or Grilled

For 4 persons: 8 *tomatoes; oil; parsley.* Cooking time: 15 minutes.

Halve ripe but firm tomatoes, squeeze to remove seeds, season and fry well in a frying pan in very hot oil or cook in the oven in a baking dish, also using oil. Sprinkle with chopped parsley.

▣ et Pommes de Terre au Gratin * with Potatoes au Gratin

For 4 persons: 2 *lb potatoes; 1 lb tomatoes; seasoning;* ¼ *pint bouillon; 4 oz butter; 2 oz grated Parmesan cheese.* Cooking time: 30 minutes.

Cook the potatoes in their skins and cut into thin slices. Peel the fresh tomatoes and cut into rounds. Butter a *gratin* dish and arrange the potatoes and tomatoes in it in alternate layers. Season. Moisten with the *bouillon.* Sprinkle with Parmesan cheese and top with butter in small pieces. Bake in a fairly hot oven, 375°F or Gas Mark 5, until all is tender.

Topinambours * *Jerusalem Artichokes*

For 4 persons: 2 lb Jerusalem artichokes. Cooking time: 20–25 minutes.

After peeling and blanching Jerusalem artichokes may be boiled, or prepared in butter, like potatoes. They may also be puréed, or sliced, dipped in batter and deep fried in oil. They are also excellent in *sauce Béchamel*. Just blanched and sliced they make an excellent salad. This is not a choice vegetable, but can be very good when properly cooked. It is also useful for soups.

Vegetable Marrow stuffed with Meat

For 4 persons: 1 medium-sized vegetable marrow; 6 oz cold cooked meat, (minced or finely chopped); 2 oz diced cooked vegetables; 1 tomato (peeled and chopped); ½ pint Béchamel sauce; salt; pepper; ½ oz chopped parsley; 2 oz grated cheese. Cooking time: 1 hour.

Cut a hole in the marrow at the end or in the top, and remove seeds. Leave marrow unpeeled. Mix meat, vegetables, tomato, salt, pepper, parsley, and half the sauce, and fill into the marrow. Place the piece cut out of marrow for the hole back in place, and wrap marrow in foil. Cook in hot oven, 400°F or Gas Mark 6, for 1 hour, or until marrow is tender. Mix grated cheese with remaining Béchamel sauce and heat. Pour hot sauce over marrow and serve, cut into slices.

Potatoes

Choose potatoes of uniform size and peel very thinly. New potatoes require only brushing and scraping.

Boiled potatoes: boil old potatoes gently, in a covered saucepan with just enough *cold* salted water to cover. New potatoes should be covered with *boiling* salted water and cooked slowly.

Pommes de Terre à la Boulangère   *   Potatoes Boulangère

For 4 persons: 2 lb potatoes; 6 oz onions; 4 oz fat; bouillon. Cooking time: 40–50 minutes.

Peel and slice the potatoes and place them in a baking dish with sliced onions. Add salt, pepper and good dripping or butter. Add ¼ pint water or *bouillon* and cook in a hot oven, 400°F or Gas Mark 6, stirring from time to time. These potatoes are usually served with mutton.

▣ Château   *   Château

For 4 persons: 2 lb potatoes; 2 oz butter; seasoning. Cooking time: 45 minutes.

Peel and trim the potatoes to the size of green olives. Place over heat in cold water with salt and bring to the boil. Drain and toss into very hot butter, salt and place in the oven, shaking them from time to time. When cooked, arrange in a mound and sprinkle with chopped parsley.

▣ Chips   *   Game Chips or Chips

For 4 persons: 2 lb potatoes. Cooking time: 3–5 minutes.

Peel and dry potatoes. Cut them to the size of a small sausage. Then cut into very thin slices, either with a mandoline or with a knife. Soak in cold water until required. Dry these slices and cook them in hot deep fat, a few at a time, for 3 minutes. Drain, reheat the fat and fry once more until crisp. These potatoes are served with roast game. They are also popular at cocktail parties.

Pommes de Terre à la Crème   *   *with Cream*

For 4 persons: 2 lb potatoes; 4 oz butter; ¼ pint cream. Cooking time: 25 minutes.

Cook the potatoes in their skins, then peel and cut into fairly thick slices. Moisten with cream, cook for a few minutes with some butter and season. Serve and pour on the remaining thick cream. Do not add any parsley.

▣ Dauphine   *   *Dauphine*

For 4 persons: ½ lb Duchess potatoes; ½ lb Choux pastry. Cooking time: 10 minutes.

Combine equal parts of Duchess potatoes and unsweetened *Choux* pastry, add a little nutmeg and drop small, round lumps of the mixture into hot fat. Gradually increase the heat of the fat. Drain the potatoes when golden brown. These are mostly served as a garnish.

▣ Duchesse   *   *Duchess Potatoes*

For 4 persons: 1½ lb potatoes; 1 oz butter; 2 egg yolks; seasoning. Cooking time: 10 minutes, using boiled potatoes.

Boil the potatoes in salted water as for *purée*. Drain as soon as they are cooked and rub through a sieve. Dry the *purée* with the butter, then remove from heat and mix with the egg yolks. Season well and pipe out into neat spirals, 2 inches high and 1 inch diameter, using a bag and large star pipe, on to a greased baking sheet. Bake in a hot oven, 375–400°F or Gas Mark 5–6, for 5 minutes. Brush lightly with beaten egg and bake for a further 5 minutes. Serve as a garnish.

▣ Frites Dites Pont-Neuf   *   *Potato Chips*

For 4 persons: about 1½ lb potatoes. Cooking time: 7–8 minutes.

Peel the potatoes and cut them into long, regular rectangles, about 2 inches long and ¼ inch thick. Soak for 10 minutes. Dry well and drop into hot fat. Fry for 7–8 minutes without browning. Remove from fat. When about to serve replace in very hot fat. Shake for 2–3 minutes and remove when they are quite crisp. Drain on a cloth, salt, serve with roast or grilled meat, or fried fish, garnished with watercress.

▣ Galettes   *   *Cakes*

For 4 persons: 1½ lb potatoes in their jackets; salt; nutmeg; 2 oz butter.

Peel the hot, boiled potatoes and mash them with butter. Season and mix well, shape into small cakes and toss in flour. Fry on both sides in just enough fat to prevent them sticking to the frying pan. Alternatively they may be cooked on a greased baking sheet in the oven. When lightly browned on first side, turn and finish by browning on other side.

▣ Gaufrettes   *   *Wafer*

For 4 persons: 1½ lb potatoes; salt. Cooking time: 10 minutes in two instalments.

Slice raw potatoes thinly with a special cutter (mandoline), which makes a wafer pattern. Throw the slices into cold, running water, drain, dry with a cloth and deep fry in plenty of hot fat. Sprinkle with fine salt. Like all other deep fried potatoes, wafer potatoes are best if fried twice.

The slicer, or mandoline, is a most useful implement for making chipped or *soufflé* potatoes and also for slicing carrots, celeriac and some other vegetables.

Pommes de Terre au Lard * *with Bacon*

For 4 persons: 1½ *lb potatoes; 2 onions; 2 oz butter; 4 oz lean bacon; flour;* 1 *tablespoon tomato purée;* ½ *pint bouillon;* 1 *tablespoon chopped parsley.* Cooking time: 40 minutes.

Brown two small chopped onions, in butter; when they turn yellow add the bacon, cut in thin strips. When everything is well browned, sprinkle with flour, brown this, add the *bouillon* mixed with a little tomato *purée* and cook for 20 minutes. Put in the potatoes, new ones if in season, or old ones cut to the same size, and cook for another 20 minutes. Serve with chopped parsley.

▣ à la Maître d'Hôtel * *Maître d'Hôtel*

For 4 persons: 1½ *lb potatoes;* ½ *pint bouillon;* ½ *pint milk; 2 oz butter; nutmeg; chopped parsley.* Cooking time: 20 minutes.

Slice boiled potatoes into a *sauté* pan, add the *bouillon*, butter, salt, pepper and grated nutmeg. Cook briskly for a few minutes and add the boiling milk. Boil up once more, and serve in a vegetable dish sprinkled with chopped parsley.

▣ à la Normande * *Normandy style*

For 4 persons: 1½ *lb potatoes; 2 leeks; 4 oz lean bacon; 1 onion; 2 oz butter.* Cooking time: 25 minutes.

Fry a large sliced onion and the sliced white of two leeks in butter, without browning, together with the blanched bacon, cut in thin strips. When this mixture begins to soften in the butter, add the thinly sliced raw potatoes. Add enough *bouillon* or, if not available, water, to cover the potatoes, season and cook over good heat. Sprinkle with chopped parsley and serve in a vegetable dish.

▣ Paille * *Straw*

For 4 persons: about 1½ *lb potatoes; salt.* Cooking time: 5–6 minutes.

Cut the potatoes into a fine *julienne*, using the mandoline cutter, if possible. Wash and dry them carefully and plunge a few at a time into very hot fat. These potatoes always contain some moisture, so that they make the fat bubble up and it may overflow; they should, therefore, be fried in a frying basket or strainer, and the pan should only be one-third full of fat. After 3 or 4 minutes remove from fat, reheat it, and replace potatoes for 1 or 2 minutes; this makes them crisp. Drain and salt. Serve with grilled meats.

▣ Persillées * *Parsley*

For 4 persons: 2 lb potatoes; 2 oz butter; seasoning; ½ *pint bouillon; chopped parsley.* Cooking time: 20 minutes.

Prepare in the same way as *Château* potatoes, and place in a baking dish with a little butter and seasoning. Half cover with a light *bouillon*, add salt and pepper. Cover with paper and bake in the oven. Serve sprinkled with fresh chopped parsley.

Pommes de Terre Sautées à la Lyonnaise *
Lyonnaise

For 4 persons: 1½ lb potatoes; chopped parsley; 5 oz butter; ¾ lb onions. Cooking time: 25 minutes.

Boil some potatoes in their jackets in salted water, partly cool them in cold water, peel and slice thinly. Brown them lightly in a frying pan with 4 ounces very hot butter. In another pan fry some sliced onions gently in remaining butter, and when cooked and yellow combine with the potatoes. *Sauté* the two together for a few minutes. Serve in a bowl sprinkled with chopped parsley.

▣ Sautées ou Roesti * *Sautéed*

For 4 persons: 2 lb potatoes; 2 oz butter; salt; chopped parsley. Cooking time: 20 minutes.

Peel and slice some potatoes cooked in their jackets. Melt butter in a frying pan, salt the potatoes and fry them golden brown. Shake from time to time to facilitate cooking, and turn over so that they fry on both sides. Serve with chopped parsley sprinkled over.

▣ à la Savoyarde * *Savoyarde*

For 4 persons: 2 lb potatoes; 2 onions; 4 oz gruyère; 1 pint bouillon; 4 oz butter. Cooking time: ¾–1 hour.

Lightly brown the sliced onions in butter and combine with raw, thinly sliced potatoes and sliced cheese. Place in a baking dish, three-quarters cover with *bouillon* and bake in a fairly hot oven, 375°F or Gas Mark 5, until tender.

Croquettes * *Croquettes*

For 4 persons: 1½ lb potatoes; 1 oz butter; 2 egg yolks. Cooking time: 10 minutes.

Prepare the same mixture as for Duchess potatoes (*p. 214*). Divide the potato mixture into even portions and shape as desired—into pears, rolls, flat cakes, etc. Egg and breadcrumb them and, at the last moment, fry in very hot deep fat. Serve at once, as a vegetable or as a garnish.

▣ aux Raisins * *with Currants*

For 4 persons: 1½ lb Croquette mixture; 2 oz currants; beaten egg; chopped almonds. Cooking time: 10 minutes.

These *croquettes* may be served with game. They are made in the same way as plain *croquettes*, but 2 ounces currants should be added to the mixture. Shape into balls, egg and roll in chopped almonds instead of breadcrumbs. Fry in very hot deep fat.

Gratin Dauphinois * *Gratin Dauphinois*

For 4 persons: 1½ lb potatoes; 1 egg; 6 oz grated cheese; 2 oz butter; 1 pint milk; salt, pepper and nutmeg. Cooking time: 40 minutes.

Thinly slice the raw potatoes. Place them in a buttered baking dish and season with salt, pepper and nutmeg. Beat a whole egg in a bowl with cold milk and 4 ounces cheese. Pour over the potatoes and sprinkle remaining cheese over. Dot with butter, cover and cook in a fairly hot oven, 375°F or Gas Mark 5, for 40 minutes.

Knepfes * *Potato Dumplings*

For 4 persons: 6 potatoes; 1 egg; 2 oz breadcrumbs; 1 oz butter; 2 oz flour; seasoning. Cooking time: 20 minutes.

Grate 6 raw potatoes and combine with 1 egg, the flour, and seasoning. Shape into balls and poach in boiling salted water. Drain and sprinkle with breadcrumbs fried in butter.

▣ au Fromage * *with Cheese*

For 4 persons: 6 potatoes; 1 egg; 2 oz gruyère; 2 oz flour; seasoning. Cooking time: 20 minutes.

Same procedure as for the previous recipe, but grate 6 boiled potatoes and add grated cheese etc. Cook the dumplings in boiling water, drain and fry golden brown. Sprinkle with cheese when serving.

Purée Mousseline * *Potato Purée Mousseline*

For 4 persons: 1½ lb potatoes; 2 oz butter; about ¼ pint milk; seasoning. Cooking time: 15 minutes.

Peel some very floury potatoes, quarter them and boil in salted water. As soon as they are ready, drain and sieve them. Dry the *purée* in a saucepan over heat with the butter, and gradually add the boiling milk. When the *purée* becomes soft, whisk it to make it fluffy and serve as soon as ready.

LES CHAMPIGNONS * *MUSHROOMS*

There are more types of edible fungi than is generally known. In Britain we are more conservative in our choice than on the continent.

The following varieties are among those obtained in this country:—

The Common or Field Mushroom, both wild and cultivated, is the variety commonly used for food in Britain.

The Horse Mushroom is much larger than the field. It is generally used for ketchup.

Champignons or button mushrooms, are grown in France. They are canned, or bottled in brine, and imported to Britain.

Cèpes or edible boletus, are larger than the *champignons*. They are a very popular variety, and may also be dried for winter use or obtained canned, or bottled in brine.

Morels are delicate in flavour. They are obtained both fresh and dried and are used mainly for seasoning. They must not be eaten raw.

Cultivated mushrooms are the most common and easily obtainable in this country, they are known as *Champignons de couche* in France.

Chanterelle—one of the best known varieties of mushrooms. Requires careful slow cooking, and is often softened in boiling water or milk before being cooked in butter.

Orange milk agaric is useful for soups, and is often preserved in vinegar and used for salad.

Parasol—a very large mushroom, excellent for cooking. The cap only is used.

St. George's—a really good Spring mushroom.

Truffles in bottled form are used mainly for garnishing. They are imported from Italy and France, and are very expensive.

CÈPES * *BOLETUS*

Cèpes à la Bordelaise * *Boletus Bordelaise*

For 4 persons: 1½ lb boletus; 4 oz butter; 1 tablespoon oil; 2 shallots; parsley. Cooking time: 10–12 minutes.

Fresh or tinned boletus may be used; both are delicious. Slice the boletus tops and cook in 2 ounces hot butter and oil. *Sauté* well until they brown, seasoning with salt and pepper. Add chopped shallots, *sauté* a few moments longer, then pour 2 ounces of *Noisette* butter on top. Sprinkle with chopped parsley.

For this recipe, cook only the tops in this way. Chop the stalks finely, fry them in oil in a separate pan and pour over the tops when they are well-fried and crisp.

▣ à la Provençale * *Provençale*

For 4 persons: 1½ lb boletus; oil; 1 clove garlic. Cooking time: 10–12 minutes.

Same method as above, using garlic instead of shallots and oil instead of butter.

CHAMPIGNONS DE COUCHE * *CULTIVATED MUSHROOMS*

à la Crème * *Creamed*

For 4 persons: 1½ lb mushrooms; 2 oz butter; ¼ pint milk; seasoning; 1 oz flour; ¼ pint cream; lemon juice; 4 slices buttered toast. Cooking time: 15 minutes.

Wash the mushrooms and stew gently with seasoning, milk and butter, in a covered pan until tender—10 minutes. Strain off the liquor. Blend flour smoothly with cold water. Add liquor and boil up, stirring all the time. Stir in the cream. Add mushrooms and boil up. Sharpen with lemon juice and serve on buttered toast.

▣ Cuisson Ordinaire * *Stewed*

For 4 persons: 1½ lb mushrooms; ¼ pint water; 1 oz butter; half lemon. Cooking time: 4–5 minutes.

Put the mushrooms into a pan with a scant ¼ pint of water, butter, lemon juice and seasoning.

Boil up and cook gently, with the lid on the pan, until tender, when the liquid is considerably reduced. Serve the mushrooms in their liquor.

Champignons Grillés * *Grilled*

For 4 persons: 8 *very large cultivated mushrooms;* 2 *tablespoons oil;* 2 *oz Maître d'hôtel butter.* Cooking time: 10–12 minutes.

Separate the stalks from the heads of cleaned mushrooms, hollow out, but do not peel. Sprinkle with oil and grill. Season with salt and fill with the *Maître d'hôtel* butter. Serve at once.

CHANTERELLES OU GIROLLES * *CHANTERELLES*

Chanterelles aux Fines Herbes * *Chanterelles with Herbs*

For 4 persons: 1½ *lb chanterelles;* 2 *oz butter; salt; nutmeg; chopped chives or parsley.* Cooking time: 30 minutes.

Heat some butter in a *sauté* pan, put the washed and drained *chanterelles* in it, cover and simmer well. Season with salt and nutmeg and add a little more butter. Cook thoroughly, add some chopped chives or parsley and serve.

▣ Sautées au Beurre * *Sautéed in Butter*

For 4 persons: 1½ *lb chanterelles;* 1 *oz butter.* Cooking time: 20 minutes.

The most popular way of serving *chanterelles* is to *sauté* them in butter. They are excellent with game or eggs.

▣ Ragoût * *Stew*

For 4 persons: 1½ *lb chanterelles;* 6 *shallots; flour; thyme; red wine; gravy.* Cooking time: 20 minutes.

Simmer some nice little *chanterelles* (or large ones cut up) in butter for 10 minutes with chopped shallots and drain in a strainer. Heat a little more butter, add a little flour and a trace of powdered thyme, a dash of red wine, some gravy and a little of the cooking liquor of the mushrooms. Stir this sauce and place the *chanterelles*, seasoned with salt and pepper, in it. Serve sprinkled with chopped parsley.

Morilles aux Fines Herbes * *Morels with Mixed Herbs*

For 4 persons: 1½ *lb morels;* 2 *oz butter; chopped parsley; lemon juice.* Cooking time: 20 minutes.

Cut up the morels or leave whole, according to size, and place in butter with a dash of lemon juice, salt and pepper. Cook in an open saucepan, so that the water they contain may evaporate. When they are dry, transfer to a frying pan, with some more butter, add parsley and cook until tender. Serve at once.

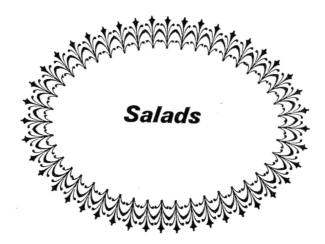

Salads

There are two different kinds of salads—simple and composite. The simple variety includes green salads such as lettuce, curled endive, etc., which are dressed with oil and vinegar and served with roasts.

Composite salads are made up of a combination of various cooked vegetables, usually bound with *mayonnaise*. (*See also p.* 41). (*See illustrations pp.* 33-36 *and* 192).

ASSAISONNEMENTS * SALAD DRESSINGS

Assaisonnement à la Crème * Cream Dressing

A special dressing for cos lettuce. Use 4 parts cream to 1 part French wine vinegar or lemon juice, with some salt and pepper.

▣ à l'Huile * Oil

Suitable for any salad. Use 3 parts oil to 1 part French wine vinegar or lemon juice, with some salt and pepper.

▣ au Lard * Bacon

A special dressing for dandelion leaves, wild chicory, cabbage and lamb's-lettuce (corn salad). Grill some streaky bacon and use the rendered fat to make the dressing adding very hot vinegar, salt and pepper.

▣ Mayonnaise * Mayonnaise

The recipe for *mayonnaise* will be found on page 28. It is used for various cooked vegetables, fish and meats.

▣ à l'Oeuf * Egg

Sieved hardboiled egg yolk blended with mustard, oil, vinegar, salt and pepper and the shredded white.

SALADE * *SALAD*

Salade d'Artichauts à la Grecque * *Greek style* *Artichoke Salad*

Proportions: ⅛ artichoke hearts (small globe artichokes); ⅛ small carrots cut to a round shape; ⅛ small white onions; ⅛ green olives; ¼ button mushrooms; ¼ chanterelles. Dressing: oil; vinegar; salt; pepper; thyme; bay leaf; coriander. Garnish: black olives; white onions and trimmed artichoke hearts.

Blanch the carrots, button mushrooms, *chanterelles*, artichoke hearts and onions. Make a marinade of 2 parts water to 1 part oil and 1 part good vinegar, peppercorns, thyme, bay leaf, salt and coriander. Bring to the boil and cook the vegetables in it for about 20 minutes, or until tender. Cool them in the marinade. Garnish with black olives, white onions and trimmed artichoke hearts. Serve very cold.

▣ Crowned Prawn Rice

For 4 persons: 2 finely chopped medium-sized onions; 1 oz butter; 4 oz mushrooms, sliced; extra 2 oz butter; 15 oz cooked long grain rice; 4 oz cooked peas; 1 green pepper, chopped; 1 oz chopped parsley; 4 oz ham, chopped; 1 lb prawns; 6 tablespoons olive oil; 2 tablespoons wine vinegar; pepper; salt; shredded lettuce; finely sliced tomatoes and cucumber.

Sauté onions in heated butter until lightly browned; remove. Add extra butter to pan, heat, *sauté* mushrooms until tender. Spoon onions and mushrooms into rice, with pan juices. Mix in peas, green pepper, parsley, ham, and shelled prawns (reserving about 1 dozen with tails still on for garnishing). Mix together lightly, pour over enough mixed oil, vinegar, pepper and salt to moisten, then mix again. Arrange rice in a ring on a large platter. Surround with shredded lettuce and alternate slices of tomato and cucumber. Fill centre of ring with shredded lettuce, arrange reserved prawns in a crown shape on top of rice ring. Serve chilled.

▣ Garden Coleslaw

For 4 persons: 12 oz shredded white cabbage; 2 oz chopped parsley; 4 shallots, chopped; 1 red pepper, finely chopped; ½ oz sugar; 2 tablespoons vinegar; 1 tablespoon oil; salt and pepper.

Combine cabbage, parsley, shallots, and red pepper; place in salad bowl. Mix together sugar, vinegar, oil, salt and pepper, and stir until sugar has dissolved. Pour over vegetables and toss lightly. Serve at once.

▣ Green Salad with Avocado

For 4 persons: 1 large lettuce; 1 avocado; salt; pepper; 6 tablespoons olive oil; 2 tablespoons wine vinegar.

Remove stalk and coarse outer leaves from lettuce. Wash thoroughly, pat dry, wrap in cloth and place in refrigerator to crisp. At serving time, break lettuce into bite-sized pieces into salad bowl. Halve avocado, remove seed, scoop flesh into bowl. Sprinkle with pepper and salt. Mix oil, vinegar, pepper and salt thoroughly, pour over enough dressing to coat salad. Toss gently and serve at once.

Salade Italienne * *Italian*

For 4 persons: 4 oz carrots; 4 oz beetroot; 4 oz potatoes; 4 oz green peas; 4 oz tomatoes; 4 oz French beans; 1 tablespoon capers; 10 anchovy fillets; 2 oz salami; 2 hardboiled eggs; mayonnaise; lemon juice; pickled tongue.

Cook carrots, beetroot, potatoes, green peas and French beans in separate pans. When cold dice the vegetables and mix them. Bind with *mayonnaise* and add the lemon juice. Chop whites and sieve yolks of eggs separately, dice the tongue and use these and the anchovy fillets to garnish the salad in a glass bowl.

▣ au Lard * *Bacon*

For 4 persons: 1¼ lb dandelion leaves; 5 oz bacon; 2 tablespoons French wine vinegar.

This recipe is used mainly for dandelions and chicory. Wash and shake dandelion leaves. Heat and slightly brown some diced bacon in a frying pan. Pour over the salad, holding it close to the stove. The melted fat replaces the oil; add hot vinegar, salt and pepper.

Note: In all salads, lemon juice may be used instead of vinegar.

▣ Marguerite * *Marguerite*

For 4 persons: 6 oz cauliflower sprigs; 6 oz sliced French beans; 6 oz asparagus tips; 8 oz potatoes; mayonnaise; 2 or 3 eggs; butter.

Boil the vegetables in salted water, slice the potatoes thinly and place the mixed vegetables in a salad bowl in a mound; coat with this *mayonnaise*. Decorate the surface attractively with some of the vegetables set aside for that purpose. In the centre make a daisy out of the white of hardboiled eggs and place some similar smaller daisies, made with a shaped cutter, round the edge. Sieve the egg yolks with butter to make the centres of the flowers. (*See illustration p. 34*).

▣ Moulée * *Moulded*

Cut out some carrots and turnips with an olive-shaped vegetable cutter, boil them separately in salted water, drain and cool. Also boil some potatoes, sliced French beans, green peas and sprigs of cauliflower. Line a domed mould with aspic and decorate with the carrots and turnips, some strips of beans and a ring of potato slices, tastefully arranged. Mix the remaining vegetables, combine with some *mayonnaise* mixed with a little aspic and fill up the mould with these. Leave to set and turn out on a round, cold dish, garnished with crisp lettuce leaves and some chopped aspic.

▣ Niçoise * *Niçoise*

For 4 persons: 12 oz French beans; 8 oz tomatoes; 8 oz new cooked potatoes; sauce Vinaigrette. Garnish: stoned black and green olives; anchovy fillets and capers.

Cook the beans and cool under the cold tap. Cut them into diamond shape. Skin tomatoes and squeeze to remove seeds. Slice the flesh coarsely. Dice the potatoes. Mix the vegetables. Season with *Vinaigrette*. Mound in salad bowl. Arrange strips of anchovy fillets over, lattice style. Sprinkle capers over and surround with stoned olives. Freshly chopped parsley and chives may be added and if liked a little finely chopped garlic. Tuna fish and hardboiled eggs are often included.

Salade aux Oeufs Durs * *Hardboiled Eggs*

Hardboiled eggs may be added to all salads; when they are used, extra seasoning is required.

▣ Orloff * *Orloff*

For 4 persons: ½ pint mayonnaise; 2 tablespoons Tomato sauce; 2 skinned and seeded tomatoes; 6 oz raw celery; 2 (tinned) artichoke bottoms; 6 oz boiled ham; 6 oz cooked chicken; 4 oz spaghetti; 1 truffle; 4 cooked mushroom caps; 4 raw mushrooms.

Cut all the ingredients into a fine *julienne*. The *spaghetti* should be only just cooked and luke-warm. Bind with well-seasoned, tomato-flavoured, thick *mayonnaise*, then arrange the salad in a mound in a salad bowl. Decorate the top with some nice white scalloped cooked mushroom tops and slices of tomato and truffle. (*See illustration p.* 34).

▣ Oyster

For 4 persons: 24 shelled oysters; 4 oz sliced celery; 1 pickled cucumber, sliced; salt and pepper; 2 chopped hard boiled eggs; ¼ pint mayonnaise; juice ½ lemon; 1 oz each chopped parsley and chives; 1 teaspoon chopped capers; lettuce leaves.

Place oysters in small pan with their liquor and heat gently until plump; drain and chill. Place oysters in a bowl with celery, pickled cucumber, salt and pepper. Add chopped egg, toss lightly. Blend mayonnaise, lemon juice, parsley, chives and capers; add to oysters, toss once again. Spoon into bowl lined with lettuce leaves and serve.

▣ Panachée aux Oeufs * *Mixed with Eggs*

Boil a cauliflower in salted water. When it is tender take it out of the pan, sprinkle with a little lemon juice and let it cool. Place it on a round dish and pour *sauce Vinaigrette* over it. Surround it with small portions of grated carrots bound with lemon juice and *mayonnaise* and with watercress salad. Garnish each portion of carrots with half a hardboiled egg.

▣ Potato Salad with Sour Cream

For 6 persons: 2 lb new potatoes; boiling salted water; ½ oz sugar; 2 table-spoons wine vinegar; ¼ pint sour cream; 1 teaspoon prepared mustard; ½ onion, finely chopped; juice ½ lemon; salt and pepper; lettuce leaves; finely chopped parsley; finely chopped chives; tomato wedges.

Scrub potatoes and cook in boiling salted water until just tender; drain, cool slightly, then peel and slice. Place in bowl, sprinkle with sugar and vinegar. Mix sour cream, mustard, onion, lemon juice, salt and pepper. Pour over salad and toss thoroughly. Serve in salad bowl lined with lettuce leaves. Sprinkle with chopped parsley and chives and garnish with tomato wedges.

▣ Rachel (recette simplifiée) * *Rachel (simplified recipe)*

For 4 persons: 4 artichoke bottoms; 8 oz asparagus tips; 8 stalks celery; 8 oz cooked potatoes; 8 oz mushrooms; brandy; port.

Peel and prepare the artichoke bottoms as explained in the chapter on vegetables; do not overcook them. Alternatively, use the tinned ones. Cut artichokes, celery and potatoes into *julienne* strips. Season separately with oil and vinegar. Add asparagus tips and the finely sliced raw mushrooms to the artichoke bottoms. Season with salt, pepper, a dash of brandy and of oil, and a drop of port wine. Arrange in separate mounds on the salad dish and place a small bunch of asparagus tips in the centre with the tips pointing upwards. This is a particularly good salad.

Salade de Riz Derby   *   *Rice Derby*

Proportions: ⅓ rice poached in salted water and drained well; ⅓ cooked fresh peas; ⅓ boiled ham and button mushroom julienne; sauce Vinaigrette slightly thickened with mayonnaise; green walnuts.

Combine all ingredients. Mix lightly with two forks. Season with dressing. Mound in the salad bowl and garnish with walnuts. (*See illustration p.* 33).

▣ de Riz Manuela   *   *Rice Manuela*

For 4 persons: 6 oz rice; 2 oz peas; 2 oz boiled ham; 1 red pepper (pimento); mayonnaise; vinegar; a little water; a little ketchup.

Boil and drain the rice. Cut the ham and red pepper into *julienne* strips. Thin the *mayonnaise* a little with vinegar, water and ketchup and mix with the other ingredients. Dress in a mound in the salad bowl and garnish with fine cress.

▣ à la Russe   *   *Russian style*

For 4 persons: 4 oz carrots; 4 oz turnips; 4 oz potatoes; 4 oz French beans; 4 oz green peas; 4 oz pickled boiled tongue; 4 oz lean boiled ham; 2 oz anchovy fillets; mayonnaise; 2 hardboiled eggs.

Cook the vegetables according to their kind. Dice them. Mix and bind with *mayonnaise*. Arrange the salad in a glass dish and garnish with anchovies, sliced eggs, and ham and tongue *julienne*.

▣ Vinaigrette Liée   *   *with Thickened Vinaigrette*

Endive is particularly popular like this. Place a yolk of egg in a salad bowl with a little dry mustard and whisk while adding 3 parts oil to 1 pint vinegar. This should not have the consistency of *mayonnaise*, but simply bind the ingredients. Hardboiled egg yolks can also be used. Salads made in this way are excellent.

Tomates Farcies au Céleri ou au Fenouil   *
Tomatoes with Celery or Fennel Filling

Choose large, firm tomatoes. Skin them, cut a thin slice off each and scoop out the centres and season. Chop the celery or fennel finely and marinate in oil, lemon, salt and pepper. Fill the tomatoes, which may also be served as an *hors d'œuvre* or as a garnish for cold meat. (*See illustration p.* 189).

Sandwiches

Originally sandwiches were only two pieces of buttered bread filled with meat. We probably owe their invention to John Montagu, Earl of Sandwich (1718–1792). He was a well-known nobleman and passionate gamester. The story goes that, being reluctant to leave the gaming table to eat, he clapped some meat between two pieces of bread in order to appease his hunger on the spot.

To make sandwiches, use brown or white bread, and cut when 1 day old. New bread will not cut easily. Sandwich rolls are used as new as possible. Wrap in a damp muslin, greaseproof paper or foil to keep moist until required. Alternatively store in deep freeze until required.

There are many varieties of sandwiches made from flavoured butter blended with the garnish. For instance:

Sandwiches aux Anchois * Anchovy Sandwiches

Spread the bread with Anchovy butter and fill with well-dried fillets of anchovies in oil. Sprinkle with chopped yolk of hardboiled egg and cut into small rectangles. The egg makes the anchovies taste less salty.

▣ de Charcuterie * Cold Meat

Fill with any kind of cold meat or sausage, *pâté*, *galantine*, boar's head, etc., and garnish with Horseradish, Mustard and Tarragon butter. Use little salt, as most of these fillings are salt enough.

▣ de Foie de Volaille * Chicken Liver

Spread the bread with roast Hazelnut butter and fill with thin slices of cooked chicken liver. Cut into triangles. The sandwiches may also be made with chicken liver *purée* mixed with one tablespoon of ground roast hazelnuts to 4 ounces liver.

▣ au Gruyère * Gruyère or Cheshire cheese

Spread the bread with Mustard butter and fill with fresh, thinly sliced *gruyère* or Cheshire cheese. Cut into triangles.

▣ au Homard * Lobster or Rock Lobster

Butter the bread with Watercress butter, fill with thinly sliced lobster or flesh of rock lobster and cut into triangles.

Sandwiches au Jambon ★ *Ham*

This is the traditional sandwich. Butter the bread with Mustard butter and fill with a thin slice of lean boiled ham. Cut into small rectangles of about 1 × 2½ inches.

▣ aux Œufs 1 ★ *Egg 1*

Spread the bread with Anchovy butter and cover with sliced hardboiled egg.

▣ aux Œufs II ★ *Egg II*

Mash hardboiled eggs with fork, add sufficient cream to make fairly moist mixture. Spread bread with Watercress butter, then with egg mixture. Season well with salt and freshly ground black pepper. Trim crusts from sandwiches and cut into four.

▣ de Poulet 1 ★ *Chicken 1*

Butter the bread, cover with shredded lettuce bound with *mayonnaise* and top with cold roast chicken cut into small, thin slices.

▣ de Poulet II ★ *Chicken II*

Cold chopped steamed or boiled chicken is more moist than roast chicken for sandwiches. Spread the bread with plain butter, then with chopped chicken, and top with mayonnaise to which some finely chopped celery has been added. Trim the crusts from the sandwiches and cut each into four triangles.

▣ aux Sardines ★ *Sardine*

Spread bread with Sardine butter and fill with halved skinned and boned sardines in oil. Cut in small rectangles containing a half sardine each.

▣ au Saumon ★ *Salmon*

Spread bread with Watercress butter, then with mashed canned red salmon. Add some very thin slices of cucumber which have been marinated in oil and vinegar dressing. Season with pepper and salt. Trim crusts from sandwiches and cut into four triangles.

▣ Toasted Corned Beef

For 4 persons: 4 *thick slices buttered toast;* 4 *thick slices cooked corned beef; prepared mustard;* 1 *tomato, sliced; little vinaigrette dressing; grated cheese; pepper and salt.*

Cover toast slices with slices of corned beef. Spread beef with little prepared mustard. Top with a thick slice of tomato, sprinkle this with vinaigrette and pepper and salt. Top with grated cheese, grill till cheese melts and turns golden.

▣ à la Tomate ★ *Tomato*

Spread bread with Horseradish butter or *gruyère* cream, fill with slices of firm skinned tomatoes from which the seeds have been removed. Cut in triangles, first cutting a square and then halving it diagonally.

Pasta and Cereals

LES PÂTES * *PASTA*

Cannelloni Farcis * *Stuffed Cannelloni*

For 8 persons: 12 *oz cannelloni;* 1¼ *lb minced beef;* 6 *oz cooked mushrooms;* 4 *oz Parmesan;* 1 *pint tomato-flavoured veal stock or Béchamel.* Cooking time of cannelloni in water: 8 minutes. Simmering time of stuffed cannelloni: 15–20 minutes.

The stuffing for the *cannelloni* may be made from some minced left-overs of cooked meat mixed with cooked mushrooms, Tomato sauce, fine herbs, eggs, etc. If pork is used for the filling, omit the eggs. Cook the *cannelloni* in boiling water with a tablespoon of oil. Remove them when three-quarters done. Drain on a cloth and fill, using a forcing bag. Roll and arrange in a baking dish, sprinkle with Parmesan, cover with tomato-flavoured stock or *Béchamel*, sprinkle once more with cheese and cook and brown slowly for 15–20 minutes to finish cooking. (*See illustration p.* 55).

Macaroni au Fromage * *Macaroni in Cheese Sauce*

For 4 persons: 6 *oz macaroni;* 4 *oz gruyère;* 1 *pint Béchamel; seasonings.* Cooking time: 20 minutes.

Cook the macaroni in boiling salted water for 15 minutes. Drain and bind with thin *Béchamel*. Simmer for a few minutes in the sauce, which will be partly absorbed. Season with fine salt, ground pepper and a trace of grated nutmeg. Finally remove from heat and combine with grated *gruyère*.

▣ au Gratin * *Cheese*

For 4 persons: 6 *oz macaroni;* ½ *pint Béchamel;* 6 *oz cheese* (*Parmesan or gruyère*)*; seasoning;* 2 *oz breadcrumbs;* 3 *oz butter.* Cooking time: 25 minutes.

Boil macaroni as above. Add 2 ounces butter, most of the cheese, seasoning and sauce. Mix well, then put into a baking dish, sprinkle with remaining cheese, breadcrumbs and melted butter, and brown in the oven.

Pâte à Nouilles * *Noodle Dough*

For 4 persons: 8 oz flour; 1 whole egg; 1 tablespoon oil; 1 egg yolk. Cooking time: 8–10 minutes.

Place the flour on a pastry board, make a well in the middle and put into it a pinch of salt, the oil, 1 whole egg and 1 egg yolk. Knead thoroughly by hand into a firm but not too dry dough. If it is dry or brittle, add either an egg yolk or some cold milk. Make the dough into a ball, wrap in a cloth and leave in a cool place for 2 hours. Divide in half and roll each piece as thinly as you can—paper-thin, if possible. It is easier and less tiring to roll out the dough in 2 parts instead of all at once. When the dough is thin enough, dredge generously with flour and fold up several times with a little flour between the folds, so that it does not stick together. Then cut into thin strips—about ⅛ inch wide—with a knife. Shake between raised hands to remove surplus flour. These noodles may be prepared 2 weeks or more beforehand, but they must be spread out on a cloth on a high shelf in the kitchen to dry, covered with paper to protect them from dust. Leave them until they are almost as brittle as those bought ready-made. They will keep in a tin in a dry place.

To cook, place in plenty of salted, boiling water and then simmer for 8–10 minutes. Rinse and prepare like macaroni.

Note: Since these noodles can be prepared beforehand, we strongly advise our readers to make some when they have a little time to spare. They are far superior to those bought ready-made.

Nouilles à la Bernoise * *Bernoise*

For 4 persons: 8 oz noodles; 2 oz butter; 4 eggs; 4 slices ham; 2 tomatoes; 4 oz mushrooms or chanterelles, cooked in butter and seasoned.

Cook the noodles, and spread with butter. Stuff the tomatoes with chopped cooked mushrooms and bake until tender. Place slices of grilled ham on top of the noodles and a fried egg on each slice. Place a stuffed tomato in each corner of the dish. (*See illustration p.* 54).

▣ à la Bolognaise * *Bolognaise*

For 4 persons: 8 oz noodles; 2 oz butter; ½ pint sauce Bolognese; 2 oz grated Parmesan cheese.

Cook the noodles, drain, add the butter and mix with the sauce *Bolognese*. Sprinkle with Parmesan cheese. (*See illustration p.* 56).

Ravioli à l'Italienne * *Ravioli Italienne*

For 4 persons: 8 oz Noodle dough; chopped meat; 1 pint sauce Demi-glace; 2 oz grated cheese; 2 tablespoons tomato purée. Total cooking time: 50 minutes.

Roll out a large square of very thin Noodle dough; moisten it with water. Using a forcing bag cover it with hazelnut-sized dabs of the filling given below, at regular intervals of about 1½ inches. Cover the whole with a second, equally thin, piece of dough, press down with the finger around each filling and cut into small squares with a pastry wheel. Poach in salted water for 30 minutes, drain and simmer for 10 minutes in tomato-flavoured *sauce Demi-glace*. Put into a baking dish, sprinkle generously with grated cheese and allow to brown in the oven for 10 minutes.

Farce de Ravioli * *Ravioli Filling*

For 4 persons: Mince 6 ounces of braised beef and combine with 8 ounces spinach *purée* well dried in butter, a raw egg yolk, the sieved yolk of a hardboiled egg, salt, pepper, nutmeg and 2 ounces very dry grated *gruyère*. An alternative filling is spinach *purée* combined with cheese and egg yolk. The sauce for the ravioli may be replaced by *Noisette* butter.

LE RIZ * *RICE*

For 4 persons: 6 oz rice if it is used as a garnish for meat; 8 oz if it is served as a vegetable.

Wash the rice thoroughly in several changes of water. Pour into a large pan of briskly boiling water, to which you have added the juice of half a lemon and some salt. Stir and cook for about 15–17 minutes. It is most important that the water is maintained at a full rolling boil throughout the cooking process. Test the rice after 12 minutes, by pressing a grain between the thumb and forefinger; it should be soft and not hard at the centre. Drain thoroughly. Melt the butter in the saucepan and return the rice. Cover with a clean cloth and leave to dry in a warm part of the stove (not over the actual burner), for about 10–15 minutes.

If preferred, the rice may be rinsed with boiling water after cooking and before being dried.

Riz au Gras * *Fried Rice*

For 4 persons: 8 oz rice; 1 oz butter; 1 bouquet garni; bouillon. Cooking time: 18 minutes maximum.

Fry the rice lightly in butter, then add boiling *bouillon, bouquet garni* and seasoning. Use 2 cupfuls of *bouillon* to each cupful of rice. Cover closely and cook for 18 minutes, by which time all the liquid should be absorbed. Fried rice is particularly suitable for chicken.

▣ à la Grécque * *Greek style*

Prepare as for Rice Pilaf, with diced cooked sausage, some cooked green peas and diced cooked pimento added.

▣ à l'Indienne ou à la Créole * *Indian or Creole style*

For 4 persons: 8 oz rice; 2 oz butter; salt; pepper. Cooking time: 15 minutes.

Throw the rice into a large saucepan of boiling, salted water and boil briskly for 12–15 minutes. Drain, rinse and dry with a lump of butter and fine salt until it no longer sticks to the fork and the grains separate easily. This rice is an essential ingredient of all dishes described as being in the Creole or Indian style.

▣ Pilaf * *Pilaf*

For 4 persons: 8 oz rice; 2 oz butter; paprika pepper; bouquet garni; bouillon. Cooking time: 18 minutes maximum.

Toss the rice in butter, then add 2 cups of *bouillon* only for each cup of rice. Season with salt, paprika pepper and *bouquet garni*. Cover and cook for 18 minutes. Then carefully stir in a small piece of butter with a fork. A well cooked pilaf is dry.

RISOTTO * *RISOTTO*

▣ Risotto aux Cèpes * *Risotto with Mushrooms*

For 10 persons: 1¼ *lb rice;* 2½ *pints bouillon;* 4 *oz grated Parmesan cheese;* 4 *oz butter; half an onion;* 2 *tablespoons oil;* ¼ *pint white wine;* 6 *oz mushrooms.* Cooking time: 18 minutes.

Chop the onion and fry lightly in the oil with a nut of butter until the onion begins to take on a slight colour. Moisten with the white wine and reduce. Add the rice and finely sliced mushrooms, then gradually add the *bouillon*. Cover closely with greased paper and a lid. Cook for 18 minutes without stirring. Add the rest of the butter and the cheese. Remove from the heat and mix well with a fork. (*See illustration p.* 54).   (*Italy*).

Risotto Milanais * *Milanaise*

For 6 persons: 8 *oz rice;* 2 *oz onion;* ¼ *pint white wine;* 3 *oz Parmesan or gruyère;* 3 *oz butter; a pinch of saffron; good* ½ *pint bouillon.* Cooking time: 16 minutes.

Fry the chopped onion in 1 ounce of butter, then add the rice and fry together for 2 minutes. Moisten with white wine and add the *bouillon* and (optional) a handful of dried boletus, softened beforehand in hot water. Season with salt, pepper, saffron and cook for 16 minutes in a fairly hot oven, 375°F or Gas Mark 5, covered closely with greased paper and a lid. Add a nut of butter and the grated Parmesan or *gruyère*. Can be served in a *timbale*.

▣ Piémontais * *Piémontaise*

For 4 persons: 6 *oz rice;* 1 *chopped onion;* 2 *tablespoons tomato purée;* ¾ *pint bouillon;* 2 *oz cheese;* 3 *oz butter.* Cooking time: 18 minutes.

Brown a large chopped onion in 2 ounces butter; add the rice and fry for another 2 minutes. Add the *bouillon* and the tomato *purée*. Cook for 18 minutes, covered closely, and when about to serve, stir in the grated cheese and remaining butter with a fork.

LES SEMOULES ET MAÏS * *SEMOLINA AND MAIZE*

Gnocchi à la Romaine * *Gnocchi Roman style*

See recipe on page 61.

Semoule au Gratin * *Semolina au Gratin*

For 4 persons: 3 *oz semolina;* 1 *pint milk;* 2 *oz grated gruyère;* 1 *egg; salt; pepper; nutmeg;* 1 *teaspoon made mustard.* Cooking time: 15 minutes.

Boil the semolina in ¼ pint of the milk, stirring with a spatula. Beat an egg with the remaining milk. Remove semolina from the heat, add seasoning. Add the egg and milk and the *gruyère*. Stir and pour into a baking dish. Place in a very hot oven, 450°F or Gas Mark 8, to brown.

Polenta à l'Eau * *Polenta*

For 4 persons: 1½ *pints water;* 6 *oz coarse ground maize; butter; cheese.*
Cooking time: 1 hour.

Stir the maize into boiling water and continue to stir all the time until it has the consistency of thick porridge—about 20 minutes. Combine with a handful of grated cheese, cover and place in the oven for 1 hour to finish cooking. Turn out on to a round dish.

Polenta has many uses, for instance when cold it is cut into slices, toasted and served instead of bread. It is sometimes served as an accompaniment to small birds.

▣ Sautée au Beurre * *Sautéd in Butter*

For 4 persons: 6 *oz ground maize;* 1½ *pints water;* 1 *oz cheese; butter.*
Cooking time: 2 hours.

Cook the polenta as above but without cheese and place in a moderate oven, 350°F or Gas Mark 4, with the lid on for about 2 hours so that it gets fairly dry. Leave to cool overnight. Cut into slices and fry them golden brown in butter. Sprinkle with grated cheese shortly before serving.

PÂTE À BISCUIT ET GÉNOISE * *SPONGE CAKE MIXTURES*

There are two main types of sponge cakes in French baking, those classified as *Pâte à Génoise* and those classified as *Pâte à Biscuit*. They are both similar but differ in that *Pâte à Biscuit* is made with separated eggs and has a firmer, slightly less fluffy texture. Most cooks agree that it is easier to make than *Génoise*, and it can often be substituted in recipes which call for *Génoise*.

▣ Pâte à Biscuit de Savoie * *Savoy or Simple Sponge Mixture*

4 oz caster sugar; ½ oz vanilla sugar; 1½ oz cornflour; 2½ oz flour; 4 eggs; 2 oz melted butter (optional). Cooking time: 30 minutes.

The true Savoy sponge does not include butter, but it may be included and improves the keeping qualities of the cake.

Beat the sugar and the egg yolks with a whisk until light and creamy, for 6–7 minutes. Whisk the egg whites stiffly. Combine the vanilla sugar with the 2 kinds of sifted flour, and fold into the egg and sugar mixture. Do this carefully and if butter is used, fold it in at the last moment. Do not overmix. Butter and flour a sandwich tin, fill it ⅔ full and bake for 30 minutes in a moderate oven, 350°F or Gas Mark 4.

▣ à Génoise * *Genoese Mixture*

4 oz sugar; 4 whole eggs; 3 oz flour (warmed); a pinch baking powder; 3 oz butter. Cooking time: 35 minutes.

This mixture must be whisked in a bowl placed over a pan of hot water. A copper bowl of the kind used by pastrycooks is ideal and fits well into a saucepan of hot water.

Whisk the sugar and eggs over heat until they are fluffy and lukewarm. Remove from heat and continue whisking until cool. Fold in half the flour and a pinch of baking powder, with a spatula. Add half the warm melted butter. Add remaining flour and butter in the same way. It is most important that you do not overmix, otherwise the mixture becomes heavy. Bake in a buttered and floured tin in a moderate oven, 350°F or Gas Mark 4. If baked too quickly *Genoese* sponge is open in texture.

If a housewife can make sponge and *Genoese* mixtures, she will never be at a loss as to how to make a cake. These two mixtures, which are among the simplest to make, enable one to bake a good dozen or so different cakes.

PÂTE BRISÉE * *SHORTCRUST PASTRY*

Pâte Fine pour Tartes et Tartelettes * *Sweet, for Tarts and Flans*

8 oz flour; 4 oz softened butter; ½–1 oz sugar; pinch of salt; about 4 tablespoons water.

Sieve the flour on a marble slab or baking board. Make a well in the flour and place the other ingredients in the centre. Gradually draw the flour into the other ingredients. Work very lightly and quickly with the fingertips in order to mix the ingredients without making the pastry tough. The consistency should be stiff. Roll into a ball, wrap in a cloth and leave to rest in a cool place for 2 hours.

It is even better to make the dough overnight; it will be firmer and will lose any toughness caused by working it. If the pastry is too elastic when raw, it will be like cardboard when baked; a long rest enables it to relax and become supple.

▣ pour Pâtes de Gibier * *for Game Pies*

8 oz flour; 4 oz butter (or lard); salt; 1 egg yolk; cold water.

Sift flour with a good pinch of salt. Rub the butter in with the fingertips. Add beaten egg and cold water, sufficient to mix to a stiff dough. Work up lightly with the hands until smooth. Wrap in a cloth and leave to relax for several hours.

▣ Sucrée * *Rich Sweet*

4 oz flour; 2 oz sugar; 2 oz softened butter; 2 egg yolks; pinch salt; zest of a quarter lemon or orange.

Proceed as for Sweet pastry but without water. Place the ingredients in a well in the centre of the flour and gradually mix together slowly drawing in the flour. Allow to rest in a cool place for 1–2 hours. This pastry is used for Strawberry Tarts, Bourdaloue Tarts and sweet pastry *petits fours*, as specified later.

PÂTE À CHOUX * *CHOUX PASTRY*

For 4 persons: 5 oz flour; 4 oz butter; ½ oz sugar; pinch of salt; scant ½ pint water; 4 whole eggs; flavouring to taste.

Put water, butter, sugar and salt into a saucepan. Sift the flour on to a piece of paper. Melt the butter in the water. When the water is boiling rapidly, slide the flour into the boiling liquid and beat with a wooden spoon until smooth. Cook until the mixture leaves the sides of the pan, stirring all the time. Cool slightly and add the eggs, one at a time, beating well between each addition. The pastry should be soft but not runny and able to maintain its shape. If the number of eggs is not sufficient, beat an egg on a plate and gradually add it to the mixture until the desired consistency is obtained. On the other hand, if the paste is already rather soft after the third egg has been added, add only part of the fourth; this is a matter of practice.

▣ pour Beignets Soufflés * *for Soufflé Fritters*

Same as for *Choux* pastry, using ¾ ounce sugar instead of ½ ounce.

233

PÂTE FEUILLETÉE * PUFF PASTRY

For 4 persons: 9 oz flour; 7–8 oz butter; ½ level teaspoon salt; 1 teaspoon lemon juice; about 9 tablespoons cold water.

It was formerly held that the basic puff pastry mixture should not be worked too much, but this directive is not in accord with the modern understanding of the reasons for the "lift" in puff pastry. Contrary to popular belief the trapping of air during the folding has no significant effect on the lift. It is caused by the change of water into steam in the gluten while the pastry is in the oven and the consequent expansion which lifts the leaves of pastry that are insulated one from the other, by the melting butter. It is therefore necessary to mix the paste well to obtain the maximum gluten hydration. The rest period of 15 minutes mentioned in the recipe will get rid of any excess elasticity.

Make a well in the flour and put salt, water and lemon juice in the middle. Mix to an elastic paste with the fingertips and work lightly until smooth. This will take about 10 minutes. Let the paste rest for at least 15 minutes. The consistency of the butter for puff paste is important; it should have the same consistency as the paste itself, that is firm rather than soft, but do not use butter which has come straight out of the refrigerator. Roll out the dough in a square. Place the lump of butter—slightly kneaded to make it softer—in the middle and fold up the 4 corners of the dough over it, and allow to rest in a cool place for 20 minutes. Then give the pastry 2 turns by rolling it out in a long strip and folding it in 3 lengthways like a serviette; allow to rest in a cool place for ½ hour. Give it 2 more turns—6 in all, 2 at a time. Each turn should be given in the opposite direction to the previous one. Now the pastry is ready for use. For small Puff pastry patties, a little less butter may be used, but not for *bouchées, vol-au-vent, Pithiviers gâteaux,* etc., which require the best Puff pastry.

PÂTE À FRIRE ET À CRÊPES * PANCAKE AND COATING BATTERS

Pâte à Crêpes Ordinaires * Plain Pancake

For 12 pancakes (4 persons): 4 oz flour; ½–1 oz vanilla sugar; 1 oz melted butter; pinch fine salt; 2 whole eggs; approx. ½ pint cold milk; brandy or rum for flavouring.

Sift the flour in a bowl, break the eggs into the middle, add the salt and sugar. Gradually add cold milk. Mix with a whisk to make a very smooth, thinnish batter with no lumps; add more cold milk if necessary. Add the melted butter; cover bowl and leave aside for 2 or 3 hours before using. Do not use more sugar, otherwise the batter will brown too quickly when fried. In any case, since pancakes are always served dredged with sugar or spread with jam, they will be sweet enough.

▣ à Frire * Frying or Fritter Batter

For 4 persons: 8 oz flour; ½ level teaspoon salt; 2 tablespoons olive oil; ½ pint lukewarm water; 2 egg whites; ¼ oz yeast.

Dissolve the yeast in the lukewarm water. Warm a bowl and put the sifted flour in it. Make a well in the centre and into it pour the oil, salt, lukewarm water and yeast. Mix briskly by hand to make a very light batter which just coats the fingers: the amount of water is variable, since it depends on the quality of the flour. Mix the batter lightly, so that it does not become elastic; it is best to add all the water at once to avoid unnecessary mixing. Cover with a napkin and put in a warm place to rise for 3–4 hours. Just before using carefully fold in 2 stiffly beaten egg whites.

PÂTE LEVÉE * *YEAST DOUGHS*

Pâte à Brioche * *Brioche*

9 *oz flour; 6 oz butter; ½ oz caster sugar; 2 whole eggs; about 4 tablespoons warm water; ¼ oz yeast; good pinch salt.*

NOTE: *the yeast in all of these recipes is baker's (fresh) yeast.*

Make a well in the centre of one quarter of the flour on a pastry board or marble slab. Pour in the water which has been mixed with the yeast, gradually working with the fingertips to make a smooth dough. Add more warm water if necessary. Continue working until smooth and elastic. Shape it into a ball, cut a cross on top and float it in a saucepan of warm water.

While this dough, known as the "ferment", is rising in the warm water, break the eggs into the remainder of the flour and knead with both hands, beating the dough to make it very elastic, until it no longer sticks to the fingers—this takes about 10 minutes. The knack is to lift the dough up with the fingers and with a flick of the wrist throw it down again.

If 2 eggs are not enough, add a little water. Add salt and sugar, then the softened butter and beat for another 5 or 6 minutes.

Drain the ferment when it has doubled in volume, combine it carefully with the dough without beating and place it in a floured bowl. Cover and put in a warm place to rise for 3–4 hours. Knead a little on a floured board, return to bowl. Cover and keep in the refrigerator or a cool place overnight.

In principle, the ferment should be made at about 5 or 6 o'clock in the evening, combined with the dough at 8 or 9 o'clock and then left to stand overnight, when it will become firmer and easier to shape.

▣ à Pizza * *Pizza Paste*

For 6 portions: 14 *oz flour; ½ oz yeast; ¾ oz salt; approx. ½ pint milk and water mixed; ½ oz lard or butter; pepper; approx. ½ pint olive oil to sprinkle on the pizza.*

Dissolve the yeast in the lukewarm water and milk. Sift the flour and salt on the table, make a well in the centre and pour the milk and water mixture into it, then add the lard or butter. Knead the dough well and place it in a bowl. Cover with a cloth and leave to rest for 1 hour (this is very important). When it begins to rise divide it into six balls each weighing about 2½ ounces. Leave to rest for 15 minutes (this is very important). Then flatten the balls with a rolling-pin and stretch the dough out into a round about ¼–½ inch thick, using the fingers. This procedure is essential to keep the dough light and pliable. Place the rounds on an oiled baking sheet. Arrange the ingredients on the dough in the order given in each pizza recipe. Sprinkle the pizza with oil. Bake for 10–15 minutes in a fairly hot oven, 375°F or Gas Mark 5. Pizza should be eaten hot, as it toughens as it gets cold.

▣ à Savarin et à Babas * *Savarin and Baba*

Savarins and *Babas* are made from the same dough. They are yeast mixtures, both enriched by the addition of eggs and butter.

Babas are made with the same dough as *savarins*, but, for the proportions given below , cleaned dried fruit is added, about 1 ounce sultanas; 1 ounce currants; 1 ounce *glacé* cherries and some shredded almonds. The fruit should be added last before the mixture is put into the tins to rise.

Special moulds of various shapes are used for baking:—

1. small boat-shaped moulds.

2. small dariole moulds.

3. shallow ring moulds.

These moulds are well greased before use, and for *babas* are lined with finely shredded almonds.

The recipe for the syrup for soaking *babas* and *savarins* is given in the section on creams, sugar boiling, etc. (*p.* 284).

4 oz flour; ¼ oz yeast; 1 oz butter; 1 oz sugar; pinch salt; 2 eggs; 5 tablespoons milk.

Cream the yeast with 1 teaspoon sugar. Add a little warm milk. Sift flour and salt into a warm mixing basin. Make a well in the centre of the flour. Pour in the yeast mixture and flick some flour over. Cover and stand in a warm place for 15 minutes or until the yeast "sponges" or cracks through the flour. Add beaten eggs, sugar, warm milk and melted butter, and beat well for 15 minutes until the dough becomes a soft, dropping consistency. The dough is now ready for use as specified in individual recipes.

PÂTE À MERINGUÉE * *MERINGUE MIXTURES*

Pâte aux Amandes ou Japonais * *Almond*

5 egg whites; 7 oz caster sugar; 6 oz ground almonds; vanilla or other flavouring.

Make in the same way as Swiss meringue (*p.* 237), i.e. combine the sugar and almonds with very stiffly beaten egg whites. The almonds may be replaced by ground roast hazelnuts, or half of each may be used.

▣ Italienne * *Cooked or Italian*

4 egg whites; 9 oz vanilla-flavoured icing sugar.

Place the egg whites and icing or caster sugar in a copper bowl over a pan of hot water. Whisk over a very low flame, as for *Génoise* mixture, until it is stiff enough to stand by itself. It should be fairly hot, but not hot enough to cook the egg whites. Remove from heat and continue whisking until cool, according to specific recipe directions. Bake in a cool oven.

This mixture is used to make light *petits fours*—almond rocks, mushrooms, etc.

▣ **Suisse** * *Swiss*

4 egg whites; 9 oz caster sugar; vanilla.

Put the egg whites in a large bowl or a special copper bowl, and whisk until very stiff. Continue whisking while adding half the sugar and a little vanilla. Whisk until the mixture stands in points. Fold in remaining sugar as gently as possible using a spatula. If the sugar is stirred instead of "folded", the egg whites will lose their stiffness and this stiffness is an essential ingredient for success.

This mixture is used to make the shells for *Meringues chantilly* and as a finish for pudding and sweets.

Creams, Icings and Fillings

Vanilla Egg Custard

2–3 oz sugar; 5 egg yolks; 1 teaspoon cornflour or arrowroot; 1 pint milk; vanilla or other flavouring.

All housewives are familiar with custard. It is served with hot and cold sweets and puddings. A more economical custard sauce is made by using 2 whole eggs instead of 5 yolks. Mix the sugar and egg yolks with a wooden spoon, add the cornflour, and mix it in smoothly. Stir in the vanilla-flavoured boiling milk. Return to the pan and cook the sauce very carefully over heat, stirring with a wooden spoon, without allowing it to boil. Remove from heat when on the point of boiling up for the first time.

▣ au Café * Coffee

Use half milk and half strong coffee.

CRÈME AU BEURRE * BUTTER CREAM

Butter creams are used to fill mocha cakes, Genoese cakes and sponges. They may also be flavoured with liqueurs—kirsch, rum, anisette; or with coffee, chocolate or fruit juices.

▣ au Chocolat * Chocolate Butter Cream

2 oz unsalted butter; 2 tablespoons Vanilla custard; 2 oz chocolate.

When the custard is cool beat in the butter in small pats, one at a time. Add the chocolate which has been melted in a bowl over a pan of hot water.

▣ au Moka * Mocha with Syrup

2 oz sugar; 4 tablespoons strong coffee; pinch cream of tartar; 2 egg yolks; 2 oz butter.

Dissolve sugar in coffee. Add cream of tartar and boil to 220°F using a thermometer—or until the syrup looks oily. Leave to settle. Beat egg yolks and run in the syrup slowly, stirring all the time. Stir over heat until the custard thickens and coats the back of the spoon. Strain and add butter in small pats, beating each one in before adding the next. If necessary, deepen the colour with a little coffee essence.

238

Crème Pralinée * *Praline*

2 oz unsalted butter; 2 oz powdered praline; 4 tablespoons Vanilla custard.

Same method as for Vanilla butter cream, adding powdered praline.

▣ Vanillée * *Vanilla*

2 oz butter; 4 tablespoons Vanilla custard, or more if required.

Put as much best butter in a bowl as you think you will need for your cake. Cream it slightly, then stir in cold custard with a whisk until the butter is sweet enough.

Crème Bourdaloue * *Bourdaloue Cream*

4½ oz sugar; 1½ oz rice flour; 1 whole egg and 1 egg yolk; 1 oz unsalted butter; scant ½ pint milk; 2–3 tablespoons kirsch; vanilla. Cooking time: 2 minutes.

Combine the sugar with the egg and egg yolk. Add the rice flour and vanilla-flavoured boiling milk. Cook in the same way as Pastry cream. When it has boiled for 2 minutes, remove from heat and add kirsch and butter in small pieces. This cream sometimes replaces Pastry cream.

Crème Chantilly * *Whipped Fresh Cream*

½ pint thick cream; 2 tablespoons milk; 1½ oz sugar; vanilla flavouring.

Add milk to cream. Whisk until almost stiff. Add sugar and vanilla to flavour. Continue whisking until thick. Avoid over-whisking or the cream will separate.

Crème Frangipane * *Frangipane Cream*

½ pint milk; 1 oz cornflour; 2 egg yolks; 2 oz ground almonds; ¾ oz sugar; vanilla flavouring.

Blend cornflour smooth with some of the milk. Boil the remainder and pour over blended mixture. Return to the pan and stir until the mixture boils and thickens. Continue boiling for a few minutes. Remove from the heat and quickly beat in the egg yolks. Reheat without boiling. Lastly, add the sugar, ground almonds and vanilla to taste. Cool and use.

Crème Ganache * *Chocolate Cream*

6 oz very good chocolate; 2 oz unsalted butter; ¼ pint fresh cream.

Melt the chocolate in a basin over a pan of hot water. Add the butter and cream slowly or, failing the latter, the same quantity of cold boiled milk added little by little. Stir the chocolate thoroughly to make it smooth. When cold use for spreading and piping and to decorate *petits fours*.

Crème Pâtissière * *Pastry Cream or Confectioner's Custard*

1 oz sugar; ¾ oz cornflour; 2 egg yolks; ½ pint milk; vanilla flavouring; 1 oz ground almonds.

Make a sauce with the cornflour and milk, and boil for 3 minutes. Add yolks, sugar, ground almonds and vanilla. Reheat slowly but do not boil. Cool and use.

Crème Sabayon * Zabaglione

Zabaglione is more of a sauce than a dessert. It is served, hot or cold, with various puddings.

Whisk 4 egg yolks and 4 ounces sugar briskly in a double saucepan. Failing this use a saucepan in a *bain-marie*. When the mixture turns white add a good ¼ pint of white wine, which may be marsala, port, Madeira or sherry. Twirl the whisk briskly between the palms of the hands until the mixture becomes very fluffy and the water in the lower container comes to the boil. Add flavouring and serve at once, otherwise the cream will go flat. If, however, the zabaglione must be made in advance, half a teaspoon of cornflour must be added to the egg yolks.

▣ Glacée * Iced

Same mixture as above, but with 2 more egg yolks; when it thickens, pour into a bowl placed on ice and whisk until quite cold. Pour into bowls.

Crème Saint-Honoré et Choux à la Crème * St. Honoré Cream

½ *pint Pastry cream;* 3 *stiffly beaten egg whites.* Cooking time: 2 minutes.

Pastry cream combined, when boiling, with 3 stiffly beaten egg whites to every 2 egg yolks. This cream is used to fill cakes made with *Choux* pastry, including *Gâteau Saint-Honoré*.

LE GLAÇAGE DES GÂTEAUX * ICING FOR CAKES

Icing a cake means covering it with a layer of sugar, coloured and flavoured to taste. There are 2 methods: one is to use fondant icing, as described below, or to use an icing made with icing sugar, which is much simpler but does not have such a high gloss. Icing sugar may be bought ready-made and is as fine as potato flour. Fondant may be bought, ready for use.

Manière de se Servir du Fondant * How to Use Fondant

Place as much fondant as you think you will need in a double saucepan or use one saucepan placed in a *bain-marie*. Add the desired flavouring. Warm it until it is luke-warm, stirring with a spatula. The water in the lower container *must not boil*. If it is too thick add a little Stock syrup. The fondant should be thick enough to cover a cake or *petit four*, but thin enough to spread easily and adhere well. If you want to make chocolate fondant icing, melt some chocolate in a bowl over a pan of hot water and then add the fondant. If you are using a liquid flavouring, such as coffee essence or a liqueur, be sure to use a good, highly concentrated product in order not to thin the icing too much.

Stock syrup: Use 1 lb sugar to ½ pint water. Dissolve sugar, and boil up to 220°F. Strain and store in a jar.

Fondant au Kirsch * Kirsch Fondant

In a small double saucepan or basin over a pan of hot water, mix a piece of fondant with a tablespoon of kirsch and a few drops of water. Warm until the warmth is just apparent when you dip your finger in it; pour onto the cake and spread quickly before it cools.

▲ *Plum pudding, p. 250*

Rhubarb pie, p. 252 ▼

▲ *Beignets de bananes, p. 248*

Croûte aux abricots, p. 249 ▼

Pommes au riz meringuées, p. 251

 Charlotte aux pommes, p. 249 ▼ 243

▲ *Poires au chocolat, p. 260*

Ananas Ninon, p. 353 ▼

If the fondant is too hot, it will dry with a dull surface instead of a shiny one; if it were not heated, it would not dry with a crust, as it should. The kirsch may be replaced by rum, curaçao, anisette, coffee, etc.; add the colouring indicated by the flavour.

GLÂCE * ICING

Glâce au Sucre Glacé * *Glacé Icing*

Put 4 ounces finely sifted icing sugar in a saucepan and make it into a thick paste with water and the desired flavouring. Warm it while mixing it with the spatula; it will become thinner. Keep it a little more than lukewarm, but no more than that. If it becomes too thin, add a little more icing sugar. It should be possible to spread it on a cake in a thickish layer; it will harden as it cools.

▣ à l'Eau * *Water*

4 oz sieved icing sugar with very little cold water.

Add the water to the sugar very slowly to make the required consistency; warm it slightly and use to ice certain cakes and *petits fours*.

▣ au Chocolat * *Chocolate*

8 oz sieved icing sugar; 4 oz plain chocolate; ½–1 oz butter; 3–4 tablespoons water; vanilla essence.

Melt the chocolate with the water in a large basin over a pan of hot water. Remove from heat and add icing sugar gradually, beating well all the time, until the desired consistency is obtained. Beat in the butter to give added gloss. Use as required.

▣ Royale * *Royal, for Decorating*

2½ egg whites; 1 lb icing sugar (approx.); 2 teaspoons lemon juice; 1 teaspoon glycerine (optional).

Beat or whisk the egg whites and lemon juice lightly, just until they are slightly frothy. Beat in the sifted icing sugar a tablespoon at a time. Beat well between each addition, continue until two-thirds of the icing sugar has been used. Add the remaining icing sugar and beat or whisk in carefully. The icing should be thick, shiny and white. Add the glycerine. If an electric mixer is used, mix with the beater on middle speed. The use of a whisk or beater at high speed will produce a light fluffy icing, useless for decorative purposes. Royal icing must be covered with a damp cloth if it is to be kept for any length of time.

Sweets and Puddings

In the past, no dinner party was complete without an elaborate course of fruit; fruit was called "dessert". Nowadays all forms of pudding, including ice cream as well as fruit are sometimes classified as dessert. They may be a combination of ice cream and fruit or sauce, fresh or cooked fruit or cooked fruit, sweet pastries, yeast mixtures or gâteaux. At a formal dinner, fresh fruit can follow a hot or cold pudding, pastry or a savoury.

When choosing a dessert consider the other courses of the meal. If these are substantial you will choose a rather light dish; if the meal is light, prepare a rich or substantial dessert.

SAUCES CHAUDES POUR ENTREMETS * HOT DESSERT SAUCES

Sauce à l'Abricot * Apricot Sauce

Cook apricot jam or *purée* with water to the required consistency. Put through a fine sieve and flavour with kirsch, Grand Marnier, Cointreau, cognac or rum.

▣ au Chocolat * Chocolate

4 oz chocolate; 2 oz icing sugar; vanilla; $\frac{1}{2}$ oz unsalted butter; about $\frac{3}{4}$ pint water; 1 teaspoon cocoa.

Break up or grate the chocolate and put in a bowl over a saucepan filled with some hot water. Add the sugar, cocoa and half the water. Stir and heat slowly, until the chocolate melts. Simmer for a few minutes and add the rest of the water and vanilla flavouring. Continue heating slowly for about 20 minutes until the sauce is thick and syrupy. Beat in the butter.

▣ aux Fraises ou Framboises I * Strawberry or Rasberry I

1 lb very ripe fruit; $\frac{1}{4}$–$\frac{1}{2}$ pint Stock syrup.

Wash the fruit well and drain, then pass through a nylon sieve. Stir in enough Stock syrup to make a thick but fluid sauce. Heat. Alternatively, mix the fruit *purée* with a little icing sugar and dilute to the desired consistency with good white wine. Serve hot.

246

▣ aux Framboises II * *Raspberry II*

1 lb raspberries; 6 oz caster sugar; ¼ pint cream.

Purée the raw raspberries, add sugar slowly and beat for 8–10 minutes. Add the half-whipped cream. This sauce may be served as a cream in glasses with sponge fingers.

▣ aux Groseilles * *Redcurrant*

Dilute some redcurrant jelly with a light syrup or a little water. Boil up once and strain. Before serving add a tablespoon of kirsch or brandy for each ½ pint sauce. The sauce should be thick enough to coat lightly.

Hot Sweets and Puddings

BEIGNETS * *FRITTERS*

Beignets de Bananes * *Banana Fritters*

*For 4 persons: 8 bananas; 2–3 tablespoons rum; vanilla sugar; approx.
¼ pint Fritter batter.* Cooking time: 4–5 minutes.

Peel the bananas, split into two and macerate in the rum and sugar for one hour. Dip the bananas in the batter and fry in very hot, deep fat. Drain on soft paper and sprinkle with vanilla sugar. Serve Raspberry sauce separately. (*See illustration p.* 242).

▣ au Pain (pain perdu) * *Bread*

For 4 persons: 8–12 slices of bread; Vanilla custard; rum; flour; 1–2 eggs.
Cooking time: 3–4 minutes.

Cut some slices of bread ⅜ inch thick, soak in hot custard flavoured with rum, roll in flour, and then dip them, one by one, in well-beaten whole egg. Drop into hot, deep fat and in 3 minutes you will have an excellent sweet, crisp outside and soft inside. Sift sugar over and serve with custard or cream.

▣ de Pommes * *Apple*

For 4 persons: 8 apples; sugar; rum or kirsch; Fritter batter. Cooking time: 5 minutes.

Slice some nice, peeled, cored dessert apples, dredge with sugar and sprinkle with rum or kirsch. Soak for 1 hour, then dip in batter and drop into very hot, deep fat. Turn over several times while they fry: drain on soft absorbent paper. Arrange in a mound dredged with vanilla sugar.

Casse-Museau * *Apple Dumplings*

*For 4 persons: 4–6 apples; 4–5 oz Sweet shortcrust pastry; 4–5 cloves;
sugar; butter.* Cooking time: 20 minutes.

Wrap some well-shaped peeled and cored apples in Sweet shortcrust pastry and place them on a baking sheet. Fill the hollow in each apple with a hazelnut of butter, a clove and sugar. Decorate top with a small crimp-edged round of pastry. Brush with egg and bake in a hot oven, 400°F or Gas Mark 6, for 20 minutes.

Charlotte aux Pommes I * *Apple Charlotte I*

For 6 persons: 1 sandwich loaf; 4 oz butter; thick apple purée; rum; Apricot sauce. Cooking time: 45 minutes.

Cut a dozen small triangles of bread, dip them in melted butter and lay them on the bottom of a charlotte mould overlapping each other so that they cover it completely. Now cut rectangular strips of bread two fingers wide and the height of the mould in length. Dip these also in butter and arrange them upright round the sides of the mould, overlapping them so that there are no spaces in between. Fill the mould with sweet apple *purée*, made with 2½ ounces of sugar to 1 pound of apples, reduced as much as possible over fierce heat, well flavoured with vanilla, sprinkled with rum and set alight. Place the mould in a hot oven, 400°F or Gas Mark 6, and bake for 45 minutes. The bread round the sides should be golden-brown and dry enough to hold the charlotte together when it is turned out. Pour fairly thin Apricot sauce flavoured with rum over the charlotte. (*See illustration p.* 243).

Charlotte aux Pommes II * *Apple Charlotte II*

The recipe given above is for the classic type of charlotte. However, it is rather difficult to bake this type of charlotte properly, and to turn it out of the mould. An easier alternative is to use a shallow square cake tin, the bottom and sides of which may easily be lined with fingers of bread dipped in butter and arranged edge to edge without overlapping. Fill with a very generous amount of reduced apple *purée* and bake in a very hot oven, 450°F or Gas Mark 8. Serve with Apricot sauce or rum-flavoured Vanilla custard sauce.

Crêpes Fines * *Pancakes*

For 12 pancakes (4 persons): Plain pancake batter as indicated in the recipe on page 234.

Lightly butter a very hot frying pan (or use lard) and pour a thin layer of batter into it. When brown on one side turn over; when cooked dredge with vanilla sugar, and a squeeze of lemon juice. Fold in half and keep hot while frying the rest of the pancakes. Butter the pan for each pancake.

Croûtes aux Abricots * *Apricot Croûtes*

For 4 persons: 4–8 slices of bread; 4 oz butter; 8 poached half-apricots; 8 red cherries; 2 oz butter; ½ pint hot Apricot sauce or apricot purée flavoured with liqueur.

Stale *brioche, savarin* or bread may be used to make the *croûtes.* Cut into ½-inch slices and brown in butter. Top each crust with one or two apricot halves, with the inside uppermost, and place a cherry in the centre of each of these. Mask with hot Apricot sauce. (*See illustration p.* 242).

OMELETTE * *OMELETTE*

Omelette à la Confiture * *Jam Omelette*

For 4 persons: 8 eggs; sugar; jam.

This omelette is made like a savoury omelette, but omitting the salt and adding a little sugar. Before folding it in the pan, fill with 1 or 2 spoonfuls of jam to taste. Place on a long dish, dredge with sugar and, using a red-hot skewer, caramelise the sugar on top to make a trellis or any other design.

Omelette au Rhum * *Rum*

For 4 persons: 8 eggs; sugar; liqueur.

Sprinkle the omelette with rum, kirsch or cognac and set it alight.

Soufflée au Citron ou à l'Orange * *Lemon or Orange Soufflé Omelette*

Rub some lumps of sugar over 2 lemons or oranges to absorb the zest and proceed as for Vanilla *Soufflé* Omelette.

Soufflée à la Vanille * *Vanilla Soufflé Omelette*

For 4 persons: 4 oz vanilla caster sugar; 2 egg yolks; 4 stiffly beaten egg whites. Cooking time: about 20 minutes.

Combine the egg yolks and sugar, and beat until thick and creamy. Then very carefully fold in the whites, which should be very stiff. Spread this mixture on a long dish buttered and sugared in a long, domed oval with a hollow in the middle. Smooth well all round with a knife and bake in a cool oven, 300–325°F or Gas Mark 2–3, for about 20 minutes. Serve as soon as ready, for it collapses even more quickly than a *soufflé*.

Plum Pudding or Christmas Pudding

For 12 persons: 8 oz suet; 8 oz breadcrumbs; 4 oz flour; 4 oz carrots; 4 oz sultanas; 3 oz currants; 3 oz seeded raisins; 2 oz stoned prunes; 2 oz finely chopped candied orange peel; 2 oz finely chopped candied lemon peel; 6 oz coarsely chopped apples; 4 oz brown sugar; 3 eggs; juice and grated rind of half a lemon and half an orange; 1 teaspoon salt; 2 teaspoons powdered spices (cinnamon, cloves, ginger and nutmeg); ½ pint cognac; ½ pint Madeira or sherry. Cooking time: 6–8 hours.

Clean and chop the suet and place in a large bowl. Add the grated carrot, dried fruit, brown sugar, breadcrumbs, chopped peel, apples, chopped prunes, eggs, salt, spices and, lastly, the cognac and Madeira. Mix well. If the mixture is too thick, add a little milk. Cover and leave in a cold place for 24 to 48 hours. Fill pudding basins with the mixture. Cover with a pudding cloth tied up securely. Place the puddings in boiling water to come half way up the sides of the basins, and continue boiling slowly but steadily. Replenish pan with boiling water when necessary. When serving the pudding, place a few small lumps of sugar on top, pour a little warmed rum or cognac over it and set it alight when about to serve. Serve accompanied by Brandy sauce, Vanilla custard sauce flavoured with rum or kirsch or Apricot sauce flavoured with kirsch. Make the pudding several months in advance. It will keep for some years if stored in a cool place. (*See illustration p. 241*).   (*Great Britain*).

POMMES * *APPLES*

Pommes Alice * *Alice Apples*

For 4 persons: 4–5 apples, peeled and cored; 4 oz candied fruit; 2 oz shredded almonds; 1 pint Pastry cream. Cooking time: 25 minutes.

Poach halved apples in a syrup made with 1 pint water and 6 ounces sugar, and place them in a baking dish, cut side up. Fill the hollow left by removing the core with finely chopped mixed candied fruit, then cover the whole generously with thinnish Pastry cream. Sprinkle top with shredded almonds, or, if these are not available, mixed sugar and breadcrumbs, and put in a hot oven, 425°F or Gas Mark 7, to brown. Serve hot.

Pommes à la Bonne Femme * *Baked Apples*

For 4 persons: 6–8 apples; sugar; butter. Cooking time: 20–25 minutes.

Core dessert apples with a corer without peeling them, then score the peel all round the centre with a knife. Place in a baking dish with a hazelnut of butter and a teaspoon of sugar in the hole of each apple; pour ½ inch water into the dish and bake in a fairly hot oven, 375°F or Gas Mark 5. Serve either hot or cold when the apples are tender.

▣ aux Riz Meringuées I * *Rice and Apple Meringue I*

For 6–8 persons: 3 oz rice; 2 oz vanilla sugar; 2 egg yolks; 1 pint milk; 6–8 apples. For the meringue: 2 egg whites; 3–4 oz sugar. Cooking time: 10 minutes.

Prepare Rice *Condé* (p. 252). Prepare a Swiss Meringue mixture (*p.* 237). Cut the apples in half, core, and fill with the rice mixture; cover with a layer of meringue, smoothing the top carefully to mask the apples, then decorate with the same meringue mixture, using a forcing bag and fluted nozzle. Dredge with sugar and place in a cool oven, 300°F or Gas Mark 2, to form a crust without colouring the meringue too much. Before serving, the spaces in the decoration may be filled with a little redcurrant or apricot jelly applied with a paper cornet.

▣ aux Riz Meringuées II * *Rice and Apple Meringue II*

For 4 persons: 3 oz rice; 2 oz vanilla sugar; 2 egg yolks; 1 pint milk; 4 apples. For the meringue: 2 egg whites; 3–4 oz sugar. Cooking time: 20 minutes.

Peel the apples and cut each into 6 segments. Poach in syrup until tender but not broken down. Arrange neatly to completely cover the rice which has been prepared as for Rice *Condé* (p. 248). Beat up egg whites stiffly, beat in half the sugar and continue beating until the mixture stands in points. Fold in remaining sugar. Pile roughly on top of the apples, sift some sugar over. Bake in a warm oven, 325°F or Gas Mark 3, until crisp and slightly coloured. (*See illustration p.* 243).

▣ Spiced Squares

For 6 persons: 4 oz butter; 4 oz caster sugar; 1 egg; 4 oz plain flour; 1 teaspoon cinnamon; 1 teaspoon mixed spice; about 1 lb stewed drained apple. Cooking time: 45 minutes.

Cream together butter and sugar until light and fluffy. Add egg, beat well. Sift flour with spices, fold lightly into creamed mixture. Spread half mixture on base of lightly greased 6-inch square cake tin. Cover with apples, spread remaining cake mixture on top. Bake in moderate oven, 350 F or Gas Mark 4, approximately 45 minutes, until golden brown. Serve hot, cut into squares, sprinkled with sifted icing sugar.

Pouding Diplomate Chaud * *Cabinet Pudding*

For 4 persons: 4 oz sponge fingers; 2 oz sugar; 2 whole eggs; 2 oz mixed currants and candied fruit; ¼ pint milk; ½ pint Vanilla custard or Jam sauce; vanilla and rum. Cooking time: ¾–1 hour.

Boil the milk with a vanilla pod and pour into the bowl in which you have beaten the eggs and sugar. Stir with a fork while pouring in the milk, then let this cream rest, skimming the foam off the top. In the meantime, butter a pudding basin, sprinkle it with sugar, then fill it with the sponge fingers broken in small pieces; *Génoise*, left-over *brioche* or any kind of sponge may be used instead. Arrange the sponge in alternate layers with the currants and finely diced candied fruit soaked in rum. The basin should be filled right up. Now pour in the cream, very slowly, so that the sponge can absorb it, until the basin is full. Allow to stand for 15 minutes. Place in a water bath and poach in the oven for $\frac{3}{4}$–1 hour. The pudding is done when the blade of a small knife thrust into it comes out dry. Turn out pudding 5 minutes after removing it from oven, and serve with Vanilla custard or Jam sauce.

Pouding aux Noisettes * *Hazelnut Pudding*

For 4–5 persons: $\frac{1}{2}$ pint milk; 2 oz roasted hazelnuts; 2 oz sugar; 2 oz butter; 2 oz flour; 3 eggs. Cooking time: 40–50 minutes.

Grind lightly grilled hazelnuts. Boil the milk with the sugar and butter. Add fine white flour and stir until the mixture cooks and leaves the sides of the pan. Add each egg yolk separately, then the hazelnuts. Fold in the stiffly-whisked egg whites. Pour into a buttered and floured dish and poach in a water bath for 40–50 minutes in a fairly hot oven, 375°F or Gas Mark 5. Serve with Vanilla or Caramel custard.

Profiteroles au Chocolat * *Chocolate Profiteroles*

For 4 persons: 5 oz Choux pastry; Saint-Honoré or Chantilly cream; Chocolate sauce. Cooking time: 20–25 minutes.

Pipe small balls of *Choux* pastry on to a greased baking sheet. Bake in a hot oven, 400°F or Gas Mark 6. When well-risen, crisp and lightly brown, remove from the oven. Using a sharp, pointed knife make an incision in each one to allow the steam to escape. Turn off the oven and replace the *profiteroles* for 5 minutes so that they can dry off. Cool on a wire tray. When cold, fill with Saint Honoré or Chantilly cream. Arrange in a pyramid on a round dish and pour hot Chocolate sauce on top. This sweet is served cold, but hot sauce is poured over it to soak right in. It is both a sweet and a cake. Alternatively use Chocolate glacé icing instead of hot Chocolate sauce. Sprinkle chopped pistachio nuts over.

Rhubarb Pie

For 4 persons: 6 oz Puff pastry; 1$\frac{1}{2}$ lb rhubarb; 6 oz sugar. Cooking time: 30–35 minutes.

Cut the rhubarb stalks into small pieces. Moisten the edge of a pie dish with water and press a strip of Puff pastry $\frac{1}{5}$-inch thick on to it all round. Fill the dish with rhubarb, cover with the sugar and add a few drops of water. Cover the dish with Puff pastry and cut a small hole to allow the steam to escape. Bake in a hot oven, 400°F or Gas Mark 6. When the pastry begins to brown, cover with buttered paper. After removing from the oven, dust with vanilla sugar. Serve accompanied by Vanilla custard sauce. (*See illustration p. 241*).

Riz Condé * *Rice Condé*

For 4 persons: 3 oz rice; 2 oz vanilla sugar; 1 pint milk; 1 oz butter; 2 egg yolks; salt. Cooking time: 25 minutes.

Blanch rice for 3 minutes. Drain, rinse and bring to the boil with the vanilla-flavoured milk. Cook slowly, stirring frequently with a wooden spoon. When the rice is thoroughly cooked and has thickened, stir in the sugar, butter and egg yolks. Continue cooking at low heat until the rice is creamy and binds well, but it must not boil. This dish is usually served as a part of other sweets but it can also be served separately.

Soufflé   *   *Soufflé (Basic Vanilla)*

For 4 persons: 2 oz sugar; 1½ oz flour; 2 oz butter; ½ pint milk; 4 egg yolks; 4 *stiffly beaten egg whites; vanilla.* Cooking time: 25 minutes.

Melt half the butter, add the flour and immediately stir in the boiling milk with vanilla. Stir briskly on the stove until it comes to the boil. Remove from heat, add the sugar, stir in the egg yolks and remainder of the butter and then fold in the beaten egg whites carefully until the mixture is even and there are no "lumps" of egg white. Pour into a buttered and sugared *soufflé* dish, which must not be more than three-quarters full. Bake in a fairly hot oven, 375°F or Gas Mark 5, for 25 minutes. This sweet must be served immediately it is taken from the oven, so be sure not to put it in to cook too soon. This, incidentally, applies to all *soufflés*, whether sweet or savoury.

▣ au Café   *   *Coffee*

Same method for Vanilla *Soufflé*, but using half milk and half strong coffee.

▣ au Chocolat   *   *Chocolate*

Same method as for Vanilla *Soufflé*, adding 2–2½ ounces of chocolate to the milk and use only 1 ounce of sugar, to allow for that in the chocolate.

▣ Ginger, with Cream

For 6 persons: ½ oz butter; 1½ oz plain flour; ½ pint milk; 4 oz sugar; pinch *salt;* ½ teaspoon ground ginger; 10 oz preserved ginger; ⅓ tablespoon brandy; 6 eggs; caster *sugar; whipped cream.* Cooking time: about 45 minutes.

Separate eggs. Wash the syrup from the ginger and chop ginger finely. Melt butter in saucepan, add flour, stir over gentle heat 1 minute. Remove from heat, gradually blend in the milk, add sugar, salt, and ground ginger. Return to heat, bring to boil, stirring; simmer a few minutes. Stir in chopped ginger and brandy; cool. Stir in beaten egg yolks, then fold in stiffly beaten egg whites. Pour into buttered 8 inch *soufflé* dish which has been dusted with a little castor sugar. Stand in tin containing boiling water, bake in hot oven, 400°F or Gas Mark 6, for 15 minutes. Reduce heat to 375°F or Gas Mark 5, cook further 30 minutes or until *soufflé* is firm to the touch. Serve immediately; top each serving with a spoonful of whipped cream, flavoured, if desired, with a little of the ginger syrup or brandy.

Ananas Ninon   *   *Pineapple Ninon*

For 6–8 persons: 1 pineapple; 1 lb wild strawberries; 2–3 bananas; 8 tartlet *cases;* ½ pint Chantilly cream; Raspberry sauce.

Cut off the top of a fresh pineapple. Loosen the flesh as follows: insert a small knife about ½ inch from the edge and cut right round as cleanly as possible almost to the bottom of the pineapple. Remove the knife and insert it ½ inch from the bottom of the pineapple. Cut round the inside without moving the handle or enlarging the opening. The central part of the pineapple can now be lifted out, leaving a hollow shell. Cut the flesh into thin slices lengthwise, and macerate in sugar and kirsch. Macerate 1 pound wild strawberries with 2 or 3 sliced bananas in the same way. Leave all the fruit and the pineapple shell on ice. Place the shell on a very cold dish, line the bottom half with the strawberry and banana mixture and stand the slices of pineapple on it, overlapping each other, to project a little way beyond the top of the shell. Fill up with Chantilly cream. Decorate with piped stars and some choice strawberries. For an extra garnish: surround the pineapple with small tartlets of Almond pastry filled with rosettes of Chantilly cream and each garnished with a choice strawberry and 2 strips of pineapple. Serve accompanied by Raspberry sauce. (*See illustration p.* 244).

Ananas et Groseilles Chantilly   *   Pineapple and Red-currants with Whipped Cream

For 4 persons: 6–8 slices of pineapple; 4 oz redcurrants; 2 oz sugar; syrup; whipped cream.

Dip 6 to 8 slices of fresh pineapple in sugar and leave for a few minutes. Arrange on a round dish and garnish generously with redcurrants or other fruit. Sprinkle with syrup and serve, well iced, with whipped cream. The recipe may be varied by using other fruit, according to season. For instance, in winter the pineapple may be replaced by sliced apples poached in syrup and the redcurrants by cherries preserved in syrup, or by apricots.

Bananes au Chocolat   *   Bananas with Chocolate Cream

Peel the bananas, slice and put them into a fruit dish. Pour a little Grand Marnier over them, sprinkle with sugar and macerate for 1 hour. Prepare some chocolate-flavoured Chantilly cream and pour over the fruit. Leave in a cool place. Decorate with *glacé* cherries before serving.

Barquettes de Bananes   *   Banana Boats

For 4 persons: 4 bananas; ¼ pint cream; 4 teaspoons maraschino; 4 oz stewed cherries.

Carefully split the whole bananas (in their skins) in half lengthwise. Remove the flesh without spoiling them. Cut the flesh into ½-inch slices, add sugar and flavour with maraschino. Fill each half banana skin with whirls of sweetened whipped cream and top with alternate slices of banana and cherries. Arrange the filled banana boats on an oval dish.

Bavarois (Crème collée)   *   Bavarian Cream (Moulded cream)

For 4 persons: ¾ pint Vanilla custard; ½ oz gelatine; 2 tablespoons water; ¼ pint cream. Cooking time: 12 minutes.

Make custard in the usual way. Flavour to taste. As soon as it thickens, remove from heat and strain. When cold, combine with whipped cream. Dissolve gelatine in water, and heat to slightly above blood heat. Stir into custard cream and stir until beginning to set. Pour at once into a moistened mould and allow to set on ice, or at least in a cool place. Turn out and serve as it is. This sweet may be flavoured in a number of ways—with chocolate, vanilla, praline, pistachio, etc. It may also be made with fruit, as below.

▣ aux Fruits   *   Bavarian Fruit Cream

For 4 persons: 8 oz fruit; 3 oz icing sugar; 4 tablespoons water; ¼ oz gelatine; ¼ pint cream; ½ lemon; carmine.

This recipe may be used for all fruit creams. Rub ripe strawberries through a nylon sieve. Put the *purée* into a bowl with the sugar, the juice of half a lemon and a little carmine. Add the gelatine dissolved to blood heat in the water. Stir until almost setting over ice. Fold in whipped cream, and when setting pour into mould as above.

Bircher Müesli * *Bircher Müesli*

Per portion: 1 large apple; 1 tablespoon chopped walnuts or hazelnuts; 1 tablespoon sweetened condensed milk or sweetened cream; 1 tablespoon quick porridge oats; 3 tablespoons water; juice of half a lemon; fresh fruit, e.g. strawberries, raspberries, gooseberries, redcurrants, bananas, oranges, etc.

Pour the water on to the oats. Soak for 20 minutes. Add the lemon juice and condensed milk, and mix. Core the apple, but do not peel it; grate it into the mixture and stir at once to prevent the apple from turning brown. Add the fresh fruit cut into dice, and mix. Sprinkle with the chopped nuts and serve.

Charlotte Russe * *Charlotte Russe*

For 4 persons: 6–8 Savoy sponge fingers; ½ pint Vanilla custard; ½ pint cream; 2 oz sugar; vanilla; 2 tablespoons sherry; 1 tablespoon brandy; ½ oz gelatine; 4 tablespoons water; lemon jelly, or paper.

Line the bottom of a charlotte mould with paper, or set a thin layer of lemon jelly in it. Split the Savoy fingers. Cut off the tip of each and trim the sides. Line the sides of the mould with these, placing them close together. Add sugar to custard and stir to dissolve. Flavour with vanilla, sherry and brandy. Half whip the cream and fold it into the custard. Dissolve the gelatine in water and when at blood heat, stir into the cream mixture. Stir until almost setting and fill up the mould. Refrigerate or leave in a cold place to set. Trim the sponge level with the cream. Dip bottom of mould in hot water. Turn out on to the serving dish. Decorate with chopped jelly, or whipped cream and *glacé* cherries.

⊡ Petites, en Coupes Fructidor * *Individual*

For 4 persons: ½ pint whipped cream; ½ pint Pastry cream; 12 sponge fingers; ½ lb wild strawberries, raspberries, pineapple or candied cherries; extra cream for piping.

Cool the Pastry cream and beat to make it smooth. Add the whipped cream. Half fill 4 stem glasses with this mixture and arrange 3 halved split sponge fingers in each. Top with fruit. Decorate with Chantilly cream piped through a forcing bag. Serve iced.

Clafoutis Limousin * *Clafoutis Limousin*

For 6 persons: 1½ lb black cherries; 4 oz sugar; 2 oz flour; ½ pint milk; 2 eggs; vanilla; salt. Cooking time: 30–45 minutes.

Work the eggs one at a time into the flour. Add the sugar, about a pinch of salt and a little vanilla and blend with the cold milk. Beat the batter well and sieve or tammy to remove any lumps. Stone very black cherries, and put them in an oval ovenproof dish and pour the batter over them. Sprinkle with sugar. Put in a fairly hot oven, 375–400°F or Gas Mark 5–6. The pudding is cooked when it has risen and browned. A needle or fine skewer inserted into the centre should come out clean. Serve cold or lukewarm. This dish may also be made in a Short pastry case, like a tart, but in this case it is not quite a genuine Limousin "*clafoutis*".

COMPOTES * *FRUIT COMPOTES*

Fruit for *compotes* should not be too ripe. Cut the fruit in quarters or halves, according to size. Poach slowly in stock sugar syrup with vanilla flavouring. The syrup used to poach the fruit varies in quantity and sweetness according to the type of fruit. Soft juicy fruits, like cherries, raspberries, and plums require a small amount of rich heavy syrup, whereas less juicy fruits, apples, pears and gooseberries, require a larger amount of thin syrup. The syrup must always be made beforehand and the fruit poached gently in it.

Syrup: 4–6 oz sugar; ½ pint water.

Dissolve the sugar slowly in the water, bring to the boil and boil for about 5 minutes, depending on the thickness of syrup required. Some fruit, such as pears, cherries and prunes, may be cooked in a syrup consisting of red wine and sugar, flavoured with cinnamon instead of vanilla. When the fruit is done, the syrup should be boiled down. Sometimes it is thickened with apricot jam, but in principle the boiled-down syrup is the only accompaniment to fruit *compote*.

Compôte d'Abricots　*　Apricot Compote*

Halve the apricots and place in vanilla-flavoured syrup. Poach for only 7 to 8 minutes, drain, boil down syrup to half and serve apricots in it. Crack the apricot stones, halve the kernels and place these on top.

▣ de Bananes　*　*Banana*

Poach the peeled whole or halved bananas gently in syrup with a little rum. Boil down the syrup and thicken with apricot jam. Strain over the fruit.

▣ de Cerises　*　*Cherry*

Stone the cherries and poach in a syrup made with wine or water and well reduced. As cherries give off a lot of water, the syrup must be well boiled down before the cherries are put into it and boiled down again after they have been drained. This syrup may be thickened with a little arrowroot—2 teaspoons per ¼ pint of syrup—and flavoured with kirsch. The cherries may be left whole.

▣ de Pêches　*　*Peach*

Same method as for apricots, but as peaches are not so soft as apricots, they may be allowed to boil gently. Skin when cooked, not before.

▣ de Poires　*　*Pear*

Poach the pears whole, halved or quartered, according to size. The syrup may be coloured with a little carmine, or they may be cooked in red wine, to make them pink.

▣ de Pommes　*　*Apple*

If you wish to cook whole apples, choose small ones, peel and core them, sprinkle with lemon juice and poach in vanilla-flavoured syrup. They may, if preferred, be quartered before cooking. Cook gently if the apples are a soft variety.

▣ de Prunes　*　*Plum*

All plums may be used for compote; some are halved.

Compôte de Pruneaux * *Prune*

Soak the prunes overnight in water or wine. Boil slowly in the liquid in which they were soaked, adding sugar after the skins are soft.

▣ de Rhubarbe * *Rhubarb*

Cut the rhubarb in 2-inch pieces, peel and poach in a little very concentrated syrup, since this fruit gives off a lot of water. If allowed to boil at all it will turn into *purée*; it is best to cover it with white paper and poach it in the oven. Drain carefully and boil down syrup before pouring over.

CRÈMES * *CREAM SWEETS*

Renversée au Caramel * *Moulded Caramel Cream*

For 4 persons: 3 oz caster sugar; ½ pint milk; 2 whole eggs and 1 yolk; vanilla pod. Caramel: 2 oz sugar; 2 tablespoons water or lemon juice.

To make the caramel: Dissolve the sugar in water or lemon juice. Cook until golden brown and use.

Beat the eggs and sugar in a bowl. When well mixed, add boiling milk in which the vanilla pod has been infused. Allow to rest for a few minutes, then skim off foam and pour the mixture through a strainer into a mould lined with the caramel. Place the mould in a tin of water in a warm oven, 325°F or Gas Mark 3. Poach without allowing to boil, until the cream resists slightly when touched with the fingers. Alternatively, creams, like cakes, may be tested with a knife, which should be dry, when the cream is done. Do not turn out the cream until quite cold.

This is the basic recipe for all inverted creams, irrespective of the flavouring used. For an inverted Coffee cream, use half milk and half very strong coffee. For Chocolate cream, use an additional egg.

▣ à l'Orange * *Orange*

2½ oz sugar; 4 egg yolks; 2 teaspoons cornflour; 1 pint milk; 2 oranges.

Beat the sugar and eggs until frothy and blend in the cornflour. Carefully grate the rind of 1 orange into the milk and bring to the boil. Pour into the egg and sugar mixture, stirring with a whisk. Return to the pan and stir until cooked. Strain through muslin, add the strained juice of 2 oranges and stir until completely cold to prevent the formation of a skin. Serve in sundae glasses.

▣ Printemps * *Strawberry*

For 4 persons: ½ pint whipped, sweetened cream; ½ pint wild strawberry purée made with 1 lb strawberries; ½ lb strawberries for decorating; kirsch; sugar.

Mix whipped cream with strawberry *purée*. Fill four *coupes* two-thirds full. Decorate with strawberries soaked and well mixed with kirsch and sugar.

▣ à la Vanille * *Vanilla*

1 pint milk; 2 oz sugar; 1 vanilla pod or 1 small packet vanilla sugar; 1 oz butter; 1½ oz cornflour; 2 egg yolks.

Heat the milk, butter and vanilla together. Put the cornflour in a bowl, mix to a smooth paste with a tablespoon of cold milk and stir in the egg yolks. Pour the boiling milk on to the paste while stirring with a whisk, return to the pan, boil up and pour into a cold bowl.

For Chocolate Cream add 3 ounces melted block chocolate to the milk when heating for the first time.

Crème Fraises à la Cardinal   *   *Strawberries Cardinal*

For 4 persons: 8 oz strawberries; 6 oz raspberries; 4 oz icing sugar; a teaspoon of lemon juice; almonds.

Cool some large round strawberries on ice, then *purée* the raspberries and combine them with the icing sugar and lemon juice. Let the sugar melt in the cold, keeping the *purée* on ice. Divide the strawberries between four iced *coupes*. Coat with the raspberry *purée* and sprinkle with fresh splintered almonds. Peaches or pears may also be prepared in this way, but they should be cooked in syrup first, cut in half and well chilled. Only add the raspberry *purée* at the last moment.

▣ Margot   *   *Margot*

For 4 persons: ½ pint whipped, sweetened cream; ½ pint strawberry purée (made from 1 lb strawberries); lemon juice; scant ½ oz gelatine; 4 tablespoons water; 8 oz strawberries; extra cream for piping; chopped pistachio nuts.

Combine cream and *purée*. Sharpen with lemon juice. Dissolve gelatine in water, heat to blood heat. Add to cream mixture. Stir, over ice, until setting, and pour quickly into a large glass bowl. Refrigerate or set on ice. Then decorate the top with large strawberries and pipe a rosette of whipped, sweetened cream between each, using a bag and fluted nozzle. Sprinkle with chopped pistachio nuts.

Fruits Rafraîchis au Kirsch   *   *Fruit Salad with Kirsch*

When peaches, apricots, strawberries, redcurrants, etc. are plentiful, make a mixture of them, quartering the large fruit. Make a syrup with 6 ounces sugar and ¾ pint water and some vanilla. When it has boiled for a few minutes let it cool and pour over the fruit in a container embedded in ice. Sprinkle with kirsch, curaçao or other liqueur when serving. If you want to serve the fruit in jelly, add ½ ounce gelatine, melted with a little water. Add at blood heat to the syrup with 2–3 tablespoons liqueur.

Île Flottante   *   *Floating Island*

For 4 persons: 2 oz peeled roasted almonds or 3 oz pounded or crushed, pink burnt almonds; 3 oz caster sugar; 3 egg whites; ½ pint Vanilla custard. Cooking time: 40 minutes.

Beat the egg whites very stiffly and combine with the sugar, vanilla and almonds. Pour the mixture into a buttered, sugared mould, and poach in a fairly hot oven, 375°F or Gas Mark 5, in a tin of boiling water for about 40 minutes. Allow to cool completely, then run a knife round the edge and turn out into a bowl filled at the bottom with cold Vanilla custard. The "island" may be sprinkled with coarsely chopped pistachios.

Lemon Self-Saucing Pudding

For 4 persons: 3 eggs; 6 oz sugar; ½ pint milk; ½ oz plain flour; grated rind and juice 2 large lemons; pinch salt; 1¼ oz desiccated coconut; extra 2 oz sugar. Cooking time: 1 hour.

Separate eggs. Beat yolks with 6 ounces sugar until light; beat in flour, milk, lemon rind and juice, salt. Stir in coconut. Beat egg whites with extra sugar until stiff but not dry. Fold into lemon coconut mixture. Bake in deep 8-inch casserole set in roasting tin of hot water in a moderate oven 350°F or Gas Mark 4, for 1 hour.

Melon Rafraîchis en Macédoine * Chilled Diced Melon

Cut off the stem end of the melon. Insert a spoon and remove the seeds and fibres, then scoop out the flesh in small pieces. Cut a slice from the other end, so that the melon will not fall over. Fill the melon with the diced flesh, sprinkle with port and decorate with a *glacé* cherry.

Mont-Blanc aux Marrons et aux Fruits * Chestnut and Fruit Mont-Blanc

For 6 persons: 1¼ *lb chestnuts boiled in milk; 4 oz sugar; vanilla; 1 oz butter.*

Score all round the peel of good quality chestnuts. Place them on the stove in a saucepan of cold water and bring to the boil. Peel quickly, remove them from water one by one so that they do not get cold, and then drop into boiling, vanilla-flavoured milk to finish cooking. Drain on a fine sieve and *purée* them. Boil the sugar to 240°F or the "softball" stage in a copper pan with ¼ pint water and a vanilla pod. Mix the chestnut *purée* and the butter with the syrup and stir. Fill the mixture into a forcing-bag with a small round nozzle. Take a buttered and sugared shallow *savarin* mould and pipe in the mixture in the form of a nest. Turn mould upside down on a round, very cold dish and lift it off carefully. At the last moment fill the hollow centre with whipped sweetened cream. Pile it up roughly to represent snowy mountain peaks. *To boil to the "softball" stage (240°F):* Drop some of the syrup into cold water. Lift between finger and thumb, and when ready, a soft ball will form when the syrup is rolled.

Mousse aux Fraises * Strawberry Mousse

For 4 persons: 1 *lb strawberries; 4 egg whites or* ½ *pint whipped cream; 4 oz caster sugar. For decoration:* ½ *pint whipped cream; 8 oz strawberries.*

Pass the strawberries through a nylon sieve and combine carefully with the stiffly beaten egg whites and the sugar. Divide between 4 individual glass *coupes.* Decorate with a piping of whipped cream and strawberries. Whipped cream may be used instead of the egg whites.

Mousseline de Pommes * Apple Mousseline

For 6 persons: ½ *pint thick apple purée;* ½ *pint Chantilly cream;* ½ *pint Vanilla custard;* ¾ *oz gelatine; kirsch; 4 glacé cherries.*

Dissolve the gelatine in 6 tablespoons water and bring to blood heat. Combine the apple *purée,* Vanilla custard and Chantilly cream. Flavour with kirsch. Stir in the gelatine, and stir until setting. Pour into 4 individual glasses and leave until cold. When set, decorate each glass with a *glacé* cherry.

Œufs à la Neige * Snow Eggs

For 4 persons: 3 *egg whites; 6 oz vanilla sugar; Vanilla custard.* Cooking time: 20 minutes in all.

Beat 3 egg whites until stiff and fold in the sugar, well-flavoured with vanilla. Very slowly boil ½ pint milk with a vanilla pod and drop moulded tablespoons of the meringue into it, poach them without boiling and turn over with a fork after 2 minutes. When the eggs are fairly firm to the touch, drain them on a cloth. Use the milk to make custard and let it cool. Pour it into a dish and place the eggs on top. Serve cold.

Orange and Raisin Pudding

For 4 persons: 2 oz butter; 2 oz sugar; grated rind 1 orange; 2 eggs; 6 oz seeded raisins; 6 oz self-raising flour; pinch salt; 4 tablespoons orange juice; 2 tablespoons milk. Cooking time: 2 hours.

Grease pudding basin thickly, press half the raisins on to the sides of the mould. Cream butter, sugar and orange rind. Add beaten eggs a little at a time, beat well. Fold in remainder of raisins, then sifted flour and salt. Add orange juice and milk. Fill carefully into prepared mould. Cover with greased paper and aluminium foil or lid. Lower into saucepan of boiling water, cover, cook 2 hours. Serve hot with custard.

▣ Oranges Stella   *   *Oranges Stella*

Halve the oranges by cutting them through the middle and remove the pulp. Serrate the edges of the skins with a pair of scissors. Cut the pulp into small cubes and macerate in Cointreau. Fill the orange skins with the pulp, pipe sweetened whipped cream on top with a fluted nozzle to decorate and sprinkle crushed crystallised violets over.

Pêches au Vin Rouge   *   *Peaches in Red Wine*

Peel the peaches, cut them in half, stone them and put them in a fruit dish or individual cups. Add sugar and pour a little sweet red wine over them. Macerate for 1 hour and serve.

Poires au Chocolat   *   *Pears with Chocolate Sauce*

For 4 persons: 4 poached, halved pears; ½ pint Chocolate sauce; 1 pint Vanilla ice cream; chocolate cigarettes.

When the pears are cold, drain them carefully and place on individual plates beside a ball of Vanilla ice cream. Mask the pears with cold Chocolate sauce and decorate with chocolate cigarettes. Serve *petit fours* separately. (*See illustration p. 244*).

▣ Poires à la Mauresque   *   *Pears Mauresque*

For 8 persons: 4 choice pears; 1 pint Chocolate egg custard; 2 teaspoons cornflour; 4 bananas; 1 tablespoon milk. Syrup: 1 pint water; 8 oz sugar; vanilla.

Use choice, juicy pears; cut them in half, peel and core. Poach in vanilla-flavoured syrup and leave until cold. Arrange them in a fruit dish or deep bowl and mask with cold Chocolate egg custard thickened with cornflour blended with cold milk. Place halved bananas, poached in syrup and left until quite cold, between the halved pears and decorate with a few whirls of whipped, sweetened cream and with halved *glacé* cherries.

Petits Pots de Crème   *   *Small Cream Pots*

Same recipe as for Caramel cream but, after flavouring, cook in small earthenware pots placed in a water bath in the oven. As these creams are not turned out, use one egg less.

260

Pouding au Citron   *   *Lemon Cream*

For 4 persons: 2 egg whites; ¼ pint cream; 2 oz sugar; juice of 1 lemon; ¼ oz gelatine; 4 tablespoons water.

Dissolve the gelatine in water and lemon juice. Whip the egg whites to a snow and fold into the whipped cream with the sugar. Add gelatine and stir slowly to setting point. Pour into a mould previously wetted with cold water. Refrigerate or leave in a cold place. When quite set, unmould and serve accompanied by Raspberry or Vanilla sauce.

Riz à l'Impératrice   *   *Rice Impératrice*

For 4 persons: 4 oz Carolina rice; 1 pint milk; ½ pint milk; 3 egg yolks; 5 oz sugar; ¼ oz gelatine; ¼–½ pint cream; vanilla; 4 tablespoons kirsch; 4 oz candied fruit; red-currant jelly. Cooking time: 30 minutes.

Soak the diced candied fruit in kirsch for 1 hour. Boil the rice in 1 pint milk with a knob of butter until tender. Add 2 ounces sugar and cool. Then make custard with 3 egg yolks, ½ pint milk and 3 ounces sugar (*see p.* 238). When it thickens remove from heat and add the gelatine, previously melted in 2 tablespoons hot water. Pass this cream through a fine strainer, combine with the rice and leave to cool. When it starts to set, mix in diced candied fruit soaked in kirsch, then fold in the lightly sugared and vanilla-flavoured whipped cream; mix thoroughly. Pour into a wetted pudding basin or charlotte mould rinsed in cold water and put in a cool place, or even on ice in hot weather. When it has set, turn out on a cold dish and surround with a sauce of redcurrant jelly, mixed with a little kirsch and well-iced. This is a delicious sweet.

Sago Fruit Pudding

For 6 persons: 1½ oz sago; ½ pint milk; 3 oz butter; 2 oz brown sugar; 2 oz soft white breadcrumbs; 1 teaspoon bicarbonate of soda dissolved in a little extra milk; ½ table-spoon rum; ½ teaspoon mixed spice; 1 egg; ½ teaspoon vanilla; 4 oz sultanas or mixed fruits. Cooking time: 2 hours.

Scald milk, add sago, butter, sugar, vanilla, rum and spice; let stand 10 minutes. Stir in breadcrumbs and bicarbonate of soda, then beaten egg and fruit. Put in greased pudding basin, cover, steam 2 hours. Serve hot with cream.

▣ Pouding de Semoule   *   *Semolina*

For 4 persons: ½ pint vanilla-flavoured milk; ½ oz semolina; 2 oz sugar; ¼ oz gelatine; 3 egg whites; Redcurrant sauce. Cooking time: 10 minutes.

Bring vanilla-flavoured milk to the boil, cook semolina in it and add the sugar. Remove from heat and add the gelatine dissolved in 3 tablespoons cold water and heated to blood heat. Quickly fold in 3 stiffly beaten egg whites and pour into a moistened ring mould. Put on ice. Turn out and serve surrounded by Redcurrant sauce, and decorate with candied fruit if desired.

Tapioca Cream

For 4 persons: 1½ oz seed pearl tapioca; 1 pint milk; 1 oz caster sugar; almond essence; ratafias; 4–6 tablespoons sherry; ¼ pint thick cream.

Simmer tapioca slowly in milk until creamy. Add sugar and flavouring. Stir occasionally while cooking. When cold, fold in half the sherry and the half-whipped cream. Soak the ratafias in serving dish in remaining sherry. Pour pudding over ratafias and serve.

Strawberry Pavlova

For 6 persons: 2 egg whites; 12 oz caster sugar; 1 teaspoon vinegar; ½ teaspoon vanilla; 4 tablespoons boiling water; 1 teaspoon cornflour. Cooking time: 1 hour.

Place all ingredients in basin, whisk until mixture is of meringue consistency. Spread mixture on lightly greased heatproof plate. Bake in a moderate oven, 350°F or Gas Mark 4, for 30 minutes, then reduce heat to cool 250°–300°F or Gas Mark 2, and bake for a further 30 minutes. Allow to cool in oven. Fill with strawberries and top with whipped cream.

Sugared Grapes with Cream

For 4 persons: 1½ lb seedless white grapes; ½ pint cream; 1½ oz brown sugar. Cooking time: about 10–15 minutes.

Peel grapes, drain on absorbent paper. Place in heatproof dish, spoon the cream over the grapes. Leave overnight in refrigerator. Just before serving sift sugar over top and place under slow griller until sugar melts. Increase heat to high, continue cooking until sugar caramelises. Serve immediately.

Turban aux Fraises   *   *Strawberry Turban*

For 4 persons: Savarin soaked in kirsch; 1 lb strawberries; raspberry purée.

Arrange strawberries in the middle of the *savarin* and cover with a mound of whipped sweetened cream. Decorate this with wild strawberries. When about to serve, pour sweetened and well-iced raspberry *purée* in top.

Ices

The best method of making ice cream is to use the special ice cream churn or bucket. However, these are not very common nowadays, so alternatives must be found. Either you can use the freezing compartment of the domestic refrigerator or you can copy the churn principle by using a basin in ice and salt.

To do this place the cold ice cream mixture in a round basin and set this in a bigger basin containing ice and salt, in the proportion of 2 parts ice to 1 part coarse salt. Turn the inner basin with the left hand while using a spatula in the right to detach the outer layer of frozen mixture from the side of the basin. Ice cream will freeze very well like this, although not so quickly as in a freezer of course.

If you use the freezing compartment of your refrigerator, set the dial at the coldest point. Every 20 minutes take the ice cream out and whisk it. Alternatively there is also a device on the market now, which is electrically driven and fits into the freezing compartment of most modern refrigerators. This churns the ice cream as it is freezing and so produces a smooth ice cream.

Ice creams always contain a high proportion of sweetening and flavouring because these seem to lose their strength during the process of freezing. Colouring, of course, should be used sparingly. Other important factors to note are that as far as possible all utensils and ingredients should be chilled before use. Sugar must always be thoroughly dissolved before starting to freeze ice cream mixtures.

Café Glacé   *   Iced Coffee

15 cups.

Make 1 pint strong coffee with very good mocha coffee. Add 12 to 14 ounces sugar and let the sugar melt while the coffee cools. Add 1 pint fresh cream and ½ pint cold boiled milk. Place the mixture in the freezer in ice in the usual way and let it cool, stirring from time to time. It should not solidify but have a creamy consistency, so that it can be drunk. Serve in well-chilled glasses.

Glace à la Crème   *   Vanilla Ice Cream (basic recipe)

For 4–6 persons: 3 oz sugar; 5 egg yolks; 1 pint milk; vanilla pod.

Cream the egg yolks and sugar, add the boiling milk, boiled with the vanilla, and thicken over low heat without allowing to boil. Strain, cool and if using the ice churn method freeze as follows: surround the freezer with crushed ice and salt in alternate layers (1 pound salt to 3 pounds ice). Pack the ice down with a piece of wood, put the ice cream in the freezer and mix steadily until a consistent mixture is obtained. Or freeze in the refrigerator as instructed above. Place the mixture in a mould filling it right up. Cover with buttered greaseproof paper, seal round the edge with lard. Bury entirely in the crushed ice and salt or put into the deep freeze cabinet. Leave for at least 30 to 45 minutes before serving. To turn out, dip mould in cold water, open it, wipe edges carefully and slip a small knife all round between the ice and the mould to let in the air. Turn out on a dish and serve.

To make extra special ice cream, add ½ pint double cream per 2 pints of mixture before freezing.

▣ au Café * *Coffee*

Proceed as for Vanilla ice cream, but use approximately 1 pint milk and 1 tablespoon of very strong instant coffee to make the cream.

▣ au Chocolat * *Chocolate*

Proceed as for Vanilla ice cream. Add 4 ounces melted chocolate per pint, and use only 2 ounces sugar.

▣ aux Marrons * *Chestnut*

When Vanilla ice cream is frozen add 8 ounces vanilla-flavoured chestnut *purée* and ¼ pint of whipped cream. Mix well and re-freeze.

▣ Plombières * *Plombières*

This consists of alternate layers of Vanilla ice cream in a shallow mould with sponge fingers soaked in kirsch and diced candied fruit macerated in kirsch. The first layer should be ice cream.

Glace aux Fraises ou aux Framboises * *Straw-berry or Raspberry Ice*

This is a true fruit ice, made from fruit, sugar and water. A saccharometer or sugar thermometer is very useful for this type of ice.

For 6–8 persons: 1¼ lb strawberries; 8 oz sugar; ¾ pint water; 1 vanilla pod; lemon juice; a few drops of carmine.

Make a syrup with the sugar, water and vanilla. Allow it to boil to 220°F (or 25° on the saccharometer). Cool it, add strawberries, puréed by passing them through a nylon sieve: the juice of half a lemon and a little carmine to improve the colour. It should now read 18° to 19° on the saccharometer. If the reading is above this, add some cold water; if less, add some caster sugar, so that it melts quickly. It is possible, in this way, to adjust the mixture to the point where it will freeze, yet still be soft. Freeze in a freezer in the usual way.

Mousse Glacée * *Ice Cream Mousse*

For 4–6 persons: ½ pint unsweetened Vanilla custard; 3 oz sugar; ½ pint cream.

Make a Vanilla custard and stir in the extra sugar until dissolved. When cold, blend with an equal quantity of whipped cream. Pour straightaway into a mould and freeze either in the ice bucket, the refrigerator or in the deep freeze cabinet. It takes 2 hours to chill. All *mousses* are made like this, whether coffee, praline, or any other flavour. Fruit *mousse* is made with puréed raw fruit, moderately sweetened, and an equal quantity of whipped cream.

Be sure to close the mould hermetically, sealing the edges with lard.

Parfait au Café * *Coffee Parfait*

For 4 *persons:* 4 *oz sugar;* 4 *tablespoons very strong coffee;* 4 *egg yolks;*
½ *pint cream.*

Boil the sugar, mixed with the coffee, to 220°F or 25° on the saccharometer. Pour this syrup over the egg yolks and whisk until the mixture is soft, add whipped cream and freeze in a well-sealed mould, for 2 hours. *Parfaits* may also be flavoured with chocolate, praline, etc.; they are not so cold as ices, and lighter.

If no saccharometer is available you may test the syrup to see if it has reached 220°F or the "thread" stage. The syrup will look thin and run off the spoon. Dip the fingers into cold water and take a little syrup between the thumb and forefinger and stretch them apart; a thin thread is formed which does not break when stretched.

Pêches Melba * *Peach Melba*

For 4 *persons:* 1 *pint Vanilla ice cream;* 2 *peaches; vanilla-flavoured syrup;*
8 *tablespoons sweetened raspberry purée; whipped sweetened cream to decorate.*

Put 1 tablespoon raspberry *purée* into each *coupe*. Fill *coupes* with Vanilla ice cream. Cover with halved peaches in vanilla-flavoured syrup and well chilled. Pour the raspberry *purée* on top. Garnish with chopped almonds and whipped sweetened cream.

Sorbets * *Sorbets*

These are half-frozen water ices flavoured with liqueur. They used to be served in special glasses between the large roast joint and before the game course in very formal meals. They refresh the palate for the better appreciation of the courses to follow. Nowadays *sorbets* are served as a light ice at buffets, parties, dances, etc. They are based on a good wine—sauternes, asti, champagne, samos, etc. The following recipe may be taken as typical.

Sorbet au Sauternes * *Sorbet with Sauternes*

For 10–12 *glasses:* 8 *oz sugar;* ½ *pint water;* ½ *pint sauternes; juice of* 1
lemon; 1 *egg white.*

Make a boiled syrup with the sugar and water, cool it and add lemon juice and sauternes. Measure the mixture, with the saccharometer—it should read 17°. Add more sugar or water if an adjustment is necessary. Now freeze like an ice cream but whisk from time to time to prevent the formation of large ice crystals. When the mixture is half frozen add the beaten egg whites, mix well. Leave until about to serve, then sprinkle with sauternes.

Soufflé Glacé * *Ice Cream Soufflé*

An ice cream *soufflé* is not frozen before being moulded. The mixture is poured into the case and frozen either in the ice bucket, refrigerator or deep freeze cabinet. To prepare the *soufflé* case: Tie a double band of oiled greaseproof paper round the outside of the case, bringing it 2 inches above the rim.

265

▣ **Grand Marnier** * *Grand Marnier*

For 6 persons: Make 1 pint Vanilla custard, sweeten and flavour with the liqueur—3–4 tablespoons should be sufficient. When cold, add 1 pint double cream. Whisk over ice until the mixture is light and fluffy. Pour quickly into the prepared case, filling it 1 inch above the rim. Deep freeze for 2 hours, or freeze in the ice box of the refrigerator for 3–4 hours. Carefully peel off the paper collar before serving and decorate quickly with whirls of whipped sweetened cream. Scatter chopped praline, nuts, etc. over and serve immediately.

Tarts and Flans

These are the simplest and best of home-made cakes. They may be made all the year round with fresh or preserved fruit. The pastry recommended in the majority of the following recipes is the Sweet shortcrust pastry on *p. 233*. Except for Strawberry tart, the pastry and filling should be baked together, even when using preserved fruit or plum jam as a filling. Tarts and flans are baked in special flan rings, but they can be made using a metal flan tin or shallow cake tin.

Below we give the recipes for the most important flans and tarts. They must not be cooked the day before, otherwise the pastry becomes soggy.

Tart aux Abricots   *   Apricot Tart

For 4–5 persons: 6 oz Sweet shortcrust pastry; 1 lb apricots; apricot jam for glazing. Cooking time: 25–30 minutes.

Half-fill the tart with slightly flattened apricots so that they overlap. Bake in a fairly hot oven, 375°F or Gas Mark 5, and then coat with apricot jam. All fruit flans are made in this way: there is therefore no need to repeat the recipe for plum tart, mirabelle tart, etc.

▣ à l'Ananas I   *   Pineapple I

For 4 persons: 1 tin pineapple slices; 2 tablespoons kirsch; ½ pint cream; 2 tablespoons sugar; 1 baked flan case (4 oz).

Finely dice the pineapple, mix with two-thirds of the whipped cream, add 6 tablespoons pineapple juice and the kirsch. Pour this mixture into the pastry case, baked beforehand as for Strawberry tart, and decorate with the remaining cream and pineapple.

▣ à l'Ananas II   *   Pineapple II

For 6 persons: Crust: 6 oz plain sweet biscuits; 3 oz melted butter. Filling: 15 oz can crushed pineapple; ½ oz cornflour; 8 oz cream cheese; 2 oz sugar; 2 eggs; 1 teaspoon vanilla. Cooking time: 25 minutes.

Crush biscuits finely and mix with melted butter. Press into base of 9-inch loose-bottomed baking tin to form crust. Drain pineapple. Mix cornflour to paste with a little of the drained syrup. Add remaining syrup over gentle heat, bring to boil, stirring until thickened. Add pineapple and mix in well, then spoon mixture into crumb crust. Beat cream cheese until smooth, add sugar, eggs, and vanilla, and beat well. Pour over pineapple. Bake for approximately 25 minutes in moderate oven, 350°F or Gas Mark 4, then turn off heat and leave pie in oven until cold. Refrigerate until chilled, serve with cream.

Tart au Banane à la Crème * *Banana Cream Tart*

For 6 persons: 1 oz butter; 3 oz brown sugar; ¼ pint water; ½ pint milk; ¼ oz gelatine; 2 eggs; ¼ pint cream; 3 or 4 bananas; lemon juice; 1 baked 9-inch pie shell.

Combine in saucepan butter, brown sugar, and half the water; cook, stirring, until sugar is dissolved, about 2 minutes; cool slightly, stir in milk. Soften gelatine in remaining water, dissolve over hot water; cool. Blend in to milk mixture. Separate eggs. Add slightly beaten yolks to milk mixture. Allow to cool; when beginning to stiffen slightly, fold in lightly whipped cream and stiffly beaten egg whites. Slice bananas, dip into lemon juice, reserve some slices for decoration. Arrange remainder on base of cooked pie case. Pour cream mixture over carefully, refrigerate until set. Just before serving, decorate with whipped cream and banana slices.

▣ aux Cerises * *Cherry*

For 4 persons: 4 oz Sweet shortcrust pastry; sugar; cherries; redcurrant jelly. Cooking time: 30 minutes.

Line the flan ring with pastry. Prick and lightly dredge with icing sugar, to absorb the juice of the cherries as they cook, and fill with raw stoned cherries. Bake in a fairly hot oven, 375°F or Gas Mark 5, and glaze with warmed redcurrant jelly, or sprinkle with vanilla sugar.

▣ aux Cerises à la Lorraine * *Cherry Lorraine*

For 4 persons: 4 oz Sweet shortcrust or Puff pastry; 1 lb cherries; 3 tablespoons cream. Cooking time: 30–35 minutes.

Line a flan ring with Short or Puff Pastry. Arrange in it stoned cherries, poached beforehand in syrup, drained and cooled. Do not place too close together. Pour on top a custard made by mixing 2 egg yolks with 2 ounces vanilla sugar and ¼ pint cold milk. Do not cook this custard before pouring it into the case. Put the tart just inside the oven before you pour the cream on, to avoid spills. Bake in a fairly hot oven, 375°F or Gas Mark 5, for 30–35 minutes. Pipe with sweetened cream, when cold.

Chocolat au Rhum * *Chocolate Rum Pie*

For 6 persons: Pastry: 1 egg; 2 oz sugar; 3 oz butter; 5 oz plain flour; ½ teaspoon baking powder; pinch salt. Filling: ½ oz gelatine; 1 pint milk; 8 oz sugar; ¾ oz cornflour; 4 oz melted chocolate; 4 eggs, separated; 1 teaspoon instant coffee; ½ tablespoon rum; pinch salt; extra 4–6 oz melted chocolate. Cooking time: 15–20 minutes.

Beat egg and sugar for pastry until thick and lemon coloured. Add softened butter and beat thoroughly. Add sifted dry ingredients. Mix well. Turn on to lightly floured board and knead lightly. Allow to chill for a few hours or overnight. Roll out and line a 9-inch pie plate. Decorate edges and prick the base. Bake in a hot oven, 400°F or Gas Mark 6, for 15 to 20 minutes. Allow to cool while preparing the filling. Soften gelatine in 4 tablespoons milk. Scald remaining milk. Blend half the sugar with the cornflour, stir hot milk into this mixture, blend well. Add to beaten egg yolks and cook over hot water, stirring constantly until mixture is smooth and thick. Blend melted chocolate, instant coffee, and softened gelatine into this mixture, stir until dissolved. Cool, but do not allow to stiffen. Mix in rum, blend well. Beat egg whites with salt and cream of tartar until soft peaks form. Add remaining sugar gradually, beating until stiff and glossy. Fold chocolate mixture into egg whites and pour into prepared pie shell. Allow to set. Pour over extra melted chocolate, forming a thin layer on top of pie. Allow to set and then drizzle thin lines of chocolate in an attractive design around the edge of pie.

Tart aux Fraises   *   *Strawberry*

For 4 persons: 4 oz Rich Shortcrust pastry; 4 oz redcurrant jelly; strawberries; sugar. Cooking time: 25–30 minutes.

Roll out the pastry to line a 6-inch flan ring, and place on a baking sheet. Bake before filling. To prevent the pastry from bulging, prick the base and line with a piece of greaseproof paper. Fill with lentils or baking beans which may be kept to be used again for this purpose. Bake at 375°F or Gas Mark 5 for 20 minutes. When the tart is almost done, take out the beans and let the pastry dry and finish cooking in a moderate oven, 350°F or Gas Mark 4; there is no longer any risk of its losing its shape. Wait until the pastry is cold, then dredge with icing sugar before filling with good, firm strawberries and brush with melted redcurrant jelly.

▣ aux Fruits   *   *Mixed Fruit*

For 4 persons: 4 oz Sweet Shortcrust pastry; 2 oz ground almonds; sugar; dessert apples; 2 oz butter; fruit in different colours (cherries, white grapes); vanilla sugar. Cooking time: 35 minutes.

Line the flan ring with pastry. Sprinkle the bottom with ground almonds. Thinly slice half the apples and arrange them to overlap on the almonds. Do not place them too close to each other. Garnish with small dabs of butter and dredge with sugar. Bake in a fairly hot oven, 375°F or Gas Mark 5. When the tart is cold, place cherries stewed in syrup and raw white-skinned and halved grapes between the apples. Dredge the whole with vanilla sugar.

▣ aux Groseilles à Maquereau   *   *Gooseberry*

For 4 persons: 4 oz Sweet Shortcrust pastry; 1 lb gooseberries. Cooking time: 20 minutes.

Bake the tart blind as for Strawberry tart, filled with dried beans so that it will keep its shape. Poach the gooseberries in vanilla-flavoured syrup, drain them and boil down the juice considerably. Fill the tart with the gooseberries, coat with the boiled-down syrup and dredge with granulated or brown sugar.

▣ de Linz   *   *Linz*

For 4 persons: 5 oz flour; 4 oz almonds ground with their skins; 4 oz butter; 4 oz sugar; 1 teaspoon ground cinnamon; a pinch of salt; 2 hardboiled egg yolks; 1 tablespoon kirsch or rum; raspberry jam; 1 egg yolk. Cooking time: 40 minutes.

Make a well in the sifted flour. In it put the almonds, butter, sugar and eggs passed through a sieve, the kirsch or rum, cinnamon and a pinch of salt. Knead to a paste, wrap in a cloth and allow to rest for 1 hour. Roll out $\frac{1}{3}$ inch thick and line a buttered flan ring on a baking sheet with it. Cover with a layer of jam. Place a strip of pastry all round the edge and pinch it. Cut out strips of pastry for the lattice with a crimped pastry wheel. Brush the lattice and edging with egg and bake in a fairly hot oven, 375°F or Gas Mark 5, for 40 minutes. Do not turn out until quite cold. This delicious tart is of Viennese origin.

▣ aux Oranges et aux Bananes   *   *Orange and Banana*

For 4 persons: 4 oz Rich Shortcrust pastry; 2 bananas; 2 oranges; $\frac{1}{4}$ pint milk; 1 egg yolk; 1 oz sugar; 1 oz flour or $\frac{3}{4}$ oz cornflour.

Make a Pastry cream flavoured with the zest of the oranges. Bake a flan case blind, using

E.F.C.

Rich Shortcrust pastry. Peel the oranges, removing all white skin, slice thinly removing the pips, and macerate in kirsch. Slice the bananas, sugar them and macerate in rum. Spread the flan with the Pastry cream and arrange the sliced fruit neatly on top.

Tart aux Pommes à l'Anglaise * *Apple Tart*

For 4 persons: 4 oz Sweet Shortcrust pastry; apple jam; apricot jam. Cooking time: 30–35 minutes, according to size.

Roll out the pastry to the size of the flan ring, $\frac{1}{8}$–$\frac{1}{4}$ inch thick, according to size. Butter the ring and line it with the pastry. Trim edges, leaving a border $\frac{1}{5}$ inch high above the edge of the ring and pinch this with pastry pincers. Place on a thick baking sheet. Prick bottom 10–15 times and half-fill with cold, well-sweetened thick apple jam. Cover completely with a layer of thinly sliced raw apples and bake in a fairly hot oven, 375°F or Gas Mark 5. Sprinkle with vanilla sugar and brush top with apricot glaze.

▣ aux Pommes Grillagée * *Latticed Apple*

For 4 persons: 5 oz Sweet Shortcrust pastry; stewed apples; egg for brushing. Cooking time: 35–40 minutes.

Line a flan ring with pastry and trim the edges, prick the bottom and fill with cold, stewed apples. Roll out remainder of pastry thinly and cut into long, narrow strips like noodles. Make a trellis of them across the top of the tart, sticking down the ends. Brush with beaten egg. Bake at 375°F or Gas Mark 5 until the pastry is ready. Dredge with icing sugar. (*See illustration p.* 277).

▣ à la Rhubarbe * *Rhubarb*

For 4 persons: 4 oz Sweet Shortcrust pastry; 1 lb rhubarb; 4–5 oz sugar. Cooking time: 30–35 minutes.

Line the flan ring in the usual way. Fill with rhubarb, carefully peeled, cut in 1-inch pieces and previously soaked for 1 hour with plenty of caster sugar. Drain fruit well before filling the tart. Bake in a fairly hot oven, 375°F or Gas Mark 5. Coat with apricot glaze made by warming apricot jam and water and then sieving it.

FLAN * *SPECIAL FLANS*

Flan à l'Andalouse * *Andalouse*

For 4 persons: 4 oz Sweet Shortcrust pastry; orange-flavoured Pastry cream; orange Fondant; candied orange peel. Cooking time: 30–35 minutes.

Line a flan ring with the pastry. Prick and fill with Pastry cream with a strong orange flavour. Bake in a fairly hot oven, 375°F or Gas Mark 5. When cold, ice with orange Fondant and decorate with small pieces of candied orange peel.

▣ Bourdaloue * *Bourdaloue*

For 4 persons: 4 oz Sweet Shortcrust pastry; $\frac{1}{2}$ pint Bourdaloue cream. Cooking time: 20 minutes.

Same method as for Frangipane flan, but fill with Bourdaloue cream. When the flan is quite cold, sprinkle with sweetened kirsch.

270

Cream Cheese Pie

For 6 persons: Crumb Crust: 5 *oz melted butter;* 1 *oz sugar;* 6 *oz biscuit crumbs;* 2 *oz chopped walnuts;* ½ *teaspoon cinnamon;* ½ *teaspoon nutmeg. Filling:* 8 *oz cream cheese; scant* ¼ *pint (4 fluid oz) sweetened condensed milk;* 2 *tablespoons lemon juice;* ¼ *pint cream, whipped.*

Mix together in basin all crumb crust ingredients; blend well, press into 9-inch pie dish. Chill while preparing filling. Sieve cream cheese, add condensed milk and lemon juice; beat until smooth. Fold in whipped cream. Pour into prepared pie-case, chill three hours. Decorate with swirls of additional sweetened whipped cream, top with strawberries or other fresh fruit.

▣ **Commun** * *Baked Custard*

For 4 *persons:* 1 *oz sugar;* 3 *whole eggs;* 1 *pint cold milk.* Cooking time: 40 minutes.

Heat the milk but do not boil it. Mix the eggs and sugar in a basin, pour on the hot milk, stirring all the time. Strain into an ovenproof dish. Bake in a warm oven, 325°F or Gas Mark 3. Some stoned raisins may be added if desired or you may sprinkle the top with grated nutmeg. This flan is made without a pastry case but you may line a greased oven-proof dish with Shortcrust pastry first, if liked.

▣ **à la Frangipane** * *Frangipane*

For 4 *persons:* 4 *oz Sweet Shortcrust pastry;* ½ *pint Frangipane cream* Cooking time: 25–30 minutes.

Fill a flan ring lined with the pastry with Frangipane cream. Decorate the top with pastry motifs—a crimp-edged band placed in a spiral or small crescents. Bake in a fairly hot oven, 375°F or Gas Mark 5.

▣ **au Lait** * *Milk*

For 4 *persons:* 4 *oz Sweet Shortcrust pastry;* 2 *eggs;* 2 *oz vanilla sugar;* ½ *oz cornflour;* ½ *pint milk.* Cooking time: 35–40 minutes.

Line a 6-inch flan ring with Short pastry and prick the bottom. Fill with a custard consisting of the eggs and sugar beaten with a fork and then combined with the cornflour and cold milk. Pass through a fine sieve and pour into tart. Bake in a fairly hot oven, 375°F or Gas Mark 5.

Cakes and Pastries

CAKES MADE WITH SPONGE MIXTURES

Biscuit Roulé   *   Swiss Roll

3 oz self-raising flour; 3 oz caster sugar; 3 eggs; ½ lemon. Cooking time: 8–10 minutes.

Have ready a shallow baking tin 7 inch × 12 inch, lined with oiled paper. Whisk the eggs and sugar together until they are thick, creamy and hold their shape when the whisk is lifted. You may find it helpful to put the bowl over a pan of hot water. Fold in the sifted flour and grated lemon rind. Tilt the tin carefully so that the mixture flows evenly over it. Bake quickly in a hot oven, 400°F or Gas Mark 6, until the mixture springs back when pressed with the finger. Be very careful not to overcook the Swiss roll. Turn out on to a sugared paper. Peel off the oiled paper. Trim the edges. Place another sheet of paper on top and roll the sponge up tightly. Leave on a wire tray until cold. Carefully unroll it, spread with Bourdaloue cream, butter cream or jam and re-roll. Brush with jam glaze and dredge with granulated sugar. (*See illustration p. 279*).

Bûche de Noël   *   Yule Log

Swiss Roll mixture—using 3 eggs. Decoration: 4 oz Mocha butter cream; 4 oz Chocolate butter cream; chopped pistachio nuts or coloured desiccated coconut; Christmas decorations. Cooking time: 10 minutes.

Make a Swiss Roll mixture, and bake as instructed above. Turn out on to a sugared paper. Peel off the oiled paper. Trim the edges and roll the sponge up tightly with the grease-proof paper in the centre. Cool on a wire tray. When cold, unroll and spread with Mocha butter cream. Re-roll tightly. Cut off ends diagonally. Spread the cut surfaces with Mocha butter cream, and toss some chopped pistachio nuts or coloured coconut over them. Using Chocolate butter cream and a forcing bag with a finely fluted nozzle, pipe the top with the cream ridged to look like a tree bark. Knots or tree branches may be added by inserting 2 or 3 pieces of sponge (from the end pieces) and piping them with Chocolate cream. Apply holly, or other Christmas decorations, as liked. Dust lightly with icing sugar and stand it on a cake board, or on a thin base of Sweet pastry, the same size as the roll, baked beforehand.

If no bag and pipe are available, spread the Chocolate cream over the roll with a knife and mark the ridges with a fork.

Easter Log: Make as above, and substitute Easter eggs and chickens for Christmas decorations.

272

GATEAUX * *GATEAUX*

Gâteau Amanda * *Almond and Praline*

4 oz sugar; 2½ oz flour; 1½ oz rice or cornflour; 5 eggs; 2 oz butter; 4 oz ground almonds; 4 oz Praline butter cream. Cooking time: 40 minutes.

Make a Savoy sponge mixture, adding 1 more egg and 4 ounces ground almonds. Bake in a greased and floured sandwich tin in a moderate oven, 350°F or Gas Mark 4. When the cake has cooled cut it through and fill with Praline butter cream. Coat the top and sides with the same cream. Mask with ground roast almonds and dredge plentifully with sieved icing sugar. Place some whole roast almonds or hazelnuts on top.

▣ d'Anniversaire * *Birthday Cake*

Savoy sponge mixture. Cooking time: 35–40 minutes. *Butter cream: 4½ oz butter; ¼ pint Chocolate custard.*

Pour the sponge mixture into a round sandwich tin and bake in a moderate oven, 350°F or Gas Mark 4. After baking, turn out on a wire tray and leave to cool. Cut through twice and spread each layer with Chocolate butter cream. Coat the sides with apricot glaze and sprinkle with chopped almonds. Ice the top with kirsch-flavoured Fondant coloured with carmine. With a forcing tube make an appropriate inscription and decoration on top. Fix on the small candles.

▣ Chocolatine * *Chocolate Fluff*

4 eggs; pinch salt; 4 oz sugar; ½ tablespoon golden syrup; 2 teaspoons cream of tartar; 1 teaspoon bicarbonate of soda; 1 oz plain flour; 3½ oz arrowroot; 1 oz cocoa; 1 teaspoon cinnamon; whipped cream; icing sugar. Cooking time: 15 minutes.

Separate eggs, beat egg whites stiffly with pinch of salt, add sugar gradually, beat well until sugar is dissolved. Add egg yolks, beat until thick and creamy. Sift combined dry ingredients 3 times. Put golden syrup in cup, stand in saucepan of hot water until syrup melts. Cool. Sift dry ingredients into egg mixture, pour golden syrup around edge. Fold all in thoroughly. Turn into 2 greased 7-inch sandwich tins. Bake in moderate oven, 350°F or Gas Mark 4, about 15 minutes, or until cooked. Cool. Fill between layers with whipped cream, sprinkle top with icing sugar.

▣ de Gênes * *Almond Genoa*

6 oz sugar; 5 oz butter; 4 oz ground almonds; 1 oz flour; 3 whole eggs; salt; 3–4 tablespoons kirsch. Cooking time: 40 minutes.

Cream the ground almonds with half the sugar. Cream the butter with the remainder of the sugar until white and soft. Combine the two mixtures and add the eggs one by one beating all the time. Do not worry if the mixture is slightly granular and not quite smooth. Add salt. Fold in flour and the desired flavouring. Line the bottom of a baking tin with oiled paper and put mixture into it. Bake for 45 minutes in a moderate oven, 350°F or Gas Mark 4, and serve without decoration or icing.

▣ Génoise Glacée * *Iced Genoese Sponge*

7 oz Genoese mixture; candied fruit; jam; butter cream; Fondant. Cooking time: 35 minutes.

Bake *Genoese* mixture in a buttered and floured tin. When cold, cut it through the centre into two halves. Fill with jam or a butter cream flavoured to taste. Ice with Fondant, in a colour and flavour to harmonise with the filling. Finally decorate with candied fruit, almonds or cream. (*See illustration p.* 277).

Lemon Cream Gâteau

For 6 persons: Base: 3 oz butter; 2 oz icing sugar; 1 egg yolk; 4 oz self-raising flour; 2 tablespoons milk. Topping: 6 oz cream cheese; 3 egg whites; 2 egg yolks; ½ oz butter; 2 oz caster sugar; ½ teaspoon vanilla; ½ tablespoon finely grated lemon rind. Cooking time: 30 minutes.

Cream together butter and sifted icing sugar until light. Add egg yolk, beat well. Add sifted flour, then milk. Spread over base of 8-inch greased sandwich tin with greased paper at base. Bake in moderate oven 350°F or Gas Mark 4, for 15 minutes. Cool slightly, spread topping over.

For topping, beat together cream cheese, egg yolks, butter, sugar, lemon rind and vanilla. Beat egg whites until stiff, fold in. Spread over base. Bake further 15 minutes in moderate oven, 350°F or Gas Mark 4, until topping is set; cool. Dust with sifted icing sugar.

▣ Marbré * Marble

7 oz Genoese or Simple sponge mixture; 2 oz grated or flaked chocolate; Vanilla butter cream and Chocolate butter cream; Fondant. Cooking time: 35–40 minutes.

This cake is original in appearance, but can be made quite easily. Make a sponge mixture and partially combine with the chocolate with only a few strokes of the spatula. Bake in an oiled paper lined tin in a moderate oven, 350°F or Gas Mark 4. When cold, split and fill with partially mixed Vanilla and Chocolate butter cream. Coat with white Fondant icing and feather with chocolate Fondant to resemble veined marble.

▣ aux Marrons * Unbaked Chocolate Chestnut Cake

1¼ lb chestnuts; 4 oz unsalted butter; 4 oz grated chocolate; 4 oz vanilla sugar.

Boil and drain the chestnuts (*see p.* 206). Peel them and pass through a fine sieve. While still hot combine with the sugar, butter and grated chocolate. When thoroughly mixed, put into a buttered tin—a square one for preference—lined with paper at the bottom. Press the mixture down well and stand in a cool place or the refrigerator for a few hours. Turn out when firm and slice. This excellent cake is not baked.

▣ Mascotte * Praline and Almond

7 oz Genoese mixture; 3½ oz Praline butter cream; 1½ oz chopped roasted almonds. Cooking time: 35–40 minutes.

Bake *Genoese* mixture in a round tin, cool and split. Fill with Praline butter cream and coat it well. Cover top and sides with chopped almonds. Dredge the whole generously with icing sugar.

▣ Moka * Coffee

7 oz Genoese mixture; 4 oz Coffee butter cream; 2 oz chopped walnuts, if liked. Cooking time: 35–40 minutes.

Make a *Genoese* mixture and bake in a *moule à manqué* or sandwich tin, buttered, floured and filled to within ¼ inch of the top. Bake for 35–40 minutes in a moderate oven, 350°F or

Gas Mark 4. If more than one tin is used the mixture will only take about 25 minutes to bake. Turn out, and leave to cool. In the meantime, make a Mocha butter cream: when the cake is quite cold, cut it through once or twice and fill thinly with the cream. Coat the top and sides with a little cream to mask the sponge. Sprinkle the sides only with crystallised sugar or finely chopped walnuts, and decorate the top with the remains of the cream, using a forcing bag and a finely-fluted nozzle. (*See illustration p.* 278). This cake is typical of all cakes garnished with butter cream. A large variety may be obtained by changing the flavouring. Decorating with a forcing bag is the most difficult part, but after a few attempts at simple designs—chequerboards, lattices, etc., the decoration will present no difficulty.

Fatless Sponge Cake

4 *eggs;* 6 *oz caster sugar;* 6 *oz self-raising flour;* 5 *tablespoons luke-warm water.* Cooking time: 25–30 minutes.

Sift flour 2 or 3 times. Beat eggs until very thick and light, add sugar gradually, and when all sugar has been added, continue beating for 10 to 15 minutes. Add 2 tablespoons water, fold in. Sift flour over top of mixture, fold in carefully, then add remaining warm water, fold in carefully and thoroughly. Divide mixture evenly into two 8-inch greased and floured sandwich tins. Bake in moderate oven, 350°F or Gas Mark 4, for 25 to 30 minutes. Turn out, cool.

Join with jam and whipped cream, sift icing sugar over top of sponge.

Gingerbread Cake

1 *lb plain flour;* ½ *teaspoon salt;* ½ *oz baking powder;* 6 *teaspoons ground ginger;* 1 *teaspoon bicarbonate of soda;* 8 *oz brown sugar;* 6 *oz butter;* 10 *oz treacle;* ½ *pint milk;* 1 *egg.* Cooking time: 1 hour.

Sift flour, salt, ginger, baking powder and bicarbonate of soda into basin. Place treacle, butter, brown sugar into saucepan, stir over low heat until sugar dissolves. Cool. Add to dry ingredients; mix in egg and warmed milk. Pour into greased and paper lined 10-inch square or oblong cake tin. Bake in a fairly hot oven, 375°F or Gas Mark 5, for 1 hour. Cool slightly before turning out on cake cooler. When quite cold, top with lemon icing.

LEMON ICING: 10 oz icing sugar; 1 oz butter; lemon juice. Sift icing sugar. Soften butter with spatula or wooden spoon, then gradually add icing sugar, working well in. Add sufficient lemon juice, a little at a time, to make a smooth spreading consistency.

Half Pound Fruit Cake

1½ *lb sultanas;* 8 *oz raisins;* 4 *oz currants;* 4 *oz glacé or crystallised cherries;* 4 *oz shredded mixed peel; scant* ¼ *pint rum, brandy, or sherry;* 8 *oz butter;* 8 *oz brown sugar;* 1 *teaspoon each grated orange and lemon rind; few drops almond essence;* 1 *teaspoon vanilla;* 2 *tablespoons marmalade;* 1 *teaspoon caramel or gravy browning;* 4 *eggs;* 10 *oz plain flour;* ¼ *teaspoon each cinnamon and nutmeg.* Cooking time: 4 hours.

Prepare fruits by washing, drying, and removing stems. Chop and place in a basin, pour over spirits, and mix well. Cover, stand overnight. Cream butter with brown sugar, grated fruit rinds and essences, and add marmalade and caramel or food colouring. Drop in eggs one at a time, beating well after each addition. Fold in prepared fruit alternately with sifted dry ingredients, mix well. Fill into an 8 or 9-inch cake tin lined with 1 thickness of white paper and 2 of brown (white paper next to cake). Level off top with knife, and decorate, if desired, with cherries and almonds. Bake in cool oven, 300°F or Gas Mark 2, for about 4 hours. When cooked, cake should feel firm, and thin skewer inserted in the centre comes out clean.

Hazelnut Meringue Torte

4 egg whites; pinch salt; 9 oz caster sugar; 4½ oz ground hazelnuts; 1 teaspoon vinegar; few drops vanilla; 2 tablespoons black coffee. Cream Filling: ½ pint cream; 2 oz sugar; ½ teaspoon vanilla; 1 rounded tablespoon cocoa. Cooking time: 35 minutes.

Whip egg whites with salt until stiff, then gradually add sugar, beating all the time. Fold in remaining ingredients. Fill into 2 greased, floured, and paper-lined 8-inch sandwich tins. Bake in fairly hot oven, 375°F or Gas Mark 5, for 35 minutes. Remove from tins and cool. When cool, sandwich together with cream filling, stand on serving stand. Cover top and sides with cream filling, decorate with whole hazelnuts.
Cream Filling: Mix, don't beat, all ingredients in bowl; refrigerate for 1 hour to blend flavours, then whip until mixture holds a soft shape. Use as directed.

Plum Cake   *   *Plum Cake*

4 oz butter; 4 oz sugar; 3 whole eggs; 5 oz flour; ½ level teaspoon baking powder; 4 tablespoons rum; 12 oz altogether raisins, sultanas and currants; 2 oz candied fruit; 2 oz chopped almonds. Cooking time: 1–1½ hours.

Soak the fruit in the rum overnight. Cream the butter and caster sugar in a bowl with a flat whisk; add 1 egg, stir vigorously and add another egg, whisk for another 3 minutes and add the last egg. When this has been thoroughly mixed in too, stir the mixture with a spoon and add the flour sifted with the salt and baking powder. Lastly add the diced macerated candied fruit, almonds and rum. Bake in a rectangular cake tin, buttered and lined with paper. Start baking in a moderate oven, 350°F or Gas Mark 4, for 5 minutes. Lower heat and finish cooking in a cool oven, 300°F or Gas Mark 2, until a heated skewer, plunged into the middle of the cake, comes out clean. Cool in the tin. Plum cake will keep fresh for several months in a sealed tin. (*See illustration p. 280*).

Quatre-Quarts   *   *Victoria Sponge*

2 eggs and their weight in butter, sugar and flour; vanilla. Cooking time: 25 minutes.

Place 2 large eggs or 3 small ones on one side of the scales and on the other the same weight in butter, sugar and flour respectively. Cream the butter in a bowl. Beat it, adding first the sugar with a little vanilla. Add two tablespoons of flour, then the eggs, singly and not too quickly. Lastly fold in the remaining flour sifted with a level teaspoon of baking powder. Bake in 2 buttered and floured tins in a moderate oven, 350°F or Gas Mark 4.

CAKES MADE WITH PASTRY

Gâteau d'Amandes, dit Pithiviers   *   *Almond or Pithiviers Cake*

8 oz Puff pastry; Almond cream (see below). Cooking time: 30 minutes.

Take one-third of the Puff pastry, shape it into a ball without handling it too much and roll out into a circle about ⅛ inch thick. Place on a baking sheet sprinkled with cold water and spread to within 1 inch of the edge with Almond cream (recipe below). Moisten the edges with water, then with the remaining two-thirds pastry, cover with a second, similar circle of Puff pastry but twice as thick. Trim with a ring cutter, allowing 1 inch all round the filling.

▲ *Tarte aux pommes grillagée, p. 270*

Génoise glacée, p. 273 ▼   277

▲ *Eclairs au café et au chocolat, Salambos, Choux à la crème et au chocolat, p. 287, 293, 286*

Gâteau moka, p. 274 ▼

▲ *Gâteau feuilleté à la confiture, p. 281*

Biscuit roulé, p. 272

▲ *Babas au rhum et petits savarins au rhum chantilly, p. 285, 290*

Plum cake, p. 276 ▼

Press the edges down well by hand, then scallop them with the back of a knife, pressing it down well without cutting through the pastry. Brush the top with beaten egg. Score curved lines right through the pastry, on the top with the point of a sharp knife, starting from the centre and radiating to the edge. Bake in a hot oven, 425°F or Gas Mark 7, for 30 minutes. Five minutes before the cake is done dredge the top with icing sugar and finish baking so that the sugar caramelises, giving the top a glossy appearance.

To make Almond cream: 3½ oz almonds; 3½ oz sugar; 1½ oz butter; 2 egg yolks; 3 tablespoons rum.

Finely pound the almonds with the sugar (or use ground almonds). Add the egg yolks, then the butter and finally the rum. Work the mixture with a spatula. This cream is used for a number of cakes, the best-known of which is the Pithiviers.

▣ Apple Cheese

For 8 persons: Pastry: 5 oz plain flour; pinch salt; ½ teaspoon cinnamon; 2 oz sugar; 1 teaspoon baking powder; grated rind of ½ lemon; 4 oz butter; 1 egg yolk; 1 tablespoon sherry. *Filling:* 2 eggs; 4 oz sugar; ½ oz plain flour; grated rind 1 lemon; ¼ pint cream; 6 oz cream cheese; ½ oz candied peel; 1 oz sultanas; pinch salt; 2 peeled, cored, sliced cooking apples. *Topping:* 1 large (29 oz) can apricots; 1 tablespoon sugar; ¾ tablespoon cornflour; 1 teaspoon rum; whipped cream for decorating. Cooking time: 1¼ hours.

Sift flour, salt, cinnamon and baking powder into bowl, add sugar and grated lemon rind, mix in. Rub in butter. Combine egg yolk and sherry, add to flour mixture and work to a dough. Turn on to lightly floured board and roll to a circle; line into a greased 8 inch loose bottomed cake tin. Prick base with fork. *Filling:* Simmer apple slices in water for a few minutes to soften slightly: drain, allow to cool, and arrange on top of pastry base. Cream eggs and sugar until thick and creamy. Beat in flour, salt, grated lemon rind, cream, cream cheese; fold in candied peel and sultanas. Spoon over apples. Bake in moderate oven, 350°F or Gas Mark 4, for about 1¼ hours, or until golden.
Topping: Drain apricots, reserving ¼ pint syrup, then sieve fruit. Stir in sugar. Blend cornflour with syrup, add to *purée*. Bring to boil, stirring; simmer 2 minutes, blend in rum. Cool, then spread over top of cake. Decorate with whipped cream.

Gâteau Feuilleté à la Confiture * *Puff Pastry Layer Cake*

8 oz Puff pastry; apricot jam; Pastry cream. Cooking time: 15-20 minutes.

Roll out the Puff pastry ¼ inch thick and cut out 3 rounds with a round cutter. Lay on baking sheet, sprinkled with cold water. Prick with a fork and bake in a hot oven, 425°F or Gas Mark 7. Leave until quite cold. Spread the first round with kirsch-flavoured Pastry cream, place the second round on top and spread this with thick apricot jam. Cover with the third round. Trim the sides and ice top heavily with *Glacé* icing. Decorate with small crescents of Puff pastry. (*See illustration p. 279*).

▣ à Galette des Rois * *Twelfth Night Cake*

7 oz flour; 5 oz butter; about 7 tablespoons cold water; salt; lucky charms. Cooking time: 15–20 minutes.

This cake may be made from Puff pastry trimmings. Shape them into a ball, flatten it and roll out about ½ inch thick. If you have no such trimmings, make a Puff pastry with the above ingredients. Place the sifted flour on a marble slab, make a well and put the salt, water and well-kneaded butter into it. Mix gently and quickly without attempting to obtain a completely homogeneous mass. As soon as the pastry holds together fairly well, roll it into a ball, wrap it in a cloth and let it rest for a good hour in a cool place. Then give it 4 turns, letting it rest for 15 minutes after the first 2. This paste only has four turns instead of six.

Roll out the pastry in a circle about ¾ inch thick. Make an opening underneath, put the lucky charm in it, place on a greased baking sheet, brush with egg and mark a lattice on top with the knife-tip. Prick 6 or 7 times and bake in a hot oven, 400°F or Gas Mark 6, for 15–20 minutes according to size.

Paris-Brest * *Paris Ring*

5 oz Choux pastry; 1 oz splintered almonds; Praline Pastry cream. Cooking time: 30–40 minutes.

Put a ring of *Choux* pastry, about 2 fingers thick, on an unbuttered baking sheet. Brush top with egg yolk and sprinkle with splintered almonds. Dredge lightly with sugar, bake in a hot oven, 400°F or Gas Mark 6, until crisp and dry. When the ring is cooked, cut it open and cool. Fill with *Praline* Pastry cream. Dredge top with icing sugar.

Gâteau Saint-Honoré * *Saint Honoré*

4 oz Sweet short pastry; 5 oz Choux pastry; ½ pint Saint-Honoré cream; macedoine of fruit. Caramel syrup: 8 oz sugar; ¼ pint hot water. Cooking time: 25 minutes.

Roll out Short pastry ⅛ inch thick and cut out a circle the size of a small plate. Prick all over and, using a forcing bag and plain nozzle, pipe a ring of *Choux* pastry all round the edge. Brush top with egg and bake in a fairly hot oven, 375°F or Gas Mark 5. Make small buns of *Choux* pastry the size of half a walnut, and bake these at the same time. Make the Caramel syrup: melt the sugar in a heavy saucepan over low heat, stirring constantly. Cook until pale gold in colour. Remove from heat and add the hot water. The sugar will form hard lumps, so stir and cook until all the lumps have dissolved. Remove from heat and cool slightly. Dip the buns in the syrup and immediately stick them on the *Choux* pastry ring of the cake, to form a basket, or raised edge. Fill with fruit and cream. Pipe with Saint Honoré cream.

Stroudel aux Pommes * *Apple Strudel*

For 8–10 persons: Strudel pastry: 12 oz sieved flour; 1 egg; pinch salt; 2 oz butter; squeeze lemon juice; ¼–½ pint water. Filling: 1½ lb apples; 3 oz fried breadcrumbs; 2 oz sultanas; 4 oz sugar; a little ground cinnamon; 1 oz splintered almonds; 1 table spoonrum; 3 oz butter. Cooking time: 40 minutes.

Beat the egg and add about ¼ pint water. Put the flour in a bowl with the salt and add the liquid. Add more water to make a soft dough. Work it well to make it elastic and pliable. Leave for 1 hour. Prepare the filling. Place it on a floured cloth, and stretch, pull and roll until parchment thin and oblong in shape. Brush with melted butter and spread with the filling of finely sliced apples, fried breadcrumbs, sugar mixed with cinnamon, sultanas and almonds sprinkled with rum. Form into a roll like a Swiss roll and shape like a horseshoe. Lift on to a greased baking sheet, brush with butter and bake in a hot oven, 425°F or Gas Mark 7, for 10 minutes. Reduce to 350°F or Gas Mark 4 for 30 minutes, brushing occasionally with melted butter. Remove from oven when baked, brush with more butter and dredge with icing sugar. Serve hot or cold. When cold, strudel is served with whipped cream.

(*Austria.*)

CAKES AND LOAVES MADE WITH YEAST MIXTURES

Brioche   *   Brioche

9 oz flour; 3 oz butter; good pinch salt; ¼ oz yeast; 1 whole egg; 4 tablespoons water. Cooking time: about 20 minutes for a loaf, 10 minutes for small rolls.

Make this dough in the same way as *Brioche* dough. Keep it soft. Make it the day before, put into a greased bread tin (½ pound) or just place small rolls on a greased baking sheet. Allow to rise, brush with egg and bake in a hot oven, 400°F or Gas Mark 6.

▣ en Couronne   *   Ring

8 oz Brioche dough. Cooking time: 15 minutes.

Roll the dough into a tight ball, make a hole in the middle with a floured finger, and enlarge it. When it is large enough to insert your hand, continue to enlarge it by turning it round and round in your hands so that it is the same thickness all round. When the ring is well-shaped and about as thick as a small rolling pin, place it on a lightly buttered baking sheet to give the finishing touch to its shape. Leave in a warm place to rise for 15 minutes, brush with egg and, using moistened scissors, cut the dough right through all round the inside of the ring, to resemble teeth. Bake in a very hot oven, 425°F or Gas Mark 7. A hotter oven is needed for Brioche ring than for the other types.

▣ de Modane   *   Modane (Fruit Loaf)

9 oz flour; 2½ oz sugar; 3 oz butter; ⅓ oz yeast; 2 eggs; salt; zest of 1 lemon; 6 oz candied fruit; 6 oz sultanas; 2 oz icing sugar; 2 oz ground almonds; 1 egg white. Cooking time: 40 minutes.

Make a *Brioche* dough with the flour, sugar, butter, yeast, eggs, salt, lemon zest and a little water. Let the dough rise and combine with finely diced candied fruit and sultanas. Leave overnight in a cool place, then shape into an oval loaf on a baking sheet and allow to rise again. Spread top with a mixture of 2 ounces icing sugar, 2 ounces ground almonds and half an egg yolk. Make a crack on top to resemble a baked loaf of bread and bake in a hot oven, 400°F or Gas Mark 6, for 40 minutes.

▣ Mousseline   *   Mousseline

8 oz Brioche dough. Cooking time: 25–30 minutes.

Similar dough to that for the Cottage loaf *brioche* is used for the *Mousseline*, but it is allowed to rise further. Roll the dough into a ball and place it in a charlotte mould or, failing this, in a deep and narrow buttered cake tin. Leave in a warm place to double its volume. Make a paper collar for the mould which should stand up at least 2 inches above it. Brush top with egg. Bake in a fairly hot oven, 375–400°F or Gas Mark 5–6. The paper collar is to prevent the *brioche* from overflowing as it rises during baking. Having risen for a longer period, this *brioche* is very light.

▣ à Tête   *   Cottage Loaf

8 oz Brioche dough. Cooking time: 25–30 minutes.

Keep back a piece of dough the size of a tangerine. Roll the remaining dough into a tight ball on a floured board after allowing it to become firm in a cool place. Place this ball in a buttered *brioche* tin which is wide-mouthed and with high sides. Shape the small piece of dough into a pear and insert into the larger, pointed side down. Leave to rise for 30 minutes in a warm place. Brush with beaten egg and define the top clearly by making 3 or 4 radial cuts round its base with a knife and bake in a fairly hot oven, 375–400°F or Gas Mark 5–6, for 25 to 30 minutes, according to size.

Brioche des Rois de Bordeaux   *   *Kings of Bordeaux Cake*

9 oz Brioche dough; orange flower water; candied lemon peel; granulated sugar. Cooking time 20–25 minutes.

Roll the dough into a tight ball on the table and make a hole in it with a floured finger. Enlarge the hole to make a ring, with a large centre hole. Place on a baking sheet and leave in a warm place until it is well-risen. Brush with well-sweetened orange flower water. Place thin slices of candied lemon peel all round, dredge with granulated sugar and bake in a hot oven, 425°F or Gas Mark 7.

Kugelhopf

9 oz flour; salt; 3 oz butter; 1 oz sugar; ½ oz yeast; 4 oz stoned Malaga raisins; 2 eggs; about ¼ pint milk; 2–3 oz blanched split almonds. Cooking time: 30–35 minutes.

This is a rich Austrian fruit loaf. Sift flour and salt together. Add the sugar. Dissolve yeast in warm milk. Make a well in the flour and pour in the yeast, add the well-beaten eggs and melted butter. Beat the mixture by hand, add more warm milk if necessary. It should have an elastic consistency. Add the raisins. Thickly butter a special Kugelhopf mould, sprinkle in the almonds and dust with caster sugar. Fill the mould with the mixture two-thirds full. Leave in a warm place until the mixture rises to the top of the mould. Bake in a hot oven, 425°F or Gas Mark 7, for 30 minutes. Before turning out, cover with a cloth for a few minutes. Cool on a wire tray. Dust with icing sugar.

Savarin (au Rhum)   *   *Savarin (with Rum)*

For 4 persons: 4 oz Savarin dough; rum or kirsch syrup (see below); whipped cream. Cooking time: 15–20 minutes.

Butter a *savarin* tin and half-fill it with the dough. Allow it to rise in a warm place until it reaches the top of the tin and bake in a hot oven, 400°F or Gas Mark 6. When it is baked, turn it out, prick it well and soak it in boiling hot sugar syrup made from ½ pint water and 6 ounces sugar with 3–4 tablespoons rum or kirsch added just before using. (The syrup should measure 19° to 20° on the saccharometer.) When the *savarin* is well soaked, sprinkle with a little undiluted rum before serving. Fill with whipped cream and decorate with cherries and angelica, if the *savarin* is to be served cold.

▣ Chantilly   *   *Chantilly*

This is a rum or kirsch flavoured *savarin*, the inside filled with fruit macedoine mixed with sweetened whipped cream. It is served cold.

Small Cakes

Use small tartlet and boat-shaped moulds for making small fruit tarts in the same way as for the large ones, rolling the pastry out more thinly and cutting it with a pastry cutter of the appropriate size and shape.

Allumettes Glacées * Iced Puff Pastry Matches

5 oz Puff pastry; Royal icing. Cooking time: 12 minutes.

Roll Puff pastry into a strip about 4 inches wide and $\frac{1}{8}$ inch thick. Cover top completely with Royal icing, trim sides and cut into strips about $1\frac{1}{2}$ inches wide. Dip the knife in water or flour when cutting the slices to prevent the pastry from sticking to it. Place on a moistened baking sheet. Bake in a hot oven, 400°F or Gas Mark 6, on the bottom shelf to avoid caramelising the icing.

Babas au Rhum * Rum Babas

Add some currants to *Savarin* dough and half-fill small moulds which have been greased and lined with splintered almonds. Allow to rise to the top of the moulds, bake in a hot oven, 400°F or Gas Mark 6, for 10 minutes and soak in Rum syrup (*see p.* 284). Serve hot, or cold with whipped cream. (*See illustration p.* 280).

Baguettes Flamandes * Flemish Batons

For 18 *cakes:* 5 *oz caster sugar;* 5 *oz flour;* 2 *oz chopped almonds;* 1 *whole egg;* 1 *egg yolk; vanilla.* Cooking time: 8–10 minutes.

Whisk the sugar, egg and egg yolks to a foam, fold in sifted flour and vanilla. Pipe strips of the mixture, the thickness of a little finger and twice as long, on to a floured and buttered baking sheet. Cover with chopped almonds and bake for 8 minutes in a fairly hot oven, 375°F or Gas Mark 5. These are excellent cakes for tea.

Brioches à Tête * Small Cottage Loaf Brioches

For 8–10 *brioches:* 7 *oz Brioche dough.* Cooking time: 8–10 minutes.

Divide the dough into pieces each weighing about $\frac{3}{4}$ ounce. Proceed in the same way as for the large *Brioche*. Put into small buttered tins and allow to rise in a warm place, then brush with egg and incise in the way described for the large Cottage loaf *brioche*; bake in a hot oven, 425°F or Gas Mark 7, for 8–10 minutes.

Bushman's Brownie

1 lb plain flour; 8 oz sugar; 8 oz butter or margarine; 1 oz currants; 1 oz raisins; 1 teaspoon cinnamon; ½ teaspoon bicarbonate of soda; ½ teaspoon cream of tartar; milk to mix (approximately ¼ pint). Cooking time: 1¼ hours.

Sift dry ingredients, rub in butter or margarine, add currants and raisins. Add enough milk to make mixture slightly stiffer than fruit cake. Spoon into well-greased baking tin, bake in moderate oven, 350°F or Gas Mark 4, approximately 1¼ hours, or until skewer inserted in the centre comes out clean.

(Australia)

Chamoix   *   Chestnut Meringues

8 Meringue shells; chestnut purée; ¼ pint sweetened whipped cream.

Make the Meringue shells round instead of oval. Fill with a border of sweetened vanilla-flavoured chestnut *purée* and put a spoonful of stiffly whipped cream in the middle, so that it emerges from the chestnut *purée* as from a nest. This is absolutely delicious.

Excellent preserved chestnut *purée*, sweetened or unsweetened, may be bought ready-made. It is more practical than using fresh chestnuts and can be used at any time of the year.

Damper

1½ lb plain flour; 1 teaspoon salt; 2 teaspoons cream of tartar; 1 teaspoon bicarbonate soda; water to mix (approximately ½ pint) or equal quantity milk. Cooking time: 1 hour.

Sift dry ingredients, add just enough milk or water to mix to a stiff dough. Knead lightly, bake in moderate oven, 350°F or Gas Mark 4, for 50 to 60 minutes. Damper is traditionally cooked in the hot ashes of the campfire. Flour the outside of the damper very well and drop into the hot white ashes, cover with hot ashes and let it bake. Or put damper into a well-greased frying pan, cover with heatproof plate. Bury pan well in the ashes, heap ashes over plate and let it bake.

Petits Chaussons   *   Small Turnovers

5 oz Puff pastry; Pastry cream or jam. Cooking time: 10–12 minutes.

Make in the same way as large turnovers, cutting thin rounds of Puff pastry trimmings, filling with Pastry cream or jam and folding over. Brush the top with egg and bake in a hot oven, 400°F or Gas Mark 6. Dust with icing sugar.

Choux à la Crème   *   Cream Buns

5 oz Choux pastry; Saint-Honoré cream. Cooking time: 20–25 minutes.

Use the same bag and nozzle as for the large *Eclairs*. Pipe small rounds on to a greased baking sheet. Bake in a hot oven, 425°F or Gas Mark 7, until quite dry. Tip on to a cooling tray and split open with a pair of scissors to allow the steam to escape. When cool, fill with Saint-Honoré cream. Dust with icing sugar. (*See illustration p.* 278).

Condés   *   Iced Puff Pastry Matches with Almonds

5 oz Puff pastry; Royal icing; chopped almonds. Cooking time: 10–12 minutes.

Make in the same way as Iced Puff Pastry Matches, but add a few finely chopped almonds to the Royal icing and dredge top with icing sugar before cutting into pieces about $2\frac{1}{2}$ inches wide. Bake in a hot oven, 400°F or Gas Mark 6.

Conversations * *Conversation Tarts*

7 oz Sweet Shortcrust pastry; Pastry cream. Cooking time: 30 minutes.

Line some tartlet tins with Sweet Shortcrust pastry. Prick and fill right up with cold, vanilla-flavoured Pastry cream. Cover all the tartlets together with a very thinly-rolled piece of Sweet Shortcrust pastry, and gently pass a rolling pin over it to cut off the pastry round the moulds. Ice thinly with Royal icing and put 4 strips of pastry on top in a cross, two in each direction. Bake in a fairly hot oven, 375°F or Gas Mark 5.

Couques ou Langues de Bœuf * *Puff Pastry Ovals or Ox Tongues*

4 oz Puff pastry; 2 oz sugar. Cooking time: 7–8 minutes.

Cut out small biscuits of Puff pastry with a crimp cutter. Put a handful of sugar on a marble slab and roll out each biscuit on it to give it an oval shape. Place on a baking sheet, sugared side up, and bake in a fairly hot oven, 375°F or Gas Mark 5.

Cuisses-Dame * *Ladies' Fingers*

2 oz butter; 5 oz sugar; 2 or 3 eggs; zest of 1 lemon; 1 tablespoon kirsch; 9 oz flour; pinch bicarbonate of soda. Cooking time: 4–5 minutes.

Cream the butter, add the sugar, beat well. Add lemon juice and kirsch and, gradually, the eggs and the flour sieved with the bicarbonate of soda. The mixture should be on the firm side. Roll it a little at a time, to the thickness of a finger, cut into pieces 2 inches long and notch each one 4 or 5 times on the same side. Place on a floured board, cover with a cloth and allow to rest. Deep fry in very hot fat until golden brown; drain and roll in sugar mixed with a little cinnamon.

Eclairs au Café ou au Chocolate * *Coffee or Chocolate Eclairs*

5 oz Choux pastry; Pastry cream. Cooking time: 20 minutes.

Using a forcing bag and round nozzle, pipe strips of *Choux* pastry the size of a little finger on to a greased baking sheet. Brush with egg and bake in a hot oven, 400°F or Gas Mark 6, for about 20 minutes, until crisp and brown. Split open immediately, otherwise they will go soggy. Fill with cold chocolate or coffee Pastry cream, and ice the top by coating with luke-warm Fondant or Glacé icing with the same flavouring as the cream filling. (*See illustration p.* 278).

Lamingtons

For 20–24: Cake: 4 oz butter; 8 oz caster sugar; $\frac{1}{2}$ teaspoon vanilla; 2 eggs; 8 oz self-raising flour; pinch salt; milk to mix. Icing: 6 oz icing sugar; 2 tablespoons cocoa; $\frac{1}{2}$ oz butter; coconut. Cooking time: 35–40 minutes.

Grease a roasting or slab tin, and line the bottom with greased paper. Beat butter with sugar and vanilla until it is soft, white, and fluffy. Add the unbeaten eggs, one at a time, beating until well mixed. Fold in the sifted flour and salt alternately with the milk, to make a thick pouring consistency. Pour the mixture into the prepared tin, and bake for 35 to

40 minutes in a moderate oven, 350°F or Gas Mark 4. Allow to stand for 30 minutes before turning on to cake cooler. When quite cold, cut into small blocks and ice as follows:
Sift the icing sugar and cocoa well together. Melt the butter in 1–2 tablespoons hot water and add a little at a time to icing sugar and cocoa until the mixture is thin enough to pour easily. Place one square of cake on the prongs of a fork, and dip in chocolate icing, coating well. Drain, toss in coconut, then place on flat plate until icing is set. Repeat until all cakes are covered. If icing begins to set while working with it, warm slightly before continuing.

Petites Galettes Amandes * *Little Almond Biscuits*

For 36: 8 oz self-raising flour; 4 oz butter; 2 oz sugar; 1 egg yolk; ¼ teaspoon almond essence; almond halves. Topping: 1 egg white; 7 oz icing sugar; ¼ teaspoon almond essence. Cooking time: 15 minutes.

Cream butter and sugar, add egg yolk, essence. Work in sifted flour. Knead well together, then roll out thinly on floured board. Cut into fancy shapes, top with little almond topping, then almond half. Bake in cool oven, 300°F or Gas Mark 2, for about 15 minutes. *Topping:* Beat egg white lightly, stir in icing sugar and essence.

Petites Galettes Feuilletées * *Small Puff Pastry Biscuits*

4 oz Puff pastry; sugar. Cooking time: 10 minutes.

Roll Three Kings' cake pastry or Puff pastry trimmings into small balls and flatten them. Dredge with sugar, bake in a hot oven, 425°F or Gas Mark 7. Serve for tea.

Petits Gâteaux Napolitains * *Small Neapolitan Cakes*

5 oz Rich sweet shortcrust pastry; apricot jam. Cooking time: 10–12 minutes.

Roll out the pastry ⅛ inch thick and cut out plain circles 3 inches across. For 12 cakes, cut 24 rounds, making a hole in the middle of half of them with a smaller cutter. Bake in a hot oven, 400°F or Gas Mark 6, then sandwich with apricot jam, placing one ring on each solid base. Coat well with apricot jam and sprinkle with granulated sugar. Garnish centre with either Bourdaloue cream, Apple compôte, Chestnut cream, jam, etc.

Macarons de Nancy * *Nancy Macaroons*

4 oz ground almonds; 6 oz caster sugar; 1 teaspoon rice flour; 2 egg whites; rice paper; pinch baking powder; vanilla. Cooking time: 12–15 minutes.

Mix the almonds with the sugar, rice flour and baking powder. Add the egg whites gradually, and continue mixing until smooth. Flavour with vanilla. Make a soft paste, but not so soft that it will spread. Shape in large buttons with a forcing bag and plain nozzle on sheets of greaseproof or rice paper. Top each with half an almond. Bake in a warm oven, 325°F or Gas Mark 3, after brushing with whipped egg white and dredging with icing sugar. To remove greaseproof paper, place on a moistened surface for a few minutes. Rice paper is edible and is not removed.

Madeleines de Commercy * *Madeleines Commercy*

For 12 madeleines: 2 oz caster sugar; 2 oz flour; 2 oz butter; 2 whole eggs; vanilla. Cooking time: 10–15 minutes.

Whisk the sugar and eggs to a foam in a bowl. With a tablespoon fold in first the sifted flour, then the melted butter and the vanilla. Butter and flour madeleine tins, fill with the mixture and bake in a hot oven, 400°F or Gas Mark 6.

Meringues Chantilly　*　*Cream Meringues*

For 4–5 persons: 2 egg white quantity of Swiss meringue mixture; ½ pint cream. Cooking time: 30 minutes.

Using a forcing bag and large round nozzle, pipe Swiss meringue mixture on to a buttered floured baking sheet in portions the size of half an egg, leaving ample room between. Dust lightly with icing sugar. Bake in a very cool oven, 250°F or Gas Mark ¼–½, near the bottom of the oven, for 30 minutes. Remove meringue shells from baking sheet and press an egg into the underside of each while still warm, to hollow it out. Replace in the oven, hollow side up, and leave them until quite dry. They may be made a long time ahead if they are kept in a dry and airtight container. When ready to use, sandwich the shells in pairs with sweetened whipped cream.

Petits Mille-Feuilles　*　*Small Cream Slices*

For 4 persons: 5 oz Puff pastry; Bourdaloue cream with almonds. Cooking time: 12–15 minutes.

Bake some thin strips of Puff pastry, 3 inches wide, well pricked, in a hot oven, 400°F or Gas Mark 6, until very dry. Sandwich 2 or 3 strips with Bourdaloue cream and ground almonds, dredge top well with icing sugar and, with a saw-edged knife, cut into strips the width of 2 fingers. It is very important to dry the pastry thoroughly when baking.

Mirlitons de Rouen　*　*Mirlitons Rouen*

For 4 persons: 4 oz Sweet Shortcrust or Puff pastry; apricot jam; 2 eggs; icing sugar; 4 macaroons. Cooking time: 15–20 minutes.

Line some tartlet tins with the Sweet or Puff pastry, and prick thoroughly. Put a little apricot jam in the bottom of each mould, then fill with a mixture consisting of 2 whole eggs and 4 ounces caster sugar whipped to a foam, 3 or 4 dry, crushed macaroons, and a little vanilla. Place a half almond on each, dredge well with icing sugar and bake in a fairly hot oven, 375°F or Gas Mark 5.

Palmiers Glacés　*　*Iced Palmiers*

For 4 persons: 4 oz Puff pastry trimmings; sugar. Cooking time: 10–12 minutes.

Work the Puff pastry trimmings gently into a ball. Roll into an oblong and give the pastry 2 turns, sprinkling it generously with sugar. Roll pastry out in a rectangle. Fold each end over twice so that the two meet in the middle, then fold up again as though you were closing an open book. You now have six layers of pastry. Cut into slices ⅔ inch thick and place these on a moistened baking sheet, cut side down, leaving enough space for them to expand. Place in a hot oven, 425°F or Gas Mark 7, and turn over after 5 minutes, so that the underside does not caramelise.

Sablés de Trouville　*　*Sandcakes Trouville*

For 18 cakes: 5 oz flour; 4 oz butter; 2 oz ground almonds; 3 oz sugar; 2 egg yolks; salt; lemon. Cooking time: 10–15 minutes.

Make the *Sablé* pastry as over, but with raw egg yolks and adding ground almonds. Roll out the pastry and cut out with a cutter. Cut each circle into 4, making triangles with one rounded side. Brush with beaten egg, decorate with the tip of a knife and bake in a fairly hot oven, 375°F or Gas Mark 5.

Sablés Vendéens * Sandcakes Vendéens

For 18 cakes: 5 oz flour; 3 oz butter; 2 oz sugar; 2 yolks of hardboiled egg; pinch salt; zest of 1 lemon. Cooking time: 10–15 minutes.

Make a well in the flour and put the other ingredients in it, the egg yolks first rubbed through a sieve. After kneading, leave pastry to rest for 2 hours in a cool place. Roll out $\frac{1}{8}$ inch thick. Cut into triangles with a pastry cutter and place on a baking sheet. Cut a lattice design into a large cork with a knife and pattern the cakes by pressing the cork on them and decorate with the prongs of a fork. Bake in a fairly hot oven, 375°F or Gas Mark 5, for 10–15 minutes.

Sacristains * Sacristans

For 4 persons: 4 oz Puff pastry; chopped almonds. Cooking time: 5 minutes.

Roll out Puff pastry trimmings in a strip the width of a hand and $\frac{1}{8}$ inch thick. Brush with egg, sprinkle with rather finely chopped almonds and dredge with icing sugar. Cut into straws the width of a little finger, take each one by the ends and twist like a corkscrew. Place on a baking sheet and bake in a hot oven, 400°F or Gas Mark 6.

Petits Savarins au Rhum * Small Rum Savarins

For 4 persons: 4 oz Savarin dough; $\frac{1}{2}$ pint Rum syrup. Cooking time: 8–10 minutes.

Pour the *Savarin* mixture into 8 well-buttered small ring moulds, filling them about $\frac{1}{3}$ full. Allow to rise in a warm place until the dough fills the mould, then bake in a hot oven, 425°F or Gas Mark 7, to crust the dough and stop it rising. While still hot soak in 18° Rum syrup (*see p.* 284). Drain, arrange on a round dish and fill centre with Chantilly or Saint-Honoré cream. (*See illustration p.* 280).

Tartelettes aux Fruits * Fruit Tartlets

For 4 persons: 4 oz Sweet Shortcrust pastry; fruit; sugar. Cooking time: 20–30 minutes.

Line tartlet tins with the thinly rolled out pastry and fill in the same way as large tarts. Bake for about 20 minutes in a hot oven, 400°F or Gas Mark 6. Dust with icing sugar, or leave plain. Serve hot or cold.

▣ au Citron * Lemon

For 24: 8 to 10 oz Shortcrust pastry; grated rind and juice 2 lemons; 2 oz butter; 4 oz sugar; 2 eggs; $2\frac{1}{2}$ oz extra sugar. Cooking time: 15-20 minutes altogether.

Roll out pastry, cut into rounds and line shallow patty tins. Bake in hot oven, 400°F or Gas Mark 6, approximately 10 minutes, or until golden. Allow to cool. Combine rind and juice of lemons with butter, sugar and egg yolks in top of double saucepan. Stir over boiling water until mixture thickens. Allow to cool, then place spoonfuls of the mixture into the pastry shells. Beat egg whites until stiff, gradually beat in extra sugar. Beat until sugar dissolves. Fill meringue into piping bag, pipe swirls of meringue over lemon filling. Return to oven and bake until meringue browns.

Tartelettes à la Vanille * Custard

For 24: 8-10 *oz Sweet shortcrust pastry;* 3 *eggs;* ¾ *pint milk;* 2 *oz sugar;* ½ *teaspoon vanilla; nutmeg.* Cooking time: 20-25 minutes.

Roll out pastry, cut into circles with a 2-inch round cutter, and press circles into patty tins. Beat eggs well with sugar and vanilla, add warm milk and mix well. Spoon carefully into pastry cases, sprinkle with nutmeg. Bake in moderate oven, 350°F or Gas Mark 4, 10 to 25 minutes, or until custard is set and pastry brown.

Tuiles aux Amandes * Almond Wafers

For 4–5 persons: 2 *egg whites;* 2½ *oz caster sugar;* 2 *oz flour;* 2 *oz melted butter;* 2 *oz splintered and roughly chopped almonds.* Cooking time: 4–5 minutes.

Whisk the egg whites stiffly and whisk in the sugar. Fold in the sifted flour, butter and chopped almonds. Place small teaspoons of the mixture on a buttered baking sheet. Spread them out a little with a fork and dredge with icing sugar. Bake in a hot oven, 400°F or Gas Mark 6. Cool slightly, turn over with a knife and press them over an oiled rolling pin until cold to give them an arched shape. Leave until hardened and remove them carefully.

LES PETITS FOURS * PETITS FOURS

Carolines au Café et au Chocolat * Coffee and Chocolate Carolines

5 *oz Choux pastry.* Cooking time: 10–15 minutes.

These are tiny *éclairs,* about the size of a plum, filled and iced in the same way as the large ones (*see* p. 287).

Choux Pralinés * Praline Cream Buns

5 *oz Choux pastry;* 1 *oz chopped almonds; beaten egg; Praline butter cream.* Cooking time: 15–20 minutes.

Pipe the *choux* pastry into tiny balls on a greased baking sheet. Brush with egg, sprinkle with chopped almonds and sugar and bake in a fairly hot oven, 375°F or Gas Mark 5. Split open immediately they are cooked. Fill with Praline butter cream when cool. Dredge with icing sugar.

Langues-de-Chat * Cat's Tongues

2 *oz butter;* 2 *oz caster sugar;* 2 *oz flour;* 2 *egg whites;* 1 *teaspoon cream; vanilla flavouring.* Cooking time: 4–5 minutes.

Cream the butter and sugar in a bowl until light and creamy. After about 5 minutes, add the unbeaten egg whites gradually, beating all the time. Add the cream and, lastly, fold in the sifted flour and flavouring. With a ½ inch plain nozzle, pipe the mixture on to a buttered and floured baking sheet in strips about as long as a little finger and the width of a thick pencil. Bake in a hot oven, 425°F or Gas Mark 7, until lightly tinged with brown round the edges.

Noix Farcies * Stuffed Walnuts (Caramel Walnuts)

Sandwich the two halves of a walnut with a ball of white or coloured

Fondant almond paste. Impale each on a cocktail stick. Leave to harden for 24 hours. Dip in Glazing syrup. To make this, dissolve 16 ounces sugar in ¼ pint water with a pinch of cream of tartar added. Stir and cook until boiling point is reached. Boil, without stirring, to 300°F or the "crack" stage. To test, dip a little syrup in cold water: it will become brittle, and break cleanly like glass. Drain carefully and lay on an oiled plate to harden. Remove stick. Serve in small paper cases.

Palais de Dame * *Ladies' Buttons*

2 oz butter; 2 oz caster sugar; 1 egg; 3 oz flour; 2 oz currants or raisins; rum. Cooking time: 10–15 minutes.

Beat the butter with the sugar for 4 to 5 minutes, add egg, beat again and combine with the flour and the currants soaked in rum. With a teaspoon put small heaps of the mixture on a buttered and lightly-floured baking sheet. Flatten them slightly with the back of a teaspoon and leave plenty of room in between. Bake in a fairly hot oven, 375°F or Gas Mark 5, until coloured round the edges.

Pâte d'Amandes Fondante * *Fondant Almond Paste*

8 oz ground almonds; 8 oz Fondant.

Put very dry ground almonds on a marble slab with softened Fondant and a little vanilla and work by hand until a fairly firm but malleable paste is obtained. Divide the paste into the desired number of pieces. Colour and shape as liked, dip in sugar or melted chocolate, and you will have some excellent *petits fours*; leave to harden on waxed paper.

If you use the paste to stuff dates, walnuts, prunes or candied fruit it will be perfect. Fondant almond paste, ready for use, may also be bought ready made.

Petits Fours aux Dattes * *Petits Fours with Dates*

4 oz Sweet Shortcrust pastry; dates. Cooking time: 10–12 minutes.

Roll out the pastry thinly. Cut into rounds and wrap round stoned dates so that both ends of the date are visible. Press the pastry down firmly. Brush with beaten egg and bake in a fairly hot oven, 375°F or Gas Mark 5.

▣ en Génoise Glacés * *Iced Genoese*

1 Genoese sponge cake; jam; Fondant; candied fruit.

Cut a *Genoese* cake (baked the day before) into small squares, triangles, lozenges, circles, crescents, etc., cut through and fill with a little jam. Heat some Fondant, flavour and colour it and dip the *petits fours* in it. Use several different flavours and colours. Decorate lightly with candied fruit, chocolate buttons, chocolate coffee beans and violets, or a piping of butter icing.

▣ en Meringue * *Meringue*

6 oz Meringue mixture. Cooking time: 10–15 minutes.

Use the Meringue mixture which is beaten over heat, following the recipe for Almond rocks (*p.* 293). Flavour with coffee, vanilla or chocolate and pipe in different shapes on to a floured baking sheet—small mushrooms, for instance. Decorate and bake in a cool oven, 300°F or Gas Mark 2.

Petits Fours à la Pâte d'Amandes * *Almond Paste*

For 5–6 persons: 7 *oz ground almonds;* 7 *oz icing sugar;* 1 *egg white.* Cooking time: 10–15 minutes.

Mix the almonds with the sugar. Moisten gradually with the egg white until it is soft enough to be piped. Flavour with vanilla. Using a fluted nozzle, pipe the mixture on to a sheet of paper in various shapes, for example, rings, buttons or S-shapes. Decorate with almonds, cherries or raisins. Bake in a fairly hot oven, 375°F or Gas Mark 5. Place the paper on a moistened board, so that the *petits fours* can be removed easily.

▣ en Pâte Sucrée * *Sweet Pastry*

4 *oz Sweet Shortcrust pastry; almonds; raisins; candied fruit.* Cooking time: 10–15 minutes.

Make Sweet pastry well-flavoured with lemon or orange. Roll out $\frac{1}{12}$ inch thick and cut out in various shapes, either with cutters or with a knife—lozenges, rectangles and little squares. Brush with egg, place on a baking sheet, and decorate each shape differently, with a half almond, a raisin or candied fruit. Bake in a fairly hot oven, 375°F or Gas Mark 5.

Rochers aux Amandes * *Almond Rocks*

For 4–5 persons: 2 *egg whites;* 5 *oz icing sugar;* 2 *oz chopped almonds; vanilla.* Cooking time: 10–15 minutes.

Place a basin in a pan of hot water over a very low heat. Beat the egg whites in it with the sugar, until stiff enough to stand between the wires of the whisk. Fold in the almonds and with a tablespoon place small mounds of the mixture on a buttered and floured baking sheet. Bake in a cool oven, 300°F or Gas Mark 2. The inside should remain creamy and the outside should be crisp. Flavour with coffee, strawberry, chocolate, vanilla, etc.

Rum Sticks

For 36: 12 *oz cooking chocolate;* 6 *oz unsalted butter;* 2 *egg yolks;* 1 *tablespoon rum. Chocolate Coating*: 8 *oz cooking chocolate;* 3 *oz unsalted butter or solid white vegetable shortening.*

Chop chocolate roughly, place in double saucepan and heat until chocolate melts. Remove from heat, cool. Cream butter until light and fluffy. Beat egg yolks to creamy consistency. Gradually add to creamed butter, about a spoonful at a time; beat until just blended. When chocolate is quite cool, gradually blend into butter mixture; beat well. Chill five minutes to stiffen slightly. Add rum and beat until thoroughly blended. Place in piping bag with plain tube, pipe in 2 inch lengths onto waxed paper. Chill in refrigerator until solid. Pour chocolate coating over each stick, return to refrigerator to set. *Chocolate Coating:* Chop chocolate and butter or shortening roughly, place in top of double saucepan. Heat until melted, blend thoroughly. Allow to cool to lukewarm before icing Sticks. (Note: if butter is used in coating, Sticks will be dark chocolate colour; if white vegetable shortening is used, the coating will be light chocolate colour).

Salambos * *Glazed Cream Buns*

For 4 persons: 4 *oz Choux pastry; whipped cream.* Cooking time: 10–15 minutes.

Small buns of *Choux* pastry, as for Saint-Honoré *gâteau*, filled with whipped cream. The tops are dipped in Caramel syrup (*p.* 292). (*See illustration p.* 278).

Simple Confectionery

Here is a selection of recipes for sweets that are very simple to make at home.

Amandes Salées   *   *Salted Almonds*

Wipe freshly peeled almonds with a clean cloth. Beat some egg white very lightly. Place almonds on a deep baking sheet, moisten with egg white and sprinkle with fine salt so that they will have a frosted crust. Place in a very cool oven, 250°F or Gas Mark ½, and remove when they start to turn yellow. They should be no more than a very pale brown. Hazelnuts or quartered walnuts can be treated in the same way. Hazelnuts should be roasted first so that they can be peeled.

Brésiliennes   *   *Brazilians*

4 oz ground almonds; 5 oz icing sugar; 5 oz chocolate; rum; coffee essence or very strong black coffee; 1–2 tablespoons milk.

Soak the almonds with a little rum and a few drops of coffee essence, add sugar, grated chocolate and milk.   It should be possible to make the paste into small balls; add more sugar if necessary to make the balls hold their shape. Roll in grated chocolate or chocolate granules. Lay on waxed paper to harden in a cool place for some hours before serving.

Cerises Marquises ou Déguisées   *   *Disguised Cherries*

These are cherries in brandy dipped in hot, white or pale pink Fondant with kirsch. Cool on a marble slab over which icing sugar has been sifted.

Chocolate Orange Peel

Rind of 2 oranges; water; 8 oz sugar; extra scant ¼ pint water; 3 oz chocolate.

Thinly peel oranges, cut peel into very narrow, thin strips, using kitchen scissors or knife. Place in saucepan of cold water, bring slowly to the boil and simmer ½ hour or until peel is tender; strain. Place sugar and scant ¼ pint water in saucepan, stir until sugar is dissolved and mixture boils; add orange peel. Boil, stirring constantly, until sugar syrup candies around peel (approximately 15 minutes). Remove from pan, cool. Place chopped chocolate in top of double boiler, melt over hot water. Add candied peel, coat well with chocolate. Place on wax paper on top of wire cake cooler; separate pieces. Refrigerate until set.

Dattes Fourrés * *Stuffed Dates*

7 oz dates; 2 oz Almond paste; boiled sugar.

Cut the fruit open down one side to remove the stone and replace it with an imitation stone in Almond paste; it should be bigger than the real one and be visible from the outside. Roll in caster sugar or dip in boiled sugar. Lay on oiled plate to harden.

Marshmallows

2 oz gelatine; 2 lb sugar; good $\frac{1}{2}$ pint boiling water; scant $\frac{1}{2}$ pint cold water; 2 teaspoons vanilla essence; $\frac{1}{2}$ tablespoon lemon juice.

Soften gelatine in cold water. Add sugar to boiling water, bring back to boil; stir to dissolve sugar. Add soaked gelatine, boil steadily 20 minutes. Allow to cool to lukewarm. Flavour with vanilla and lemon juice. Beat until very thick and white. Pour into large shallow tins which have been rinsed out with cold water. Allow to set. Cut into squares, roll in icing sugar or toasted coconut.

To toast coconut: Spread coconut on baking trays, bake in moderate oven 8 to 10 minutes. Shake tray occasionally. Or the coconut can be put in a large heavy frying pan and cooked over moderate heat. Shake the pan continuously so coconut does not burn, or stir it with fork.

▣ Chocolate-Topped

Make marshmallows as above, pouring into trays to set. Melt 6 ounces dark chocolate and 1 ounce of unsalted butter over hot water. Cut set marshmallow into squares. Dip top of each marshmallow into melted chocolate mixture. Set aside until chocolate sets.

Marquisettes * *Chocolate Almond Balls*

4 oz ground almonds; 4 oz icing sugar; 4 oz chocolate; 2 egg yolks; $\frac{1}{2}$ oz butter.

Combine almonds with the sugar and grated chocolate and stir in egg yolks and softened butter to make a paste; divide into hazelnut-sized pieces, form into balls and roll in grated chocolate. Leave in a cool place for not more than 2 hours.

Rainbow Jellies

1 oz gelatine; 1 orange; 1 lemon; 1 lb sugar; $\frac{1}{4}$ pint water; 2 tablespoons sherry; red and green food colouring.

Soften gelatine in a little of the cold water. Thinly peel half the rind from orange and lemon, cut into small pieces. Squeeze juice from fruit. Place rind, juice, sugar and water into saucepan, stir over low heat until sugar is dissolved; allow to boil. Add softened gelatine and sherry; simmer until gelatine is dissolved. Strain, then divide equally into 3 basins. Colour one portion green, another red, leave third plain. Pour red jelly into wetted baking tin, place in freezer to set quickly. Whip third portion until white and commencing to set, pour evenly over red jelly, then finally cover with green jelly. When set, cut into squares, roll in caster sugar or coconut.

Schoolboy's Toffee

3 lb sugar; scant 1¼ pints water; 1 tablespoon vinegar.

Combine all ingredients in saucepan. Heat slowly, stirring until sugar has dissolved. When mixture boils, place lid on saucepan for a few minutes to dissolve any sugar which may have adhered to sides. Remove lid, cook quickly until syrup is a pale amber colour and a little dropped into cold water forms hard ball. Spoon or pour quickly into paper patty cases standing in muffin tins, or into lightly greased patty tins. Sprinkle with chopped nuts and allow to set.

Toffee Apples

1½ lb sugar; scant ½ pint water; ½ tablespoon vinegar; red food colouring; small red apples; wooden skewers.

Wash apples well. (The oil on skin of apples sometimes prevents toffee from sticking to apples). Dry well. Remove stems, pierce apples with wooden skewers (these can be obtained from the butcher). Chill apples while preparing toffee. When the hot toffee meets the cold apple it will set immediately, making coating easier. Combine sugar, water and vinegar in small saucepan. Bring slowly to the boil, stirring constantly and making sure that sugar has dissolved before bringing right to the boil. Do not stir once mixture has boiled. (Undissolved sugar, and stirring after the mixture has boiled, can cause candied toffee). Cook toffee steadily and quickly until it turns a deep straw colour. The toffee should bubble slowly and thickly, and when a small portion is dropped into cold water it should form a hard ball. (Undercooked toffee is one of the main causes of failure when making toffee apples.) Add a few drops red food colouring, stir in quickly. Dip apples in toffee, twirl around, coating well. Stand upright on waxed paper to set.

Do not store in refrigerator, as this will cause sticky toffee.

Toffee Strawberries

For 6 persons: 1 punnet of strawberries; 16 oz sugar; scant ½ pint water.

Wash strawberries gently, spread on absorbent paper to dry. Place sugar and water in small saucepan and stir over a gentle heat until all sugar has dissolved. Raise heat and bring to boil. Brush the sides of the pan with water to remove any sugar particles. Boil syrup until it becomes a pale gold colour. Remove from heat immediately. Using tongs, hold strawberries by the stem in the syrup, coating the entire fruit except the stem. Place on greased baking trays and leave until toffee has hardened. Serve just one or two to each person with after dinner coffee.

These are best made 1 or 2 hours before they are to be used. Grapes can also be treated in the same manner.

Truffes au Chocolat I   *   *Chocolate Truffles I*

2 oz Fondant; 3 oz ground almonds; 2 oz softened butter; 2 oz melted chocolate.

Take an egg-sized piece of Fondant icing and crush it by hand with the ground, roasted almonds, butter and chocolate. Make into small balls and roll in chocolate vermicelli. Keep in a cool place for a few hours.

296

Truffes au Chocolat II * *Chocolate Truffles II*

8 oz chocolate; 4 oz unsalted butter; 1–2 tablespoons fresh cream; 1 tablespoon cocoa; 1 tablespoon kirsch or rum.

Grate the chocolate, sift it and keep back the coarser part. Add to the creamed butter, cream, cocoa and kirsch or rum. Work well until thoroughly mixed. Shape into truffle-sized balls with 2 teaspoons and roll in the coarse chocolate or in chocolate vermicelli.

Preserves

The housewife will find this section most useful in enabling her to preserve the yield of garden and orchard in the best possible way.

Considerable progress has been made with preserving equipment. Jars which are easy and practical to seal can be obtained everywhere.

All produce to be preserved must be absolutely fresh; use the fruit as soon as picked or bought. Fruit should be firm ripe rather than over ripe.

GENERAL PRINCIPLES OF BOTTLING

The principle of preservation by bottling is to create a vacuum in the bottle or jar; once the container is filled it must, therefore, be boiled until sterilisation is complete.

Sterilising is one of the most convenient ways of preserving fruits and vegetables. A sufficient degree of heat must be used to kill off infection, and as soon as that is destroyed the container must be hermetically sealed to prevent the entrance of unsterile air. If the heat is insufficient, later spoilage will result. 165°F is a general temperature for fruit bottling, but certain fruits, lacking in acid, require greater heat, that is, 190°F, which is equivalent to simmering point. So, for all practical purposes, if no thermometer is available, simmering point gives a satisfactory result with all fruits.

Bottles used are important, because their lids must give a perfect seal. Two types of bottle are recommended:

Clip-top bottles—fitted with rubber bands, lids and clips, and

Screw cap bottles—fitted with rubber bands and screwbands.

Both types are easily procured.

Covering Liquid 1) Water—preserves the natural flavour.

2) Syrup—8–12 ounces sugar per pint of water. Make the syrup by dissolving the sugar in water, boiling for 3-5 minutes and straining before use.

Fruit—firm ripe gives the best results.

Packing—tight pack is best.

Steriliser—fish kettle or large pan may be used. Both must have a false bottom and a tight-fitting lid. Bottles should neither touch each other nor the sides of the pan. Bring *slowly* to *simmering point*—1–1½ hours—and hold this for 10–20 minutes or the time recommended in individual recipes.

Sealing After sterilisation, bale out some of the water. Remove bottles and if screw bands have been used, these are screwed up tightly. If clips have been used, leave these on. Leave the bottles undisturbed until cold.

Testing When cold, remove screw bands and clips and lift each bottle *by the lid*. If this remains on, there is a good vacuum and the fruit will keep, providing sterilisation was properly carried out.

Storage Keep in a cool, **dry,** airy cupboard.

Jams, Jellies, Marmalades and Fruit Paste

The making of jams, jellies, marmalades and preserves is very important in most families even today, when good commercial brands are available. This is because home-made preserves are very economical and easy to make. Apart from these two factors, though, there is a great sense of achievement to be gained from a store cupboard of preserves to be enjoyed during the winter.

LES CONFITURES * JAMS

Abricots * Apricot

To make 6½ lb jam: 4 lb firm ripe apricots; 4 lb sugar; ¾ pint water; juice of 1 lemon.

Wash fruit. Cut in halves and remove stones. Simmer fruit in water and lemon juice with some of the split blanched kernels—until fruit skins are soft. Add the sugar. Stir until dissolved. Boil up and boil to setting point, i.e. a little poured on a plate skins on cooling, this takes about 15 minutes. Skim, cool for 15 minutes, stir up and pot. Tie down and label.

Blackberry (Bramble)

6 lb blackberries; ¼ pint water; juice of 2 lemons; 6 lb sugar.

Make sure the blackberries are clean and free from worms. Wash, put in a pan with the lemon juice and water. Heat slowly until they are cooked, soft and reduced. Add sugar, bring to the boil and boil till setting point is reached; this takes about 10 minutes. Cool and pot.

▣ de Cassis * Blackcurrant

To make 12 lb jam: 4 lb blackcurrants; 3 pints water; 6 lb sugar; 2 oz fresh butter.

Remove stalks from fruit, wash and put into pan with the water. Simmer until the skins are really soft, stirring occasionally to prevent sticking. Add the sugar. Stir until dissolved, boil up for 10 minutes or until "setting" point is reached. Stir in the butter to disperse the scum. Cool until a skin begins to form. Stir up and pot.

300

Confiture de Cerises * *Cherry*

To make 6 lb jam: 5 lb cherries; 3½ lb sugar; juice of 3 large lemons.

Stone the fruit and cook it very slowly at first, with the stones tied in muslin and the lemon juice. Boil up and simmer until the skins are tender. Add sugar and stir until dissolved. Boil up quickly to setting point—10–15 minutes. Remove stones, skim, cool and pot.

▣ de Fraises * *Strawberry*

Make in the same way as Cherry jam, but using only 1½ parts of sugar to 2 of fruit, that is 1½ pounds sugar to 2 pounds strawberries, and the juice of 2 lemons.

▣ de Framboises * *Raspberry*

4 lb raspberries; 4½ lb sugar.

Heat fruit in pan to extract juice and soften the fruit. This takes 15–20 minutes. Add sugar. Stir until dissolved. Boil up quickly to setting point—5–10 minutes. Cool slightly. Stir up and pot. This jam is delicious!

▣ de Marrons ou de Châtaignes * *Chestnut*

Skin the chestnuts (*see p.* 8) and cook in unsalted water. Drain and rub through a sieve. Weigh the *purée*; put an equal weight of sugar in a preserving pan with half a glass of water per pound of sugar and a vanilla pod. Cook this syrup gently for 10 minutes, then add the chestnut *purée* and continue cooking, scraping the bottom of the pan with a spatula for some time. Cook for about 2 hours (if the heat is kept fairly low there is no need to stir all the time, except towards the end when the jam has thickened). Fill into jars when cooked to a very thick consistency.

▣ de Melon * *Melon*

Peel a fairly ripe, but not over-ripe, melon and dice the flesh. Macerate for 24 hours with ½ pound sugar to 1 pound melon. Drain off the juice and boil it to 215–220°F or the "thread" degree. To test: dip the fingers in cold water, take a little syrup between the thumb and forefinger and stretch them apart; a thin thread is formed which does not break when stretched. Add the melon pulp and a piece of tangerine or orange peel and continue cooking until the jam has reached the consistency of a thick *purée*. Flavour with vanilla. Stir up and pot.

▣ Passionfruit-skin Jam

12 passionfruit skins; juice 1 lemon; warmed sugar; 3 pints water.

Place skins in saucepan, add lemon juice, cover with water. Boil approximately 20 minutes, until insides of skins puff up and become soft enough to be easily removed with a spoon. Drain water carefully from skins, reserve. Scrape out inside pulp with teaspoon, measure, and allow 1 cup of sugar for each cup of pulp. This will be approximately 12 ounces sugar. Place pulp and sugar back into reserved liquid, boil quickly until liquid jells when tested (about 45 minutes). Bottle while hot, seal when cold. (*Australia*)

▣ Pineapple Honey

Peelings and core from 1 pineapple; 2 small lemons; 2 cloves; water; sugar.

Slice lemons thinly, remove seeds, add to pineapple peelings in preserving pan. Add cloves, cover with water. Boil approximately 35 minutes, until lemon peel is softened and liquid is reduced to about half original quantity. Remove from heat, strain liquid through muslin or fine strainer, and measure liquid. Add 1 cup warmed sugar to each cup of juice (this will be approximately 2 pounds 4 ounces of sugar). Boil quickly, until mixture jells when tested on cold saucer (approximately 30 minutes). Pour into clean warm jars immediately. Seal when cold.

Confiture de Pomme * Apple Jam

6 lb apples; 4 pints water; sugar.

Chop 4 pounds of the apples roughly, without peeling. Place in large saucepan, cover with 4 pints of water. Peel, core, and slice thinly remaining 2 pounds apples. Place in basin, cover with water. Cover and reserve. Add peelings and cores from these to saucepan with chopped apples, boil quickly to pulp. Strain liquid through fine muslin. Do not squeeze as this would cloud the jam. When liquid stops dripping, measure it; allow 8 ounces sugar to ½ pint liquid, add extra 1½ pounds sugar for the sliced apples. Return liquid to saucepan, add all sugar, stir until its dissolves. Boil 10 minutes, add strained sliced apples. Continue boiling, stirring occasionally, 1 to 1½ hours until jam jells when tested on a cold saucer. Leave in saucepan 10 minutes before bottling into sterilised jars. Seal when cold.

▣ de Prunes * Plum

Plum jam is made in the same way as Apricot jam, but the proportion of sugar varies according to the sweetness of the variety, from an equal weight for the more acid plums to three quarters the weight of the fruit for the sweeter ones, such as greengages and mirabelles. Mirabelles are not halved, only stoned.

▣ de Quatre Fruits * Four Fruit

Use equal weights of peaches, apricots, greengages and mirabelle plums. Stone the fruit, macerate for 12 hours with ¾ pound granulated sugar to 1 pound fruit and cook in the same way as Apricot jam.

▣ de Rhubarbe * Rhubarb

String the rhubarb. Cut it into small pieces and place in a bowl with an equal weight of granulated sugar. For every 2 pounds fruit, use the grated rind of 1 lemon and 2 teaspoons ground ginger. Macerate for 2 days, then pour off the juice. Boil for ten minutes. Add rhubarb and boil for 15 minutes longer. Pot, tie down and label.

▣ de Sureau * Elderberry

The elderberry is not only a medicinal shrub, its fruit also makes a very good household jam. Seed some very black elderberries, place them in a pan with three-quarters their own weight in granulated sugar and boil, stirring the bottom of the pan well to prevent sticking. When setting point is reached, cool slightly. Stir up and pot.

Farmhouse Lemon Curd

2 oz butter; 8 oz sugar; 2 eggs; juice 2 lemons; grated rind of 1 lemon.

Mix together the butter and sugar. Add the well-beaten eggs, lemon juice, and rind. Place in top of double saucepan. Cook over medium heat, stirring all the time, until mixture becomes smooth and thick. Bottle into clean jars and seal.

LES GELÉES * JELLIES

Gelée de Coing * Quince Jelly

5 lb quinces; 1 lb apples; lemons; sugar.

Peel the quinces, rubbing each one with lemon immediately. Cut them in quarters, remove core and pips and tie these in a muslin bag. Place the fruit in a pan with 3 pints water. Add the cores, which contain more pectin than the fruit. Simmer until the fruit is soft and rub through a nylon sieve. Measure and add 1 pound sugar and the juice of 2 lemons to each pint of *purée*. Put all into the pan. Dissolve sugar. Boil to setting point. Skim and pot.

◙ de Cassis * Blackcurrant

Wash the fruit without removing the stalks. Allow 2-3 pints water per 4 pounds fruit. Simmer currants with water until pulpy. Strain through a jelly bag overnight. Reboil pulp, adding water to make a thin mash. Strain, and add juice to first boiling. Measure and allow 1 pound sugar to each pint of juice. Boil up juice, add sugar and dissolve. Boil quickly to setting point. Skim and pot.

◙ de Framboise * Raspberry

Pulp the fruit by heating slowly in a pan, *no water is added*. When well broken down, mash and strain through a jelly bag overnight. Allow 1 pound sugar to each pint of juice. Finish as for Blackcurrant jelly.

◙ de Groseille * Redcurrant

Crush the redcurrants by hand, boil them up once and drain. When they have cooled off a little, press them through a jelly bag. Measure the juice and boil up. Add 1¼ pounds sugar per pint of juice. Dissolve and boil quickly to setting point. Skim carefully until it thickens. This jelly is made very quickly, so be careful not to overcook it. A little raspberry juice may be added if liked.

◙ de Pomme * Apple

Wash and remove any bruised parts from the apples. Do not peel or core the apples. Quarter them and simmer with the juice of 1 lemon and enough water to cover them. Cook until the apples are really soft and the mixture well-reduced. Strain and cook the juice with its own weight in sugar. Bring to the boil and stir until the sugar has dissolved and the mixture jells. Apple jelly is used chiefly for sweets. The juice may be added to fruit which is lacking in pectin, e.g. blackberries—when this fruit is used to make jam. A slice or two of raw beetroot boiled with the apples improves the colour of the jelly.

Jus de Pomme * Apple juice

Cook 2½ pounds apples, cut into quarters but not peeled or cored, barely covered with water until well pulped. Strain and keep the juice, which contains all the pectin (the substance that makes fruit set as jam). Apple juice made in this way is required to make any fruit with a low pectin content set without altering the flavour. Dessert apples should not be used for Apple juice.

LES MARMELADES * MARMALADES

Dundee Marmalade

To make 3½ lb: Wash 1 pound Seville oranges and 1 lemon thoroughly. Place in a saucepan. Add water and cover. Simmer for about 1½ hours, until the skins are soft enough to pierce easily. Remove fruit. Leave until cool, then slice neatly. Tie pips in muslin and add to the juice. Bring to the boil and boil steadily for 10 minutes, then remove pips and add fruit pulp. Bring to the boil. Stir in sugar. When dissolved, stir until boiling, then boil rapidly without stirring, to setting point. This will take about 20 minutes.

▣ d'Oranges * *Orange*

Wash 12 oranges. Then peel to remove the zest, shred this finely and tie in muslin. Prick the oranges all round with a needle and soak for 4 days in water with the zest, changing it several times. Cook until soft, cool and slice very finely. Weigh the oranges, then boil them with their own weight in sugar, plus the juice of 6 other oranges and the zest of the first ones. Add 1 pint Apple juice, boil to 215-220° F or "the thread", add the cooked orange slices and simmer until it thickens.

▣ de Tomate * *Ripe Tomato*

---

15 medium-sized tomatoes; 2 small oranges; 2 small lemons; 3 lb 12 oz sugar; 1 teaspoon salt; 2 sticks cinnamon.

Scald tomatoes, remove skins. Mash tomatoes, retaining all juice and discarding hard cores. Measure pulp and juice (there should be 4 pints). Thinly slice oranges and lemons, including rinds; leave slices whole. In large saucepan combine tomato, orange and lemon slices, sugar, salt, and cinnamon sticks. Bring to the boil and boil gently, stirring frequently, until thickened (about 1½ hours). Remove from heat, discard cinnamon sticks. Pour into hot sterilised jars. Seal immediately.

LES PÂTES DE FRUITS * FRUIT CHEESES

The fruit cheeses sold commercially usually consist of apple or apricot cheese containing colouring and acidulating substances and flavoured with the appropriate essence. Fruit cheeses may be made at home and are particularly good made with apricots, plums and apples. The main method of preparing them is as follows:—

Prepare a *purée* of raw fruit. Add slightly more sugar than the weight of the *purée* and cook until very thick, taking great care that the mixture does not burn. When cold the mixture should be firm enough to cut in slices. These are rolled in sugar and served as a sweetmeat or as an accompaniment to certain cold meats.

Pâte de Coings * *Quince Cheese*

Boil the quinces and pass them through a fine sieve. Place the *purée* in a pan with 3 parts of sugar to 2 of quince. Cook for a long time, until you can see the bottom of the pan, without letting the paste stick; it is better to cook it too much rather than too little. Dredge a marble slab with caster sugar and spread the quince paste out on it evenly. Let it cool, cut in pieces, roll them in granulated sugar and allow to dry in the air before storing in a tin kept in a dry place.

⊡ **de Pommes** * *Apple*

Proceed as for Apple Jelly but use 1¼ pounds sugar to 1 pound *purée*, with a piece of lemon rind and vanilla. Boil the ingredients together, stirring all the time with a spatula until the mixture is stiff enough not to flow back behind the spatula. Pour the cheese on to caster sugar or sheets of white paper, spread evenly, leave until cold and cut up.

LES CONSERVES DE FRUITS * *FRUIT PRESERVES*

Conserve d'Abricots pour Tartes * *Bottled Apricots for Tarts*

Halve some almost ripe apricots, place them in glass jars, pressing them down, and cover with the syrup as used for Bottled cherries. Close the jars. If using a thermometer, raise to 165°F very slowly: it should take about 1½ hours. If heated too quickly the fruit will rise to the top of the jars. Hold at this temperature for 10 minutes, then remove the jars as explained in the general instructions.

If you are not using a thermometer, fill the steriliser with enough cold water at simmering point to almost cover the jars. Place jars half an inch apart. Bring water to boiling point in 1¼ hours. Cover steriliser and the moment the water is at full boil allow a processing time of 5 minutes. Proceed as explained in the general instructions.

⊡ **d'Abricots au Sirop pour Entremets ou Compôtes** * *Apricots in Syrup for Sweets or Compotes*

Prepare as above, but use syrup made with 12 ounces sugar per pint of water. Boil and cool the syrup before pouring it on to the fruit.

⊡ **de Cerises pour Tartes** * *Bottled Cherries for Tarts*

Remove stalks and stone the cherries. Boil a little water with sugar in the proportion of 12 ounces per pint. One quart of syrup is enough for 10 pounds of cherries. Put the cherries into the boiling syrup, boil up once and drain. Put the cherries into wide-necked jars, tapping the jar on a folded cloth on the table so that the cherries settle. Half-fill the jars with cold syrup, apply the lids and place the jars in a large pan and wedge them so that they cannot move during sterilisation. Fill pan with cold water. Bring slowly to boiling point in 1 hour. Simmer for 10 minutes.

⊡ **de Cerises pour Compôtes** * *Cherries for Compotes*

In this recipe it is better not to stone the cherries and to leave part of the stalk. Put the cherries directly into the jars and pour cold syrup, made with 1 pound sugar to 1 pint of water. Put on in cold water, raise to simmering point in 1 hour. Simmer for 15 minutes. Tap the jars on a cloth to pack the cherries more tightly before applying the lid.

⊡ **de Jus de Fraise pour Glaces** * *Bottled Strawberry Juice for Ices*

Clean some ripe, sound strawberries and pass them through a nylon sieve. Fill some strong ½ pint bottles with the pure juice, cork loosely. Put on in cold water. Bring to the boil and boil for 15 minutes. Cork tightly and when cold seal by dipping corks in melted paraffin wax.

Conserve de Pêches au Sirop   *   *Peaches in Syrup*

Prepare in the same way as Apricots. The peaches should not be too ripe. Simmer large jars for 15 and small jars for 10 minutes.

Vegetable Preserves, Chutneys and Pickles

Vegetables are much more difficult to sterilise than fruits, as they are liable to be contaminated by bacteria and micro-organisms. Therefore, the *only safe* way to sterilise them is to use a pressure cooker, raising this to 10 pounds pressure or 240°F. It is very important to follow the instructions very carefully as faulty processing can cause food poisoning.

Conserve de Cornichons à Chaud * Hot Pickled Gherkins

Wrap the gherkins in a cloth with a large handful of fine salt and rub and shake energetically until they become moist with the water they give off. Then hang them up over the sink, in the cloth, until the next day. Wipe each one with a clean cloth. Heat enough vinegar to cover the gherkins in a copper pan. When it boils, pour it over the gherkins in a container and leave for 24 hours. Repeat this operation the next day, boiling up the same vinegar. Repeat once more the next day but using fresh vinegar with pickling onions, pimento, peppercorns and tarragon. Pack in jars, cover with vinegar. Cover the jars and store. These gherkins may be used three weeks later.

▣ de Cornichons à Froid * Cold Pickled Gherkins

The gherkins, brushed and soaked in salt overnight, may simply be placed in jars with pickling onions, tarragon and a bay leaf and covered with spiced vinegar. Six weeks later they will be ready for use. They will be soft because the water they contain dilutes the vinegar.

▣ d'Estragon * Preserved Tarragon

Use good quality tarragon; remove the leaves one by one and drop into boiling water. Boil up once, refresh, place in small jars filled with lightly salted water. Cap loosely. Put jars in cold water and boil for 10 to 15 minutes. Tighten caps on removal from steriliser.

▣ de Haricots au Sel * Beans Preserved in Salt

String the beans, slice and blanch them for 3 minutes over a fierce heat. Drain and leave to cool on a cloth. When cold, arrange in layers in a wooden tub or earthenware jar, covering each layer with coarse salt. Finish with a layer of salt and place a board, held down by a heavy weight, on top, so that the beans will be immersed in the brine which forms after the fourth or fifth day. Beans preserved in this way must be well-washed in several changes of cold water and then boiled in unsalted water when they are to be eaten.

▣ de Demi-Tomates pour Farcir * Bottled Half Tomatoes for Stuffing

Halve some medium-sized, firm tomatoes and carefully remove the seeds.

Place tomatoes in jars, cut side down, cover with slightly salted cold boiled water (use ½ ounce salt per quart of water). Close jars and heat gently to simmering point (190°F) taking 90 minutes. Maintain at this temperature for 30 minutes. Tighten stoppers on removal from steriliser.

Conserve de Tomates en Purée * *Bottled Tomato Purée*

Simmer the tomatoes with an onion, a *bouquet garni*, salt and pepper and leave them to soak until the next day. Pass them through a nylon sieve and boil the *purée*, stirring with a spatula. Pour *at once* into warm, dry jars or bottles, stopper loosely and boil 10 minutes for half pints, 30 minutes for pints. Immediately tighten stoppers to effect a seal. Store when cold.

Piccalilli

2½ lb green tomatoes; ¼ lb cabbage; 1 large green cucumber; ¾ lb brown sugar; ½ teaspoon black peppercorns; ¼ oz mustard seed; 1 teaspoon mustard; 1 pint wine vinegar; ½ pint malt vinegar; 3 onions; salt; 1 teaspoon turmeric; 1 teaspoon celery seed; 4 tablespoons olive oil.

Chop the vegetables and arrange in layers in a basin alternately with a sprinkling of salt. Leave overnight, then drain and discard the brine. Heat up the wine vinegar with sugar and turmeric and the seeds and peppercorns tied in muslin. Pour over the vegetables and leave for 48 hours. Drain off the liquid. Mix the olive oil, vinegar and mustard and pour over the vegetables. Pack in sterilised jars and cover closely.

Pickles

Use gherkins, sprigs of cauliflower, slices of carrot, onions, celery and fennel or a selection of other raw vegetables. Brine the vegetables (1 pound salt—1 gallon water) for 48 hours—weighed down to keep them under. Rinse thoroughly in cold water. Pack in jars and cover with spiced vinegar and crushed peppercorns. Cover and leave for 1 month before using.

DRIED VEGETABLES AND FRUIT

If no special drying equipment is available, vegetables and fruit may be dried by the following methods.

Champignons, Cèpes, Morilles * *Mushrooms and Fungi*

Clean and wash the mushrooms; the large ones should be cut in fairly thick slices after wiping them carefully. Thread them on a string and hang them in the sun or in a warm, airy room covered with gauze to protect them from dust. Do not put them in a tin or box until absolutely dry.

Abricots * *Apricots*

Halve the apricots, which should not be too dry, and place them on wicker fruit trays without letting them touch. Put them in a very cool oven and leave the door open. The temperature should be 120°F–150°F and no more, or use a drying cupboard. Leave them there for several hours for three days in succession. Now take the apricots one by one and flatten them by rubbing them slightly, as the heat will have shrivelled them; lay them side by side and condition them by exposing them to the air and, if possible, sun, for 2 to

3 days. Take them in at night so that they are not softened by the dew, and store them in a box when quite dry.

Pommes   *   *Apples*

Peel and core the apples and slice them ½ inch thick. Dry them in a very cool oven with door open so that there is no risk of cooking them. Then leave them in the oven or drying cabinet overnight and finally put them in the sun, turning them over several times. When ready, the apple rings should feel like chamois leather. Store in wooden boxes, or jars with lids.

FRUIT IN BRANDY

Cerises à l'Eau-de-Vie   *   *Cherries in Brandy*

Take some nice, sound cherries and cut off half the stalk and prick to the stone with a needle. Place them close together in a wide-mouthed jar, sprinkling with granulated sugar from time to time. Then cover generously with good brandy (40 to 50 degrees). Seal the jar as tightly as possible and leave for 5 to 6 weeks before eating. A piece of vanilla pod may also be put in the jar.

Mirabelles et Quetsches   *   *Mirabelles and Plums*

Mirabelles and plums may be preserved in brandy in the same way as greengages.

Prunes Reines-Claudes   *   *Greengages*

This is a little more complicated. Take some nice, not too ripe greengages picked before sunrise. Wipe them and prick them to the stone 7 or 8 times with a silver fork. Throw each into cold water as it is pricked, then blanch in lightly salted water. Place on moderate heat and as each greengage rises to the surface, remove it with a skimmer and cool in iced water. If the greengages are to be a good green, they must then be replaced in lukewarm salted water over moderate heat and kept there, without boiling, for some 15 minutes. Drain and rinse once more, then place them in glass jars and soak in good (50 degree) brandy for 4 to 6 weeks. Drain off the brandy and combine it with one-third its volume of 32° syrup, replace the plums in jars and cover with the sweetened brandy.

To measure the correct degree a density thermometer (saccharometer) is used for the syrup, good makes being Balling or Beaumé.

Raisin Muscat   *   *Muscat grapes*

Put some nice firm muscat grapes in glass jars, but do not fill too full. Cover with brandy and soak for 3 weeks. Finish off by filling up the jars with cold syrup made with 14 ounces sugar to ½ pint water. Shake jars well to mix the contents. Other kinds of grapes may also be used, so long as they are sound.

All fruit—redcurrants, raspberries, strawberries, blackcurrants, etc., may be preserved in this way.

Drinks, Syrups and Liquers

A few commonly used recipes are set out below.

LES BOISSONS CHAUDES * *HOT DRINKS*

Lait de Poule * *Chicken Milk*

Heat some milk, sweeten and flavour with rum or brandy; beat up an egg yolk in a bowl, beat in milk away from heat. Serve slightly foamy.

Punch à l'Orange * *Orange Punch*

Make tea as described below, but not as strong. Squeeze out 6 oranges and 1 lemon; add with 6 oranges cut into thin slices, ½ pint rum and 6 tablespoons curaçao. Pour into a punch or salad bowl and set alight, stirring meanwhile. When it has burnt out, serve in large cups with a few slices of orange.

▣ Rhum * *Rum Punch*

For 15 glasses: Make 1¼ pints rather strong tea and sweeten with 12 ounces sugar. Strain and add slices of lemon and half a bottle of rum, then set alight. Serve with a slice of lemon in each glass. Kirsch punch may be made in the same way.

▣ Vin Blanc * *White Wine Punch*

Dissolve 8 ounces sugar in a bottle of good white wine (e.g. Sauternes) over the heat. When the wine begins to froth, but before it reaches boiling point, add a piece of orange or lemon peel, a little cinnamon and a clove and leave to steep. Strain, add a coffee-cup of liqueur brandy and set alight. Serve with a thin slice of lemon in each glass.

Vin Chaud Réconfortant * *Hot Wine Tonic*

Place in a saucepan 5 ounces honey, 2 bottles claret, ¼ pint of port or Madeira and 4 cloves. Stir while heating but *do not* allow to boil. Pour this on to 6 egg yolks, well-beaten with a cup of water. Replace over heat, whisk without boiling and serve in hot cups.

LES BOISSONS FROIDES * *COLD DRINKS*

Cidre * *Cider*

Wash 6 pounds of sweet juicy apples and put through the mincer together with the skin and pips. Cover with 2 gallons of water and 1¼ pounds granulated sugar, stir well. Allow to stand for 5 days. Stir daily. Strain through a jelly bag and squeeze well. Pour into bottles, cork and fasten this on with string. Store in a cool place. This may be used after several days but it improves with keeping.

Citronnade * *Lemonade*

For 12 glasses: Rub the zest of 2 or 3 lemons off onto several lumps of sugar to impregnate them with the essential oil which provides the flavour. Place the lumps of sugar in a bowl with 7 ounces sugar, approximately 1 pint water and the juice of 5 lemons. Leave in a cool place for 2 hours until the sugar has melted. Add soda water or plain water and serve with a slice of lemon in each glass.

Limonade * *Sparkling Lemonade*

This fizzy lemon drink is made with 1¾ pints aerated water, 1 pint very sweet syrup (1½ pounds sugar per 1 pint water), the juice of 5 lemons and a little grated lemon rind.

Orangeade

For 12 glasses: Proceed as for Lemonade, adding half a bottle of good white wine and the juice of 1 lemon to the water used to dissolve the sugar.

Ratafia de Framboise * *Raspberry Ratafia*

Put 4 pounds raspberries and 2 pints 85° alcohol in a jar. Seal hermetically and allow to soak for at least a month. Pour into a nylon sieve and collect the juice in a bowl. Add a syrup made from 2 pounds sugar dissolved in 2½ pints water and 1 pint kirsch or brandy. Strain through a cloth and bottle.

LES SIROPS * *SYRUPS*

Fruit which is too ripe for bottling or jam-making can be used to make delicious fruit syrup.

The bottles must be tightly corked or they will blow off during sterilisation. Use a screw stopper or cork tied down with wire or string. Make sure all bottles, corks and stoppers are sterilised by boiling for 15 minutes.

To sterilise: fill the bottles with prepared syrup to within 1½ inches of the top. Seal. Place bottles in a deep pan padded with thick cloth. Fill with cold water to the base of corks or stoppers. Heat to simmering point and maintain for 20 minutes. Bale out some water and remove bottles. If using corks only seal with melted paraffin or candle wax. Store in a cool, dry place.

Sirop de Cassis * *Blackcurrant Syrup*

Boil 7 pints of water and 5 pounds sugar for 10 minutes, add 3 pounds picked ripe currants and boil for another 10 minutes. Squeeze out the juice through a cloth, boil up once more and put into bottles. Cork tightly, and sterilise. When cold, seal with melted paraffin wax.

Sirop de Framboise * *Raspberry Syrup*

Macerate raspberries with an equal quantity of sugar for 24 hours, crush and pass through a sieve. Cook the juice for 15 minutes over low heat. Cool and bottle. Cork tightly, and sterilise. When cold seal with melted paraffin wax.

▣ de Groseille * *Redcurrant Syrup*

Press out 5 pounds redcurrants and let the juice rest for 24 hours. Then boil up in a preserving pan with double its weight in sugar. Allow to boil up 4 or 5 times, skim, cool and pour into bottles, sterilise. Do not overcook, or you will have jelly instead of syrup. *To seal:* When cold, dip corked bottle necks in melted paraffin wax.

▣ d'Orgeat * *Orgeat Syrup*

Pound 9 ounces shelled sweet almonds and 1 ounce bitter almonds in a mortar, moistening gradually with $1\frac{1}{4}$ pints cold water. When you have a very fine paste, squeeze out the juice through a cloth, add 2 pounds lump sugar and let it melt on the stove until it reaches boiling point. Cool and add 6 tablespoons of orange flower water. Bottle, cork well and keep in a cool place.

LES LIQUEURS DE MÉNAGE * *HOME-MADE LIQUEURS*

Curaçao pour Parfumer Crèmes et Gâteaux *
Curaçao for Flavouring Creams and Cakes

Dry some orange on top of the stove until it is brittle enough to break. Place in a bottle and cover with rum. Leave for 4 to 6 weeks. Filter the rum and combine with the same syrup as for Quince liqueur.

Liqueur de Cassis * *Blackcurrant Liqueur*

Soak 4 pounds picked ripe blackcurrants for 2 months in 90° alcohol. Make a boiling syrup with 2 pounds sugar and $\frac{1}{4}$ pint water, add the currants and alcohol, press through a cloth and bottle.

▣ de Coing * *Quince Liqueur*

This liqueur is very easy to make. We are not here concerned with vintage products, but with producing delicious home-made drinks. Wipe the quinces thoroughly. Plunge into boiling water, then dip in cold. Peel them and place the peel in a jar with some good brandy of about 60°. Macerate for 6 weeks, then take 12 ounces sugar and $\frac{1}{4}$ pint water to a bottle of brandy and boil together for 5 minutes. Cool and blend with the quince juice after pressing it through a cloth. This is an excellent liqueur for stomach disorders.

Wines

It is difficult, not to say impossible, to imagine good food served without quality wines. Even at a simple, everyday meal, a glass of pleasant, clean though unpretentious wine imparts its glow to the family table. The choicer Sunday bottle or the grand vintage wines served in honour of friends or to celebrate a happy occasion are indispensable complements to the dishes carefully prepared and watched over by the hostess.

For this purpose, the map of the wine-growing districts of France offers us a many-coloured, infinitely varied palette from which it is a real pleasure to choose the wine or wines to set off a menu.

A few words, first of all, to explain wine-growing legislation so that the reader may be certain of recognising the origin of any wine.

The words "Appellation contrôlée" (guaranteed vintage) on a label mean that the wine in the bottle is authentic and has not been blended or interfered with in any way. They also mean that the producer has agreed to comply with strict, well-defined rules to ensure the good quality of his wine. The letters "V.D.Q.S." stand for "Vins Délimités de Qualité Supérieure" (Delimited Superior Quality Wines): these are regional wines, the quality and authenticity of which have been subjected to controls.

A quick survey of the great wine-producing regions seems appropriate to help the reader to understand and interpret the table at the end of this chapter of wines and foods which go together, and to appreciate more fully the diversity of French wines.

BORDEAUX AND THE SOUTH-WEST

Bordeaux

The Bordeaux vineyards all lie within the boundaries of the Gironde department, on the land bordering the Garonne, Dordogne and Gironde rivers, which is very suitable for vine-growing. The Bordeaux wine district is divided into broad regions, each with its own distinctive wines.

Médoc

To the north of the city of Bordeaux, on the left bank of the Garonne and the Gironde and in the southern part of the district called Upper Médoc, are found the wonderful wines of Margaux, St. Julien, Pauillac and St. Estèphe, as well as Moulis and Listrac. These are red wines combining great elegance with a sound, well-balanced "Structure", reminiscent of the purest classicism. Médoc wines have the virtues of ageing extremely well. Their great qualities are best appreciated with roast or grilled meats.

Graves

The vineyards surround the city of Bordeaux and extend southwards, beyond the town of Langon. The red wines are closely related to Médoc; in addition, they are full-bodied and preserve their quality well. The white wines are dry; they possess a fine bouquet and "breeding". They are served with shellfish and poached or grilled fish. In the southern part of the region the white wines are mellow or sweet and soft, not unlike Sauternes.

Libourne

On the right bank of the Garonne the vineyards of St. Emilion, Pomerol and Fronsac surround the town of Libourne. These are warm, potent, full-bodied red wines, which are drunk with red meat, game and cheese.

Sweet white wines

Sauternes, Barsac, Cérons, Loupiac, Ste.-Croix-du-Mont—all these white wines with their taste of honey and mild bouquet are among the glories of the Bordeaux vineyards. Served as an appetiser, with desserts that are not too sweet, with "foie gras" or certain kinds of fish, they shed a ray of sunshine on a meal.

Other varieties

The Gironde department produces a large number of other wines—red or white Bordeaux and Bordeaux supérieur, Bordeaux claret (light-red); Entre-Deux-Mers, Premières Côtes, Ste. Foy, Graves de Vayres, etc. All these deserve a favoured place on our tables.

The South-West

Red and white Bergerac, sweet white Monbazillac, Jurançon—a favourite of Henry IV—still or semi-sparkling Gaillac, Blanquette de Limoux—all these have the charm and savour of the South of France.

BURGUNDY

Burgundy wines, which bear the name of one of the most renowned provinces of France, come from vineyards of four departments—Yonne, Côte d'Or, Saône-et-Loire and Rhône. Red or white, their diversity and manifold personalities are the delight of the epicure.

Chablis

The white Chablis wines, which are very dry and have an aroma all their own, go well with molluscs and fish; they are made from grapes grown in the Yonne department, round the small town of Chablis. All of them—"Great Growth", "First Growth", Chablis and Petit Chablis have the same freshness and pale golden colour with a slight sheen of green.

The Côte d'Or

From Dijon to Chagny, through Nuits and Beaune, the vineyards cover a narrow line of hillsides. From the northern part, called Côte de Nuits, come potent, full-bodied, aromatic red wines which may be drunk with venison and fermented cheese. They include wines from the famous Chambertin, Clos Vougeot and Romanée-Conti vineyards.

The southern part of the Côte d'Or, called Côte de Beaune, produces the most famous white Burgundy wines—Montrachet, Meursault, Corton-Charlemagne. The red wines are lighter and more subtle, having a more flowery bouquet than those of the Côte de Nuits. They are Beaune, Volnay, Savigny and the potent Corton and Pommard.

Saône-et-Loire and Mâcon

The region of Chalon-sur-Saône produces white Rully and Montagny and red Mercurey and Givry. The actual Mâcon vineyards yield white, red and rosé wines; they provide, in particular, an esteemed, heady, dry white wine, Pouilly Fuissé.

Beaujolais

The Beaujolais vineyards, known throughout the world for their delicate wines, extend over the southernmost communes of Saône-et-Loire and the whole of the Rhône department to the north of Lyon. Beaujolais should be drunk chilled with ham, continental sausage and goat cheese; Beaujolais Village, Chiroubles and Brouilly are delicious carafe wines.

Other fuller-bodied wines, such as Juliénas, Morgon, Fleury or Moulin à Vent, may be drunk with red meat or meat served in a sauce.

CHAMPAGNE

The name of the province of Champagne immediately calls to mind "Champagne", the gay, sparkling wine so appropriate to festive occasions which may be drunk with equal pleasure as an appetiser, at the end of a meal, throughout the meal, or at any time of the day or night.

There are different growths of Champagne but, with certain exceptions, the bottles are not marked with their names. What gives Champagne its personality is its "brand". All the large firms of blenders in Rheims, Epernay and elsewhere consider themselves honour bound to offer under their label blends of the best growths from the main regions, which are:

La Montagne de Rheims (the Rheims hills)

La Vallée de la Marne (the Marne valley)

La Côte des Blancs (to the south of Epernay).

Although Champagne is a white wine, it is not made from white grapes only, unless it is labelled "blanc de blancs" (white wine from white grapes). The vine-growers of Champagne make white wine from black grapes by fermentation of the juice alone, without the pulp which contains the colour pigments.

Champagne making includes a number of very delicate operations—fermentation of the still wine, secondary fermentation in the bottle to produce the effervescence, riddling and disgorging to remove the sediment and, finally, the addition of a sweetening agent to give the different types of Champagne: "brut" (extremely dry), "extra dry" (dry), "sec" (fairly dry), "demi-sec" (medium sweet) and "doux" (sweet.)

Champagnes are only dated (i.e. bear the vintage date on the label) in great years. Otherwise the wines of several years are blended in the same way as those from the various growths in the region.

ALSACE

The Alsace vineyards lie on the slopes of the Vosges overlooking the Rhine plain, from south of Strasbourg to Mulhouse. The wines are white and fruity; except for Gewürztraminer and Muscatel, they are dry. They usually accompany shellfish, fresh-water and sea fish, as well as local ham or sausage, sauerkraut and Munster cheese. The names of Alsace wines correspond to the varieties of vine that produce them—Chasselas, Sylvaner, grey pinot (called Tokay), Riesling, Muscatel and Gewürztraminer. Zwicker and Edelzwicker wines are blends of several varieties.

JURA

The most original wine of this region is a yellow wine which acquires an unusual flavour all its own, reminiscent of walnuts, by a special process of vinification and by remaining in the cask for six years. The most famous is Château-Chalon.

The region also produces Arbois and Côtes-du-Jura red, white and rosé wines, as well as the Etoile wines.

CÔTES-DU-RHÔNE

The Côtes du Rhône vineyards extend for 125 miles along the Rhône valley, from Vienne, south of Lyons, to the river delta. There are two main regions—northern and southern.

I. Northern Côtes-du-Rhône

The steep hillsides under terraced cultivation yield elegant red wines with a good bouquet—Côtes-Rôties, Cornas, Hermitage and Crozes-Hermitage, Saint-Joseph. These rich wines are mainly drunk with red meat and game. There are some heady white wines—those of Condrieu, Château-Grillet, Hermitage and Crozes-Hermitage, Saint-Joseph; Saint-Péray is also made in a sparkling variety by the Champagne method.

II. Southern Côtes-du-Rhône

Besides the potent, aromatic Châteauneuf-du-Pape, this region provides Gigondas, Vaqueyras, Cayranne and the Tavel, Lirace and Chusclan rosé wines. In addition, it produces a much-prized dessert wine, Beaumes de Venise Muscatel.

We may also include in this region Clairette de Die, an excellent sparkling wine with a musky perfume, and the fresh, light white wines of Savoy, such as Crépy and Seyssel.

THE MEDITERRANEAN COAST

In Provence, the very dry white wines served with "bouillabaisse", fish soup and Mediterranean sea-food, are found side by side with rosé and strong red wines. Cassis, Bandol and Bellet, Côtes-de-Provence and Côteaux d'Aix are the wines of this region.

The Languedoc wines are Corbières, Minervois, Fitou and Quatourze. This region and Roussillon produce the great dessert wines—Frontignac Muscatel, Riversaltes, Maury, Côtes d'Agly, Haut-Roussillon, Banyuls and Banyuls Grand Cru.

THE LOIRE VALLEY

The Loire basin occupies the centre of France. A large number of vineyards adorn the banks of the river and its tributaries. Despite their diversity and individual characteristics, these wines are grouped together under the Val de Loire; red and white alike have grace, freshness and distinction in common.

Nièvre and Berry

The wines of Pouilly-sur-Loire and Sancerre are produced practically opposite each other, on the right and left banks of the Loire respectively. They are made from the same grapes—Sauvignon—and are also alike in that they are dry white wines served with fish and molluscs. Each of them, however, has its own special bouquet, its own native tang.

White Pouilly is a Nièvre wine, Sancerre comes under Berry, like its cousins Ménetou-Salon, Reuilly and Quincy.

Touraine

The white wines of Vouvray and Montlouis, both of the same parentage, are fruity, dry or a little mellow and possess a very elegant bouquet. In their semi-sparkling and sparkling forms, too, they are by no means devoid of charm. Their counterparts are two closely related red wines, Chinon and Bourgueil, with the fragrance of violets and raspberries. These wines, as well as those which are simply called "Touraine", are excellent with regional Touraine food, "matelote" of eel (stewed eels with onions), chicken in wine, "rillettes" (potted rabbit and pork), crackling and goat cheese.

Saumur

White Saumur is a light, dry wine tasting of "gunflint" which is also successfully made in a sparkling variety. Saumur-Champigny is a red wine related to Bourgueil.

Anjou

Anjou white wines, which all possess finesse and "breed", may be dry, like the Côteaux de la Loire or Savennières (Coulée-de-Serrant and Roche-aux-Moines growths) or soft and sweet with a taste of honey, like the Côteaux du Layon (Bonnezeaux and Quarts-de-Chaume growths). Anjou also produces good red wines and rosés held in very high repute.

Muscadet

The Nantes region is the birthplace of this very dry white wine which is perhaps the best one to serve with oysters and shellfish in general. It derives its name from a variety of vine of Burgundian origin which was acclimatised in the region several centuries ago.

Two distinct kinds of Muscadet are Sèvre et Maine and Côteaux de la Loire. Special mention may be made of the V.D.Q.S. Gros Plant Muscadet from the Nantes region.

AUSTRALIAN WINE

Australia, the only continent entirely in the southern hemisphere, stretches from the rain forests of the tropical north to snow covered mountains in the south.

In such a great land mass there must be great variations in soil and climate, ranging from rich alluvial to granite, shale and calcareous, from hot to temperate climate. A small population in relationship to area has enabled the viticulturist more or less to choose the sites of his vineyards at will and this choice is far wider than that in Europe.

Good rainfall during the dormant period coupled with a dry, sunny atmosphere during the vintage time, must and does produce wines of excellent quality and great variety.

The transfer of the vine stocks of Europe to the new climatic conditions of Australia has produced wines with a different palate and bouquet, differed and intriguing, thereby establishing themselves in their own rights as wines of purity, quality and character.

The variety of choice of vines can best be exemplified by the weight of crop. The shy bearers from areas of average rainfall yield up to 3 tons per acre, the *"cépages d'abondance"* from the river valleys average 15 tons per acre. These crops may be either delicate red and white table wines or the robust and full-bodied table wines; sherries, ports and herbal wines such as vermouth.

The history of Australian wines has been one of continual progress from the day in 1788 when Captain Arthur Phillip planted the first vine, to the present day. Free of violent atmospheric changes and deadly pests, the vines have progressed and proliferated over this newly discovered continent. A great name in Australian viticulture—Gregory Blaxland—who was awarded the Silver Medal in London in 1822 and the Gold Medal in 1827 for his red wines, pointed clearly to the potentialities of Australian wine culture. Other great *vignerons* followed, men of experience and enthusiasm, who were well acquainted with the great vineyards and *vignerons* of Europe, knew their land was a land of promise and planted accordingly.

With an established oenological research department, constant revision of cellar manipulation and great storage cellars, wines of purity and quality are constant.

There are five great wine producing States: New South Wales; Victoria; South Australia; Western Australia and Queensland.

Queensland the youngest of the States and youngest and smallest of the wine producers whose first wines were not planted until 1899 produces principally red and white table and dessert wines.

Western Australia next to Queensland in volume of production, specialises in red and white table wines as well as a variety of others.

New South Wales. The oldest State where the first vines were planted produces a great variety of wines including red and white table wines, dry fortified white and red wines, sparkling, sherries, ports, vermouths, muscats and brandy.

Victoria has a similar production to New South Wales.

South Australia. The largest wine producing State in Australia which produces 75 per cent of the total quantity. South Australia has good rainfall during the dormant period, a sparkling climate and the summer sun tempered by the waters of the St. Vincent Gulf. Here celebrated vineyards extend for mile upon mile on the undulating hills. Here grow the Rieslings, Cabernet, Pinots, Shiraz, Tokay, Verdelho, Malbec, Grenache, Carignan and Mataro vines, producing every variety of wine.

Table of wines to be served with various foods

HORS D'ŒUVRE

1. LIGHT WHITE DRY WINES: *Bordeaux supérieur, Entre-deux-Mers, Aligoté Burgundy, Petit Chablis, White Mâcon, Pouilly-Fumé, Sancerre, Montlouis, Edelzwicker, Sylvaner.*
2. LIGHT RED WINES: *Bordeaux supérieur, Burgundy Passe-Tous-grains, Givry-Mâcon, Beaujolais, Chinon, Bourgeuil.*
3. ROSÉ WINES: *Bordeaux claret, Burgundy rosé, Anjou, Touraine, Provence, Côtes-du-Rhône.*

ENTRÉES

1. DRY WHITE OR MELLOW WINES: *Graves, Cérons, Puligny-Montrachet, Meursault, Champagne, Vouvray, Samur, Anjou, Riesling.*
2. SUPPLE RED WINES: *Margaux, Moulis, Beaune, Savigny, Mercurey, Beaujolais, Chinon, Bourgueil.*
3. FRUITY ROSÉ WINES: *Sancerre rosé, Anjou or Touraine rosé, Alsatian pinot rosé.*

OYSTERS AND SHELLFISH (MOLLUSCS)

1. DRY WHITE WINES: *Graves, Entre-deux-Mers, Chablis, Pouilly-Fuissé, Chassagne-Montrachet, Puligny-Montrachet, Champagne Nature, Riesling, Pouilly-Fumé, Sancerre, Quincy, Savennières, Muscadet, Cassis, Bandol, Arbois.*

GRILLED OR POACHED FISH OR SHELLFISH

1. DRY WHITE WINES: Same as for molluscs.
2. DRY ROSÉ WINES OF SOUTHERN FRANCE: *Cassis, Bandol, Côtes-de-Provence, Tavel, Lirac, Côtes-du-Rhône.*

FISH OR SHELLFISH IN A SAUCE

A. HIGHLY-SEASONED SAUCES:
   FULL-BODIED DRY WHITE WINES: *Graves, Chablis, Meursault, Chassagne-Montrachet, Corton-Charlemagne, Pouilly-Fuissé, White Hermitage, Condrieu, Riesling, Arbois yellow.*
B. MILD SAUCES:
   MELLOW OR SEMI-DRY WINES: *Monbazillac, Vouvray, Anjou, Côteaux-du-Layon, Gewürztraminer.*
C. FISH STEW (MATELOTE) WITH RED WINE: Same wine as that used for cooking.

GRILLED MEAT

A. WHITE MEATS:
   WHITE WINES: *Graves, Cérons, Vouvray, Anjou, Champagne.*
   FAIRLY LIGHT RED WINES: *Médoc* and *Graves, Beaune, Savigny, Beaujolais, Chinon, Bourgueil, Saumur-Champigny.*
B. RED MEATS:
   FULLY MATURE RED WINES: *Pauillac, St. Estèphe, Graves, St. Emilion, Pomerol, Côtes-de-Beaune, Côte-de-Nuits, Morgon, Fleurie, Moulin-à-Vent, Hermitage, Châteauneuf-du-Pape.*

MEAT SERVED IN A SAUCE

A. WINE SAUCE:
Same wine as that used for cooking.

B. HIGHLY-SEASONED SAUCES, STEWS:
FULL-BODIED, BUT NOT FROM GREAT GROWTHS: *Bordeaux supérieur, Canon-Fronsac, Sautenay, Mercurey, Juliénas, Côtes-du-Rhône, Côtes-de-Provence, Touraine-Amboise.*

C. MILD SAUCES:
Graves, Sauternes, Montrachet, Meursault, Riesling, Vouvray, Anjou, Champagne.

GAME

A. WINGED GAME:
Médoc, Graves, St. Emilion, Pomerol, Chambolle-Musigny, Vosne-Romanée, Wines of the Côte-de-Beaune, named *Beaujolais, Arbois, Hermitage, Cornas.*

B. GROUND GAME:
Médoc and *Graves,* good years, *St. Emilion, Pomerol,* Wines of the Côte-de-Nuits, *Corton, Pommard, Côtes-Rôties, Cornas, Châteauneuf-du-Pape.*

CHEESE

A. HARD OR SEMI-HARD CHEESES:
Médoc, Graves, St. Emilion, Pomerol, Wines of the Côte-de-Beaune, *Beaujolais, Chinon, Bourgueil.*

B. SOFT FERMENTED CHEESES:
St. Emilion and *Pomerol,* good years, wines of the Côte-de-Nuits, *Côtes-de-Beaune,* good years, named *Beaujolais, Hermitage, Cornas, Côtes-Rôties, Châteauneuf-du-Pape, Bandol, Cassis, Banyuls Grand Cru.*

C. BLUE-VEINED CHEESES:
WHITE: *Sauternes, Barsac, Meursault, Chassagne-Montrachet, White Hermitage, Condrieu, Jura* yellow wine, *Gewürztraminer.*
RED: Rich wines of the Côte-de-Nuits, *Côtes-du-Rhône, Châteauneuf-du-Pape, Banyuls Grand Cru.*

D. GOAT CHEESES:
WHITE: *Sancerre, Pouilly-Fumé, Quincy, White Arbois.*
RED: *Mercurey, Mâcon, Beaujolais, Chinon, Bourgeuil.*
ROSÉ: *Bordeaux claret.*

SWEETS AND DESSERTS

1. WHITE: *Champagne,* sparkling wines made by the Champagne method, *Sauternes, Barsac* and all sweet white vintage *Bordeaux, Monbazillac, Vouvray, Saumur, Côteaux-du-Layon, Gewürztraminer, Alsatian Muscatel,* Muscatel wines of Southern France: *Rivesaltes, Lunel, Frontignan, Beaunes-du-Venise.*
2. RED: *Maury, Rivesaltes, Grand-Roussillon, Banyuls.*

FRANÇOIS-MF D'ATHIS
*General Secretary
of the "Revue du Vin de France"*

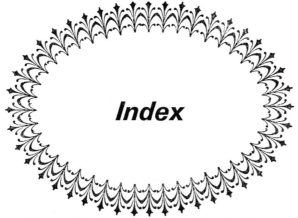

Index

Page number in **bold type** refers to illustrations.